PUBLISHED FOR THE
GERMAN AFRICA SOCIETY

JANHEINZ JAHN,
ULLA SCHILD, ALMUT NORDMANN

Who's Who
in African Literature

BIOGRAPHIES, WORKS, COMMENTARIES

Sole distributors
in North America
The Baker & Taylor Co.

HORST ERDMANN VERLAG
Tübingen · Federal Republic of Germany
1972

IN COLLABORATION WITH
INTER NATIONES

*Contribution of the Federal Republic of Germany
to the International Book Year*

ISBN 3 7711 0153 0

© 1972 by Horst Erdmann Verlag
für Internationalen Kulturaustausch, Tübingen - Basel
Jacket design by Karlheinz Groß
Printed in Germany by Becht-Druck & Co., Pfäffingen
Bound by Großbuchbinderei Josef Spinner, Ottersweier

CONTENTS

PORTRAITS

Plate I, facing page 64

Olaudah Equiano, Nigeria
Jacobus Eliza Joannes Capitein,
    Ghana
Phillis Wheatley, Senegal
Ignatius Sancho

Plate II, facing page 65

Samuel Adjai Crowther, Nigeria
Joseph Ephraim Casely Hayford,
    Ghana
Carl Christian Reindorf, Ghana
Hamed bin Muhammed el
    Murjebi (Tippu Tib), Tanzania

Plate III, facing page 80

Samuel Edward Krune Mqhayi,
    South Africa
Peter Abrahams, South Africa
Ezekiel Mphahlele, South
    Africa
Bloke Modisane, South Africa

Plate IV, facing page 81

Dennis Brutus, South Africa
Alex La Guma, South Africa
Lewis Nkosi, South Africa
Richard Rive, South Africa

Plate V, facing page 144

Léopold Sédar Senghor, Senegal
Birago Diop, Senegal
Alioune Diop, Senegal
Sembene Ousmane, Senegal

Plate VI, facing page 145

Keita Fodeba, Guinea
Camara Laye, Guinea
Yambo Ouologuem, Mali
António Aurélio Gonçalves,
    Cape Verde Islands

Plate VII, facing page 160

Paul Hazoumé, Dahomey
Jean Pliya, Dahomey
Bernard B. Dadié, Ivory Coast
    Coast
Ahmadou Kourouma, Ivory
    Coast

Plate VIII, facing page 161

Efua Theodora Sutherland,
    Ghana
Ayi Kwei Armah, Ghana
Kofi Awoonor, Ghana
Cameron Duodu, Ghana

7

INTRODUCTION

African literature has established itself as a new and genuine branch of world literature. It has become subject of scholarly research and is taught at universities and schools. Research needs basic information such as a reliable bibliography and the background information about the creative individuals. Jahn's "Bibliography of Creative African Writing" already listed the entire creative literary works of African authors. This "Who's Who in African Literature" is the first endeavour to supply biographical data on the creators of this new literature. The book makes interesting reading and gives a fresh insight into the life and the fate of the modern African elite.

"African" in the context of this book means "sub-Saharan African" or "Black African". Excluded are the literatures of North Africa and Ethiopia because they constitute separate literary entities.

Some writers could not be traced, official and inofficial means to find out their whereabouts proving equally inefficient. Other writers believe that it is their work that counts and not their person and they refused to submit more data than were already known. A third, though small group, is in prison. The result of our endeavour therefore is a collection of biographies not wholly balanced. But we decided rather to leave the uneven lengths, which reflect the unevenness of the sources, than to cut down our material for the sake of equality.

We collected biographies of African authors writing in European and African languages. We are particularly proud to include a number of biographies of African writers using the Portuguese language, though these biographies are often fragmentary.

Included are also biographies of essayists and critics concerned with African literature. We also included politicians if they have written some creative literature, at least an autobiography. These articles, however, have been intentionally kept short as full political biographies are mostly available.

9

The writers are listed alphabetically according to their names, as they appear on the title page of their books. If their real name is different, this is made evident in the text.

The birthplaces have been checked on maps. Districts and provinces were added, except for capitals of countries. The French administrative unit "département" has been translated by "district". For countries and administrative units the most modern designations have been used, but recounting an author's life story, the historical terms have remained. Thus an author would be born in Ghana or in the Western State of Nigeria, but he would be representing the Gold Coast in a delegation, or he would be Premier of the Western Region of Nigeria.

The spelling of geographical names follows as far as possible the English language. Where an English form of spelling exists, as is the case with most big cities, the English form has been used. Thus one will read Whydah, and not Ouidah, Wagadugu and not Ouagadougou, Yaunde and not Yaoundé, Buake and not Bouaké. In the case of small places, where a standardised English spelling does not exist, local official spelling has been adopted, for instance Yamoussoukro and Fadougou. In cases of doubt the New Library Map of the London Geographical Institute was consulted.

Although the best available maps have been used, some villages could not be located. It proved that these maps, drawn during colonial times, were fairly accurate only within the respective colonial frontiers. Maps are particularly disappointing in Rhodesia, where many villages are indicated by dots only, with no names supplied.

If the country's name is not mentioned after the name of a town, this town is situated in the country mentioned last.

Supplying full bibliographical details of the authors' works would go far beyond the aim and the limits of this book. Thus numbers are added in brackets after most titles. They refer to Janheinz Jahn's "Bibliography of Creative African Writing", Nendeln, Liechtenstein 1971, where all necessary data are supplied and all editions and translations listed. If a book was not included in the Bibliography, because it was either not creative or appeared after the publication date of the Bibliography, place and year of the first publication are added. A translation of a title in an African language is provided only when this title is not listed in the Bibliography.

Where possible, a selection of critical voices and comments has been added to an author's biography. This selection is not meant as a final judgement of an author or his work, but as a kind of orientation and stimulus for further studies.

There was no need to supply the sources of quotations. The name of the author in brackets is sufficient. Full bibliographical citations can be found in the "Bibliography of Creative African Writing" under the name of the author concerned. Books and journals that have appeared after the publication date of the Bibliography and from which quotations are taken, are included in the bibliography attached to this book.

If biographies in book form, studies, theses and dissertations have been written on a writer, no comments or criticisms were quoted. Instead authors and titles of these studies were listed with a short indication of their character.

At the end of the book two lists are attached: "Authors Grouped by Languages" and "Authors Grouped by Countries". They do not hold an equal quantity of names, because some writers write their works in two or even more languages.

The authors hope that this book will be a useful guide to the understanding of African literature and the people who create it, that it will stimulate African writers to further production and will further critical studies in the field.

Many thanks are due, firstly to the writers who helped to compile this "Who's Who", by submitting their biographies and patiently answering letters when ensuing points had to be clarified.

Special thanks are due to Professor Chinua Achebe (Nsukka, Nigeria), Professor Chief Ulli Beier (Ife, Nigeria), Mr. Dennis Duerden (London), Professor Lyndon Harries (Madison, USA), Mr. James J. R. Jolobe (Lovedale, South Africa), Mrs. Kayper-Mensah (Bonn - Bad Godesberg), Professor Bernth Lindfors (Austin, Texas), Herr Gerd Meuer (Cologne, Germany), Sybill

Baronin von Tiesenhausen (Lagos, Nigeria), Herr Wolfgang von Wangenheim (Abidjan, Ivory Coast).

Quotations have been taken from the following books to whose authors and publishers the authors of this book express their thanks:

Gérard, Albert S., *Four African Literatures,* Berkeley 1971.

July, Robert W., *The Origins of Modern African Thought,* London 1968.

July, Robert W., *A History of African People,* London 1970.

Kunene, Daniel P. and Kirsch, Randal A., *The Beginning of South African Vernacular Literature,* Los Angeles 1967.

Segal, Ronald, *Political Africa,* London 1961.

WHO'S WHO IN AFRICAN LITERATURE

A-Amang, Boé   Cameroon

Born on January 30, 1938, at Rionong, near Bafia, district
Mbam, Cameroon, Boé A-Amang is the son of a Muslim father
and a Protestant mother. He attended the Koran school, then the
Protestant school of his village, then the Ecole principale at
the town centre of Bafia. In 1952 he entered the Collège
moderne of Nkongsamba where he met his friend Jacques
Muriel Nzouankeu, with whom, in 1959, he started the literary
journal "Le Dattier".

After he got his Brevet d'Etudes, Boé A-Amang, now Director
of "Le Dattier", settled at Duala and taught at the Institut
Moderne et Technique d'Epoupa Mooh Mbella, and later at the
Ecole de Sécretariat at Bali, district Bamenda, West-Cameroon.
In 1969 he became Superintendent of the Centre d'Etudes
Commerciales et Financières at Nliba, and General Secretary
of A.P.E.C. (Association des Poètes et des Ecrivains Came-
rounais) in Duala.

In 1960 Boé A-Amang founded the "Théâtre Populaire
Camerounais" for which he wrote his plays, the didactical
satire *La Course à l'Argent* (1), and *Les Amants de Nulle Part*
(2) a comedy about the marriage of a girl. "The style is very
natural, easy, without affectation, rather poetic" (Emmanuel
E. Moukory).

Abrahams, Peter   South Africa

Peter Abrahams was born on March 19, 1919, in the slum area
of Vrededorp, Johannesburg, South Africa, of a "Cape Coloured" mother and an Ethiopian father. When he was five years
old his father died, the family was broken up, and the boy
was sent to relatives in Elseberg. Three years later he returned
to Vrededorp. At the age of nine he went to work at a tinsmith's

13

for the weekly wage of two shillings and sixpence. It was while working there that a young Jewess, a typist in the office, told him during one lunch hour the story of Othello from Lamb's "Tales from Shakespeare". From that day on Abrahams determined to read for himself and went to school. He attended school regularly for three years. After that he attended school sporadically, working at intervals as dish-washer, carrier in the market and office boy.

While working as an office boy he met a white missionary who was the head of a training school for native teachers. The missionary agreed to find him a place at the school, provided he worked his way. In 1935 Abrahams left school and wandered about South Africa. With another young man he started a school in the Cape Flats, just outside Cape Town.

Towards the end of 1939 he signed on as a ship's stoker, hoping to work his passage to England, but the ship went East, and it took him two years, working as a steward, cabin boy and stoker again, till he finally reached England in 1941 and settled there.

In 1952 Abrahams returned to Africa to do a series on Kenya and South Africa for the London "Observer". In 1953 he visited West Africa. In 1956 he went to Jamaica to prepare an official report on the British West Indies, and he decided to settle there with his family. He thereafter became editor of the "West Indian Economist", controller of the daily radio news network "West Indian News", and a commentator on Jamaica's radio and television programmes. In 1964 Abrahams resigned from most of his duties in order to devote himself more fully to writing.

Peter Abrahams' first work was a collection of stories, *Dark Testament* (1474). This was followed by the novel *Song of the City* (1475). *Mine Boy* (1476) was one of the first books to draw attention to the black's situation in South Africa. It calls for a future in a multiracial society by describing the adventures of Xuma, the man from the North, in Johannesburg. *The Path of Thunder* (1477) has been translated into at least twenty-five languages. It is a love story between the coloured boy Lanny and the white girl Sarie, a union that gives hope to overcoming the laws that lead to a racially segregated society, but which ends tragically, leaving several deaths on the scene.

In *Wild Conquest* (1478) Abrahams goes back to the Great Trek, following the Boer family Jansen from their leaving home to their joining of the trek and the ensuing battle with the Matabeles.

"The tone he obviously intends in *Wild Conquest* is poetic, but often his striving for it fails in marshes of inarticulateness, sterile preciosities painfully inferior to the rich authority of metaphor and implication that glorifies the work of the greatest masters" (Blyden Jackson).

Return to Goli (1479) is primarily a political book in the form of an itinerary, in which Abrahams discusses the social and racial problems in South Africa, dedicating a chapter each to the Coloureds, the Indians, the Africans and the Whites. *Tell Freedom* (1480), which has been translated into eight languages, tells his autobiography from the days in Vrededorp to his employment on a ship. "Wherever is takes us, the great, unforgettable features are the virulence and the obduracy of South African color caste" (Blyden Jackson).

In *A Wreath for Udomo* (1481) Abrahams evokes a future African society. The central figure is a political leader with a progressive view, who is overcome by the force of tradition. Senghor stated that this novel is more than a "political novel", that it is "the novel of Man" ("le roman de l'Homme"), and he continues: "If Peter Abrahams is a great novelist, it is because he is, first of all, a great writer. A classic who borrows less from Europe than from Africa. ... Peter Abrahams is the classic of Négritude" (Léopold Sédar Senghor).

"Mr. Abrahams demonstrated his ability to handle a story which could easily take on epic proportions. ... Mr. Abrahams' unquestioned talents and the immediacy of the theme to which he has committed himself give promise of a strong and authentic historian of the Africa which is in the making" (John S. Lash).

A Night of Their Own (1482) tells the story of a black South African who has been away from his homeland for many years, and returns as a courier with money for the underground movement. "Abrahams draws his characters with compassion and with sense of romanticized humanity" (Wilfred Cartey).

Abrahams's last novel so far is *This Island Now* (1483), a political novel about present-day Carribbean. "Because Mr. Abrahams's relationship with his new country has not yet jelled, one finds that where he grasps for power and poetry, he achieves only a mawkishness; where he sets out to give vivid portrayals of his islanders, he does them only a great disservice. He makes them even more unbelievable to their already sceptical eyes." "... *This Island Now* is an Instant novel-now coffee powder blend, easily digestible. And forgettable" (Sylvia Wynter).

Portrait on Plate III.

Abruquah, Joseph Wilfred   Ghana

Abruquah was born on May 8, 1921, in Saltpond at the coast, Central Region, Ghana, and educated at Mfantsipim School, Cape Coast, Ghana, King's College and Westminster College, London, where he received his diploma in Education and Geography. He was a teacher then at Mfantsipim School in Cape Coast from 1949 to 1957 and at Keta Secondary School from 1957 to 1963. In 1963 Abruquah returned to Mfantsipim School to become its Headmaster, but was refused further employment by the Ghana government in 1970 after the military handed over the government to Dr. K. A. Busia. Abruquah left Ghana for the United States and is a lecturer in African Literature at the University of Iowa, Iowa City, and a member of the International Writers' Workshop at the same university (1971).

Abruquah is the author of two novels, *The Catechist* (4) and *The Torrent* (5).

Joe de Graft wrote about *The Catechist*: "No pretensions to African avant-gard fiction writing; none of the rather over-played conflicts between 'traditional' and present-day Africa; not larded with folk wisdom concealed in proverbs; no attempt to show off or put over 'our beloved Africa'; no striving towards a hybrid of the English language that will pass for African — a language which, almost alas! is becoming such a tiresome feature of so much West African fiction in English. And yet this novel is well written und very readable, because it says what it wants to say without fumbling, without straining" (Joe de Graft).

Abubakar Imam, Alhaji   Nigeria

Born in 1911 at Kagara, Kintagora Province, Northwestern State, Nigeria, Abubakar Imam was sent to the Katsina Provincial School in 1922, from where he entered the Katsina Training College in 1927. As a teacher at the Katsina Middle School he won a prize in an essay-competition organized in 1933 by the Translation Bureau, a branch of the Education Department of Northern Nigeria. In 1934 Abubakar Imam was appointed the first Honorary Secretary of the Katsina Provincial Board, a local parliament of district heads; in 1935 he was delegated to the Translation Bureau in Zaria for six months.

In 1939 Abubakar Imam became editor of a newly founded Hausa newspaper "Gaskiya Ta Fi Kwabo", published by the British administration. In 1943 he was nominated by the Northern House of Chiefs to join the first West African Press Delegation to the United Kingdom. On this occasion he met Lord Lugard and criticized his policy of Indirect Rule in Northern Nigeria.

In 1951 Abubakar Imam was elected to the House of Assembly and House of Representatives. In the same year he gave up his post as editor of "Gaskiya Ta Fi Kwabo" to become the Head of the Book Section of the Corporation. In 1954 he resigned his political appointment to become Superintendent of the Government Literature Agency.

In 1962 Abubakar Imam was awarded the Margaret Wrong Memorial Fund Scholarship of the University of London, in appreciation of "his distinguished editorial services as Hausa editor of 'Gaskiya Ta Fi Kwabo', Editorial Superintendent with the Northern Region Literature Agency, and for his authorship of fiction, history and miscellaneous writings in Hausa".

Together with Alhaji Abubakar Mahmud Gumi and Alhaji Haliru Binji, Abubakar Imam is working on a translation of the Koran into Hausa.

Abubakar Imam is the author of seventeen books in Hausa, the majority of which deals with Islam history and culture. Education is also the subject of his fiction, *Tafiya mabudin ilimi* (6), *Ruwan Bagaja* (7) and *Magana jari ce* (8).

Abubakar Tafawa Balewa, Alhaji Sir   Nigeria

Born in December 1912 in Tafawa-Balewa, Bauchi-Province, Nigeria, Alhaji Abubakar Tafawa Balewa, the son of a district head, was educated locally, then went to Katsina College, where he qualified as a teacher. He was first a teacher, then from 1943 to 1947, superintendent, of Bauchi Middle School, passing his Senior Teacher's Certificate by private studies. In 1945/46 he studied at the Institute of Education, London University, England.

Returning to Nigeria he became Education Officer, and was almost immediately appointed to the first Northern Region House of Assembly, being elected from there to the Nigerian Legislative Council. In September 1951 he was, with the Sardauna of Sokoto, one of the founders of the Northern Peoples Congress (N.P.C.) and was elected to the Northern House of Assembly and, from there, to the Federal House of Representatives. In 1952 he became Federal Minister of Works, in 1954 Federal Minister of Transport, and in 1957 he became Chief Minister. In 1960 he became the first Federal Prime Minister. The same year he received the title of Sir from Queen Elizabeth II, and in 1961 he became Privy Councillor of the United Kingdom.

During several changes in constitution and Cabinet, Abubakar Tafawa Balewa remained Prime Minister of Nigeria until his death during the military revolt of January 15, 1966. His body was found a few days later.

Abubakar Tafawa Balewa wrote a very popular novel, *Shaihu Umar* (9). It is a portrayal of Hausa family life and Islamic society — a statement of the values and philosophy of orthodox Islam. The book, published in Hausa as early as 1934, was translated into English in 1967 (9 a). His speeches were collected in the volume *Nigeria Speaks*, Ikeja 1964.

Achebe, Chinua   Nigeria

Born on November 15, 1930, in Ogidi near Onitsha, East Central State, Nigeria, Chinua Achebe, an Ibo, is the son of a teacher in charge of the Church Missionary Society's village school. He attended this school and in 1944 went to Government College in Umuahia. In 1953 he was one of the first students to obtain his B. A. from the University College of Ibadan. In 1954 he began a career in broadcasting as Talks Producer for the Nigerian Broadcasting Service. In 1956 he attended the BBC Staff School, and in 1961 he was appointed Director of External Broadcasting for Nigeria, "Voice of Nigeria". From 1960 to 1962 he visited East Africa on a grant from Rockefeller Foundation, and in 1963 he was awarded a Fellowship for Creative Artists by UNESCO and travelled to the United States, Brazil and Great Britain.

In 1966, after the massacre of Ibos in Northern Nigeria, Achebe relinquished his post at the radio and moved back to Eastern Nigeria. In 1967 he, together with the poet Christopher Okigbo, launched a publishing company in Enugu. Their aim was to publish relevant literature for African school children based on local thought. When, however, the Nigerian civil war broke out, Okigbo joined the Biafran army and later that year was killed in action. Achebe subsequently threw in his lot with his fellow-Ibos in Biafra. His house was destroyed during the war.

In the latter part of 1969 Achebe, in the company of Gabriel Okara and Cyprian Ekwensi, toured the United States, lecturing at universities. Shortly after the war, he was appointed Research Fellow in the Institute of African Studies at the University of Nigeria, Nsukka, East Central State. He is editor of the campus magazine of the University of Nigeria in Nsukka, "Nsukkascope", editor of the cultural review "Okike", published by Nwamife publishing house, editorial adviser of Heinemann's "African Writers Series" and of the newly founded publishing house Nwankwo Ifejika & Co, Enugu. In August 1972 Achebe has been awarded an honorary Doctorate of letters by Dartmouth University, USA, for his "unique contribution to the literature of the world".

Achebe's first novel, *Things Fall Apart* (11), translated into thirteen languages, is set in Iboland at the turn of the century. It is concerned with the dislocation of the African society caused by the impact of Western civilisation, as heralded by the arrival of the missionaries. Besides it is a lovingly drawn reconstruction of a traditional Ibo community. *No longer at Ease* (12) depicts the story of Obi Okonkwo, the grandson of the hero of *Things Fall Apart* and a man with a Western education, who can't fall in with the social demands of his surrounding. He falls and his fall is the result of the profound gulf between his intellectual awareness and his individual place in his society. *Arrow of God* (14) describes the Ibo society at the onmarch of the British administration. With the fight of the old priest Ezeulu for the upkeep of the old power relations, the individual and the social drama are woven into a unity. *A Man of the People* (17), Achebe's most recent novel, is set in modern Nigeria and deals with a corrupt politician and political deeds, that are the outcome only of personal conflicts.

Achebe published two collections of short stories, *The Sacrificial Egg* (13) and *Girls at War and Other Stories,* London 1972. The latter combines all the stories previously published in *The Sacrificial Egg* and scattered in various journals, added by the hitherto unpublished title story. *Chike and the River* (16) is a children's book. Achebe ventured into poetry with his volume *Beware, Soul Brother, and Other Poems,* first published in Enugu in 1971, and republished in 1972 in London.

His essays comprise the following: *The Role of the Writer in a New Nation* (S 1); *English and the African Writer* (S 2); *The Novelist as Teacher* (S 3); *Le fardeau de l'écrivain noir* (S 4), translated also into English under the title *The Black Writer's Burden* (S 4 a); and *The African Writer and the Biafran Cause* (SW 206).

Books on Chinua Achebe are G. D. Killam, *The Novels of Chinua Achebe,* London 1969, and Arthur Ravenscroft *Chinua Achebe,* London 1969. Both studies are more descriptive than critical, supplying mainly explanations for the use of schools.

"One can observe his mastery of the English language, his skill in choosing the right words to convey his ideas, his keen sense of what is in character and what is not, his instinct for appropriate metaphor and symbol, and his ability to present a thoroughly African world in thoroughly African terms" (Bernth Lindfors).

Portrait on Plate XI.

Adali-Mortty, Geormbeeyi   Ghana

Born in 1916 at Gbogame near Ho, Volta Region, Ghana, Geormbeeyi Adali-Mortty was educated in the Roman Catholic School at Kpandu, and at Achimota College near Accra. As a graduate student he had an extended stay at Cornell University, Ithaca, New York, USA.

After leaving school Geormbeeyi Adali-Mortty worked for nine years as a teacher. In 1946 he became a social worker, transferring to the Institute of Extra-Mural Studies of the University of Accra, in 1949. From 1966 to 1968 he was Ghana's Special Commissioner for Redeployment of Labour.

In 1961 Geormbeeyi Adali-Mortty was a co-founder of the literary magazine "Okyeame". His poems and essays have appeared in journals and anthologies.

He coedited one of these anthologies, *Messages: Poems from Ghana* (AW 121).

His poems mark the deep attachment to his mother and to his birthplace. Though fiercely traditional in his material, he knows how to cope with the harsh realities and problems of modern African life, a vision at once romantic and realistic.

Adotevi, Stanislas Spéro   Dahomey

Born on February 4, 1934 in Lome, Togo, Stanislas Spéro Adotevi is, on his father's side, a Mina from Degbénou, and on his mother's side a descendant from Foli Bébé, the king of Glidji. After his primary and secondary education done at the Séminaire Saint-Gall at Whydah, he continued his education at Caen, France, and then in Paris, at the famous Lycée Henri-IV. He studied Philosophy at the Sorbonne and specialised in "myths and ideologies of a dawning society", and "primitive mentality".

With his examinations he returned to Dahomey in 1963, taught some months at the Lycée Béhanzin in Porto-Novo, became Technical Councillor to the Cabinet of the President of the Republic, and in 1964 he was appointed Director of Cabinet of the Minister of Foreign Affairs. As the result of a disagreement he resigned in September 1965. Two months later he was called back and became General Secretary of the Government. In February 1966 he joined the government as High Commissioner for Information. He resigned from the Soglo Government in March 1967, to continue teaching at the Lycée Béhanzin. In October 1967 he was appointed Director of IRAD (Institut de Recherches Appliquées du Dahomé) in Porto-Novo. And on April 24, 1969 he has been appointed General Commissioner for Youth and Sports.

Stanislas Spéro Adotevi is one of the leading Dahomeyan intellectuals, his articles on literature, culture and politics having been published in Dahomey — *Etudes dahoméennes* — and abroad.

Aggrey, James Emmanuel Kwegyir   Ghana

Born on October 18, 1875, at Anomabu, a town 15 miles East
of Cape Coast, Central Region, Ghana, as son of Princess
Abena Annuah of Ajumaku, and Prince Kodwo Kwegyir, Chief
Linguist in the court of King Amonoo V of Anomabu, James
Emmanuel Kwegyir Aggrey was the fourth of eight children.
He entered the Wesleyan School at Cape Coast in 1883, where
he and 23 other lads received instruction in joinery, black-
smithery, home decorating and painting, in addition to formal
literary education.

In 1891 Aggrey completed his course at this college, and
accepted the post of temporary pupil-teacher at Abura-Dunkwa
(20 miles East of Cape Coast) at a monthly salary of 35 shillings. A year afterwards, he was transferred to Cape Coast,
where he joined the staff of the Wesleyan Memorial School, of
which he became Headmaster in 1898. He made Cape Coast
Wesleyan School, with its 400 enrolled students, the best school
in the colony.

The years 1895 to 1898 saw him, besides his remaining a
teacher, as politician and soldier. He became Secretary of the
Aborigines Rights Protection Society, fighting the Public Lands
Bill of 1897. During the Fanti-Ashanti War he was attached
to the Telegraph Unit as interpreter, and marched with his
unit from Cape Coast to Kumasi in December 1896, where he
took part in the battle in 1897, but returned to Cape Coast
unhurt.

On July 10, 1898, Aggrey left for America. In 1902 he
became Registrar and Professor of Livingstone College, North
Carolina, USA. In 1903 he was ordained Elder of the Zion
Methodist Church; in 1912 he obtained his Doctoral Degree at
Hood Theological Seminary. In 1914 he became Pastor at Miller's Chapel and Sandy Ridge; in 1923 he obtained his Ph. D.
at Columbia University.

Aggrey served as the only African member on two inter-
nationally reputed education commissions for Africa — the
Phelps-Stokes Commissions, which toured almost every country

in Africa. Thus we hear of Aggrey in Sierra Leone and Liberia in September 1920, in the Gold Coast from October to November 1920, in Nigeria and Fernando Poo from November to December 1920, the Cameroons in December 1920, the Belgian Congo in January 1921, Angola from January to March 1921, South Africa from March to June 1921, Abyssinia from January to February 1924, Kenya from February to March 1924, Uganda in March 1924, Tanganyika and Zanzibar from March to April 1924, Nyasaland and Rhodesia from April to June 1924, South Africa again in June 1924, and again in the Gold Coast in October 1924.

On his return home on October 15, 1924, Aggrey became a founder-member of the staff of Achimota College. He left again for America in July, 1926, and returned in November that year. Achimota, his dream, was formally opened on January 28, 1927, and in May that year he left for England and America once more. He died on July 30, 1927, in New York, of pneumococcal meningitis.

"Aggrey of Africa" or "Aggrey the Great" was a famous educator and speaker. His sayings were selected by C. Kingsley Williams in the pamphlet *Aggrey Said,* London 1945. His most famous utterance was: "You can play a tune of sorts on the white keys, and you can play a tune of sorts on the black keys, but for harmony you must use both the black and the white." The journal of the West African Students' Union, "The Keys", was named after this saying.

"The saintly J. E. K. Aggrey was far too impracticable in his theorizing about co-operation between the races" (Robert W. July).

Agunwa, Clement   Nigeria

Born in 1936 (not 1933, as stated elsewhere) in the village Ukunu near Agulu, Njikoko Division, East Central State, Nigeria, Clement Agunwa had his primary education at Agulu. He could not go on to secondary school because of lack of funds,

though he had passed the entrance examination to the famous
D.M.G.S. Onitsha in 1948. He was trained as a teacher instead,
from 1951 to 1952 at the Bishop Lasbrey Teachers College in
Irete near Owerri, and at St. Mark's Teachers Training College
at Awka from 1955 to 1956. In 1953 he passed the Cambridge
Overseas School Certificate, as an external candidate, and in
June 1957 the General Certificate of Education. From 1958 to
1961 Clement Agunwa continued his education at the University of Ibadan. In 1964/65 he received a Diploma in Teaching
of English from the University of Edinburgh.

He has been a teacher since. In 1962 he became Principal of
the Obazu Grammar School. From 1964 to 1972 he was Principal of the Agulu Grammar School. Since 1972 he has been
Principal of the Oaukwa Grammar School, and he is a senior
examiner in English Literature for the West African Examinations Council.

Besides a school reader, *Day-by-Day English for Primary
Schools in Eastern Nigeria,* 1963 to 1966, he wrote a novel,
More Than Once (36), born of the author's personal exper-
iences in perseverance.

"The reader, bogged down in the irrelevant passages and
sloppy writing, is simply bored" (Charles R. Larson).

"The book is perhaps reminiscent of Onitsha market literature" (Hans Zell).

"This kind of moralising may appeal to a large section of
the society needing re-awakening" (Rose Mukuria).

Aidoo, Ama Ata   Ghana

Born on March 23, 1942, near Saltpond, at the coast, Central Region, Ghana, Christina Ama Ata Aidoo — this is her full name —
was educated at the Wesley Girls' High School at Cape Coast
and at the University of Ghana at Legon, near Accra, where she
graduated in 1964 and became a Research Fellow in African
Studies. In summer 1966 she participated in the Harvard

International Seminar at Harvard University, Cambridge, Massachusetts, USA. She taught African Literature at the University of Nairobi, Kenya, and participated in the Pan-African Festival in Algiers, in 1969. From there she returned to Ghana after a two-year trip that had also taken her to London and East Africa. She is now lecturer in English at the University College, Cape Coast, Ghana.

Ama Ata Aidoo wrote two plays, *The Dilemma of a Ghost* (39), and *Anowa* (41), and many short stories which appeared in anthologies and journals like "Journal of the New African Literature and the Arts", "Okyeame", "Black Orpheus", etc. and were finally collected in the volume *No Sweetness Here* (40).

The Dilemma of a Ghost "explores the situation in which an American Negro bride returns 'home' with her Ghanaian husband, to find herself a complete stranger, color not withstanding" (Eldred Jones). "Most of the dramatical interest comes from the fact that western culture in this case is represented not by a man or a woman of white race, but by a young black woman ... The subject needs a more elaborated treatment than the one that is offered here" (Mbella Sonne Dipoko).

"The dialogue has authenticity, as well as sparkle and wit, though there are occasional failures in the use of American slang" (C. J. Rea).

"The pace of the play is too slow, the climax too weak, and too many characters spend too much of their time feeling sorry for themselves" (Bernth Lindfors).

"... *Anowa* is a dramatization of an old Ghanaian legend: The beautiful Anowa refuses the suitors chosen by her parents and decides to marry the man of her own choice" (Hans Zell).

Portrait on Plate IX.

Aig-Imoukhuede, Frank   Nigeria

Born on January 8, 1935, in Edunabon near Ife, Western State, Nigeria, Frank Abiodun Aig-Imoukhuede grew up in Benin

Province, Mid Western State. He is the son of a clergyman who died just before completing a translation of the New Testament into Ora, a widely spoken Bini dialect. He attended at least fifteen primary schools, then Igbobi College, Lagos, and University College, Ibadan, where he graduated. He was employed by the Broadcasting House in Lagos, later as a reporter by the "Daily Express", Lagos, with John Pepper Clark. He then worked at the Ministry of Information in Ibadan. Since 1971 he has been Editor of "Nigeria Magazine" in Lagos.

Much of Aig-Imoukhuede's poetry is in Pidgin-English. It has been published in journals like "Black Orpheus", "The Horn", and "Présence Africaine", and in Anthologies like "Poems from Black Africa" (A 42), "Modern Poetry from Africa" (A 75), "The African Assertion" (A 98), and "Nigeria Student Verse" (AW 122).

While he was at University College, Ibadan, he wrote two plays for campus production, which were later published in Lagos, *Ikeke* (42) and *Day of Sasswood* (43).

"Aig-Imoukhuede delights in remaining close to the people" (Langston Hughes).

Ajao, Motolami Aderogba   Nigeria

Born in 1930 in Awe near Oyo, Western State, Nigeria, Motolami Aderogba Ajao was educated at the Baptist Academy in Lagos. He then attended the George Watson's Boys' College in Edinburgh, Scotland, and the College of Technology and Commerce in Leicester, England. He later studied at the University of Leipzig, East Germany. His only novel, *On the Tiger's Back* (48), translated into three languages, depicts his experiences in East Germany.

Ajao, S.   Nigeria

Born in Awe, near Oyo, Western State, Nigeria, S. Adedeji
Ajao received a secondary education. After finishing school he
became Secretary of the USA Pat-Boone-Fan Club led by Femi
Phillips. In 1966 the club changed its name into "Osumare
Concert Party" and staged plays in and around Lagos. Later
Ajao founded his own theatre group, the "Melody Theatre"
and changed its name after a year into "Oriyomi Players".

Ajao's play *Suru Baba Iwa* was first performed for the "Eko
Akete Association" at their anniversary. It was successfully
staged again at a drama competition organized by the Goethe
Institute in Lagos in January 1971. Other plays performed are
Iforiti, Inawo Eko, Eruku Jomu, and *Iwa Lewa.*

Akar, John   Sierra Leone

Born on May 20th, 1927, at Rotifunk, Southern Province, Sierra
Leone, John Joseph Akar was educated at the E.U.B. Day School,
Rotifunk from 1934 to 1942, and the Albert Academy, Freetown from 1943 to 1946. He proceeded to the United States
of America in 1947 and entered Otterbein College, Westerville,
Ohio. In 1950 he obtained his B.A. degree at the University of
California at Berkeley. He continued his postgraduate studies
at the London School of Economics for two years and later was
a Nuffield Scholar at the African Studies Centre, University
of Edinburgh, Scotland. Akar then worked as a freelance journalist for the B.B.C. from 1950 to 1955, for the Voice of
America from 1955 to 1956, and for the Worldwide Broadcasting System in New York from 1956 to 1957.

On his return to Sierra Leone in 1957, Akar was appointed
Head of Programme in the Sierra Leone Broadcasting Service.
Three years later he was promoted Director of Broadcasting.

In 1959 John Akar was decorated Officer of the Most Distinguished Order of the Cedars of the Lebanon by the Lebanese

Government, and in June 1966 he was awarded in the Queen's Birthday Honours List the M.B.E. (Member of the Most Distinguished Order of the British Empire) in recognition of his contribution to culture in Sierra Leone.

In September 1967 Akar became Secretary of the Commonwealth Broadcasting Conference Secretariat in London, and in June 1969 was appointed Sierra Leone's Ambassador to the United States, acting also as High Commissioner to Canada and Jamaica. On April 20, 1971 he resigned and is now Professor at the University of California, Berkeley, USA.

John Akar's versatility led him to broadcasting, writing, acting and composing the Sierra Leone National Anthem. His two plays are *Valley Without Echo* (52) and *Cry Tamba* (53), which won him a prize in the "Independence Competition" sponsored by the Congress for Cultural Freedom.

Akiga   Nigeria

Born in 1898 in Tivland, in the village of Sai, a senior of the Shitire clan, Nigeria, Akiga was the first of his tribe to come under the influence of the missionaries. After his conversion he wandered round Tivland to preach the gospel. It was then that the idea was formed in his mind to write down his tribal traditions, "in order that the new generation of Tiv, which is beginning to learn this New Knowledge, should know the things of the fathers as well as those of the present generation". Later Akiga served his people in Gaskiya Corporation as editor of a Tiv news-sheet. For five years he was a member of the Northern House of Assembly, and afterwards with the Tiv Native Authority in the field of literature and adult education.

Akiga wrote down the history and the customs of his tribe in the Tiv language. The manuscript was translated by Rupert East and published only in English under the title *Akiga's Story* (55).

Akpabot, Samuel   Nigeria

Born in October 1930 in Uyo, South Eastern State, Samuel
Akpabot was educated at King's College, Lagos. From there, in
1954, he went to study at the Royal College of Music, London,
for five years. In 1959 he was appointed Senior Music Producer
in the Nigerian Broadcasting Corporation in Lagos, then Assistant Lecturer at the University of Nigeria. From 1964 to
1967 he continued his studies at the University of Chicago,
USA, where he obtained his M. A. in Musicology.

Samuel Akpabot writes music for films, ballets, festivals and
orchestras. He published a volume of poetry, *Masters of the
Music* (70).

Akpan, Ntieyong Udo   Nigeria

Born in 1924 in the Ibibio village of Mbiabong, Uyo division,
Calabar province, South Eastern State, Nigeria, Ntieyong Udo
Akpan was sent to the school of the Scottish Mission in Calabar.
When his father died in 1934, his mother could not afford his
school fees. So it was the missionary Rev. A. T. H. Taylor, who
virtually took a father's place. In return Akpan acted as a
steward in Mr. Taylor's household.

Later he was expelled from Hope Wadell College in Calabar
and settled down to private study for his London Matriculation.
In 1944 he passed, just in time to become a third class government clerk before the edict came into force that for a time,
government jobs were to be reserved for ex-service men. While
working in the Resident's office in Calabar, he continued to
study, and in 1950 passed the London B. A. in Economics,
History, and Law. He became a clerk. In 1952 he was finally
accepted for the Administrative Service.

Apart from his field postings, he has been official secretary
at the Eastern Region's London office, Permanent Secretary of
a number of ministries, clerk to the Executive Council, Officer

in Charge of Establishments in the Premier's Office, and Secretary to the Public Service Commission. During the Military Régime, as Permanent Secretary to the Ministry of Commerce and Industry, he acted as Chairman of the Marketing Board and Director of several government-owned companies. In 1966 he became Head of the Eastern Civil Service in Enugu.

Ntieyong Udo Akpan always finds time for writing. A novel for school children *The Reservoir*, has been followed by *The Wooden Gong* (71), a novel of Ibibio village life, and a story for children, *Ini Abasi and the Sacred Ram* (72).

"*The Wooden Gong* is a 'life and customs' novel but its easy narrative, the author's sense of identity with his scene and characters and his eye for interesting incident keep it clear from artificiality. Akpan's story brings in social change, the mushroom growth of new churches, local custom, the clash with the colonial administration and, guiding everything, the tradition and power of the tribal secret society" (Edgar Wright).

Alapini, Julien   Dahomey

Born on August 28, 1906, in Abomey-Calavi near Cotonou, Southern District, Dahomey, Julien Alapini received his primary education at the Ecole Primaire in Whydah. From 1926 to 1929 he visited the Ecole William Ponty at Gorée, Senegal. After some teaching appointments he was, from 1959 to 1967 primary-school inspector in Dahomey. In 1967 he died in his house in Cotonou.

Julien Alapini wrote several books, religious and educational, *Les initiés*, Paris 1941, *Le petit Dahoméen*, Avignon 1950, *Les noix sacrées*, Monte Carlo 1950, and *Les Dahoméens et Togolais au centenaire des apparitions*, Avignon 1959. His only creative work is a collection for use in schools of short scenes to make children play themselves and their environment, *Acteurs noirs* (76).

Alegre, Costa
vid. *Costa Alegre, Caetano da*

Aluko, Timothy Mofolorunso   Nigeria

Born on June 14th, 1918, in Ilesha, Western State, Nigeria,
where he also received his early education, Timothy Mofolo-
runso Aluko visited the Government College, Ibadan from 1933
to 1939 and from 1939 to 1942 the Higher College in Yaba,
Lagos. From 1943 to 1946 he served as a junior engineer in the
Public Works Department of Lagos and Ilorin. From 1946 to
1950 he studied Engineering and Town Planning at the University of London and continued at the University of Newcastle
upon Tyne from 1968 to 1969. From 1950 to 1956 he was
Executive Engineer in the Public Works Department and held
the position of District Engineer in Oyo (1951—52), Oshogo
(1952—54), and Ikoyi (1954—56). From 1956 to 1960 he was
Town Engineer in Lagos, from 1960 to 1966 Controller of
Works Services and Permanent Secretary in the Ministry of
Works and Transport, Western State. He was also Chief Technical Adviser to the Government from 1963 to 1966. Now he
is Director of Public Works in the Western State and since 1966
has also been Senior Research Fellow in Municipal Engineering
at the University of Lagos.

T. M. Aluko was encouraged to write fiction by F. N. Lloyd
Williams, first Representative of the British Council in Nigeria.
He won prizes in short story contests organized in Nigeria by
the British Council in 1944 and 1945. A number of his short
stories and articles have been published in the "West African
Review" and broadcast by the B.B.C. West Africa Service.

Aluko's first novel, *One Man, One Wife* (80), describes the
conflict between Christians and "heathens" in a Yoruba village
community. "The author leaves us in no doubt where his
sympathies lie. Any reference to traditional religion is clothed
in abusive language! . . . Mr. Aluko's harangue against the

'pagans' is based on complete ignorance of the facts. He uses imperialist vocabulary, like 'juju' and 'idol' ... One can look forward to better work from this author. But this time he set out to write a novel about a conflict of cultures in an African village, but instead of a novel his book has become an harangue that ends with a sermon" (Ulli Beier).

"*One Man, One Wife* is a very funny book written with sympathy and real understanding of the conflicts involved" (Mbella Sonne Dipoko).

Aluko's next two novels, *One Man, One Matchet* (81) and *Kinsman and Foreman* (82), also deal with the cultural clash in a small town.

"For another 'conflict' story, full of a clear and objective understanding of the problems of the period, written with marvellous lucidity, and full of humour without irritating, belaboured flowery language, I recommend *One Man, One Matchet*" (Nunasu Amosu).

"Mr. T. M. Aluko displays in *Kinsman and Foreman* not only humour and mild sarcasm but also a penetrating understanding of the psychology of his people, and particularly the difficulty of a certain type of educated African to adapt himself as an individual to the demands of a virile traditional society" (Sunday Ogbonna Anozie).

In his latest novel, *Chief the Honourable Minister* (83), set in an imaginary state called "Afromacoland", Aluko "has a very keen eye for the foibles of politicians, and has drawn on his wide experience of them ... The characters, however, are imaginary, and are mostly types, each playing his role in what otherwise would be a textbook on political corruption and malpractice" (D. W.).

Amadi, Elechi   Nigeria

Born in 1934 in Allua, near Port Harcourt, Rivers State, Nigeria, Elechi Amadi was educated at Government College, Umuahia, and University College, Ibadan, where he took a degree in Mathematics and Physics. After a spell of land surveying and teaching, he was commissioned in the Nigerian army. He was attached to the Military School in Zaria, where he held the rank of Captain in 1966. During the Nigerian civil war he was a Captain in the Federal Army in Port Harcourt. He later left the army and returned to teaching.

His first novel, *The Concubine* (84), is about a woman whose first husband died and who brings suffering and death to her lovers. The second novel, *The Great Ponds* (85), concerns the rivalry of two villages over the ownership of a fishing area. In both novels Amadi depicts a picture of rural life without any kind of Western influences.

The Concubine "is the first African novel to deal exclusively with tribal life" (Theo Vincent). "*The Concubine* offers an evocation of Igbo life whose interest is to be partly in its strangeness to the reader (nothing is left to make its own impression; every variation on a cultural norm is busily pointed out and explained, as by a garrulous anthropologist) ... Elechi Amadi's slack energyless prose, that threatens to reduce everything to the same level of triteness. Every situation, however dramatic, labours under the weight of the vapidity that's attributed to it" (David Thompson). "The overall effect of such explanations is to ruin for the reader the significance of some of the most psychologically realistic scenes" (Kalu Uka).

"*The Concubine* is not only the best novel, in English, so far written by a Nigerian, it is also great literature and of potentially classic value" (Ukpabi A. Asika).

"... *The Great Ponds* already demonstrates a clear advance stylistically and technically on *The Concubine*" (Alastair Niven).

Amali, Samson O. O.   Nigeria

Samson O. O. Amali was born on January 29, 1947, in Upu-Oturkpo, Oturkpo Division, Benue Plateau State, Nigeria. He went to Up-Methodist Primary School in Oturkpo, New Nigerian Primary School in Lagos, and Alafia Institute Mokola in

Ibadan from 1952 to 1957, Christ High School in Lagos from 1958 to 1960, Methodist Boys' High School in Lagos from 1961 to 1962, and The International Secondary School, University of Ibadan from 1963 to 1966. Amali entered the University of Ibadan in 1966 and passed his B. A. Hons. degree in English with Sociology as his subsidiary in 1970. He also had one year of Phonetics, one year of Linguistics, two years of French, and one year of History. He has been working since in the Institute of African Studies, University of Ibadan, mainly assisting Prof. Robert Armstrong with various works concerning the Idoma language and conducting tape-recordings of Idoma oral texts. At the moment he is working temporarily in this institute as a Research Assistant in Idoma.

Amali speaks Idoma, English and Yoruba, he understands some Ibo and Tiv. Poems and articles of his are published in various newspapers and journals, among them "L'Afrique Actuelle" and "Black Orpheus". His poems and plays were published privately, as for example *Selected Poems* (87), *God Poems*, and *World Within Worlds & Other Poems*. His play, *Onugbo Mloko* (88), was first written in Idoma and published privately too, but has been translated into English and published by the Department of Linguistics and Nigerian Languages of the University of Ibadan. His second play, *The Downfall of Ogbuu* (86), has been staged three times in Amali's hometown Oturkpo. In 1970 Amali published another small book of poetry, and in 1971 another play in Idoma and English, *Nigeria*.

Besides these creative works Amali is occupied with the collection of Idoma oral texts and folktales, the history of the Tivs and a documentation of the Nigerian Civil War. Amali has won several literary awards.

Amar, Andrew Richard   Uganda

Born in 1934 in Amogu, Lango district, Uganda, Andrew Richard Amar, a Lango, was educated at Kalaki and Lira, and then at Makerere College in Kampala. In 1957 he came to London and studied Physics, Chemistry and Zoology at the Paddington Technical College and the Regent Street Polytechnic as a preliminary to studying Medicine. He went to Moscow in 1959 to read Medicine at Moscow University and left the Soviet Union late in the summer of 1960 to continue his studies in Europe.

Andrew Richard Amar is probably a pseudonym. All efforts to trace his whereabouts or to reveal the real name have been in vain.

Amar is the author of an autobiography, *A Student in Moscow* (1232).

Amo, Anton Wilhelm   Ghana

Born about 1703 near Axim in what is today Ghana, Amo came to Amsterdam in 1707, and was then given to Duke Anton Ulrich of Brunswick-Wolfenbüttel, who handed him over to his son August Wilhelm. In 1708 Amo was christened Anton Wilhelm after his patrons. In 1721 he was confirmed, in 1727 he went to Halle University, where in 1729 he graduated in Law with his dissertation *De jure Maurorum in Europa,* which unfortunately has not yet been traced. In 1730 he went to Wittenberg University and there in the same year gained a degree as Doctor of Philosophy. In 1733, on the visit of Augustus the Strong, Elector of Saxony and King of Poland, Dr. Amo led the students' procession in the monarch's honour. In 1734, after having his dissertation published, he was made Professor of Philosophy. In 1736 he returned to Halle as lecturer and there taught Psychology, 'Natural Law', and Decimal System — a universality which was then customary.

In 1738 Amo's *Tractatus de arte sobrie et accurate philosophandi* (96) was published in Halle; he himself had become quite a bright star in the firmament of Halle's Enlightenment. The following year he moved to Jena University, where he gave his inaugural lecture on 'The Frontiers of Psychology', and no doubt stayed there till May 1740. The two sons of Duke Anton Ulrich had died in 1731 and 1735 respectively; Johann Peter von Ludewig, Chancellor of Halle University, died in 1742; and Amo probably found no other patron in Germany. At any rate we hear no more of him until 1753, when he was back home in Axim, venerated apparently as a sort of witch doctor. We do not know when he died.

The only creative writing of Amo which has come down to us, is a short dedicative poem in German, written in 1737.

Amon d'Aby, François-Joseph   Ivory Coast

François-Joseph Amon d'Aby was born on July 17, 1913, in Abi, South District, Ivory Coast, and was educated in administration at the Ecole Normale William Ponty, Gorée, Senegal, where he received his diploma in 1937. In December 1937 Amon d'Aby did a course at the national archives and library, and in June 1938 he became Director of the national archives, a post he held till 1961. In 1961 he got his diploma from the Centre des Hautes Etudes sur l'Afrique et l'Asie Modernes, Paris, and in the same year a diploma from l'Institut des Hautes Etudes d'Outre-Mer, also in Paris.

Amon d'Aby returned to the Ivory Coast to work in the civil service. In September 1961 he was appointed Inspecteur des Affaires Administratives, and in 1966 Inspecteur Général des Services Administratifs, along with the post of Director of the national archives.

Besides his professional career, Amon d'Aby developed various other activities. From 1938 to 1942 he was a member of La Jeunesse Ouvrière Chrétienne (Young Christian Workers' Union), he has founded the weekly magazine "La Semaine Sportive", and he is one of the founder-members of the Théâtre Indigène in the Ivory Coast. After joining La Jeunesse Ouvrière Chrétienne, Amon d'Aby began writing plays for the stage of these young people: *La conversion des habitants de Yabi* (98), *Le Mando* (99), *Un mariage difficile* (101), *Noel! Noel! Jésus est né* (103), *Joseph vendu par ses frères* (105) and *Le supplice de Jeanne d'Arc* (107).

For the Théâtre Indigène de la Côte d'Ivoire he wrote the play *Boussatié* (102), *La mort de la Princesse Alloua* (106) and *L'entrevue de Boundoukou* (100).

In 1951 Amon d'Aby was one of the founder-members of the Cercle Culturel et Folklorique de la Côte d'Ivoire. He acted as general secretary to this association and brought its theatrical section to life. He wrote for this Cercle: *Entraves* (108), *Kwao Adjoba* (109), *La sorcière ou Le triomphe du 'dixième-mauvais'* (107) and *La couronne aux enchères* (111).

Besides plays, Amon d'Aby has published several studies on Ivorian sociological and ethnological problems, such as *La Côte d'Ivoire dans la Cité Africaine*, Paris 1951, *Le problème des chefferies traditionnelles en Côte d'Ivoire*, Paris 1958, and *Croyances réligieuses et coutumes juridiques des Agni de la Côte d'Ivoire*, Paris 1960.

This research work is more to Amon d'Aby's liking, and he intends to follow this new line now.

François-Joseph Amon d'Aby is a member of the Académie des Sciences d'Outre-Mer, of the Institut International des Civilisations Différentes (INCIDI), of the Société des Auteurs et Compositeurs Dramatiques and of the Société Française d'Histoire d'Outre-Mer. He received many decorations.

Anahory, Terêncio   Cape Verde Islands

Born in 1934 on the island Boa Vista of the Cape Verde Islands, Terêncio Casimiro Anahory Silva spent most of his youth in Portuguese Guinea. He studied Law at the University of Lisbon before he became a journalist.

Terêncio Anahory contributed to the "Boletim de Cabo Verde" and to the journal "Bolanense" published in Bissau. His volume of poetry, *Caminho longe* (112), shows a poet who tries to liberate himself from the influence of the "Claridade" poets.

Ananou, David   Togo

Born on August 17, 1917, in Lome, Togo, David Ananou had his primary education in Lome and his Primaires supérieures in Porto Novo, Dahomey. He was trained as a teacher and received his diploma in 1936. Most of his life he was Principal of a private school in Lome, where he is still living in retirement.

His only novel *Fils de Fétiche* (113), favourable to the western civilisation, gives a summary history of two generations in a rural Ewe area.

"The day-to-day life is drawn with great warmth of sentiment" (Robert Pageard).

Andrade, Fernando Costa   Angola

Fernando da Costa Andrade was born in 1936 in Lepi, district Huamba, Angola. For a time, he lived in Brazil where he was arrested during the overthrow of the Government of Goulart. He later studied Architecture in Yugoslavia. In Portugal he was one of the animators of the cultural movement of the Casa dos Estudantes do Império. He is one of the fighting members of the MPLA (Movimento Popular de Libertação de Angola).

He has published two volumes of poetry, *Terra de acácias rubras* (1491) and *Tempo angolano na Itália,* São Paulo 1963, and a poetical pamphlet for MPLA, *Um ramo de miosotis* (1492). His poems have appeared in journals like "Présence Africaine" and anthologies like "Literatura africana de expressão portuguesa" (A 5) and "La poésie africaine d'expression portugaise" (A 6).

Andrade, Mario de   Angola

Born on August 21, 1928, in Golungo Alto, district North
Cuanza, Angola, Mário Pinto de Andrade had his secondary
education in Luanda. In 1948 he went to Portugal to study
Philosophy at the University of Lisbon. In 1954 he fled to Paris
and studied Sociology at the Sorbonne in Paris. At that period
he became Secretary of "Présence Africaine" and of the African
Society of Culture and he helped to organise the First Congress
of Negro Writers and Artists in Paris in 1956 and the Second
Congress in 1958 in Rome. He became a member of the MPLA
(Movimento Popular de Libertação de Angola) and in 1959,
with the death of Ilidio Machado, Mario de Andrade became
the new President. He was first based in Conakry, Guinea,
from where he travelled widely, later in Kinshasa. In 1962,
when Agostinho Neto escaped from Portuguese prison, Mario
de Andrade handed over the presidency to him and became
General Secretary, based in Algiers.

  Mario de Andrade is one of the leading intellectuals of Angola and has contributed many essays on literature and politics
to "Présence Africaine", "Europe" and many political journals.
He published quite a number of anthologies in which he introduced and commented African writing in Portuguese to the
international audience: *Anthologia da poesia negra de expressão
portuguesa* (A 4), *Literatura africana de expressão portuguesa*
(A 5), *La poésie africaine d'expression portugaise* (A 6), *Lette-
ratura negra* (A 67), and *Poesia negra de expressão portuguesa*
(A 105).

Andriananjason, Victor Georges   Madagascar

Born on July 4, 1940, in Tananarive, Madagascar, Victor
George Andriananjason is the son of a surveyor. He received his
education in Madagascar and in France. In Paris he studied

journalism at the Ecole Supérieure de Journalisme and at the Ecole des Hautes Etudes Internationales.

In 1962 he went to Germany with a group of musicians and dancers from Madagascar performing in Protestant circles. He sang, danced and played the clarinet. Since 1964 he has been contributing programmes to Deutsche Welle (Voice of Germany), Cologne, where he settled. He later was employed by Deutsche Welle in the editorial department. In 1971 he was transferred to the Antilles Radio Cooperation in Plymouth on the island Montserrat, British West Indies, as representative of Deutsche Welle.

Victor George Andriananjason has published a book on Madagascar in German, *Im Lande der Malagasy,* Hangelar 1969, the original being written in French.

Anozie, Sunday O.   Nigeria

Born on September 27, 1940, in Owerri, East Central State, Nigeria, Sunday Ogbonna Anozie received his primary education from 1945 to 1949 at CMS (Church Missionary Society) School Owerri, and from 1950 to 1952 at Government School, Owerri. From 1953 to 1957 he was at Holy Ghost College, Owerri. From 1958 to 1959 he taught English, Latin and History at the Okigwi National Grammar School at Umunna, then he began his university education. From 1960 to 1963 he was at the University of Nigeria at Nsukka, from 1963 to 1964 at the University of Toulouse, France, from 1964 to 1965 at the Sorbonne in Paris. In 1965 he studied at the University of Cambridge, England, and from 1966 to 1969 at the Sorbonne again, where he received his Ph. D. in 1969. Since 1969 he has been teaching English and French Literature and West African Literature in English and French at the University of Texas at Austin, USA. Since September 1972 Anozie has been Associate Professor in the Department of African Studies, State University of New York, New Paltz, N. Y.

Sunday Ogbonna Anozie, as a scholar, has applied structuralist theories to African literature, both oral and written. He is editor of "The Conch", the leading structuralist African journal. His book, *Sociologie du roman africain* (SW 210) is based on his Sorbonne doctoral dissertation. *Christopher Okigbo: Creative Rhetoric*, London 1971, analyses the poetry of this writer.

Articles and essays of Sunday O. Anozie have appeared in numerous journals, such as "The Conch", "Présence Africaine", "The African Writer", "Cahier d'Etudes Africaine", "Insight" and others.

António, Mário   Angola

Born on April 5, 1934, in Maquela do Zombo near Luanda, Angola, Mário António Fernandes de Oliveira who uses only his first two names as a writer, went to school in Luanda and became a meteorologist. In 1959 he was arrested as a "threat to inner peace and the unity of the nation", but some years later he was free again. He lives in Lisbon, Portugal.

Mário António has written three volumes of stories: *Gente para romance: Álvaro Lígia, António* (1497), *Crónica de cidade estranha* (1501), and *Farra no fim de semana* (1502). All his other books, besides a volume of essays, *Luanda 'île' créole*, Lisbon 1970, are collections of poems: *Poesias* (1495), *Amor* (1496), *Poemas & canto miúdo* (1498), *Chingufo; poemas angolanos* (1499), *100 poemas* (1500), *Era, tempo de poesia* (1503), *Rosto de Europa* (1504), and *Coração transplantado*, Braga (Cape Verde Islands) 1970. Some of his poems have been translated and published in foreign journals and anthologies.

"The book *100 Poemas* unites nearly all the poetry by Mário António ... a real poet, able to see the world from the point of real nature ..." (José Blanc de Portugal).

"From his initiation into poetry not very long ago until his last lyrical documents ... which recall the strange Negro music he gathers from his musical instrument, Mário António presented himself always as the little boy who is disenchanted that nothing cures him from his disenchantment" (Amândio César).

Portrait on Plate XIII.

Armah, Ayi Kwei   Ghana

Born in 1939 in Takoradi, Western Region, Ghana, Ayi Kwei Armah received his secondary education at Achimota College near Accra. In 1959 he left for the United States, where he studied at Groton, Massachusetts, and at Harvard University, Cambridge, Massachusetts. He graduated in Sociology, and went to Algiers where he worked as translator for the weekly "Révolution Africaine".

Returning to Ghana in 1966, he taught English at the Navrongo School and began script writing for Ghana Television. In 1967 he left Ghana again to participate in the Graduate Writing Program of Columbia University, New York, on a grant from the Farfield Foundation. Then he went to Paris where he was on the staff of "Jeune Afrique". In 1968 he left Paris to become Visiting Lecturer in African Literature at the University of Massachusetts, USA. Since 1972 he has been teaching in Dar es Salaam, Tanzania.

Ayi Kwei Armah wrote poems, published in the journal "Okyeame", short stories, published in "Okyeame", "The New African", "Harper's" and "Atlantic Monthly", essays published in "Présence Africaine" and "The New York Review of Books", and three novels, *The Beautyful Ones Are Not Yet Born* (135), *Fragments,* (136) and *Why Are We So Blest?*, New York 1972.

The Beautyful Ones Are Not Yet Born denounces filth and corruption in Ghanaian life and society. *Fragments* draws its major theme from the conflict between the shattered spiritual vision and the grotesque material expectations of Africa today, *Why Are We So Blest?* depicts three characters trying to break out of their cages: the African student longing to free himself from the strictures of privilege by revolutionary action, the

43

white American girl trying to overcome her prejudices, and the African intellectual trying to overcome his paralyzing pessimism. But they all fail.

"What is impressive about *The Beautyful Ones* is the way in which it expresses the disillusion and cynism engendered in Ghana in the last years of Nkrumah, which his fall only seemed to compound" (Kaye Whiteman).

"The style is deliberate, cumulative and successfully contrived to heighten the feeling of disgust and revulsion. Its invocation of disgust and nausea strongly recalls Swift, and as in Swift's satire the moral, physiological and atmospheric states are studiously fused to produce a unified and powerful moral suggestion" (E. N. Obiechina).

"The novel hits your senses, especially those of sight, smell and touch, with an insistence and pungency that are almost choking: unbearable" (Jonathan Kariara).

"The fact that Armah's presentation of a universe of spiritual poverty and moral decay is directly related to the present social situation in Africa is indicative of the novelist's growing awareness of the predicaments which the individual in modern Africa is beginning to live with" (Abiola Irele).

Portrait on Plate VIII.

Armattoe, Raphael Ernest Grail   Ghana

Born on August 20, 1913, at Keta, Volta Region, Ghana, son of Mr. Glikpo Armattoe, a prosperous merchant of Palime, Togoland, Raphael Ernest Grail Armattoe had his early education in Lome, Togoland, and Denu, Gold Coast. In 1925 he entered Mfantsipim School in Cape Coast, where he received his Cambridge School Certificate in 1928. With funds from his father he left for Europe to study Medicine at the University of Hamburg, Germany, French Literature at the University of Lille, France, Anthropology and Ethnology at the Sorbonne of Paris, Medicine at the University of Edinburgh, Scotland, and Physical

Sciences at the University of Londonderry, Northern Ireland. He held doctorate degrees in Philosophy, Anthropology and Medicine.

Between 1939 and 1945, Raphael Ernest Grail Armattoe was Honorary Physician in charge of Brook Park Post (E. M. S.), Londonderry, in 1944 he was a Patron of the German Institute of Science and Learning in London, and in 1946 President of the North West of Ireland Amateur Radio Society. He mainly worked at Londonderry at the Lomeshie Research Institute of Anthropology and Racial Biology, which he founded.

Dr. Armattoe was an adversary of Kwame Nkrumah, and opposed the incorporation of Western Togoland into Ghana.

On November 17th, 1953, he addressed the United Nations in New York, speaking for an independent, re-united Togoland. A month later, in London, he fell ill. He was flown to Hamburg, Germany, and died there on December 21, 1953.

His many writings reflect his three primary interests in Medicine, Anthropology, and Letters. There are two volumes of poetry, *Between the Forest and the Sea* (137), and *Deep Down the Blackman's Mind* (138).

Some of Armattoe's "poems are charming for their pathos and romantic idealism, (and) there is another group ... brusque and severe ... they possess all the virtues of satire, being brief, ironical and witty" (Ras Khan).

Aromire, Abayomi   Nigeria

Born in 1944 in Lagos, Nigeria, as son of a "native doctor", Abayomi Aromire received his primary education at St. Stephen WAEC School in Lagos. At school he acted in plays like "Ten Commandments", "Trust No Friend", "King Solomon's Judgement", etc.

In 1965 he joined the theatre troupe of Duro Ladipo. In 1969 he formed his own troupe, the "Aromire Theatre Group". He produces his plays, which are in Yoruba, together with Amos Folorunsho.

Asalache, Khadambi   Kenya

Born on February, 28, 1935, in Kaimosi, Rift Valley province,
near Kisumu, Kenya, Khadambi Asalache grew up in Nairobi,
and was educated at Mangu High School, Thika. He started to
read Architecture at the Royal College in Nairobi, but while
attending a students' conference in Tunisia, changed his plans
and proceeded to Rome, Geneva and Vienna before coming to
London in 1960. Since then he has been living in London where
one of his first jobs was teaching Swahili at the Berlitz School.
At present he is working as a literary adviser in the educational
section of Macmillan's, London.

His novel, *A Calabash of Life* (1237), is set in pre-colonial
Africa, and deals particularly with the Vatirichi tribe, a sub-
division of the Abaluhya. "Asalache sees his characters not as
entities unto themselves, but as extensions of humanity, and in
this light he is fairly successful. For the most part the language
of the characters remains artificial and static — they converse
and even express their deepest emotions like a bunch of con-
servative Englishmen might be expected to and in a similar
style" (Valerie D'Cruz).

Atta Koffi, Raphaël   Ivory Coast

Raphaël Atta Koffi was born on March 27, 1942, in Broukro,
division Tanda, Eastern District, Ivory Coast, into the Agni-
Bonda tribe. He entered the primary school of Bondoukou in
1949. In 1956 Atta Koffi continued his education at the secondary school of Abidjan, and left three years later with his B.E.P.C.
In 1961 Atta Koffi found employment with what is now Caisse
Nationale de Prévoyance Social. He is still working there as a
controller.

Raphaël Atta Koffi's first stories were published by "Bingo"
in 1957. His novel, *Les dernières paroles de Koime* (573), was
a failure. In 1967 he presented a play to the Concours Théâtral
Interafricain 1967—1968, *Le trône d'or* (574), which was
awarded a prize.

Autra, Ray
vid. *Traoré Mamadou*

Awolowo, Obafemi   Nigeria

Born on March 6, 1909, in Ikenne, Western State, Nigeria, Obafemi Oyeniyi Jeremiah Awolowo, an Ijebu-Yoruba, was educated in Ikenne, Itesi, Abeokuta. In 1927 he entered Wesleyan
College, Ibadan, to become a teacher. In 1930 he was employed
as shorthand typist by a German firm in Lagos. He returned to
Wesleyan as secretary in 1932, but left again in 1934 to become
a reporter-in-training at the "Nigerian Daily Times". Subsequently Awolowo ventured into the money-lending business
and became a trader, organizing the Nigerian Produce Traders
Association in the late thirties and becoming Secretary of the
Nigerian Motor Transport Union. Studying in his spare time,
he matriculated in 1939 and received his Bachelor of Commerce
Degree in 1944. The same year he went to London to study Law.
In London he founded the Egbe Omo Oduduwa, a Yoruba
tribal association, and wrote *Path to Nigerian Freedom,* London
1966. Qualifying in 1946, he returned to Ibadan in 1947 and
set up in practice with A. Akerele.

In 1950 Chief Awolowo, together with Bode Thomas,
founded the Action Group. From 1951 to 1954 he served as
Minister of Local Government in the Western Region, where he
became Prime Minister in 1954. After the elections of 1959
Awolowo became Leader of the Opposition in the Federal
House of Representatives.

In 1962 a fight broke out between Chief Samuel Ladoke
Akintola and Awolowo. Martial law was declared, under which
Awolowo and other leaders of the Action Group were convicted
of subversion. Awolowo received a sentence of fifteen years in
prison, but in summer 1966 he was released by the Military
Government, and in 1967 he was appointed Minister of Finance
in General Gowon's cabinet. He resigned his post in 1971.

Awolowo has phrased his ideal of a Nigerian state as follows: "Under a true federal constitution each group, however small, is entitled to the same treatment as any other group, however large." He tells of his life in his autobiography, *The Autobiography of Chief Obafemi Awolowo,* Cambridge 1960, reedited under a new title, *My Early Life,* Lagos 1968.

Awoonor, Kofi   Ghana

Born on March 13, 1936, in Wheta, District Anlo South, Volta Region, Ghana, near Keta, "the flood town, with the sea in my ears", Awoonor was educated at Keta Presbyterian Mission School and Achimota College in Accra. He studied at University College of Ghana, Legon, London University, where he got his M.A. in Modern English, and State University of New York, Stony Brook, where he obtained his Ph. D. in Comparative Literature.

His career includes posts as Lecturer in the English Department, University of Ghana from 1960 to 1963, Research Fellow and Lecturer at the Institute of African Studies, University of Ghana, from 1963 to 1965, and Managing Director of the Ghana Film Industries Corporation from 1965 to 1967. From 1967 to 1968 Awoonor was awarded a Longmans scholarship to do post-graduate work at the University of London. In 1968 he became Associate Professor in the English Department, State University of New York, Stony Brook. From 1970 to 1972 he was Chairman of the Comparative Literature Programme at State University, Stony Brook, and in 1972 was appointed for one year as a Visiting Assistant Professor in the Department of English at the University of Texas, Austin.

Formerly known as George Awoonor-Williams, Kofi Awoonor assumed his new legal name in October 1968. He writes of himself: "Pet aversions: poseurs and hypocrites and righteous men."

Kofi Awoonor established his reputation with his first volume of poetry. He is influenced in his verse by the landscape of his childhood. The tides of the lagoon-city, the fishermen and seagulls, mingle with the gods of his ancestors to a *Rediscovery* (167), as he entitled his first publication, of the traditions of his people. This first success was backed up seven years later by another volume of poetry, *Night of My Blood,* New York 1971, and a novel, *This Earth, My Brother,* New York 1971. Examples of his art have appeared in many anthologies, such as "Modern Poetry from Africa", "African Writing Today", "Commonwealth Poets of Today", and "Younger Poets of the Commonwealth". Awoonor also contributed to the following journals "Transition", "Alcheringa", "African Arts", "Okyeame", "Black Orpheus" and "Greenfield Review". Parts of his works have been translated into German, French, Russian and Chinese.

"In the poetry of George Awoonor-Williams, there is an attempt to describe the plight of the younger generation who have been educated away from the norms of their fathers. But his poetry is a conscious attempt to deploy imagery from the oral vernacular poetry to give added effect to this feeling of loss" (O. R. Dathorne).

"Awoonor-Williams' poems are single moments selected out of a pattern of rediscovery. The points of crystallisation are recorded — both low and high, the moments of inglorious desire, the moments of discovering the strength that his own soul possesses" (Paul Theroux).

Portrait on Plate VIII.

Awoonor-Williams, George
vid. *Awoonor, Kofi*

Azikiwe, Nnamdi   Nigeria

Born in 1904 in Zungeru, Northwestern State, Nigeria, Nnamdi Azikiwe was educated at mission schools in Onitsha, Lagos and Calabar. From 1921 to 1925 he worked as a government clerk in the Treasury at Lagos. In 1925 he went to the United States to study at Storer College in West Virginia, at Howard University and at Lincoln University. He studied History and Political Science, earning his livelihood as a coal miner, casual labourer, dish-washer and even as boxer. He took a postgraduate course at the University of Pennsylvania. In 1934 he returned to West Africa and became editor of the "African Morning Post" in Ghana. In 1937 he went back to Nigeria, joined the Executive of the Nigerian Youth Movement (N.Y.M.) and started a chain of newspapers. In 1944, the Nigerian National Council — later to become the National Council of Nigeria and the Cameroons (N.C.N.C.) was formed. Azikiwe became the Secretary-General of the party and later its President. In 1951 he was elected to the Western Region House but could not go on from there to the Federal House because of the predominance of the newly founded Action Group. He remained therefore, as Leader of the Opposition in the Western Assembly. In 1952 he went to the Eastern Region, first as Chief Minister and then as Premier. In 1959 he became President of the Senate, and then Governor-General. With Nigeria's independence in 1960, Azikiwe became President of the federation. He was removed from the office in 1966 by the military coup, and lived in London. Since December 1971 Azikiwe has been Chancellor of the University of Lagos.

Besides numerous articles in newspapers, Azikiwe has published *Liberia in World Affairs,* London 1934, *Renascent Africa,* Lagos 1937, and *Zik: a Selection from the Speeches of Nnamdi Azikiwe,* London and New York 1961.

Kwatei Asoasa Brempong Jones-Quartey's, *A Life of Azikiwe,* Harmondsworth 1965, is an extensive biography of Azikiwe.

Azuonye, Chukwuma   Nigeria

Born on March 31, 1945, in Okigwi, district Owerri, East Central State, Nigeria, Chukwuma Azuonye studied English Literature and Art History at the University of Nigeria, Nsukka. He was editor of "The Muse", the literary journal of the English Association at Nsukka. He is now Secretary of the University's Writers' Club and editor of "Odunke Monographs". He has contributed regularly to the Radio in Enugu. Poems have been published in the German anthology "Gedichte aus Biafra" (AW 133); a short story has appeared in the anthology "The Insider", Enugu 1971. Azuonye is also the editor of the anthology *Nsukka Harvest*, Nsukka 1972.

Ba, Amadou Hampaté   Mali

Born in 1899 in Bandiagara, Mopti region, Mali, Amadou Hampaté Ba began his studies of the Koran under Tierno Boka, "le sage de Bandiagara", of whom he later became a disciple. Shortly after his studies, he began a long career in administration and diplomacy, holding positions such as cabinet secretary in the government of Upper Volta and as a member of the French ethnological service IFAN (Institut Français d'Afrique Noire) in Guinea, Sudan and Senegal. He was Mali's ambassador to the Ivory Coast, and a member of the executive council of UNESCO where, during eight years, his work was centred around the preservation of traditional African cultures.

Ba is a leader of the Black African Tidjanist Congregation. He is fluent in five African languages and in French. At present he continues his research and abstains from all political activity due, says he, to his religious convictions.

Ba has devoted his life to the preservation of oral tradition, mainly of the Fulbe people. He collected epics, initiation texts, legends, court tales, and chronicles. Besides several articles in "Présence Africaine" and "Abbia", he published, together with Jacques Daget, *L'empire peul du Macina*, Paris, La Haye 1962, and, together with Marcel Cardaire, *Tierno Bokar, le sage de Bandiagara*", Paris 1957.

Babalola, Adeboye   Nigeria

Born on December 17, 1926, in Ipetumodu, Western State, Nigeria, Solomon Adeboye O. Babalola went to secondary school in Lagos and studied at Achimota College near Accra, Ghana, and Cambridge University, England. From 1952 onwards he taught English and Yoruba at Igbobi College in Lagos. In 1963 he got his Ph. D. at the University of London with a thesis on "ijala", the Yoruba hunter songs. From 1962 to 1964 he was a lecturer at the Institute of African Studies of the University of Ife. He left to become a lecturer in Yoruba at the School of Modern Languages in African Studies at Lagos in 1965, Acting Dean of the newly established School of African and Asian Studies in 1967, Associate Professor in 1968, and Professor of African Languages and Literatures in 1969.

Babalola is Chairman of the Department of Yoruba in the School of Humanities at Lagos and President of the Yoruba Studies Association of Nigeria.

His treatise *The Content and Form of Yoruba Ijala*, London 1966, won the Amaury Talbot Prize for the year's best contribution to literature on West African peoples.

Badian, Seydou   Mali

Born on April 10, 1928, in Bamako, Mali, Seydou Badian Kouyaté — this is his real name — had his elementary and the first part of his secondary education in Bamako at the Lycée Terrasson de Fougères. He then continued his studies at Montpellier, France, where he was called Kouyaté Saïdou. At the University of Montpellier he received his degree as a medical doctor, after his thesis on *Nine African Treatments of Yellow Fever*.

When Mali became independent in 1960, Seydou Badian Kouyaté was appointed Minister of Rural Economy and Planification. From 1965 to 1966 he was Minister of Development.

He then worked in Bamako as a medical doctor.

In November 1968, when a military coup overthrew the regime of president Modibo Keita, Seydou Badian Kouyaté was arrested and detained. He is still in prison.

Seydou Badian — as he calls himself as a writer — wrote a play about the murder of the Zulu king Shaka, *La Mort de Chaka* (179), in English *The Death of Chaka* (179 a), and a novel on forced marriage and the conflict of generations, *Sous l'orage* (178). His book, *Les dirigeants d'Afrique noire face à leur peuple*, Paris 1964, "is, in the first place, a defense against the accusation, the leading persons of the new states would betray the purity of the revolution" (Franz Ansprenger).

"Badian's play has its weaknesses. The language is eloquent, but lacks dramatic power, and, because there is so little action on the stage, the play seems rather static" (Clive Wake).

"*Sous l'orage* is rich in ideas which are expressed in dialogues on politics and economy" (Robert Pageard).

Balogun, Ola   Nigeria

Born on August 1, 1945, in Aba, East Central State, Nigeria, Olatunbosum Balogun — this being his full name — received his first schooling in Aba, and continued at King's College in Lagos from 1957 to 1961. The year 1962/63 saw him at the University of Dakar, Senegal, where he took up French. From 1963 to 1966 he studied at the Université de Caen, France, and obtained his Licence de Lettres Modernes in 1966. From 1966 to 1968 he studied film making at the Institut des Hautes Etudes Cinématographiques in Paris. Coming home to Nigeria at the end of 1968, he was employed by the Federal Ministry of Information as a film director, then sent to Paris as Press Attaché to the Embassy of Nigeria in 1969.

Balogun's first works were published in French, *Shango, suivi de Le Roi Elephant* (182). Short stories in English appeared in various Nigerian magazines.

Balewa, Abubakar Tafawa
vid. *Abubakar Tafawa Balewa, Alhaji Sir*

Bamboté, Pierre   Central African Republic

Pierre Makambo Bamboté was born on April 1, 1932, in Wadda
on the River Pipi, district Haute Kotto, Central African Republic. He had his school education in Bambari until 1949. The
same year he went to France to complete his studies at the
Collège de Die in Drôme and different Collèges in Nérac, Le
Havre, Saint-Germain-en-Laye and Paris where he studied at
the Sorbonne, at the Ecole Supérieure du Journalisme, and at
the Ecole d'Hautes Etudes Internationales.

On March 18, 1965, he was appointed Director of the Information Service in Bangi, the capital of the Central African
Republic. In this capacity he travelled through Europe during
1966. From 1966 to 1970 Bamboté held various official positions. Among others he was Director of the museum in Bangi.
In 1970 he was appointed Professor of African Literature at the
University Laual, Quebec, Canada. He resigned in April 1970
to become his country's delegate to UNESCO in Paris.

Besides a novel for children *Les randonnées de Daba* (1160),
Pierre Bamboté has published four volumes of poetry, *La poésie
est dans l'histoire* (1157), *Chant funèbre pour un héros d'Afrique*
(1158), *Le grand état central* (1159), a historical poem, and *Le
dur avenir* (1161).

"With a language vibrating like a drumskin, pointing like
a spear of war, juicy like a fruit of the tropics, (Pierre Bamboté)
decorates the colourful and animated reality which surrounds
him and which shaped him so much that he can no longer
distinguish his flesh from the flesh of the star, his blood from
the sap of the trees" (André Laude).

Barbosa, Jorge   Cape Verde Islands

Born in 1902 in Praia, Island St. Jago, Cape Verde Islands, Jorge Barbosa was educated in Praia and became a customs official and a journalist. He rose to be head of customs on the island Sal.

He wrote three volumes of poetry, *Arquipélago*, São Vicente (Cape Verde Islands) 1935, *Ambiente* (184) and *Caderno de um ilhéu* (185).

"Jorge Barbosa .. has begun to use everyday language and free verse in the manner of the Brazilians in disturbing poems about the isolation and poverty of the Islanders" (Gerald M. Moser).

"The sacrosanct Jorge Barbosa, ... the pope of evasionism ... passes from the spontaneous period of books like *Ambiente* and *Arquipélago* to another, decadent period of *Caderno de um ilhéu*, which by its conventionality of subject and artificiality of poetical form disappoints the expectant reader" (Onesimo da Silveira).

Bart-Williams, Gaston   Sierra Leone

Born on March 3, 1938, in Freetown, Sierra Leone, Gaston Bart-Williams went to the Prince of Wales School in Freetown and to Bo School in Bo, Sierra Leone. In 1958 he founded the African Youth Cultural Society to promote mutual understanding through culture and a year later attended the World Assembly of Youth in Bamako, Mali, as Sierra Leone's delegate. From 1961 to 1963 Gaston Bart-Williams studied Theatre Directing under Clifford Williams of the Royal Shakespeare Company and passed the ADB — Associate of the Drama Board of Great Britain and Northern Ireand, also the Board of Adjudicators.

In 1962 Bart-Williams won the London Writers' Poetry Prize, and the All-African Short Story Award sponsored by the International Congress for Cultural Freedom, Paris. A year later, in 1963, he won the Michael Karolji International Award, France, and stayed in Vence, France. In 1964 he won the German London Embassy Cultural Grant.

Bart-Williams served his country as a delegate to various cultural conferences.

In 1970 Gaston Bart-Williams founded the Pan African Youth Movement at the University of Njala, Sierra Leone, and The Mud Hut, Pan African Centre in Cologne, Federal Republic of Germany.

Gaston Bart-Williams lives in Cologne as a freelance writer and film director. Poems and plays of his have appeared in various British anthologies. A play, *A Bouquet of Carnations* was produced by BBC, London. Two others, *In Praise of Madness* (188) and *Uhuru* (189), were produced in Germany in translation.

Bazarrabusa, Timothy B.   Uganda

Born in 1912 in the district Bunyoro, Uganda, Timothy B. Bazarrabusa was educated at the Nyakasura School in Fort Portal. From 1931 to 1934 he studied at Makerere College. He was a teacher, and later, from 1951 to 1961, a principal. Then he was appointed Uganda's High Commissioner to London. Bazarrabusa died in a car accident in London in April 1966.

Bazarrabusa published two long stories and a volume of short stories in his mother tongue Runyoro-Rutooro, *Ha munwa gw'ekituuro (1240), Kalyaki na Marunga* (1241) and *Obu ndikura tindifa* (1242).

Bebey, Francis   Cameroon

Francis Bebey was born on July 16, 1929, in Duala, Cameroon, where he obtained his Baccalauréat Mathématique. He studied

English at the Sorbonne in Paris, and then learnt Broadcasting at the Studio-école de la Radiodiffusion Outre-Mer, Paris. He continued his studies of Broadcasting and Television at the New York University. Bebey is living now in Paris, working for the information service of UNESCO (1972).

Francis Bebey is a man of many talents and untiring activity. Besides his studies of communication problems in developing countries he produces many radio programmes, writes, plays the guitar and composes music for this instrument. Bebey is a famous guitar-player, who has toured the United States, Canada, Europe and Africa, performing classical guitar pieces and his own compositions. He is also the author of a book on African music, *Musique de l'Afrique*, Paris 1969.

He entered the field of creative writing with a novel, *Le fils d'Agatha Moudio* (190), which won him the Grand Prix Littéraire de l'Afrique Noire in 1968. This novel, set in a Cameroonian village, deals humourously and wittily with the problems of emancipation. A collection of narratives and poems, *Embarras & Cie.* (191), followed a year later.

"This little book" *Le fils d'Agatha Moudio* "which is easily read because it is well written contains a great danger: to convince the reader easily of the authenticity of the painting, that has been created of a certain African community by an African author" (Iwiyé Kala-Lobe).

Portrait on Plate XII.

Belinga, Samuel-Martin Eno
vid. *Eno-Belinga, Samuel-Martin*

Bello, Alhaji Sir Ahmadu   Nigeria

Born in 1909 at Rabah in Sokoto Province, North Western State, Nigeria, Ahmadu Bello was the son of a District Head, and grandson of Abubakar, known as Atiku na Rabah, the seventh Sultan of Sokoto. Bello's first schooling was with Mallam Garba, the Liman of Rabah, where he learnt the Holy Koran by heart and elementary Arabic. From 1926 to 1931 he went to Katsina College, where he learnt perfect English. From 1931 to 1934 he was a teacher and from 1934 to 1938 District Head of Rabah. On his transfer to Sokoto Central Office Bello was given the title of Sardauna of Sokoto. In the olden days a Sardauna led the aristocrats into war, and the title carries with it a sword of office.

The Sardauna first entered the national political scene, as a member of the Northern House of Assembly, in 1949. In 1952 he became leader of the Northern People's Congress and was elected to the House of Representatives in Lagos. His first ministerial appointment was as Minister of Works. Then, when it was decided that the North, like the other regions, should have a Minister of Local Government, Ahmadu Bello became Premier of the North in 1954. He held this office until his assassination on January 15, 1966.

Ahmadu Bello was a great-great-grandson of Shehu Usuman dan Fodio, the founder of the Fulani Empire. He was thus a member of the Sultan family and a potential Sultan himself. In the Muslim world he gained fame as the Vice-President of the World Muslim League.

Ahmadu Bello's only literary work is his autobiography, *My Life* (195), written in English, but translated into his mother tongue Hausa as *Raynwata* (196).

Bemba, Sylvain
vid. *Malinda, Martial*

Bengono, Jacques   Cameroon

Born in 1938 in Tsinga near Yaunde, Cameroon, Jacques Bengono received his school leaving certificate in 1953. Then he started working selling lettuce to the people of Yaunde. Later he ventured into all kinds of creative work as poet, artist, guitar player — he even trained himself as a boxer.

His short stories, *La perdrix blanche* (198), are based partly on oral, partly on Christian legends.

Bereng, David Cranmer Theko   Lesotho

Born in 1900 in Rothe, Lesotho, David Cranmer Theko Bereng was a member of the royal family of Lesotho. He was educated at the mission schools in Morija and Lovedale, Cape Province. He was a member of the National Assembly of Basutoland, and was acting as chief for Chief Theko Makhaola. Traces of him were lost after he did his military service in the forties.

Bereng published *Lithothokiso tsa Moshoeshoe le tse ding* (1512), the first collection of original poems to appear in Southern Sotho. The poems centre round Moshoeshoe, who is identified with the Sotho nation, and most of them are composed in the manner of traditional praise poetry.

Besolow, Thomas E.   Liberia

Born around 1867 in Bendu, district Montserrado, Liberia, Thomas E. Besolow, a Vai, was educated at Wilbraham Academy, USA. His autobiography, *From the Darkness of Africa to the Light of America — The Story of an African Prince*, Boston 1891, is the first written literature from Liberia.

Bessa Victor, Geraldo   Angola

Born on January 20, 1917, in Sâo Paulo de Luanda, Angola, Geraldo Bessa Victor was educated at the Licéu of Luanda. For ten years he was a bank clerk at the Bank of Angola. In 1946 he went to Lisbon to study Law. Since his examinations in 1951 he has been working as a lawyer in Lisbon.

Except for a volume of short stories, *Sanzala sem batuque* (1518), all his books are collections of poetry, *Ecos dispersos* (1513), *Ao som das marimbas* (1514), *Debaixo do céu* (1515), *Cubata abandonata* (1516) and *Mucanda* (1517), most of which inspired by African traditions which he described and analysed in his volume *Quinjango no folclore angolense*, Braga 1970.

"The style, the characters, the subjects, the new language for a new world, the new syntax, the behaviour of each person, the value of each case and of each story, the spirit of observation, the careful analysis... all these values give Geraldo Bessa Victor a special place in modern Portuguese literature" (Amândio César).

"... a Negro lawyer, Geraldo Bessa Victor, began to write verse in defense of his race, while paying homage to Portuguese nationalism" (Gerald M. Moser).

Beti, Mongo   Cameroon

Born on June 30, 1932, in Mbalmayo, district Nyong et Sô, Cameroon, Mongo Beti, whose real name is Alexandre Biyidi, was educated at the local Catholic mission school. At the age of fourteen he was evicted for being rebellious. In 1945 he entered the Lycée Leclerc in Yaunde and took his baccalauréat in 1951. He left for France the same year, studying first at the Faculty of Letters at the University Aix-en-Provence, later at the Sorbonne, where he received his licence ès lettres. He taught at a high school in Lamballe (Côtes du Nord) and in Brittany. He is now teaching at the Lycée Corneille in Rouen, France. Mongo Beti did not supply biographical data.

The first novel, *Ville Cruelle* (201), was published under the pen-name Eza Boto. It describes the cruelties of the colonial regime, under which Greek merchants, in collaboration with

French policemen, cheated African cocoa farmers out of their earnings. *Le pauvre Christ de Bomba* (202) was the first novel under the pseudonym Mongo Beti. It depicts the story of a Catholic missionary, who discovers on a tour through his parish, that all evil, fornication, venereal disease and social disorder, have their origin in the mission station. The book is a formidable satire and a stinging criticism of European colonialism. The book was also translated into English under the title *The Poor Christ of Bomba*, London 1971.

His next novel was *Mission terminée (203)*. The American edition is entitled *Mission Accomplished*, New York 1958 (203 c); a new English edition appeared under the title *Mission to Kala* (203 c). It tells the story of a schoolboy who failed his baccalauréat and who discovers, on his return home, that responsibility is laid upon him to bring back the runaway wife of his cousin. "Prejudices, passions, ideals, purity are all corrupted by Beti's unrelenting laughter and insistence on the physical nature of things" (Anthony Brench). *Mission terminée* received the Saint Beuve literary award in 1958. Beti's fourth novel is *Le roi miraculé* (204), translated into English under the title *King Lazarus* (204b). This too is a satire. It centres round King Essomba, whose illness brings many people nearer to their wishes including a missionary who succeeds finally in baptising him on his deathbed. But the king recovers and does not want to reject his wives.

Beti's most recent book, *Main basse sur le Cameroun*, edited at Maspero in Paris 1972 was seized by the French police.

"Beti delves into his characters' personalities presenting them through their own words and actions which, in the actual situation, are ridiculously pompous or foolish" (Anthony Brench).

A study on Mongo Beti has been done by Thomas Melone, *Mongo Beti: l'homme et le destin*, Paris 1971.

Portrait on Plate XII.

Bhêly-Quénum, Olympe   Dahomey

Born on September 26, 1928, in Cotonou, Dahomey, Olympe
Bhêly-Quénum received his primary education at Cotonou and
Grand Popo, his C.E.P.E. (Certificat d'Etudes Primaires Elé-
mentaires) in Whydah. He spent one year at Achimota Grammar School near Accra, and some time travelling in Nigeria,
Niger, Togo, and Ghana. From 1945 to 1948 he worked at the
firm John Walkden & Cie., Cotonou, — a Unilever branch —
where he rose to be the youngest junior director of a division.

In 1948, with his own savings and the money he got from
his mother, he left for France and had his secondary education
at the Collège Littré in Avranches (Manche) and at the Lycée of
Rennes. As a Lauréat of the Bourses Zellidja he returned to
Africa to study and to describe *The virtues of the oil palm
tree in French West Africa*, in 1954. Back in France he prepared
his admission to the Ecole Normale Supérieure, working as
tutor in the collège of Eu (Seine Maritime). In 1957 he got the
Certificat d'Etudes Littéraires Générales (C.E.L.G.) at the Faculty of Arts in Caen (Calvados), and his Certificat d'Etudes
Supérieures de Littérature Française in 1958. From 1958 to 1961
he was Assistant Teacher at the Lycée Paul Langevin in Suresnes
(Seine).

With Dahomey's independence, Olympe Bhêly-Quénum
abandoned teaching and studied Diplomacy at the Institut des
Hautes Etudes d'Outre-Mer (I.H.E.O.M.), in Paris. In 1962 he
worked at the Ministry of Foreign Affairs in Paris, at the International Court of Justice in The Hague, at the French General
Consulates in Genoa, Milan, and Florence, finally at the French
Embassy in Rome. In July 1962 he received his diploma of
the I.H.E.O.M. for his thesis *La presse italienne et les problèmes africains*. This study of the press changed his career:
journalism became his vocation. After a short holiday in Dahomey, August to October 1962, he was appointed Director and
Editor of the journal "La Vie Africaine", published in Paris
from 1962 to 1965. In 1965 Olympe Bhêly-Quénum founded
his own company SAGEREP (Société Africaine d'Edition et

de Réalisation de Presse) in Paris, in which he published his journal "L'Afrique Actuelle", until it ceased to exist in April 1968. Since then Bhêly-Quénum has been a functionary of UNESCO in Paris.

Olympe Bhêly-Quénum, besides writing in his own journals, has contributed to many papers and reviews, "Communauté France-Eurafrique", Paris, "Liberté", Montreal (Canada), "Bingo", Dakar, "The Student World", Geneva, "Il Mulino", Bologna, "Le Monde Diplomatique", Paris.

Besides a school reader for African children, *Un enfant d'Afrique,* Paris 1970, and a language course of seven volumes and three records, *Practical French,* 1965 to 1970, Olympe Bhêly-Quénum has written two novels, *Un piège sans fin* (206), and *Le Chant du Lac* (208), which received the Grand Prix de l'Afrique Noire in 1966. His stories have been collected in his volume *Liaison d'un été* (209).

"The dominant atmosphere in *Un piège sans fin* does not allow any chance of redemption for the individual. Progressively Olympe Bhêly-Quénum's hero discovers the reign of the evil and the absurdity of the world" (Bernard Mouralis).

"This novel is a picture of Dahomey, full of reality and of lyrism — there are beautiful love stories — written in a beautiful language. An 'inside view' of a Dahomean" (A. C.).

Bitek, Okot p'
vid. *p'Bitek, Okot*

Blay, J. Benibengor   Ghana

Born in 1915 in Half Assini, Western Region, Ghana, J. Benibengor Blay went to the Mission School in his coastal home town and later studied Journalism at the Regent Street Polytechnic in London. In 1958 he was Deputy of the Constituency of Western Nzima, his home district. In 1965 he became Minister of Art and Culture. Since the end of the Nkrumah regime little has been heard of him. He lives, presumably, in Ghana as a private person.

Benibengor Blay published five volumes of poetry, *Immortal Deeds* (213), *Memoirs of the War* (215), *King of the Human Frame* (216), *Thoughts of Youth* (223) and *Ghana Sings* (224), quite a number of stories, published one by one in small volumes, *Parted Lovers* (217), *Dr. Bengia Wants a Wife* (218), *Operation Witchcraft* (219), *Love in a Clinic* (220), *Stubborn Girl* (221), *Here and There Stories* (222), *Tales for Boys and Girls* (225), and *Alomo,* Aboso 1969, and two novels, *Emelia's Promise and Fulfilment* (214) and *Coconut Boy,* Accra-Tema 1970. His radio talks have been collected under the title *On the Air,* Aboso 1970.

Blay's works are popular reading, with a strong moral, most of it for the benefit and the education of children.

"Mr. Benibengor Blay, a versatile writer, has the knack for creating characters that are true to life. This intellectual gift of his has permeated the entire gamut of his past literary works already published" (J. Abedi-Boafo).

Bognini, Joseph Miezan   Ivory Coast

Born on September 18, 1936, in Grand Bassam, Southern District, Ivory Coast, Joseph Miezan Bognini completed his primary education at a private Catholic school. He was then trained in cabinet-making at the Trade School of Abidjan from 1952 to 1956. After his military service from 1956 to 1967, he obtained a scholarship to Paris, France, where he studied architectural design.

His only volume of poetry, *Ce dur appel de l'espoir* (227), reflects his cultural conflict and combines a nostalgic attitude for a rural past with Paris tristesse.

"Perhaps alone among the poets of West and Central Africa who write in French, Bognini composes in the regular meter and

Olaudah Equiano

Jacobus Eliza Joannes Capitein

PLATE I

Phillis Wheatley

Ignatius Sancho

Samuel Adjai Crowther

Joseph Ephraim Casely Hayfor

PLATE II *Hamed bin Muhammed el Murje*
(Tippu Tib)

Carl Christian Reindorf

formal rhyme schemes of classical French poetry" (Ellen Conroy Kennedy).

Bokwe, John Knox   South Africa

Born on March 18, 1855, at Ntselamanzi, near Lovedale, Cape Province, South Africa, John Knox Bokwe, a Xhosa, was educated at Lovedale. At the age of ten, he was a pupil of William Kobe Ntsikana, a son of the first Christian oral poet of the Xhosa, Ntsikana. From 1869 to 1872 Bokwe attended Lovedale's College Department, and was private secretary to the principal, James Stewart. In 1873 he was put in charge of the Lovedale Telegraph and Post Office.

In 1875 Bokwe began to compose hymns — the words and the music.

"A gifted musician, Bokwe not only delighted Lovedale audiences with his singing and conducting of choirs, but also with his playing of the piano and the organ and with his musical compositions" (Z. K. Matthews).

From time to time his hymns were published in "Isigidimi", a Xhosa journal, and a number of them were collected in *Ama-Culo ase-Lovedale* (1529), such as *Ntsikana's Hymn* and *Vuka Deborah* (Come, Deborah), which were both sung on the occasion of the Royal Family's visit to Lovedale in 1947.

In 1874 Bokwe visited the United Kingdom, where he sang his hymns with marked success at numerous public gatherings. Back in Lovedale he resigned as Postmaster, in order to help John Tengo Jabavu in the editorship of "Imvo Zabantsundu" at King William's Town. He contributed articles in Xhosa and English, but soon left journalism again to return to preaching. He was ordained a minister around the turn of the century, and was placed in charge of the Presbyterian Congregation at Ugie. He had differences, however, with the church authorities about the use of money he had collected in Scotland, whereupon he set up his own church. Together with John Tengo Jabavu he founded the South African Native College at Fort Hare.

In 1920 Bokwe retired from public service and returned to his hometown Ntselamanzi. John Knox Bokwe died on February 22, 1922.

Besides his collection of hymns Bokwe published *Ibali lika Ntsikana* (1530), a biography of the preacher Ntsikana.

Bolamba, Antoine-Roger   Zaire

Born on June 17, 1913, in Boma, near the mouth of the Congo River, province Congo-Central, Zaire, Antoine-Roger Bolamba, received his secondary education at the school of the Frères des Ecoles Chrétiennes. He later became chief editor of the journal "La Voix du Congolais" in Kinshasa.

Of his two small volumes of poetry, *Premiers essays* (1165) and *Esanzo* (1166), only the latter became known outside his country.

"Sometimes the image shoots forth, colourful, ardent, bulged by a genuine African sap" (David Diop).

"These texts are only geysers of images with a syntax of juxtaposition which dissolves this syntax, for all words are soaked in the impetus of desire, and anguish is only the reverse of desire" (Léopold Sédar Senghor).

Boni, Nazi   Upper Volta

Born in 1912 in Bwan near Dédougou, district Black Volta, Upper Volta, Nazi Boni was a member of one of the tribes independent of the powerful Mossi people who dominate the political life in Upper Volta. After his elementary education he entered the famous Ecole William Ponty at Gorée, Senegal in 1930.

Trained as a teacher he began teaching in Wagadugu in 1931. Later he changed schools very often. In 1941 he was appointed Headmaster of the Ecole Primaire at Treichville, a suburb of

Abidjan, Ivory Coast. In 1945 he entered into the local politics of Upper Volta.

Elected to the French National Assembly as a member for Upper Volta, he joined the IOM group (Indépendants d'Outre-Mer) led by Léopold Sédar Senghor, who remained one of his closest political allies. In 1957 Boni's parti MPEA (Mouvement Populaire de l'Evolution Africaine) became a section of the federalist PRA (Parti du Regroupement Africain) formed by Senghor, and later supported membership of the Mali Federation. After the accession to power of Maurice Yaméogo in 1959, Boni's party was dissolved, and in 1960 he fled secretly to Dakar where he lived in exile until the 1966 coup that overthrew Yaméogo. He returned to Upper Volta and tried to form a new party, based in the Bobo-Diulasso area. This was stopped short when the army suspended all political activity. Nazi Boni subsequently went back to teaching. On his way to Wagadugu to lecture on *Traditional and modern foundations of power in Africa,* he was killed in a road accident in May 1969.

Nazi Boni has expressed his political ideas in quite a number of articles published in "Afrique Nouvelle", "Paris-Dakar", "L'Essor", "Volta-Presse", "L'Incorruptible". During his exile he studied the sociology and history of Africa. A result of these studies is his historical novel, *Crépuscule des temps anciens* (228), which gives a vivid picture of traditional life in Bwawa (Bobo) society.

"The author has tried to use as far as possible an African terminology to give local colour to his report, and we can only felicitate him" (Bernard Mouralis).

"The weakness of *Crépuscule des temps anciens* is in its style which sins by using slang and vulgar terms" (Robert Pageard).

Brew, Kwesi   Ghana

Born on March 14, 1928, at Cape Coast, Central Region Ghana, Osborne Henry Kwesi Brew — this is his full name — finished his studies at the University College of the Gold Coast (today University of Ghana) at Accra. Since 1953 he has worked in the administration. When Ghana became independent, he joined the Ministry of Foreign Affairs, where, for a time, he was Chef de Protocole. Since then, he has represented his country at Embassies in Great Britain, France, India, Germany, the Soviet Union, and, as Ambassador, in Mexico, Senegal, and now, at Beirut, Lebanon.

Kwesi Brew's poetry, widely spread in journals and anthologies, has been collected in the volume *The Shadows of Laughter* (231).

"The vagueness of the language is accompanied by a failure to articulate convincingly the argument which he is presenting" (Angus Calder).

"The poems are in fact capable of interpretation simultaneously on two planes: many people will read them as sheer impressionistic pieces, but the more sophisticated will find in them symbols and universalist interpretations" (Oyin Ogunba).

Brutus, Dennis   South Africa

Born in 1924 in Salisbury, Rhodesia, of South African parents, Dennis Brutus was educated at Fort Hare College, South Africa and the University of Witwatersrand in Johannesburg, South Africa. He taught in South African high schools till 1962, when he lost his job and was unemployed for some time. Then he worked as a tea boy at the University of Witwatersrand. Brutus participated in many anti-Apartheid campaigns, particularly those concerned with sports. The South African Government eventually banned him from holding political and social meetings and made it illegal for any of his writings to be published in South Africa. In 1963 he was arrested for holding a meeting. When released on £ 200 bail, he fled to Swaziland and from there tried to make his way to Baden-Baden in Germany to meet the Olympic executive committee, but the Portuguese

Secret Police at the Mozambique border handed him back to the South African Security Police. Realizing that no one would know of his capture, he made a desperate attempt to escape and was shot in the back in a Johannesburg street. On recovery he was sentenced to eighteen months hard labour on Robben Island off Cape Town. When he was released on July 8, 1965, he was permitted to leave South Africa with his wife and seven children on an "exit permit", a document which makes it illegal for him to return. After some years in London, Brutus is now teaching at Northwestern University in Evanston, Illinois, USA.

Dennis Brutus was President of SANROC (South African Non-Racial Olympic Committee), the organization that led the movement to exclude South Africa from the Olympic Games because of its discriminatory sport policies.

Brutus was awarded the Mbari Prize for Poetry in 1962. Mbari Publications in Ibadan, Nigeria, published his first collection of poems, *Sirens, Knuckles, Boots* (1532), in 1963, while he was in prison.

Letters to Martha (1533) are poems chiefly of experience as a political prisoner on Robben Island. Since he was not permitted to write anything that could be published, he camouflaged these poems as "letters" to his sister-in-law, after his brother had been sent to Robben Island. In his latest work, *Poems from Algiers* (1934), he questions Africa and himself.

"I worked out the problem . . . in assertion of myself and my (South) African experience, but especially in my re-discovery of the 'variousness' of Africa and the extent to which my own difference was a part of it."

"Vigour, integrity, defiant hopefulness — these wholesome qualities are impressed upon us by the compelling force of the poet's trained intellectual capacity, by the brilliant intensity of his imagery, by the way he presses language urgently and aptly into service, by the confident modulation of rhythm and gross structure" (Daniel Abasiekong).

"Dennis Brutus language and themes are almost prosy. But there is a maturity of feeling and above all a *precision* of phrase, that lifts this verse far above the common protest cry coming from South Africa" (Ulli Beier).

Portrait on Plate IV.

Camara, Condetto Nénékhaly
vid. *Nénékhaly-Camara, Condetto*

Camara, Laye
vid. *Laye, Camara*

Bukenya, A. S. Uganda

Born in February 1944 in Masaka, district Masaka, Uganda, Austin S. Bukenya, after absolving his secondary education in Kampala, joined the University of Dar es Salaam, Tanzania, where he read Literature, Linguistics and French. He was founder and co-editor of the journal "Darlite". After graduating in 1968, he took an M. A. degree in Traditional African Literature at Makerere University, Kampala, Uganda, where he is now Tutorial Fellow in the Department of Literature.

A. S. Bukenya has published a one-act play, *The Secret* (in AE 159), a handbook on public speech in Luganda, his mother tongue, and a novel, *The People's Bachelor*, Nairobi 1971.

Capitein, Jacobus Eliza Joannes Ghana

Born about 1717 in Ghana, Capitein was seven or eight years old when he was bought by a slave-dealer, who gave him as a present to one of his friends. This man gave him the name Capitein and took him to the Netherlands, where Capitein learnt Dutch and devoted himself to painting. He began his preliminary studies in The Hague, where the pious and learned

Miss Roscam taught him Latin, Greek, Hebrew and Chaldean. He proceeded then to the University of Leiden to study Theology. He got his doctor's degree in 1742 with his thesis *Dissertatio politico-theologica de servitute, libertati christianae non contraria* (237), in which he argues, "rich in erudition, but with poor reasoning" (Abbé Grégoire), that the keeping of slaves did not contradict Christian teachings. In the same year he was sent as a Calvinist missionary to his home town, Elmina, Ghana. From 1742 to 1746 he was headmaster of the school of the Dutch-Reformed Church in Elmina, which flourished only under him. Capitein died in 1747.

Besides his dissertation, translated also into Dutch, Capitein wrote Dutch sermons, *Uitgewrogte predikatien, zynde de trouwhertige vermaaninge van den apostel der heydenen Paulus ...* (238).

Portrait on Plate I.

Cardoso, António   Angola

Born 1933 in Luanda, Angola, António Cardoso received his education in his home town. He was a business clerk until his arrest in 1961, when he was accused of nationalist machinations and sentenced to fourteen years hard labour. He is still serving time in the concentration camp on the Cape Verde island of Chao-Bom.

With the story (?) *São Paulo* (1510), he contributed to an anthology in which four Angolese writers were presented: Benúdia, Arnaldo Santos, Luandino Vieira and António Cardoso.

Casely Hayford, Gladys May   Ghana

Born in 1904 in Axim, Western Region, Ghana, as daughter of Joseph Ephraim Casely Hayford, Gladys May Casely Hayford received her secondary education in Wales. After five years in

Britain she returned to Africa to teach at a girls' school in Sierra Leone, where she died in 1950.

Her earliest poems, which she wrote under the pen-name, Aquah Laluah, appeared in "Atlantic Monthly" and American Negro anthologies. Her short stories were published in anthologies, as "Darkness and Light" (A 90). Some of her poetry, partly written in Krio, the Créole of Sierra Leone, was collected in the volume *Take um so* (243).

Casely Hayford, Joseph Ephraim   Ghana

Born on September 29, 1866, in Cape Coast, Ghana, Joseph Ephraim Casely Hayford was the fourth son of Joseph de Graft Hayford of the Anona Clan of Anomabu. The father was one of the important politicians of his period, a most active member of the Fanti Confederacy of 1867, imprisoned for a short time by Her Majesty's Government for the Confederacy's extremist views, and reputed to have been the first British Ambassador to Ashanti in about 1860. This family could give Joseph Ephraim the best education.

He went to the Cape Coast Wesleyan Boys' School, then to Fourah Bay College in Sierra Leone. From there he returned to be appointed Principal, at the age of 23, of the only secondary school of the country, the Collegiate School (now Mfantsipim School) in Cape Coast in 1889. At the same time, he became editor of the "Gold Coast Echo". After some years his family sent him to England where he studied and graduated from St. Peter's College, Cambridge. He entered the Inner Temple London, from where he was called to the Bar on November 17, 1896, after which he returned home to set up a lucrative practice in Cape Coast, Axim, Sekondi and Accra. With this background he earned the reputation of being competent in every field in which he was engaged.

In politics, he was a member of the Legislative Council from 1916 to 1926, and from 1926 to 1930. He was the first Vice-

President and co-founder of the National Congress of British West Africa. He contributed to the activities of the Aborigines Rights Protection Society and was in more than a dozen commissions dealing with all kinds of industrial, commercial and political activities. He suggested two stages of development for political organization, first a regional Congress, and second a Continental unity. Thus he was regarded the "Uncrowned King of West Africa" and is one of the fathers of Pan-Africanism.

In journalism, he was sub-editor to the "Gold Coast Echo", became editor of the "Gold Coast Chronicle" and a joint editor with the Rev. Attoh-Ahuma of the "Wesleyan Methodist Times". At the time of his death he was editor of the "Gold Coast Leader". He died in Accra on August 11, 1930.

Most of his writings deal with economics and politics, as do his works *The Gold Coast Native Institutions*, London 1913, *Gold Coast Land Tenure, The Truth About the West African Land Question, The Forest Bill*, and *United West Africa*. In all of them he defended the rights of his people in the heyday of imperialism.

His only creative work, *Ethiopia Unbound* (244), mixes the elements of a novel with essays on all kinds of political affairs.

"The language of the book is discoursive, rhetorical, and elusive despite occasional quaintness and archaism. The influence of the Bible and 'Pilgrim's Progress' is evident, and there are many passages from Homer. *Ethiopia Unbound* is without doubt the matrix of all the nationalist and cultural ideas of one of the ablest African political and intellectual leaders in West Africa" (F. Nnabuenyi Ugonna).

Portrait on Plate II.

Chafulumira, English William   Malawi

Chafulumira was born on June 25, 1908, in Chief Chapananga's village, Chikwawa District, Southern Region, Malawi. His father died when he was six years old. Chafulumira went to a Catholic village school, but had to leave it when he was thirteen years old to work for English farmers as a goatherd and kitchen boy. In 1925 he went to St. Michael's Catholic Mission School and was baptized the same year. In 1926 Chafulumira was sent to St. Joseph's Teacher Training College in Nguludi, District Chiradzulu. He qualified as a teacher, but because the salary was too low, worked first as a court-clerk for a year, then as a cook in Rhodesia. In 1937 he proceeded to South Africa, working again as a cook for an English couple. There he wrote *Banja Lathu,* and sent it to his District Commissioner, who presented it to the Education Department, which recommended it for publication. *Banja Lathu* (Our Family), which teaches how an African family could best be run, was published in 1942.

Returning home to Malawi, Chafulumira took up teaching again. From 1941 to 1948 he was headmaster of Kadikira Central School, interrupted only from 1944 to 1945, when he went to the Teachers' Training College in Nguludi to obtain a degree in English.

From 1949 to 1956 he worked for the Nyasaland and Northern Rhodesia Joint Publications Bureau in Zambia. In 1956 he went back to Malawi to train teachers at the Montford Teacher Training College, from where he retired in 1968.

In 1958 Chafulumira joined a pilgrimage to Lourdes and Rome and was received by Pope Pius XII. In 1959 he was appointed Member of the Legislative Council.

Chafulumira published three volumes of narratives in his mother tongue Nyanja; *Kazitape* (1541), *Kantini* (1542) and *Mfumu watsopano* (1543). He is also the author of educative booklets and school readers in Nyanja and a Nyanja grammar.

Chakaipa, Patrick   Rhodesia

Born in 1932 at Mhondoro Reserve of pagan parents, Patrick Chakaipa went to St. Michael's Primary School and then to

R. C. Chishawasha Seminary, where he studied Theology. He is now a priest and the Principal and Supervisor of the All Souls Mission at Mtoko, Rhodesia.

Chakaipa is the author of four novels, *Pfumo reropa* (1546), *Rudo ibofu* (1547), *Garandichauya* (1548), and *Dzasukwa Mwanaasina-hembe* (Beer for Sale), Salisbury 1967, and a narrative, *Karikoga gumiremiseve* (1545), all in his mother tongue Shona.

Chaparadza, L. Washington   Rhodesia

Chaparadza was born in 1926 at Zvimba Reserve, Lomagundi, Rhodesia, and died on August 22, 1964. He was a schoolteacher and freelance journalist. He supported the World Crusade Organization with his writings. He was interested in Metaphysics, Philosophy and Hypnotism.

Chaparadza is the author of a narrative in Shona, *Wechitatu muzvinaguhwa* (1549).

Chidyausiku, Paul   Rhodesia

Chidyausiku was born on January 1, 1927, at Domboshawa, Chinamora Reservation, Rhodesia, his father being the son of Chief Chinamora, his mother the daughter of Chief Chiweshe. He went to Kutama Secondary School and to Domboshawa Government School, where he received a diploma in agriculture. For thirteen years he was teaching agriculture in elementary schools.

In 1958 Chidyausiku won the second prize in an essay competition organized by the Southern Rhodesia Literature Bureau with his first narrative *Nhoroondo dzukuwanana* (1551). Later followed two more narratives, *Pfungwa dzasekuru Mafusire* (1552) and *Nyadzi dzinokunda rufu* (1553), a play, *Ndakambokuyam-*

bira (1554) and a novel *Karumekangu* (1555). All his works are in Shona.

In 1960 Chidyausiku became editor of the Shona newspaper "Moto".

Chona, Mainza Mathias   Zambia

Born on January 1, 1930, in Monze, district Mazabuka, Southern Province, Zambia, Mainza Mathias Chona, the son of a chief, was educated at the Chona Out School, Chikuni Training School and Munali Secondary School. Until 1955 he was clerk and interpreter at the High Court of Northern Rhodesia, now Zambia, in Livingstone. From 1955 to 1959 he was in Britain on a scholarship by the Government of Northern Rhodesia to study Law. In 1959 he did his Bar Final Examination in London as the first African from Northern Rhodesia, and returned to Zambia to become a solicitor. In 1960 he was first President of the National Independence Party (UNIP), but resigned after Kenneth Kaunda's release. From 1961 to 1962 he was Secretary of UNIP, in 1964 he was a Member of Parliament, from 1964 to 1966 he was Minister of Justice, and from 1966 to 1967 he was Minister of Home Affairs. From 1967 to 1968 he was Minister without Portfolio, and from 1968 to 1969 he was Minister for Central Province. From March 1969 to September 1969 he again was Minister without Portfolio, and from September to November 1969 he was Minister of Provincial and Local Government. From 1969 to 1970 he was Zambia's Ambassador to the United States of America. Since 1970 Chona is Vice President.

Chona is a member of the United National Indepedence Party (UNIP). Since 1967 he has been the party's National Secretary. He is also a member of the Law Society of Zambia.

Chona, a Tonga, is the author of a novel in Tonga, *Kabuca Uleta Tunji* (Each new day brings many things), Lusaka 1956.

Cissoko, Siriman   Mali

Born in 1934 at Balandougou, Canton Saboula, district of Kita, Mali, Siriman Cissoko spent his early youth herding cattle and fishing in the swamps. His father and his mother were both blacksmiths. He had his elementary education from 1942 to 1949 at the Regional School of Kita, his secondary education from 1949 to 1954 at Banankoro near Segu, where he was also trained, from 1954 to 1955, to be an assistant teacher. He did his military service from 1955 to 1956 at Bamako, Segu and Timbuktu.

Since 1956 he has been teaching, first as an assistant teacher in Gundam (from 1956 to 1958), Sèféto (in the Kaarta, the home of his mother, from 1958 to 1959), in Toukoto (from 1959 to 1962). In 1962 he went to school again to continue his training at the Ecole Normale Secondaire at Katibongou, four kilometres from Kulikoro. When in 1964 he got his diploma as a qualified teacher he left for Senegal to live in the country of his admired master Léopold Sédar Senghor, who had invited him in December 1959 and August 1960. In Senegal Siriman Cissoko taught in Toumbakounda (from 1964 to 1966), Djourbel (from 1966 to 1967), and, since 1967 he has been teaching in Dakar.

In 1956 he started to write poetry. His volume of poetry, *Ressac de nous-mêmes* (255), is deeply influenced by Senghor, "whose deep mark in my way of singing I recognise", Sissoko wrote in a letter.

Clark, John Pepper   Nigeria

Born on April 6, 1935, in Kiagbodo, Western Ijaw division, Delta province, Mid Western State, Nigeria, John Pepper Clark was educated in Okrika and Jeremi, and at Warri Government College in Ughelli. He completed his formal education with a B.A. degree in English at Ibadan University in 1960. While a student, he founded "The Horn", a magazine of student poetry, in which some of his verses appeared. After graduating he began work in journalism, first as Information Officer for the government of Nigeria for a year, then, in 1961, he became a features and editorial writer of the Nigerian "Daily Express" in Lagos. In 1962 he became a Parvin Fellow at Princeton University, United States, where he wrote *The Masquerade* and *The Raft*. From 1963 to 1964, he was a research fellow at the Institute of African Studies in the University of Ibadan, doing work on Ijaw traditional myths and legends. As of 1966 he has been teaching English at the University of Lagos, and since February 1969, he has been co-editor (with Abiola Irele) of the literary magazine "Black Orpheus".

Clark ventured into poetry, theatre, essay and travelogue. His first play *Song of a Goat* (256 and 259), is a tragedy about an impotent man, who is substituted by his brother. At the end of the work both husband and brother commit suicide, while the wife has a miscarriage. The play has been produced in Kampala, Uganda, and in Nigeria. *The Masquerade* (259) depicts the tragedy of a father, who kills his daughter, because he does not want her to marry a man with a curse on his head. Together with *Song of a Goat,* it was presented at the Commonwealth Arts Festival in 1965. *The Raft* (259) depicts the gloomy destiny of four men on a timber raft in a Niger creek. *Ozidi* (261) is based on a Ijaw epic. Revenging his tyrant father the hero, Ozidi, becomes a tyrant himself.

Clark's first collection of poetry is simply entitled *Poems* (257). It was followed by *Casualties* (262), a lament for the casualties, living and dead, of the Nigerian civil war. *America, Their America* (258) is a sharp indictment of the sins of American society against him during his academic year at Princeton. His last work to date is an essay *The Example of Shakespeare,* London 1970.

Song of a Goat "opens a new era in Nigerian writing, for it deals in purely local and personal terms with a human problem, and thereby manages to achieve universality" (Robert G. Armstrong).

Song of a Goat "succeeds as poetry, but not as drama" (Adrian A. Roscoe).

"So far as Clark's verse-style in concerned, he has chosen a rather slow-moving blank verse of predominantly Elizabethan flavour. *The Masquerade* is particularly full of phrases and inversions of words which are oddly Shakespearean" (Gerald Moore).

"In contrast to *Song of a Goat*, *The Masquerade* seems much too frail to bear weight of the tragedy with which it is overloaded" (Margaret Laurence).

"The main effectiveness of *The Raft*, lies not in its underlying meaning but in the picture it gives of the life on the creeks and swamps, set down lovingly and with the kind of close-up detail that shows a lifelong knowledge and an inner understanding of the place" (Margaret Laurence).

"It is possible to give *The Raft* an existentialist interpretation ... (it) would represent the world ... in which man is doomed from the start and is left to drift to inevitable destruction" (Oyin Ogunba).

"Paradoxically, in *The Raft,* Mr. Clark has created ... a play of considerable power and beauty" (Geoffrey Hill).

"It is amazing that the Ark ever rose from the ground. It is more amazing that *The Raft*, sailing as a poertical symbol of the twentieth century in general, and Nigeria in particular, ever got into print, and onto the stage" (James Morel Gibbs).

"*Ozidi*, although apparently based on a traditional Ijaw cycle, is a highly episodic dramatic poem rather than a play" (Gerald Moore).

"Clark's plays are the result of the battle between his strengths and his weaknesses. His weaknesses include a tendency to melodrama, an adolescent attitude toward sexuality, a narrow range of form, and a determination to be 'impressive'" (James Morel Gibbs).

"*Poems* show Clark in search of a style. The awkwardness, the verbal indirections, the angularity and unevenness of the language indicate a partially developed technique which together contribute to the general obscurity" (Edwin Thumboo).

"It is poetry which makes heavy reading but which is moving because it is always nourished by immediate experience and because the author's harassed, tormented and irrepressible personality is present in every line" (Ulli Beier).

"Whereas his earlier poems were punctuated with humour and irony, a polarity of visions that were at times real and imaginary, his *Casualties* is a somber lament" (Syl Cheyney-Coker).

In *America, Their America* "Clark is anxious to tell any American who would not care to listen, just how black he is. It is the poor American women that come off worse ..." (Ronald Dathorne).

Portrait on Plate X.

Cole, Robert Wellesley   Sierra Leone

Robert Benjamin Wellesley Ageh Cole was born on March 11, 1907, in Kossoh Town, a district of Freetown, Sierra Leone. Belonging to a Krio family, he is the son of a strict Church of England Christian. He began his primary education in 1914 at elementary school, then attended the Prince of Wales School, the CMS Grammar School and Fourah Bay College, all in Freetown.

He later went to Britain for further studies. He became a medical doctor and was the first African to be elected a Fellow of the Royal College of Surgeons of England. For more than twenty years he had been active in the movement for the independence of his country.

In his autobiography, *Kossoh Town Boy* (263), he looks back on the days of his childhood in Freetown.

Conton, William   Gambia

Born on September 5, 1925, in Bathurst, Gambia, William Conton had his primary education from 1930 to 1935 in Co-

Samuel Edward Krune Mqhayi

Peter Abrahams

PLATE III

Ezekiel Mphahlele

Bloke Modisane

Dennis Brutus

Alex La Guma

PLATE IV

Lewis Nkosi

Richard Rive

nakry, Guinea, and from 1935 to 1938 he attended the C.M.S. Grammar School in Freetown, Sierra Leone. From 1938 to 1947 he continued his education in Great Britain, up to 1943 at the Bible College of Wales at Swansea, Wales, and from 1943 to 1947 at St. John's College at Durham, England. He returned to West Africa and, from 1948 to 1949, studied at the Fourah Bay College in Freetown, Sierra Leone.

Since 1947 William Conton has held different positions in education. From 1947 to 1953 he was Lecturer in History at the Fourah Bay College, Freetown, from 1953 to 1960 Headmaster at Accra High School in Accra, Ghana, from 1960 to 1963 Principal of different government secondary schools in Sierra Leone, from 1963 to 1964 Assistant Chief Education Officier in the Ministry of Education in Freetown, and from 1964 to 1971 Chief Education Officer in the Ministry of Education. Since then he has been Director of the Division of Equality of Access to Education in the Department of Advancement of Education at UNESCO, Paris.

William Conton's novel *The African* (264), touches tribalism, nationalism, panafricanism, and racialism. "Finally, the key sentence to Mr. Conton's novel may well be that uttered by Greta, the South African girl of Boer descent to Kamara, the student, 'Racial hatred is wicked, whoever shows it and against whom it is directed'" (Erisa Kironde).

Costa Alegre, Caetano da   São Tomé

Costa Alegre was born on April 26, 1864, in São Tomé and died on April 18, 1890, in Alcobaça, Portugal. He was educated at the Escola Acadèmica in Lisbon and later at the Escola Medical, where in 1887 he began his studies, to become a naval medical officer. He died of tuberculosis during his easter holidays and thus ended the career of the first poet from São Tomé. He had time only to publish one volume of poems, *Versos* (165), many of which deal with African themes.

Born on January 30, 1900, in Whydah, Dahomey, Félix Komla
Dossa Couchoro had his primary education at the Catholic
mission school of Grand Popo, and his secondary education
at the Séminaire Sainte-Jeanne-d'Arc at Whydah. From 1917
to 1927 he was monitor at the Catholic school of Grand Popo,
and from 1927 to 1939 at the school of Grand Popo. In 1939
he went into business in Anecho, Togo. His function as public
letter writer and his association with the Nationalist Party of
Sylvanus Olympio made him a wellknown figure all through
Eweland and the southern part of Dahomey. Forced in 1951
to flee from French colonialist repression, he sought asylum in
Aflao, the Ghanaian border town. He returned to Togo in 1959
and was appointed assistant editor of the Togolese Information
Service. In this capacity he was able to republish several of his
novels, and he wrote numerous others: they all appeared in the
local newspaper "Togo-Presse" and made him the most famous
writer in Togo. Couchoro retired in 1965. He died in Lome on
April 5, 1968.

Only one of his novels, *L'esclave* (266), was published in
Paris; the others which appeared in book form were printed
locally, in Whydah or Lome: *Amour de féticheuse* (267), *Drame
d'amour à Anecho* (268), *L'héritage, cette peste* (269). His other
novels, of the chapbook type, were published in the newpaper
"Togo-Presse" in serials: *L'esclave* (27/IV/62–30/IX/62), *Max
Mensah* (1/X/62–14/XI/62), *Béa et Marilou* (31/XII/62–16/II/
63), *Les secrets d'Eléonore* (16/II/63–17/IV/63, in bookform
269), *Pauvre Alexandrine* (I/X/64–18/XI/64), *Sinistre d'Abidjan* (12/II/65–1/IV/65), *La dot plaie nociale* (14/II/66–3/IV/
66), *Le passé resurgit* (4/IV/66–7/VI/66), *Les caprices du destin*
(8/VI/66–2/VIII/66), *Accusée, levez-vous!* (24/II/67–6/IV/67),
Amour de féticheuse au Togo (10/VII/67–30/VIII/67), *Gang-
sters et policiers* (31/VIII/67–20/X/67), *Les gens sont méchants*
(21/X/67–4/XII/67), *Ici bas tout se paie* (5/XII/67–16/I/68),
Le secret de Ramanou (17/I/68–2/III/68), *L'homme à la mer-
cédés-benz* (4/III/68–25/IV/68), *Les dix plaies de l'Afrique*

(26/IX/68—11/XI/68), *Fille de nationaliste* (13/II/69—17/IV/69) and *D'Aklakou à El Mina* (23/I/70—13/III/70). "All these serials were carefully typeset and paginated since a contract with Editogo, the Togolese National Publishing Company, stipulated that his novels were to appear subsequently in separate volumes" (Alain Ricard).

"We can say that Félix Couchoro was the first regional African novellist" (Robert Cornevin).

"Unique in French speaking West Africa, the case of Félix Couchoro is very instructive: it demonstrates that an audience is establishing itself which is keen on adventures with local colour" (Alain Ricard).

Coulibaly, Augustin-Sondé   Upper Volta

Augustin-Sondé Coulibaly was born in 1933 in Tin-Orodara, district Haut Bassin, Upper Volta. He obtained his primary education in Orodara from 1942 to 1946 and his secondary education in Abidjan, Ivory Coast, from 1946 to 1950. From 1950 to 1962 Coulibaly was employed by the administration. In 1962 he entered the University of Strasbourg, France, to study journalism at the Centre International d'Enseignement Supérieur de Journalisme.

Coulibaly collaborated with the journals "Encres vives", "Poésie vivante", and "Dialogue et Culture", for the pages of which he contributed poems and essays. In reward for his work and ideas he was selected "Chevalier de l'ordre des arts et lettres" by the French Republic in 1962.

In 1966 Coulibaly was appointed Director in the Ministry of Justice, a post he held till 1971. At the same time he devoted his life to literary and artistic activities in Upper Volta. He is the founder of the Cercle d'activités littéraires et artistiques de Haute-Volta and directed it till 1969.

Coulibaly is now doing research work in Bobo-Dioulasso for the Information Centre.

Minuit-Soleil, a collection of poems published in various journals won the prize of "Encres Vives" in 1965. Fragments of *Quand chante le Nègre,* a volume of poetry finished in 1966, were published in "Virage d'Afrique" and the Upper Volta journal "Carrefour africain". Four novels, written in 1955, 1956, 1958 and 1968 are still awaiting publication.

Craveirinha, José — Mozambique

Born on May 28, 1922, in Lourenço Marques, Mozambique, José Craveirinha was educated in his home town and lived there as a journalist until he was arrested in 1964 with other writers for support of FRELIMO (Frente de Libertação de Moçambique). He is still in prison.

Poets like Craveirinha "hail from the rapidly growing cities in Portuguese Africa — Luanda, Beira, and Lourenço Marques. They represent not only the 'assimilados' but the mass of detribalized Africans that crowd the squalid 'native' quarters of these cities" (Gerald M. Moser). From his volume of poetry, *Chigubo* (1572), some poems have been translated into English and anthologized in *Modern Poetry from Africa* (A 75).

Crowther, Samuel Adjai — Nigeria

Born about 1807 at Oshogun in Yorubaland, Nigeria, Samuel Adjai Crowther in 1822 happened to be on a Portuguese slave ship that was captured by the English. The slaves were liberated and brought to Freetown, Sierra Leone. Thus Samuel Adjai Crowther was the first and most distinguished alumnus of Fourah Bay College, having been enrolled in its initial class in 1827, even before it had achieved seminary status. He graduated to become a school teacher in mission and government schools in and around Freetown. He gained recognition as a sober and down-to-earth but high-minded Christian and was invited to join the Niger expedition of 1841. Two years later he was in England where he was ordained, and in 1845 he went to Abeokuta (in today's Western Nigeria) as a missionary, one of the early Sierra Leone emigrés to go home again.

Two more voyages up the Niger in 1854 and 1857 followed a visit to England in 1851. The expedition of 1857 was expressly for the purpose of establishing inland missions along the Niger and the Benue, and at Onitsha. In June 1864, Crowther was consecrated as Bishop of the territories of "Western Equatorial Africa beyond the Queen's Dominions". He was untiring in his missionary activities. In 1869, while addressing his clergy of the Niger Mission, he dwelt at length on the question of Africa's ability to make her way without the assistance of others.

From 1873 Crowther's authority over his diocese was eroded away bit by bit. Underlying the whole process was a fundamental scepticism over the competence of the Negro race for leadership. To the new generation of English missionaries he was wanting in the necessary qualities of leadership. Step by step, his mission was divided, his helpers were suspended, and his authority circumscribed, until by 1891 he had been stripped of all practical control over his diocese. Later in the same year he died.

He wrote diaries and numerous letters. His works include *A Grammar and Vocabulary of the Yoruba Language,* London 1852, *Journal of an Expedition up the Niger and Tshadda Rivers,* London 1855, and, written together with J. C. Taylor *The Gospel on the Banks of the Niger,* London 1859.

Portrait on Plate II.

Cruz, Tomaz Vieira da   Angola

Born on April 22, 1900, in Constância, province Ribatejo, Portugal, Tomaz Vieira da Cruz, was the son of poor landowners. After an elementary school education, he became a hand in a pharmacy and remained one for the rest of his life. In Lisbon he frequented the circles of literature and arts. On February 20, 1924, he left Portugal for Africa and settled down in the little costal town of Novo Redondo, district South Cuanza, where, from 1929 to 1931, he edited the journal "Mocidade" in which he published his first poems. In 1937 he moved to Luanda. On the occasion of his visit to Brasil he was appointed member of the Academia Brasileira de Letras. He died in Lisbon on June 7, 1960.

During his life time three volumes of poetry were published, *Quissange — saüdade negra* (1573), *Tatuagem, Poesia d'Africa* (1574), and *Cazumbi, Poesia de Angola* (1575), which brought him several awards between 1938 and 1940. Posthumously his poems were reedited in the collection *Poesia angolana de Tomaz Vieira da Cruz* (1576).

"The attachment of the poet to the Angolan world, the enrichment of his language by the elements offered by this world, all that has been called, in social science, by the name of 'Luso-Tropicalism' has found in the poet Thomas Vieira da Cruz its most brilliant confirmation" (Mario Antonio).

Cruz, Viriato da   Angola

Born on March 25, 1928, in Porto Amboim, district South Cuanza, Angola, Viriato da Cruz received his secondary education in Luanda. He was trained as an accountant, a profession he held for some years. In 1957 he left Angola for Lisbon, where he continued his activities for the liberation of Angola. He soon left Portugal for Paris, and from there to Frankfurt, Germany, where he tried in vain to receive a scholarship. In 1958 he moved to East Germany, until he could work more actively with the UPA (União das Populaçoes de Angola) in Kinshasa, Zaire, in 1964. In 1966 he moved to Algiers to become General Secretary of the MPLA (Movimento Popular de Libertação de Angola). In 1969 he became secretary of the organization of Asian and African writers in Peking, China.

His only collection of poems, *Colectânea de poemas 1947–1950* (1577), has been suppressed together with its publishing house, "Casa dos Estudantes do Império".

"... they express the new racial solidarity of common blackness, negritude, on a continental, even a universal, scale ..." (Gerald M. Moser).

Cugoano, Ottobah   Ghana

Born around 1748 in Agimaqua (Ajumako?), Mfanti district, Central Province, Ghana, Ottobah Cugoano was caught, together with twenty other children, by slave dealers and brought onto the ship Grenada. He was freed by Lord Hoth, who took him to Britain. There, in 1788, he was in the service of the artist Cosway. He married an Englishwoman and worked zealously for the abolition of slavery, whose horrors he graphically described in his *Thoughts and sentiments on the evils and wicked traffic of the slavery and commerce of the human species, humbly submitted to the inhabitants of Great Britain, by Ottobah Cugoano, a native of Africa* (274).

Dadié, Bernard B.   Ivory Coast

Born in 1916 in Assinie, a coastal village some 40 kilometres east of Grand Bassam, Ivory Coast, Bernard Binlin Dadié, an Agni, was sent to school in Dabou in 1925. From 1928 to 1930 he continued his education at Grand Bassam, then at Bingerville. From there, he was transferred after three years, in 1933, to the famous Ecole William Ponty at Gorée, Senegal. He left it with a diploma in Administration.

87

From 1936 to 1947 he worked at the IFAN (Institut Français de l'Afrique Noire) in Dakar. In 1947 he returned to Ivory Coast where he became responsible for the press in the Comité Directeur of the Parti Démocratique, the local branch of the RDA (Rassemblement Démocratique Africain). After the events of February 6, 1949, he was arrested and sentenced to three years detention. In prison, he wrote his first poem, *Le Corbillard de la Liberté*. After sixteen months he was released, and continued work with IFAN, at the IFAN library in Abidjan.

In 1933 his play, *Les Villes* (276), was performed by the pupils of Bingerville at the First Children's Feast of Abidjan. Since then he has been working for the theatre. His historical chronicle of the Agni people, *Assémien Déhylé* (277), was performed in 1937 in Paris, during the International Colonial Exposition, at the Théâtre des Champs Elysées.

From 1957 to 1959 he was Chef de Cabinet in the Ministry of Education, and from 1959 to 1961 Director of the Information Service of Ivory Coast. Since 1961 he has been Director of the Service des Beaux-Arts et des Traditions Populaires. He is also lecturer in African Literature at the National School of Administration and President of the Ivory Coast section of the African Society of Culture.

Bernard Binlin Dadié has been active in all genres of literature. His plays *Min Adja-o, Situation difficile,* and *Serment difficile* have been compiled in the anthology *Le théâtre populaire en République de Côte d'Ivoire* (AW 120). *Monsieur Thôgô-Gnini* (290) was successfully performed at the Pan-African Festival in Algier in 1969. The play is about a king's speaker who collaborates with the colonialists to enrich himself. *Les voix dans le vent* (291) depicts a rebel who overthrows the government and becomes a dictator himself. *Béatrice du Congo,* Paris 1970, is a historical panorama of the time of Portuguese trade with the kingdom of Congo.

Dadié's poetry, *Afrique debout* (278), *La ronde des jours* (283) and *Hommes de tous les continent* (288) follows the style pattern of négritude.

Dadié's interest in oral literature is documented by his collections, *Légendes africaines* (279), *Le pagne noir: contes africaines* (280), and *Les belles histoires de Kacou Ananzé, l'Araignée* (284), in which he recreated oral tales in French.

Besides his autobiographical novel, *Climbié* (281), in which he recalls the period of childhood and school, he wrote books which give an African's view of a big town mixed with novelistic elements and travelogue: *Un nègre à Paris* (282), *Patron de New York* (285) and *La ville où nul ne meurt (Rome)* (289).

Though sections of his works have been widely used in anthologies and journals, to date no book of his has been translated into English.

"Dadié's poetry can have a gentle beauty, but all too often his feelings are too vague to produce precise and striking images" (Ulli Beier).

"*Climbié* does not live before our eyes; we are told about him. He discusses, he reasons. He does not exist really, he is a symbol. What exists is the country, the Ivory Coast, which lives fully in front of our eyes, without exotism" (Raymond Lavigne).

"*Un Nègre à Paris* ... is magnificent in its formal diversity. Certain passages give us a true poetical inspiration. At others we have the impression of reading Voltaire or Montesquieu" (Joseph Miezan Bognini).

"*Patron de New York*, a 'cronie' ... where, with an irony which touches incessantly the smiling derision, his African eye screens the madhouse of prejudices which 'justify', come what may, that pilotless universe in which the Black Man, for many generations, has drifted along, devotely" (Yambo).

Portrait on Plate VII.

Danquah, Joseph Kwame Kyeretwie Boakye   Ghana

Born on December 21, 1895, at Bepong, district Kwahu, Ghana, Joseph Kwame Kyeretwie Boakye Danquah was the son of an evangelist for the Basel Mission. He received his education at the grammar school at Begoro. In 1913, he was employed as a High Court Official. Between 1915 and 1921, he acted as Secretary in Kibi to his elder brother, Nana Sir Afori-Atta, Paramount Chief of the major southern state of Akim Abuakwa, and for years the most important public figure in the country.

In 1921 Danquah came to London. By 1925 he had graduated in London, and two years later he was a Doctor of Philosophy with his thesis: *The Moral End as Moral Excellence.*

He had become a member of the Inner Temple in 1922 and was called to the Bar in 1926. That year he went on his travels; to Helsinki for a world conference of missionaries, to Berlin and The Hague. He was offered a mastership at Achimota College to succeed Dr. Aggrey, but decided to join, instead, the local Bar.

By 1928 he was back in England with his brother; and published his first book, *Akan Law and Customs*, London 1928. In 1931 Danquah founded in Accra "The Times of West Africa", which ceased publication in 1939, when he was deep in politics. In 1934 he again went to London, as secretary to a delegation and stayed on for two years, reading at the British Museum and writing about Gold Coast history.

After World War II, in 1947, he was one of the founders of the UGCC (United Gold Coast Convention) and invited Nkrumah to come from London and occupy the position of General Secretary for the party. In the Watson Commission report on the 1948 disturbances Danquah was regarded the "doyen" of Gold Coast politicians. This led to the "banishment" of Danquah and five others, including Nkrumah.

During Nkrumah's regime, Danquah was considered the symbol of opposition. In 1960, at the elections for presidency, he opposed Nkrumah, and received 124 000 votes, in Accra 9000 against 16 800 for Nkrumah. In 1961, after the strike of the railway workers, Danquah was put into detention. In 1962, he was released. In 1964, after the attempt on Nkrumah's life in Flagstaff House, Danquah was put into prison again. He died in the Nsawam Prison near Accra on February 4, 1965.

Joseph Boakye Danquah's scholary works include *The Akim Abuakwa Constitution*, London 1928, in the same volume as *Akan Laws and Customs*, and *The Gold Coast Akan*, London 1945, which also has become a classic. His plays are written in Twi, the language of the Akan, such as *Nyankonsɛm* (296) and *Biribi wɔ baabi* (299), and in English respectively, such as *The Third Woman* (297), and *Liberty* (298), which is an autobiographical story.

Danquah was one of those allround personalities as they are born in times of deep cultural conflict. He was outstanding as a politician, lawyer, scholar, and writer.

Daskalos, Alexandre   Angola

Born in 1924 in the district Huambo in Angola, Alexandre Daskalos was trained as a veterinary surgeon. He died in 1961 in Caramulo, Portugal.

His poems were published under the title *Colectânea de poemas* (1579) in a now prohibited publishing house. The only critical evaluation obtainable is Amândio César's attack: "The poetry of this group, because of the demagogy of the subject, simply has nothing left of art or even of the human feeling of art."

Dei-Anang, Michael Francis   Ghana

Born on October 16, 1909, in Mampong, district Akwapim, Eastern Region, Ghana, Michael Francis Dei-Anang grew up as an only child. His father was clerk to the District Commissioner. He went to Mfantsipim School in Cape Coast, then to Achimota College in Accra in 1932 to study for his Intermediate Arts examination. After passing his examination there seemed disappointingly little in the way of openings, so Dei-Anang went into the Printing Department for £ 3 a month, but was soon asked by his old headmaster to teach at Mfantsipim. There he had the chance to study for another degree, with which he obtained a scholarship to Westminster Training College — a Methodist College — in London. He also took up a postgraduate course at the Institute of Education of the London University.

In 1938 Dei-Anang attended a Youth Conference at Vassar College in the United States, then went back to Ghana via London in 1939 to teach Latin at Mfantsipim School till 1943, when he was appointed Assistant Education Officer in Ashanti.

In 1949 Dei-Anang was asked to be Secretary in Charge of the Common Entrance Examination papers, a post he held for two years. In 1952 he was appointed Senior Assistant Secretary in the Ministry of Defence and External Affairs, and in 1953 moved to Recruitment and Training in the Establishment office.

Dei-Anang has travelled widely, to Britain and the United States. He was a member of the Ghana Government party to the Bandung conference in 1954.

After Independence, Dei-Anang became Secretary to the Governor-General, then Principal Secretary in Nkrumah's Ministry of Foreign Affairs. At the same time he was Head of the State Publishing Corporation.

With Nkrumah's fall Dei-Anang was detained from February to April 1967, then retired from Ghana's Diplomatic Service and dedicated himself to writing.

In 1970 Dei-Anang took up his studies again. He was a Nuffield Research Fellow at the Institute of Commonwealth Studies at London University from January to November 1970, and a Distinguished Visiting Scholar in Residence, State University of New York, U.S.A. from December 1970 to June 1971. Since September 1971 Michael Francis Dei-Anang has been Professor of History in the Black Studies Department, State University College at Brockport, New York.

Michael Dei-Anang has published several volumes of poetry, all revealing his great pride in his race and colour. *Wayward lines from Africa* (305) appeared as early as 1946. It was followed by a play in 1949, *Cocoa comes to Mampong* (306),

Africa speaks (307), another collection of poems, *Okomfo Anokye's golden stool* (308), another play, and two more volumes of poetry, *Ghana semi-tones* (309), and *Ghana glory* (310).

Delano, Oloye I. O.   Nigeria

Born in 1904 in Western Nigeria, Chief Oloye Isaac Oluwole Delano was educated at mission stations and has been a teacher for most of his life. At present he is Lecturer for Yoruba at the Institute of African Studies of the University of Ife, Western State, Nigeria. Because of his contributions to Yoruba studies he has been appointed a chief.

Chief Delano is a well known Yoruba writer who wrote several short stories and two novels, *Aiye d'aiye òyinbo* (311) and *L'ojó ojó un* (312), both concerned with Yoruba life in the modern world.

His earlier writing is concerned with the Christian missions. In *The Soul of Nigeria*, London 1937, he describes several aspects of Yoruba life. *The Singing Minister of Nigeria*, London 1942, is a biography of the life of the Rev. Cannon J. J. Romsane Kuti. *Notes and Comments from Nigeria*, London 1944, is the report of a travel through Nigeria and shows Delano's interest in the development of Christianity. *An African Looks at Marriage*, London 1945, sees the problem from a Christian point of view. *One Church for Nigeria*, London 1945, suggests a unification of the different Christian denominations.

More important are his contributions to Yoruba studies and linguistics. *Atúmò ede Yoruba* (Explanation of the Yoruba language), London 1958, includes a grammar with a Yoruba-Yoruba dictionary. *Agbékà oro Yoruba* (Yoruba idioms), London 1960, is a Yoruba style manual. His volume *Iránti anfani* (History) depicts Yoruba local history, *Itan Egba*, London 1963, depicts the history of the Egba, and *Itan Oyo*, London 1964, the history of the Oyo. *Owe l'esin oro*, Ibadan 1966, explains

Yoruba proverbs, their meaning and usage. Two books in English introduce the foreigner to Yoruba: *Conversation in Yoruba and in English*, New York 1963, and *A Modern Yoruba Grammar*, London 1965.

Demand Goh, Gaston   Ivory Coast

Born on September 6, 1940, in Port-Bouet, a suburb of Abidjan, Ivory Coast. Gaston Demand Goh was sent, at the age of seven, to the regional school at Treichville, another suburb of Abidjan. When he was fourteen he went to Saint-Louis, Senegal, to the preparatory military school. At the age of nineteen he had to leave school, having become deaf because of meningitis. Instead of sending him to a hospital, his parents brought him to a traditional medicineman in Sassandra, Ivory Coast, and thus wasted a year. Meanwhile his hearing nerves had been damaged to such an extent that it was too late for operation.

In 1962 Gaston Goh returned to Agboville where he tried to end his life in suicide. Discovered in time, he was saved in hospital. While there, his friends brought him books, among which was "Terre des hommes" by Antoine de Saint-Exupéry. This story gave him new courage and the will to write. In the course of two weeks he wrote a play, *Toussio*. In a letter course he taught himself the profession of an accountant. Since that time he has been working as accountant at the Compagnie Fermière des Huiles de Palme at Dabou.

In January 1971 his play, *Toussio* has been performed by the Ecole Nationale de Théâtre in Abidjan.

"*Toussio* . . . a fine story of love and death, of cultural conflict challenging certain ancestral tradition . . ." (Jean Favarel).

Born on March 20, 1921, at San, province Segu, Mali, in a family
of farmers, Dembele went to primary school at San from 1929
to 1934, to the Ecole primaire supérieur at Bamako from 1934 to
1937, and to the Ecole Normale William Ponty at Dakar, Senegal, from 1938 to 1940. He enrolled then at the Ecole Féderale
des PTT. In 1941 he was called up for military service and
stayed in the army till the end of the war in 1945.

Sidiki Dembele helped to found the RDA (Rassemblement
Démocratique Africain) at Bamako in 1946, and edited its
journal "Réveil" from 1946 to 1954. He has been a member of
this party ever since. Dembele is also a unionist. He was general
secretary of the PTT workers in the federation A.O.F. (Afrique
Occidentale Française) and Togo from 1948 to 1954. From 1954
to 1959 he was general secretary of the PTT trade union in the
Ivory Coast, and at the same time general secretary of the
"Union des Syndicats autonomes" of the Ivory Coast.

Dembele visited Paris in 1950 to attend a course for super-
visors of the PTT. He returned to Paris in 1965 to study the
administration and management of government enterprises.

In 1960 Dembele was appointed Director of Information and
Broadcasting in the Federation of Mali at Dakar. After the
break-up of the federation he became Director of Radio Mali at
Bamako. From 1967 to 1968 he was General Director of In-
formation and Broadcasting of Mali. Since 1968 he has been
General Supervisor of PTT in Mali.

Sidiki Dembele is a Mohammedan. He likes boxing, classical
music, cinema and theatre. He calls himself "liberal" and says
of himself: "N'aime pas lire. A horreur du socialisme".

Sidiki Dembele is the author of *Les Inutiles* (313), a novel
that won him the "Grand Prix Littéraire 1959 de Côte
d'Ivoire". *Le Chant du Madhi* (314), a play he wrote in 1950,
was produced in Paris, Abidjan and Bamako. Two other plays
are not yet published, but have been staged: *Les hommes*,
written in 1962, at Bamako and Algiers, and *La Bourgeoise*,
written in 1964, also at Bamako. A radio play *Une femme, un*

amour, written in 1969, was broadcast by Radiodiffusion- Télévision Française in Paris.

Dempster, Roland Tombekai   Liberia

Born on December 9, 1910, at Tosoh (from "wo tosoh" meaning
"keep quiet") on the shore of the Piso or Fisherman Lake, Cape
Mount, Liberia, Roland Tombekai Dempster had his early
schooling from 1920 to 1927 at the missionary school at St.
John's Protestant Episcopal Church, his secondary schooling
from 1927 to 1929 at Cuttington College in Cape Palmas, and
from 1929 to 1931 at Liberia College, Monrovia. From 1932 to
1941 he passed through all grades of Liberia College to receive
finally his Master of Literature degree.

Roland T. Dempster was employed by the administration. In
1938 and in 1945 he was Chief Clerk of the Bureau of Public
Works and Utilities. From 1936 to 1948 he taught shorthand,
typing and office management at the Community Commercial
School. From 1948 to 1954 he was Editor-in-Chief of the
"Liberian Age", a bi-weekly newspaper in Liberia. From 1948
to 1960 he was Professor of English and History at Liberia
College, and of Latin, World Literature and Creative Writing
at the University of Liberia.

In 1951 he travelled to the United States to attend a course
in Journalism, in 1953 to Ghana and Nigeria, and in 1957 to
Europe.

He spent his last years of life both in Monrovia and in his
home in Tosoh, and died in Monrovia in September 1965 as
Liberia's first poet laureate.

His prose works which include a satirical treatise on moral
philosophy, *The Mystic Reformation of Gondolia* (317), and
his poetical works are of local importance. They are *Echoes
from the Valley* (316), a collection including also poetry from
Bai Tamia Moore and Harmon Carey Thomas, *To Monrovia
Old and New* (318), *Anniversary Ode to Dr. William V. S.*

Tubman (319), *A Song out of Midnight, Souvenir of the Tubman-Tolbert Inauguration* (320), and *Tubman* (321). Though it was his "highest ambition to become one of Africa's most outstanding poets, writers and philosophers" (Roland Tombekai Dempster), he only achieved to be the late President Tubman's court poet.

Dhlomo, Herbert I. E.   South Africa

Herbert I. E. Dhlomo, a Zulu, the younger brother of R. R. R. Dhlomo, was born in 1905 in Siyama Village near Pietermaritzburg, Natal, South Africa. In the thirties he was appointed to the staff of the "Bantu World", a weekly journal. In October 1936 he was the only Zulu representative at the African Authors' Conference hald at Florida, Transvaal. In late 1936 he was appointed Librarian-Organizer by the Transvaal Committee of the Carnegie Library Service for Non-Europeans, the first African to hold such a job. On September 30, 1937, he attended the second African Authors' Conference, which was held in Johannesburg. For a while he was assistant editor of "Ilanga laseNatal".

Herbert I. E. Dhlomo died at King Edward Hospital in Durban on October 23, 1956.

Dhlomo's first work is also the first drama published in English by a black South African author. Entitled *The Girl Who Killed to Save* (1581), it is based on an episode of the Xhosa history, the cattle-killing tragedy of 1857. *The Valley of a Thousand Hills* (1582) is a long elegiac poem, based on the contrast between the harmony of nature and the cruelty and ugliness of human society. Dhlomo also composed a number of plays. Three of them, dealing with the Zulu kings Shaka, Cetshwayo and the paramount chief and founder of the Sotho nation, Moshesh, "were meant to be published in one book, which the author intended to call *The Black Bulls*" (B. W. Vilakazi). Apparently, none of these works ever reached print.

Chaka — a Tragedy (1583), however, was performed by the African Dramatic and Operatic Society in Johannesburg.

Dhlomo also dealt with Zulu oral art in a series of articles. His controversy with B. W. Vilakazi about form and content of Bantu literature is probably the first controversy in the history of African literature.

"Dhlomo provides one of the most lucid expositions of the societal significance of folk art, and especially praise poetry, to have come from the pen of an African" (Albert S. Gérard).

Dhlomo, R. R. R. South Africa

Born in 1901 in Zululand, South Africa, Rolfes Reginald Raymond Dhlomo — this is his full name — was educated at the Zulu Christian Industrial School at Ohlange, called Ohlange Institute in brief, founded by John L. Dube. He proceeded then to the American Mission Board School at Amanzimtoti, Zululand, where he obtained his teacher's certificate. In the early twenties he became a regular contributor to Dube's journal "Ilanga laseNatal", writing under various pen names such as "Randite", "Rollie Reggie", and "The Pessimist". In 1928 he was working as a mine clerk with the City and Suburban Mine in Johannesburg. In the thirties, he was appointed to the staff of the "Bantu World", another weekly, where he signed "R. Roamer, Esq.". In 1951 Dhlomo was selected by the University of the Witwatersrand as the first recipient of the Vilakazi Memorial Award. In 1961 he became editor of "Ilange laseNatal".

Rolfes Reginald Raymond Dhlomo died in 1971.

Dhlomo's first novel was *An African Tragedy — A Novel in English by a Zulu Writer* (1584). As he stated in the preface, his purpose was to describe the decline of native life in large cities, but the work also contains some cogent criticism of traditional customs. *An African Tragedy* "is the first piece of genuine prose fiction by a Zulu writer. It is the first fairly extensive and realistic treatment of the moral evils of city life to be written in a spirit of social criticism" (Albert S. Gérard).

Dhlomo's next book was *Izikhali zanamuhla* (1585), which was followed by a series of semibiographical narratives about the Zulu dynasty. The first of these, *UDingane kaSenzanga-khona* (1586), centres around Dingane, Shaka's half-brother and murderer. *UShaka* (1587) is an attempt to reassess the manifold personality of the great Zulu king, Shaka.

Shaka "is a tyrant and a merciless despot; a humorous, respected, loving king; a warrior, a founder of an aristocratic nation, and a prophet; a man who always wanted to solve some difficulties. ... It is the best book on Shaka for it contains facts and very little of fictitious tales that have shrouded Shaka's history" (B. W. Vilakazi).

UMpande kaSenzangakhona (1588) deals with Shaka's younger half-brother, who succeded Dingane on the Zulu throne, *Indlela yababi* (1589) is a dramatic account of Zulu life in the slums of Johannesburg. *UNomalanga kaNdengezi* (1590) is a love story involving two of Shaka's lieutenants and the daughter of a prominent warrior. *UCetshwayo* (1591) is the story of Mpande's eldest son, who followed him on the throne and who was the last independent Zulu king. Dhlomo's last novel is *UDinuzulu kaCetshwayo* (1592), centred around Dinuzulu, the king who succeeded Cetshwayo.

"In handling the plot of his stories, Dhlomo shows a masterful and adept treatment not found in the writers of the earlier age" (B. W. Vilakazi).

Dia, Amadou Cissé   Senegal

Born on June 2, 1915, at Saint-Louis, Senegal, Amadou Cissé Dia studied Medicine in Dakar, and was, until May 1959, Medical Superintendent of the Hygiene Service at Kaolack, Senegal. Then he went into politics.

He was President of the Commission of Delegates of the Federal Assembly of Mali; from October 9, 1959, to March 3,

1960, Secretary of State for Commerce and Industry of the Republic of Senegal, and then on many different ministerial assignments: Minister of Commerce and Industry, of Health and Social Welfare, of Technical Cooperation, of the Armed Forces. On March 19, 1965, he was appointed Minister of Home Affairs. In 1968, at the death of Lamine Gueye, he was appointed President of the National Assembly of Senegal, and he also is Secretary General of the Union Progressiste Sénégalaise, the ruling party, and President of the Senegalese Red Cross.

Amadou Cissé Dia wrote two historical plays, *La mort du Damel* (326), and *Les derniers jours de Lat Dior* (327), the latter being performed with great success at the First Festival of Negro Arts in Dakar, in April 1966.

Diabaté, Massa Makan   Mali

Born on June 12, 1938, in Kita, region of Kayes, Mali, Massa Makan Diabaté, a Malinke, had his education at the Lycée Donka in Conakry, Guinea. From 1958 to 1959 he studied in Paris, France, where he obtained his B. A. He then studied Politics and Social Science at the Ecole des Hautes Etudes Européennes in Strasbourg. In 1966 he returned to Mali to teach at the Institut des Sciences Humaines in Bamako. In 1969 he was appointed General Director of Information in Bamako. He is now (1972) Head of the Department of Culture in the Ministry of Information in Bamako.

His stories, collected in the volumes *Si le feu s'éteignait...* (329) and *Kala Jata*, Bamako 1970, and his songs, *Janjon et autres chants populaires du Mali*, Paris 1970, are inspired by the oral tradition of the Malinke and Mende.

"Exceptionally privileged, the young student of the university has inherited from his uncle all the wisdom of the region of Kita ... Massa Makan writes in Bambara language in traditional forms which he enriches with his experience of the modern world. Massa Makan proves that French is only one way to make us known" (Djibril Tamsir Niane).

Diagne, Ahmadou Mapaté   Senegal

Born between 1894 and 1899 in or near Louga, region of Diour-bel, Senegal, into the family of a Wolof chief, Ahmadou Mapaté Diagne went to school in Saint-Louis, was a teacher in Dakar and then the headmaster of a school in a suburb of Dakar. After that he became the secretary of Georges Hardy, the founder and Director of the Ecole Normale William Ponty in Gorée. When Georges Hardy left West Africa in 1919, he recommended Ahmadou Mapaté Diagne to enrol as guest student at the Ecole Normale at Sedhiou, where he received his Brevet Supérieur. He then became School Superintendent of the Casamance.

Besides his short novel, *Les trois volontés de Malic* (330), the first fiction in French from West Africa, he published some ethnological studies in journals. Once he travelled to France and visited Georges Hardy. When Joseph Mbelolo finished his thesis on the beginnings of Senegalese writing in 1968, Ahmadou Mapaté Diagne was still living in Sedhiou, Casamance.

"Diagne puts the finger on many problems like western education, cultural conflict and conflict of generations, the presence of colonial powers, problems that are the treasure of later novels much better written" (Joseph Mbelolo).

Diakhaté, Lamine   Senegal

Born on September 18, 1928, in Saint-Louis, Senegal, Lamine Diakhaté spent his first years in his home town, then his family moved to Louga. He went to school in Saint-Louis and Kati-bougou, Mali, where he founded a students' journal which was not allowed to appear by the French administration.

Lamine Diakhaté was working with IFAN (Institut Français de l'Afrique Noire), when, in 1960, he became Director of Cabinet of President Léopold Sédar Senghor. In 1962 he was appointed Minister of Information. On May 29, 1964, he was dismissed and became administrator of the Société Africaine de Culture in Paris. In July 1971 he was appointed Ambassador of Senegal to Nigeria.

Lamine Diakhaté wrote three volumes of poetry, *La joie d'un continent* (331), *Primordiale du sixième jour* (333), and *Temps de mémoire* (334), and he adapted a story of Birago Diop, *Sarzan* (332), for the theatre.

"*Primordiale du sixième jour* (Primer for the sixth day) is essentially a set of songs to build a nation by . . . (It) draws heavily upon the Senegalese folk myths whose influence on other modern African poets Diakhaté discussed in a 1962 article in Présence Africaine . . . Diakhaté's patriotism is admirable. His style, merely the feeblest echo of Senghor, is simply not sufficient to transmute his engagement into art" (Ellen Conroy Kennedy).

Diallo, Bakary   Senegal

Born in 1892 at M'Bala near Podor, division Sovanabe-Botol, district Dagana, River Region, Senegal, Bakary Diallo herded the cattle of his noble Fulani parents until he went to Saint-Louis to enter the French army on February 4, 1911. On May 2 of the same year he was shipped to Casablanca in Morocco to fight against Moroccans who resisted French occupation. In 1914 he was sent to France to fight against the German army. At Marne he was wounded and then spent much time in hospitals at Epernay, Neuilly, Paris, and Menton. In 1920 he was given the French citizenship, he left the army and became a doorman at the Hotel National, Monte-Carlo. After a period of very poor life in Paris he published his book *Force-Bonté* (336) in 1926, the first autobiography of an African written in French.

On February 6, 1928, Bakary Diallo returned to Senegal and was appointed messenger at the Residence of Dagana. Six months later he was made Chef de Canton for the nomads of Dimar. Four years later he became functionary at the local administration of Podor, but as this job did not suit his intellectual and moral education he resigned and became interpreter for the administration. He retired in 1953, and since then lives in his village from his pension and his cattle. In 1960 he was awarded the Légion d'honneur.

"I have chosen the ideal of writing, trying to give my contribution to the determination of the writers of the Universe to seek day and night to be brave auxiliaries to the Gods of the world" (Bakary Diallo).

Diallo, Georges

Georges Diallo, author of the novel *La nuit du destin* (337), is no African. Georges Diallo is the pseudonym for the Révérend Père Georges Janssens of the Catholic Mission in Kolongo par Massina, Mali.

Diallo, Mamadou   Ivory Coast

Born on October 26, 1920, in Tiassalé, Southern District, Ivory Coast, Diallo was a student of the Ecole Normale William Ponty in Senegal. From 1961 to 1963 he studied law at the University of Abidjan, but broke off to join the Ecole Nationale d'Administration in Paris, where he stayed from 1963 to 1965. Then he returned to the Ivory Coast and became Director of Financial Affairs in the Ministry of Education. He held this office from 1966 to 1970, then became Inspecteur de Service Administratif. His small collection of poems *Tam-Tam noir*, Abidjan 1969, received the Prix Houphouet-Boigny in 1969.

Diop, Alioune   Senegal

Born on January 10, 1910, in Saint-Louis, Senegal, Alioune
Diop received his secondary education at the Lycée Faidherbe
in his home town. He later went to France via Algiers. He
became Professor of Classical Literature in Paris, and Senator
of Senegal. In 1947 he was the founder of the journal "Présence
Africaine" which became the dominant journal not only for
French speaking Africans. The influence of "Présence Africaine"
extended to the Caribbean, to Afro-America and to the intellectual world in general. Alioune Diop founded a publishing
house of the same name. In 1956 he organized the First International Congress of Negro Writers and Artists in Paris. On
this occasion he founded the Societé Africaine de Culture, the
African Cultural Society. As General Secretary of the society,
he organized the Second Congress of Negro Writers and Artists
in Rome. He became President of the Association of the World
Festival of the Negro Arts which, because of Diop's organizing
talents, was held in Dakar in 1966. Alioune Diop has represented his journal, his publishing house and his society at
numerous international conferences and meetings, and he is
a member of many organizations which try to unite the African
peoples.

With his friend Léopold Sédar Senghor he has been a philosopher of and a fighter for Négritude, always trying to transform
ideology into practical and human action. Numerous articles,
essays, introductions and addresses in his own journal and in
many papers have demonstrated his clear concepts, his insistence
and his sense for measure and perspective.

Portrait on Plate V.

Diop, Birago   Senegal

Born on December 12, 1906, in Ouakam, a suburb of Dakar,
Senegal, Birago Diop is the son of a Wolof father and a mother
from Sine-Saloum. He received his primary education from

1914 to 1920 at the school in Rue Thiong, Dakar. In 1920 he failed the exam for the school William Ponty, but succeeded in winning a scholarship for the Lycée Faidherbe in Saint-Louis. He attended this already coeducational and multi-racial school from 1921 to 1928. In 1928, as he was trying to get a new scholarship, he was called for eleven months of military service. During this time, he was a nurse in the military hospital of Saint-Louis. Obtaining a scholarship in Veterinary Medicine, he left for France to study at the University of Toulouse from 1929 to 1933, when he received his degree as veterinary surgeon. This doctorate opened up for him the opportunity to attend the school for the necessary specialisation, the Institut d'Etudes Vétérinaires Exotiques in Paris where he spent six months in 1933/34. Here he came into contact with Léopold Sédar Senghor who was just preparing to start the journal "L'Etudiant Noir" to which Birago Diop contributed.

In 1934 he went, via Dakar and Bamako, to Kayes, where he had been appointed Head of the Cattle Inspection Service for the whole of western Mali. He remained in this position until 1937, travelling widely on horseback, in canoe, by car. Near the place where the river Falémé joins the Senegal he met an old Griot, Amadou Koumba Ngom, sixty years old, who became the protagonist of his tales.

In 1937 he returned to France to spend his leave, then went for his second term in Africa, from 1937 to 1942. During his leave in Paris in 1942, he worked at the Institut de Médicine Vétérinaire Exotique to avoid compulsory labour service, and remained there until November 1944. After the Liberation of Paris, Birago Diop regained his position as cattle inspector in Dakar, but it took him four months and six days to arrive there. Shortly afterwards, from 1945 to 1950 he worked as a veterinary surgeon in the Ivory Coast and Upper Volta. In 1950 he returned to Senegal, to Saint-Louis which was then the capital of Senegal and Mauretania to whose administration he belonged. He was present when in 1955 the famous theatre troupe of Keita Fodeba performed his *Sarzan* in the adaptation of Lamine Diakhaté.

In 1961 Birago Diop retired to be appointed Ambassador of Senegal to Tunisia. In 1965 he resigned from diplomatic life and returned to Dakar to open his private veterinary clinic.

His tales, *Les contes d'Amadou Koumba* (341), *Les nouveaux contes d'Amadou Koumba* (342) and *Contes et lavanes* (344) adopt subjects and style of oral tradition, as told by the Griots, recreating the tales in a most modern French. A selection of these tales has been published in English, *Tales of Amadou Koumba* (346). Birago Diop's poetry, *Leurres et lueurs* (343), comprises verses from 1925 to 1966.

"Amadou Koumba recounted to me the tales which had lulled me to sleep as a child. He taught me others, too, sudden with maxims and morals, in which can be found all the wisdom of our ancestors" (Birago Diop).

An analysis of the work of Birago Diop by Mamadou Kane has been published at the University of Dakar in 1968: *Les Contes d'Amadou Coumba* (!). Mamadou Kane has also published a study: *Birago Diop, l'homme et l'oeuvre*, Paris 1971.

"In presenting these stories in a written form Diop had to recreate" (Anthony Brench).

"*Les Contes d'Amadou Koumba* give a complete panorama of the rural life ... this care for realism is a heritage of the popular tale mirroring the way of life and the deepest sorrows of the audience" (Mohamadou Kane).

"As a faithful disciple of Amadou the son of Koumba, he resumes the tradition and restores the fable and the ancient tales, in their spirit and in their style. But he renovates them by translating them into French with an art which, respecting the genius of the French language, conserves at the same time all the virtues of the negro-African languages" (Léopold Sédar Senghor).

Portrait on Plate V.

Diop, Cheikh Anta   Senegal

Born on December 29, 1923, in Diourbel, region Diourbel,
Senegal, Cheikh Anta Diop received his primary and secondary
education in Senegal. He passed his Baccalauréat and went to
Paris, France, just after World War II. He studied at the Sorbonne and received his Ph. D. His thesis, in which he tried to
prove the Negro character of ancient Egyptian civilization,
Nations Nègres et culture, Paris 1954, was rejected by the university but printed by " Présence Africaine".

In the fifties he was one of the leading African intellectuals
in Paris, and helped to shape the ideology of the Négritude
movement. After the independence of Senegal he returned home
and formed his own party, Bloc des Masses Sénégalaises, which
broke up in 1963. The majority of its members joined Senghor's
UPS (Union Progressiste Sénégalais). Cheikh Anta Diop then
founded another party, the Front National Sénégalais, an opposition party which was proscribed in 1965. Cheikh Anta
Diop has subsequently become Director of the research department of IFAN (Institut Fondamental de l'Afrique Noire) in
Dakar, a position he still holds.

The studies of Cheikh Anta Diop centre around African
History and African Culture. His essays were published in the
journal "Présence Africaine". His books are still widely discussed: *L'unité culturelle de l'Afrique noire*, Paris 1959, *Les
fondements culturels techniques et industriels d'un futur état
fédéral d'Afrique Noire*, Paris 1960, *L'Afrique noire pré-colo-
niale*, Paris 1960, *Antériorité des civilisations nègres: mythe ou
vérité historique?*, Paris 1967.

Diop, David   Senegal

Born on July 9, 1927, in Bordeaux, France, of African parents
— his father from Senegal, his mother from Cameroon — David
Diop spent his youth partly in France, partly in West Africa.

He studied Medicine, and he taught History of Literature at High Schools. After Guinea became independent in 1958, he taught Literature at the Ecole Normale of Kindia, Guinea. He died in a plane crash in Dakar on September 6, 1960.

His poetry, collected in his book *Coups de Pilon* (348), is only a small part of what he wrote, but all his manuscripts perished with him and his family. But "that little pamphlet was enough to establish David Diop as the most interesting and talented new African poet of the fifties. Its appearance in 1956 aroused hopes of a career which never happened, but the unifying passion and fire of these few poems earn Diop a place as the spokesman of a new age ... the age of the Guinéan Revolution ... He is the Mayakovsky of the African Revolution" (Gerald Moore).

"Characteristic for his poems is the simple force of his verse and a humour which scourges, quickly, like the lash of a whip" (Léopold Sédar Senghor).

Diop, Massylla   Senegal

Born in 1885 in Dakar, Senegal, of a Wolof family, Massylla Diop, the elder brother of Birago Diop, had his education in a Koran school in the province of Cayor. After having received a solid islamic education he was one of the first pupils of the School Jery in Saint-Louis which later became the Lycée Faidherbe.

After school he was sent to Guinea as a functionary of the Administration. Then he became a journalist. He founded "Le Sénégal Moderne", a political journal. In 1925, under the direction of M. Sableau, a Frenchman, he became chief editor of the "Revue Africaine Artistique Littéraire" in Dakar, in which he published his sonnets and his novel *Le réprouvé* (349), the first novel on Senegalese town life, anticipating subjects later dealt with by Ousmane Socé and Abdoulaye Sadji. Massylla Diop died in 1932.

Massylla Diop "makes of each character the representative of a category of individuals. He changes continually between portraits and personal reflections. He condemns prostitution, and his moral concern is evident" (Joseph Mbelolo).

Dipoko, Mbella Sonne   Cameroon

Born on February 28, 1936, in Duala, Cameroon, as son of the Paramount Chief Paul Sonne Dipoko and Ebeny'a Mpa'a Bwanga, the daughter of the Chief of Bonaberi, Mbella Sonne Dipoko was educated in Western Cameroon and Nigeria where he attended St. Paul's Commercial College in Aba, Eastern Region. Here he began writing, and in 1956 had his first book, a volume of poetry, printed locally. In 1957 he joined the Nigeria Broadcasting Corporation and became a news reporter. The following year he went to the Southern Cameroons to cover the decisive elections which saw the fall of the local pro-Nigerian Government and the rise to power of the K.N.D.P. which later negotiated reunification with the Cameroon Republic.

In September 1960 he went to France. In Paris he resigned from the Nigerian Broadcasting Corporation and joined the editorial staff of "Présence Africaine" for a year. "I flirted with law studies at Paris University", he writes, "visited London and Holland, returned to France and paid a number of visits to the Provinces". In 1969 he moved to Spain.

Mbella Sonne Dipoko wrote poetry, some of which appeared in reviews, was broadcast by B.B.C., and translated into German. Between spring 1964 and winter 1965 he wrote novels of which the first, *A Few Nights and Days* (350), is a love story in Paris, between an African man and a French girl. His second novel *Because of Women* (352), is set in rural Cameroon, where a young fisherman and farmer tries to make his choice between several women.

Dipoko "is especially good in clipped exchanges, where the situation behind the fragments of conversation charges them with force and significance beyond themselves" (Gerald Moore).

"*A Few Nights and Days* is a French novel about France by a man who writes like a European woman" (Paul Theroux).

Djoleto, Amu   Ghana

Amu Djoleto was born on July 22, 1929, in the little village of Bana Hill, Manya Krobo, Eastern Region, Ghana. He is part Ga, part Ewe and considers himself "happily detribalized". His father is a Presbyterian minister, his mother the daughter of a Christian chief. Djoleto grew up in school compounds, for his father was a teacher for 24 years.

Djoleto received his higher education at Accra Academy, Accra, and at St. Augustine's College, Cape Coast, Ghana. He continued his studies at the University of Ghana, Legon, and received his Honours degree in English. He then joined the Institute of Education, London University, where he attended a course in textbook production.

In 1967 Djoleto became editor of the "Ghana Teachers' Journal". In the same year he moved to the headquarters of the Ministry of Education in Accra, being now the Principal Education Officer in charge of the Information, Public Relations and Publications Schedule of the Ministry. He is responsible for the following publications: "Ghana Journal of Education", "Brochure on Pre-University Education in Ghana", "Handbook of Education in Ghana", "Annual Report on Education in Ghana".

Amu Djoleto is the author of a novel, *The Strange Man* (356), which reflects his experience with schools and education.

Richard Dogbeh was born on December 31, 1932, in Cotonou, Dahomey, of Peda parentage, got his primary education at the Ecole Catholique Saint-Michel in Cotonou (from 1940 to 1946), and his secondary education at the Collège Moderne Victor-Ballot, Cotonou (from 1946 to 1950). From 1950 to 1953 he did a teacher's course at the Ecole Normale de Dabou, Ivory Coast, then went to Dakar to get his Certificat d'Etudes Littéraires et Générales (from 1953 to 1954). His brilliant results enabled him to continue his studies in psychology at the universities of Toulouse, Marseille and the Institute of Child Psychology in Bordeaux (from 1954 to 1957). During his studies he was a member of the African Students Union (F.E.A.N.F.) and the National Liberation Movement (M.L.N.). He also wrote for student journals.

Back in Dahomey Richard Dogbeh entered the service of Inspection Académique in Porto Novo and was in charge of schooling and pedagogical questions. In 1962 he received a scholarship from UNESCO to do another practical course in pedagogy in Paris, Nairobi and Kampala, then returned to Porto Novo in 1963 to become a Director in the Ministry of National Education, a post he held till 1966. From 1966 to 1967 he was again Director of the Institut Pédagogique National in Porto Novo, then was appointed to the French section of the Ghana Academy of Sciences to work on the African Encyclopedia. Since 1968 Richard Dogbeh has been an expert to the UNESCO, and since 1969, a teacher at the Ecole Normale Supérieur in Atakpame, Togo.

Richard Dogbeh has a long list of articles, on psychology and pedagogy, on African culture and literature, to offer. His own creative writing comprises the volumes of poetry *Les eaux du Mono* (359), *Rives mortelle* (360), and *Cap Liberté* (362). *Voyage au pays de Lénine* (361) is the literary result of an invitation to the Soviet Union by the Russian Writers' Union in 1966. His narrative, *Les trois princesses et les trois brigands* (in "Bingo", no. 110, 1962), won the Prize of the IFAN (Institut

Français de l'Afrique Noire) of Dahomey in 1948 as the best African narrative. Several other works are in preparation.

Dolamo, Elon Ramarisane   South Africa

Born on January 24, 1927, in Marishane, District Middelburg in Transvaal, Republic of South Africa, Dolamo got his primary education at Marishane school, passing Standard VI with distinction, then went to Ngwana-Mohube School near Pietersburg in the Northern Transvaal for his secondary education. He enrolled for the Joint Matriculation Board Examination at his school, but owing to financial difficulties had to leave at the end of the same year. Dolamo then took up a course at Mokopane Training College in Potgietersrust to become a teacher. After leaving college, he was appointed Principal of Aapjesboom School in the Lydenburg District, then moved to Madibong School near Jane Furse Hospital, District Middelburg, on account of ill health, holding the same position. After his health improved he completed the Senior Certificate privately, obtained a Second Class and then enrolled with University of South Africa for a B.A. degree.

Dolamo is the author of a narrative, *Mononi (1595)*, a novel, *Mahlale* (1596) and a volume of poems, *Ithute go reta* (1597), all in North-Sotho.

Doutéo, Bertin B.   Ivory Coast

Bertin B. Doutéo was born in 1927 in Jacqueville, Ivory Coast. He received his education at the Ecole Primaire Supérieure in Bingerville, and then at the Ecole Primaire Supérieure in Yaundé, Cameroon. From 1949 to 1952 he was a contributor to the journal "Côte d'Ivoire" in Ivory Coast.

Bertin B. Doutéo started to write poetry at the age of fifteen. At school in Bingerville he edited a journal, "Echos Hebdomadaires", together with Dinan Mokey who became a producer at the "Ballets Africains" of Keita Fodeba. Between 1943 and 1946 he contributed poetry to the school journal "L'Appel du Tam-Tam" in Yaunde.

Bertin B. Doutéo published three volumes of poetry, *Cloches et grelots* (367), *La maison isolée* (368), and *L'harmonica oublié* (369), full of well-rhymed poems.

Dox   Madagascar

Dox is a pseudonym for Jean Verdi Salomon Razakandrainy, born on January 13, 1913, in Manankavaly, Madagascar, as son of a medical doctor. After elementary school in Antsirabe and the school of Abohijatovo in Tananarive, he entered the Collège Paul Minault, a private protestant school, where he edited a school journal. In his articles he did not want to contradict the general opinion, he did not cultivate the "paradox", and therefore was surnamed "DOX" by his co-students, a name he adopted as a pseudonym to express his intention to be a popular poet. He also composed quite a number of Malagasy songs and studied drawing and painting by correspondence courses.

Since 1940 he has written poetry, and many of his poems — all written in Malagasy language — have become very popular, for example *Mionona* (Renounce!) which he wrote after the death of one of his daughters, or *Atataovy* (Help me to put my jar on my head). Many of his poems were collected in his volume of poetry, *Folihala* (1253).

He also wrote historical plays. *Ny Ombalahibemaso* was produced in 1958, as was *Estera,* a play inspired by the bible. Other plays like *Le Cid, Horace,* and *Andromaque* he translated from French into Malagasy.

"Dox manipulates ideas, images, and sentiments with great facility. He gives the feeling that he vibrates in concord with everybody, especially in his melancholy and his love" (Victor-Georges Andriananjason).

Dramani, Bazini Zakari   Dahomey

Born on August 22, 1940, at Djougou, district Atakora, Dahomey, Issifou Zakari Dramani — this is his official name — had his first education in his home town. He got his Certificat d'Etudes Primaires at Adjohoun, district Ouémé, his Baccalauréat at Porto Novo, his Propédeutique at the University of Dakar, Senegal, and his Licence d'Histoire-Géographie at the University of Caen in France. He is a teacher at the Lycée A. Charnier at Bayeux, France, where, since 1957, he has also been representative of different students' organizations.

A small volume of poetry *Le nouveau cri* (370) sings of nature, women, brotherhood, the African past and revolt.

Dube, John Langalibalele   South Africa

Born on February 22, 1871, near Inanda Mission Station, Natal, South Africa, as son of a Zulu chief, John Langalibalele Dube got his primary education at Inanda and then went to Adams College where he trained as a teacher. He had a great desire to get a higher academic and theological education than was then possible in Natal, and thus went to America to attend Oberlin University, at which he graduated in Arts and Theology and was ordained. In America Dube was influenced by Booker T. Washington, W.E.B. Du Bois and John Hope of Atlanta University.

Returning home to Natal Dube was eager to found a school for black South Africans along the lines of the Tuskagee Institute in America. But the Anglo-Boer War interrupted his plans, and Dube had to go back to America and raise money by giving lectures. Returning home he was able to realise his dream. He founded the Ohlanga Institute, fifteen miles from Durban, a primary and a secondary school and an industrial school with classes in such commercial subjects as bookkeeping, shorthand and typing, and in carpentry, building, shoemaking and tailoring.

In 1903, with the assistance of Ngazana Luthuli, John Dube founded the first Zulu newspaper "Ilanga laseNatal" (The Natal Sun), which was printed in Ohlanga both in Zulu and English.

In 1912 Dube founded the South African Native National Congress (later the African National Congress) in Bloemfontein and was elected its first President-General. In this capacity Dube led the deputation to London in 1914 to protest against the infamous Land Act of 1913.

In 1926 John Dube attended the International Conference of Christian Missions at Le Zoute, Belgium. In 1936, the University of South Africa conferred upon him the degree of Doctor of Philosophy — the first of such awards to an African. In 1937 Dube was elected to represent Natal at the Native Representative Council which met twice a year in Pretoria, and remained a member until his death. John Langalibalele Dube died on February 11, 1946, at the age of 74. His successor in the council was Chief Albert J. Luthuli.

Besides being a journalist for "Ilanga laseNatal" John Dube was the author of five books. In 1922 he published *Isita Esikhulu Somuntu nguye Uqobo Lwake* (The Greatest Enemy of the Black Man is himself), a book for self-help. This was followed by *Ujeqe, Insila ka Shaka* (1601), a novel depicting the time of the great Zulu King Shaka, and *U-Shembe* (1602), a biography of the prophet. *Ukuzipatha Kahle* teaches young people manners and behavior.

"Dube tells the story *(U-Shembe)* well, with a masterly flow of language — he is one of the finest exponents of Zulu" (C. M. Doke).

Duodu, Cameron   Ghana

Born on May 24, 1937, in Asiakwa, District East Akim Abuakwa, Ghana, Duodu went to elementary school in Kibi, then
continued his education privately. At the age of nineteen he left
for Accra and joined the Ghana Broadcasting Corporation as
news editor, a job he held from 1956 to 1960. From 1960 to
1965 he was chief editor of "Drum", and in 1970 he became
chief editor of Ghana's largest daily newspaper, the "Daily
Graphic". He lost his job in January 1971 when he wrote an
editorial criticizing Prime Minister Busia's intention of entering
into a "dialogue" with South Africa. Duodu now lives as a
freelance journalist in Accra, writing mainly for the "Observer"
and the "Financial Times", both in London. His main interest
lies in financial politics.

Duodu likes travelling. He has visited several African
countries, Western Europe, the Soviet Union, China, USA and
Cuba.

Cameron Duodu writes radio plays, short stories and poetry.
In his novel *The Gab Boys* (371) he describes village boys, who
have been to school and cannot find adequate jobs afterwards.
Dealing with rural education and migration to town, he emerges
as a severe critic of Nkrumah's Ghana and touches on a problem
typical for modern Africa in general.

Portrait on Plate VIII.

Easmon, R. Sarif   Sierra Leone

Raymond Sarif Easmon was born on January 15, 1913, in Freetown, Sierra Leone, into a family of doctors, and was educated
in Sierra Leone. He studied medicine at the University of Durham, now University of Newcastle-upon-Tyne, where he was
Biology Prizeman, Honoursman in Anatomy and Physiology,
winner of the Stephen Scott Scholarship for Anatomy. In 1936,
at the age of 23, he obtained his degree Bachelor of Medicine

and Surgery and got his Diploma in Tropical Medicine at the University of Liverpool in the same year. Returning home Easmon served for two years in the Colonial Medical Service, but found the "colonialist" atmosphere insupportable and left to establish a practice. He is still practising as a doctor in Freetown.

Not a politician, Easmon is nevertheless strongly active in politics, and has been a commentator for years. He was actively engaged in the struggle for independence, which was gained in 1961, and has also watched the post-independence political scene closely. This brought him seventy-five days of political detention in October 1970.

Easmon has a study full of manuscripts. His first play, *Dear Parent and Ogre* (373), wom him the Encounter Magazine Prize. Then followed another play, *The New Patriots* (374), and a novel, *The Burnt-out Marriage* (375). Many short stories were published in English and American anthologies.

"Dr. Raymond Sarif Easmon's *Burnt-out Marriage* stands out like the Rock of Gibraltar in so far as a realistic portrayal of the cultural interaction of an African tribal society is concerned" (Bankole Timothy).

"Though by most West African writers' standards he uses much less idiomatic language, he is nonetheless very precise and natural in his expressions, especially in the numerous dialogues" Cerned" (Bankole Timothy).

Portrait on Plate IX.

Echeruo, Michael J. C.   Nigeria

Born in 1937 in Okigwi, East Central State, Nigeria, Michael J. C. Echeruo was educated in Nigeria at the University of Ibadan and in America at Cornell University, Ithaca, New York, where he obtained a Ph. D. in English Literature. He subsequently became Lecturer in English at the University of Nigeria, at Nsukka.

Michael Echeruo's poems have been widely anthologized and published in journals like "Journal of the New African Literature and the Arts", "Présence Africaine", "Busara", etc. They have been collected in his volume *Mortality* (376). He also has published literary criticism in various journals and anthologies.

"Echeruo writes with a cold, crisp, controlled sensuality which is utterly convincing; and sometimes he communicates with startling directness" (Angus Calder).

"The appearance of difficulty ... is the result of the poet's technique of describing states of mind or persons or incidents through the imagery of natural phenomena, presented in fantastic forms which conform to the violence of the poet's feelings" (Donatus Ibe Nwoga).

"It is in his jealous husbandry of words, as well as in his fondness for 'recherché' literary allusions, that he displays most clearly the influence of the late Christopher Okigbo" (Gerald Moore).

Egbuna, Obi   Nigeria

Born on July 18, 1938, in Ozubulu near Onitsha, East Central State, Nigeria, Obi Benue Egbuna grew up in Nigeria. In 1961 he went to London on a scholarship and he has been living there since first as an editor of "The Voice of Africa", a journal in the service of Ex-President Nkrumah, then as President of the Universal Coloured Peoples' Association, the British organ of Black Power. In 1970 he was held in custody for six months pending trial at the Old Bailey on the charge of masterminding a plot to kill police officers at Speakers Corner, London. While in Brixton Prison he wrote a book, *Destroy This Temple*, London 1970, in which he relates and analyses the experience that prompted him to compose the document that led to his arrest.

Obi Egbuna has written a novel, *Wind Versus Polygamy* (393), a discussion of the pros and cons of polygamy. The work was also turned into a play. He published a volume of short stories *Daughter of the Sun and Other Stories* (397), and three plays, *The Anthill* (394), a comedy about rather rude tricks, *Divinity* (395), a radio play about intellectual re-Africanisation in a setting of cultural conflict between a secret society and an African clergyman, and *The Agony* (396) which was first performed at the Unity Theatre, Kings Cross, London, on March 15, 1970. A pamphlet, *The Murder of Nigeria,* London 1968, discusses the Nigerian civil war.

"In *Wind Versus Polygamy* an African writer from Nigeria amuses us endlessly by giving us a documentation about what can soon be the most controversial subject of our time: polygamy! I have never had so much fun reading a work on this institution ... Mr. Egbuna has written an extraordinary novel with world-wide implications" (Mbella Sonne Dipoko).

"This is the worst African novel I have ever read" (Ronald Dathorne).

"*The Anthill* ... lacks in my opinion the essential magic of good theatre — warmth and realism" (Joe Chukwuemeka Brown).

The Agony "... as a whole is gripping, especially when it concerns the harsh realities of prison life, but in the third act, when a curious symbolism takes over, with the psychiatrist appearing in a white fur-lined robe, it seems to lose the direction and control of the first two acts" ("Griot").

Egharevba, Jacob U.   Nigeria

Born on January 27, 1893, at Idanre, Western State, Nigeria, Jacob Uwadiae Egharevba is of noble descent, on both sides from famous Benin families. He was educated at St. James' C.M.S. School in Ibadan, St. David's C.M.S. School at Akure, and St. Mathew's C.M.S. School in Benin City. From 1913 to 1914 he was a shop boy in Benin City, from 1915 to 1917 a sunday school teacher, from 1916 to 1917 a water rate clerk in Benin, in 1917 to 1921 a road overseer at Warri, a time keeper in Port Harcourt, a clerk to a prison contractor.

Since 1921, Chief Jacob Uwadiae Egharevba has been a confidant of Akenzua II, the Oba of Benin, even when he was yet a Crown Prince. He was in charge of the Oba's house, entertained the guests, collected taxes, accompanied the Oba to conferences, and grew with time into the role of a councillor. His knowledge of oral traditions which he has used to write about Benin history, is valuable material to historians. On November 17, 1967, Chief Egharevba received the honorary degree of Doctor of Literature of the University of Ibadan.

Chief Egharevba has written twenty-eight books, the most famous of which are: *A Short History of Benin*, Ibadan 1935, Lagos 1953, *Benin Law and Customs*, Benin 1949, *Some Stories of Ancient Benin*, Benin 1951, *Some Tribal Gods of Southern Nigeria*, Benin 1951, *Brief Autobiography*, Benin 1968.

Ekwensi, Cyprian   Nigeria

Born in 1921 in Minna, North Western State, Nigeria, Cyprian Odiatu Duaka Ekwensi, an Ibo, had his secondary education at the Higher College, Yaba, and the Achimota College near Accra, Ghana. In England he studied Pharmacy. Then he taught Biology and Chemistry at the Igboby College in Lagos, Nigeria, and at the School of Pharmacy at Yaba. In 1951 he joined the staff of the Nigerian Broadcasting Corporation in Lagos, where he eventually was Head of Features, a position which he held for many years. He then became Director of Information in the Federal Ministry of Information in Lagos, a position from which he resigned in 1966 before the outbreak of the civil war so that he could do the same work in the East. After the capitulation of Biafra he said he was "happy to be a Nigerian again".

Cyprian Ekwensi began his career as a writer with an Onitsha market publication, *When Love Whispers* (406), the first of many short stories which were published in journals throughout the English-speaking world. His short stories were collected in the volumes *The Leopard's Claw* (407) and *Lokotown and Other Stories* (421), and for children, *The Drummer Boy* (409), *The Passport of Mallam Ilia* (410), *An African Night's Entertainment* (412), *The Great Elephant-Bird* (416), *The Rainmaker and Other Stories* (417), *The Boa Suitor* (418), *Juju Rock* (420) and *Trouble in Form Six* (422).

People of the City (408), in 1954, was the first Nigerian full-length novel about contemporary life. The plot is loosely strung together, but the details build up the complex structure of the city life in Lagos. In his second novel, *Jagua Nana* (411), centred around a Lagos prostitute who is a lady and becomes a market queen, "he has created an unforgettable character in Jagua Nana herself, and he conveys an excellent picture of Lagos — not everybody's Lagos but Jagua's Lagos" (Ulli Beier).

His novel *Burning Grass* (413) is set in northern Nigeria among the migrating Fulani people who graze their cattle and open the season of hunting and entertainment by burning the high grass. The Lagos atmosphere is grasped again in his next novel, *Beautiful Feathers* (415), where a respected leader of a political movement lacks all authority in his own home. His last novel, *Iska* (419), reveals the rising tensions between Ibo and Hausa which eventually caused the civil war.

"Despite minor excursions into the area of rural and traditional Africa (*Burning Grass . . .*), he is above all an urban writer: it is city life that he loves and mirrors best. One might go even further and call him West Africa's first picaresque author, for he excels in the depiction of the criminal side of city life: and a random selection of his characters reads like a roll-call for West Africa's underworld. Pimps, forgers, burglars, prostitutes crowd into his pages . . ." (Adrian Roscoe).

"His writing is full of events, narrated in a brisk and snappy style that owes much to journalism . . . He is able at one moment to take on a warning tone when speaking of the city's prostitutes and thugs, and the next moment to show a genuine compassion towards these lost and fallen, seeing them as victims of the city which they victimize" (Margaret Laurence).

"I remember the first impression I had of reading the novel of Cyprian Ekwensi, *People of the City* (the first West African novel I read) and how very excited I was about it ... It was talking about us, as it were, of people in the city and their problems. ... I didn't care to try and evaluate it. The sheer fact that this novel was there in itself was sufficient to stimulate a number of us to read more of what was coming out from West Africa" (David Rubadiri).

Ela, Jean-Marc   Cameroon

Born in 1936 in Ebolowa, district Ntem, Cameroon, Jean-Marc Ela studied at the Faculty of Catholic Theology of the University of Strasbourg where he did a biblical study on the first of all Ecumenical Councils and received a Doctorat d'Etat in Theology for his thesis on the Transcendence of God and the Human Existence according to Luther.

At present he is a priest in his home region and divides his time between parochial duties and private research.

His sociological study, *La plume et la pioche*, Yaunde 1971, tries to show how to bridge the gap between town and village in modern African society by reconciling the pen and the hoe.

Elébé, Philippe   Zaire

Born on September 27, 1937, at Bumba on the River Congo, Equator Province, Zaire, Philippe Elébé had his secondary education in Kinshasa. From 1958 to 1960 he spent twenty-four months in the Armée Congolaise. From 1960 to 1966 he was in Germany (East), received a diploma of the Trade Union University, and read journalism at Karl Marx University at Leipzig. From 1966 to 1967 he worked as a journalist for the Agence Congolaise de Presse. From 1967 to 1970 he was Press

Attaché at the Zaire Embassy in Algiers. At present he is Chef du Service de Presse in the Ministry of Foreign Affairs in Kinshasa.

Under the pen-name "Philippos" he contributed to several Congolese journals: "Présence Congolaise", "Horizons", "Emancipation, Congo et Indépendence".

His works comprise two volumes of poetry, *Mélodie africaine* (1167), and *Uhuru*, Paris 1970, and two plays published in one volume, *Simon Kimbangu ou le messie noir*, and *Le sang des noirs pour un sou*, Paris 1972.

"Philippe Elébé has succeeded in evoking the melodies of those African songs with their interminable refrains" (Boguo Makeli).

Enahoro, Anthony   Nigeria

Born in July 1923 at Uromi, Ishaw division, Midwestern State, Nigeria, Chief Anthony Eronsele Oseghale Enahoro — this is his full name — was educated at government schools in Uromi and Owa and at King's College in Lagos. In 1942 he went to work for the chain of newspapers started by Dr. Nnamdi Azikiwe. In 1944 he became editor of the "Southern Nigeria Defender", and from 1945 to 1947 he edited the "Daily Comet". Gaoled for a seditious article he was released and then gaoled again for delivering a seditious speech. Again released, he became assistant editor of the "Nigerian Star". In 1951 he was a founder-member of the Action Group, elected to the Western Region House of Assembly, and from there to the Federal Assembly. In 1954 he became Minister of Home Affairs in the Western Region Government, adding in 1957 Mid-West Affairs to his Portfolio. In December 1959, he was one of those chosen by Chief Awolowo, Leader of the Action Group, to contest the Federal Elections, and became one of the outstanding members of the Parliamentary Opposition to the Federal Government in Nigeria. During the state of emergency from 1962 to 1963, Enahoro was able to make his way to England, but was arrested on an application by the Federal Nigerian authorities for an extradition warrant. He spent six months in Brixton Prison and was eventually extradited to Nigeria. Released again, Chief Enahoro was made Commissioner for Information and Labour in the Federal Federal Nigerian authorities for an extradition warrant. He spent six months in Brixton Prison and was eventually extradited to Nigeria. Released again, Chief Enahoro was made Commissioner for Information and Labour in the Federal Government. He is still holding this office (November 1971).

While restricted to his home at Uromi, Chief Enahoro wrote the early chapters of his autobiography, *Fugitive Offender* (423).

Enahoro, Peter   Nigeria

Born on January 21, 1935, at Uromi, Ishaw division, Midwestern State, Nigeria, Peter Enahoro, the brother of Chief Anthony Enahoro, received his education at Government College, Ughelli, before he joined the Federal Government Information Service in Lagos in 1954. In 1955 he became sub-editor of the "Daily Times", Lagos. From 1956 to 1957 he was Assistant District Manager of the Rediffusion Services in Ibadan. Then he went back to the "Daily Times", as sub-editor, but in 1958, when he was 23, he was appointed editor of the mass-circulation Nigerian "Sunday Times". Four years later, in 1962, he was appointed editor of the daily paper, becoming the youngest editor of West Africa's most influential newspaper. He became the group's editor-in-chief in 1966, but in the same year left Nigeria in self-exile, following the upheavals which led to the Nigerian civil war. He has travelled widely, and now lives in Cologne, Germany. He is an editor of "Africa", the Paris-based English edition of the magazine "Jeune Afrique", and he broadcasts to Africa over Radio Deutsche Welle.

Peter Enahoro gained fame in Nigeria for his witty thrice-weekly column under the pseudonym of "Peter Pan". He is the author of two books of critical essays, *How To Be A Nigerian*, Lagos, 1966, and *You Gotta Cry To Laugh*, Cologne, 1972.

Eno-Belinga, Samuel-Martin   Cameroon

Born on December 6, 1935, in Ebolowa, District Ntem, Cameroon, Samuel-Martin Eno-Belinga had his elementary schooling
in his home town from 1944 to 1950. From 1951 to 1957 he
was at Collège Vogt, and from 1957 to 1958 at Lycée Leclerc
where he got his Baccalauréat. From 1959 to 1962 he was at
the University of Strasbourg where he studied Zoology, Geology, Mineralogy, Botany, Phytosociology, and Pedology. From
1963 to 1966 he studied at the Faculty of Science, University
of Paris, receiving the doctorate in Practical Geology for his
thesis: *Contribution à l'etude géologique, mineralogique, et géo-
chimique des formations bauxitiques de l'Adamaoua, Cameroun.* Then he completed his Doctorat d'Etat ès-Sciences with
the thesis *L'alteration des roches basaltiques et le processus de
bauxitisation dans l'Adamaoua, au Cameroun.* Eno-Belinga has
continued to do research in Adamaua, on the spot as in the
laboratory, so that he published nineteen texts about his geo-
logical findings between 1965 and 1971.

Eno-Belinga now teaches Geology at the Faculty of Science,
University of Yaunde, Cameroon. Simultaneously he serves in
the administration. In 1968 he was appointed Assistant Director of Higher Education in the Ministry of Education, and in
November 1970 he rose to the position of Director.

Samuel-Martin Eno-Belinga's interests are not limited to
science. His book on oral literature and music, *Littérature et
musique populaire en Afrique noire*, Paris 1965, was awarded
a prize at the First Festival Negro Arts in Dakar, 1966. He
contributed articles on African music, literature, and art to
journals like "Sentiers" and "Abbia".

His creative works are two volumes of poetry: *Masques Nègres* (426), *Equinoxes*, Yaunde 1970, and *La prophétie de Joal*
Yaunde 1971.

Epanya Yondo, Elolongué   Cameroon

Born on March 8, 1930, in Duala, Cameroon, Elolongué Epanya
Yondo had his elementary education in Duala. As a boy he was
a partisan of the Moumié wing of the opposition party UPC
(Union des Populations du Cameroun), was caught, beaten, and
spent a year in prison. When he was released, at the age of
sixteen, he went to Paris, France, where he lived in the family
of Alioune Diop, the Director of "Présence Africaine". He was
a friend and a cousin of the poet David Diop, and a cousin of
Iwiya Kala Lobé, secretary of "Présence Africaine".

In 1966 he was a Research Fellow at the Centre Fédéral Lin-
guistique in Yaunde, but meanwhile he has returned to live in
Paris.

His collection of poetry, *Kamerun! Kamerun!* (427) is bilingual, in Duala and French, expressing his nationalist feelings
and his sensibility for the rural life with its rhythms.

His poetry has been widely anthologized, and his poems and
essays have appeared in journals like "Présence Africaine" and
"Abbia".

"... wrath and violence change into music and beauty"
(Olympe Bhêly-Quénum).

Epée, Valère   Cameroon

Born in December 1938 in Duala, Cameroon, Valère Epée had
his secondary education in Duala and in the United States
where he received a B. A. and a Master's Degree in Linguistics
at Georgetown University, Washington, D. C. He is presently
Lecturer for English and Spanish at the Ecole Normale Supérieure of Cameroon, in Yaunde.

Valère Epée, besides his theatrical and musical activities, has
published a dramatic poem, *Transatlantic Blues*, Yaunde 1972,
in a bilingual edition of French and English, the English version
having been translated by Samir M. Zoghby.

Equiano, Olaudah   Nigeria

Born around 1754 at Essaka, near Benin, Nigeria, Olaudah
Equiano, who was also called Gustavus Vassa, was sold into
slavery when he was twelve and taken to the West Indies. He
was resold to a British naval officer, who enabled him to have
a good education, and then came into the service of a trader
from Philadelphia, for whom he sailed in the West Indies. He
bought himself free and settled in London, where, in 1787, he
was appointed a "Commissary of Provisions and Stores for
the Black Poor going to Sierra Leone". He too, was supposed to
go to Sierra Leone, but had difficulties with the authorities and
desisted. In 1788 he handed over a petition for the supression
of the slave trade to the British Parliament. He married an
Englishwoman and died around 1801.

Equiano wrote *The interesting narrative of the life of Olaudah Equiano, or Gustavus Vassa, the African, written by himself*
(429). It was a very popular book in his time, had eight English
editions and one American and translations into German and
Dutch.

"Frequently he can write with an irritating sense of patro-
nage, . . . but he was obviously a man who, in spite of his education away from his own culture, still managed to maintain a
fierce energetic pride in his race" (O. R. Dathorne).

Portrait on Plate I.

Espírito Santo, Alda do   São Tomé

Born on April 30, 1926, on the island São Tomé, Alda do
Espírito Santo was educated in São Tomé, where she became a
school teacher. In the sixties she was arrested with others. Since
1969 she has been forced to live in Lisbon.

Alda do Espírito Santo is one of the few women writers in
the Portuguese tropics. Her poems have been published in many
anthologies like "Poesia negra de expressão portuguesa" (A 105),

"Literatura africana de expessão portuguesa" (A 5), "La poésie africaine d'expression portugaise" (A 6), "Poesia africana di rivolta" (A 102) and in many journals.

She deals with the motley plantation labour and has "strong solidarity with the dispossessed" (Gerald M. Moser).

Ezuma, Benjamin James   Nigeria

Born around 1937 at Arondizuogu, Orlu division, East Central State, Nigeria, as son of Chief J. N. Ezuma, the head of the local council, Benjamin James Ezuma had his elementary education at the C.M.S. School at Arondizuogu, his secondary education at the Iheme Memorial Grammar School. He studied Classical Philology at the University of Ibadan and then worked at Worcester College, Oxford, England. Back in Nigeria he became a teacher at the Pricilla Grammar School in Oguta, then Principal of the Eastern Regal Grammar School at Nri.

Benjamin James Ezuma wrote three ironic and critical plays, *The Flight of Omenuku* (448), *Ph. D.s on Parade, and, Beentos' Symposium* (449), and an introduction into a novel of Chinua Achebe, *Chinua Achebe's "Things Fall Apart" in Questions and Answers*, Onitsha 1965.

Fabo, Paul   Dahomey

Born in Dahomey, Paul Fabo was enlisted in the French army during World War II, serving on a destroyer. In June 1940 he was in Nunkirk, then left the army and went to Brussels to join the Resistance. He became an actor, then a journalist and subsequently director of the weekly "Afrique et le Monde" in Brussels. Later he was appointed Ambassador of Dahomey to Kinshasa.

His only play, *Ombrages* (450), is a normal French boule-
vard comedy about a poor student who is to marry the daughter
of a factory owner.

"The play which he brought me today is good handicraft and
good writing. The subject is well observed and of high morality"
(René Lyr).

Fagunwa, Daniel Olorunfemi   Nigeria

Fagunwa was born of Yoruba parentage around 1910 at Okeig-
bo near Ondo in Western Nigeria. His parents were farmers and
associates of the Egungun-cult who were later converted to
Christianity and sent their son to school. Chief Fagunwa was a
teacher for thirty years, then became head of Heinemann's
agency for educational books. Fagunwa died on December 7,
1963, when his car plunged into the River Wuya near Bida,
Northern Nigeria.

Fagunwa's father was already a good story-teller, and the
boy liked to listen to his stories, but he was even more attracted
by the stories the hunters told coming from the bush. These
reminiscences of his youth were later woven into his most
famous novel *Ogboju ode ninu igbo irunmale* (451), in which
he tells of the hunter Akara-Ogun, who, first on his own later
on orders from his king, explores the secrets of the forest in a
series of remarkable adventures. The following five works *Igbo
Olodumare* (452), *Irèké-oníbùdó* (453), *Irinkerindo ninu igbo
Elégbèje* (454), *Asàyàn ìtàn* (455) and *Adììtu Olódùmare* (456)
are also set in the traditional Yoruba world of imagination, in
which the line that separates reality from myth is so thinly
drawn as to be practically non-existent.

Content and form of Fagunwa's novels belong essentially to
the traditional Yoruba folktale, but Fagunwa brought them into
a more sustained narrative form. He can be said to have created
the present trend of modern Yoruba literature.

Fagunwa "does not deal with contemporary social problems,
... he does not 'analyse' characters and is completely dis-

interested in the 'African Personality'. But then he makes up for this by his charm, his humour, his vividness, his baroque imagery" (Ulli Beier).

Faik-Nzuji, Clémentine
vid. *Nzuji, Clémentine*

Faleti, Adebayo   Nigeria

Born about 1937 in Western State, Nigeria, Adebayo Faleti has been working for many years at Western Nigerian Television in Ibadan.

All his works are in Yoruba, the plays *Eda kò l'aròpin* (457) and *Nwon ro pe wèrè ni* (458), and his collection of short stories, *Ogun àwìtélè* (459).

Fiawoo, F. Kwasi   Ghana

F. Kwasi Fiawoo was born in 1891 in Wuta, district Keta, Volta Region, Ghana — at a time when this area was part of the German colony Togoland. He entered the Wesleyan Methodist School in Kpong in 1903 and the Basel Mission School in Akuse in 1905. He matriculated at the Johnson C. Smith University, Charlotte, North Carolina, USA in 1928. In 1933 he was ordained at Gloverville, New York. He holds diplomas in English, Greek, Psychology and Ethics, and a teacher's certificate for secondary schools from the State of North Carolina.

From 1934 to 1936 Fiawoo was General Manager of the Zion Mission Schools. In 1937 he founded the Zion College of West Africa in Anloga, Ghana. He became the first Deputy Speaker of Gold Coast's Legislative Assembly in 1951 and was reelected in 1952, 1953 and 1954. He lost his seat in the General

Elections of 1956 and was appointed Chairman of the Board of Governors Zion College of West Africa and of Keta Secondary School, Keta, Ghana.

Fiawoo wrote the first play in West Africa, *Tɔkɔ atɔlia* (465) in Ewe language. The play was first translated into German and then into English, *The Fifth Landing Stage* (465 b), and is still being performed.

Fodeba, Keita   Guinea

Born in February 1921 at Siguiri, region Siguiri, Guinea, Keita Fodeba — Keita being his family name — a Malinke, the son of a male nurse, was educated at mission schools and at the famous Ecole William Ponty in Dakar, Senegal. For a while he worked as a teacher, then, in 1948, he went to Paris, France, to study Law at the Sorbonne. Having no grant, he wrote short stories and poetry in his spare time to pay his living and study expenses. From 1951 onwards, his poems were banned throughout French Africa because of their nationalist tendency. An accomplished singer and dancer, carrying a banjo with him everywhere he went, he eventually gave up his Law studies altogether in favour of the theatre and formed the "Ballets Africains", a group of African singers and dancers with whom he toured the world.

In May 1957, when the first African Government was formed in Guinea, he became Minister of the Interior, later becoming Minister of National Defense and Security. In March 1969 he was accused of having participated in a plot against President Sékou Touré, and was sentenced to death. He was killed in Camayenne Prison, on May 27, 1969.

His works are a mixture of poetry and prose: *Poèmes africains* (466), *Le maître d'ecole, suivi de Minuit* (467), and *Aube africaine* (468).

"Keita Fodeba ... has reinterpreted all the rhythmic images of his country. In his poetical work ... you find a constant care to specify the historical moment of the struggle, to define the field for the actions and the ideas around which the will of the people will crystallize" (Frantz Fanon).

Portrait on Plate VI.

Fonseca, Aguinaldo   Cape Verde Islands

Born on September 12, 1922, on the island São Vicente, Cape Verde Islands, Aguinaldo Brito Fonseca grew up without a mother and without financial prospects. He went to Lisbon, Portugal, where he became an office clerk.

Aguinaldo Fonseca published a volume of poetry, *Linha do horizonte* (470) and poems in the journals "Claridade", "Cabo Verde", "Seara Nova", "Atlântico" and "Mundo Literário". Once he received an award from the newspaper "Diário Popular".

"Fonseca's poetry preserves on the whole a basically Cape Verdean quality, although written in Lisbon where the writer pursues his stolen destiny. ... The presence of the African element is perhaps the most valuable aspect of Fonseca's poetry" (Norman Araujo).

Fula, Arthur   South Africa

Born on May 16, 1908, in East London, Cape Province, South Africa, Arthur Nuthall Fula, a Xhosa, moved to Johannesburg with his parents at an early age and attended the Siemert School at Doornfontein and the Eurafrican Normal College and Secondary School. In 1925 he began as a clerk in the hospital of the Wollhuter goldmine and was later employed as a labourer in this mine. From 1930 he worked in the New Pioneer gold mine. Having decided to learn a trade, he entered the service of a cabinet-maker and after two years opened his own workshop. He had to give up his business, however, and went to work in a furniture shop. In the meantime he continued his education privately and studied several subjects, French among them, at the Alliance Française. In 1947 he began writing novels in English but could find no publisher for his first two efforts. A consolation prize in an essay competition run by a newspaper encouraged him, however, and Fula produced the first Afrikaans novel written by a black South African, *Jôhannie giet die beeld* (1608). The book expresses the view of a black South African on Johannesburg life. A short story, *Pfarrer Kalashe, der Xosalehrer*, appeared in German translation in the anthology "Christ erscheint am Kongo" (A 100). His second novel, *Met erbarming, o Here* (1609), depicts the struggle of modern, educated black South Africans against traditional religion and magic.

Arthur Nuthall Fula died on May 17, 1966 in Johannesburg.

Gadeau, Germain Coffi   Ivory Coast

Born in 1913 in Gbomizambo, sub-division of Tiébissou, Baule country, Central District, Ivory Coast, Germain Coffi Gadeau went to school at Tiébissou until 1924 when he entered the regional school at Buake. In 1929 he was transferred to the Ecole Primaire Secondaire in Bingerville. From 1932 to 1935 he studied at the famous Ecole William Ponty at Gorée, Senegal. In 1935 he became a treasurer in Abidjan, a profession he practiced for twenty years.

In 1945 he entered politics as an activist of the RDA (Rassemblement Démocratique Africain) of Félix Houphouet-Boigny. Gadeau was local councillor, then, from 1955 to 1960, a Deputy of the Ivory Coast. When his country won independence, Gadeau became its Minister of the Interior, combining political with cultural functions, being General Secretary of the "Théâtre Indigène de la Côte d'Ivoire". "Wrongly molested during the year 1963, at the period when certain political intrigues were spun in Ivory Coast, involved in an imaginary conspiracy by malevolent spirits who wished to compromise him, he lived for seven years in a total retirement, the causes and conditions of which it is useless to ask him about" (Philippe Decraene).

In June 1971 he was appointed Minister of State and Controller in the Ministry of Economic and Financial Affairs.

Germain Coffi Gadeau has written many plays. In 1940 his play *Nos femmes* (472) was seized by the police, and his play *Les recrutés de M. Maurice* (474) was banned by the French Governor in 1942 because it attacked the forced labour system of certain plantations. Other plays too, like *Les anciens combattants* (475) and *Le mariage de Sogona* (476), have never seen print. Others, *Kondé Yao* (471), *Mon mari* (473), *Yaou N'Da* (477) and *Adjo-bla* (478), have been collected in the anthology *Le Théâtre Populaire en République de Côte d'Ivoire* (AW 120).

His own theatre, "Théâtre Indigène de la Côte d'Ivoire" which staged his plays and those by other Ivory Coast writers, was very successful because of its both popular subjects and actors. In 1956 the troupe arrived in France for the first time on July 14th, and remained for six months. In November 1956 the troupe performed at the Théâtre de l'Etoile in Paris, and in May 1960 at the Théâtre Sarah-Bernhardt, where it was awarded a prize by the Theatre of Nations.

"The lady Kouassi Afoué, whom Coffi Gadeau had rejected some weeks before was present at the first performance of *Nos Femmes* with most of her friends and lovers. She cried for shame and had to leave the hall without waiting for the end of the play, which had an enormous success" (François Amon d'Aby).

Gatheru, Mugo   Kenya

Born in 1925 as son of squatters on a European's farm called "Kwa-bara-bara-miti" (The Place of the Trees planted in a Line), Rift Valley Province, Kenya, Renel Mugo Gatheru belongs to the Ethaga clan. He first went to a one-teacher school in Stoton, then to a privately organized one-teacher school on the Kibogoro-Farm, seven miles Northeast of Stoton, then for two months to an evening school on Bwana Tennett's Farm. He received his first regular schooling in 1936 at Kahuti elementary school in Githiga, which he attended for two years. From 1939 to 1940 he attended Weithaga Sector School of the Church Missionary Society which had higher grades than Kahuti. In 1941 he entered Kambui Primary School near Nairobi, where he took the Kenya Primary examination in 1944. In 1945 he joined the Medical Research Laboratory in Nairobi to train as a laboratory technician. In 1949 he left Kenya to study at St. Joseph's School in Allahabad, India, and in 1950 left India again for England, from where he obtained a visa to the United States of America. There he studied Sociology, Political Science, Biology, English Language, Literature and History at Bethune-Cookman College in Daytona Beach, Florida. In 1951 he received a scholarship to Lincoln University, Lincoln, Pennsylvania, and obtained his B. A. degree in History and Political Science in 1954.

Before he started his post-graduate studies, Gatheru worked for the New York Standard Manufacturing Company in Brooklyn as a general factory hand making hampers, baskets and stools. He then registered at New York University in the Political Science Department, obtained an M. A. degree, and decided to study Law in Great Britain. He finished in 1963 and worked for the Lord Chancellor's Department. He returned to Kenya, but could not be traced.

Mugo Gatheru wrote his autobiography, *Child of Two Worlds* (1257).

Gicaru, Muga   Kenya

Muga Gicaru is the pen-name for John Mwangi who was born about 1920 in the Kikuyu Country, Kenya. Although it was difficult his father, a poor field-hand, managed to send him to a mission school and later to a college of the protestant mission. He then went to Nairobi to work in all kinds of odd jobs and to continue his education in evening classes. This enabled him to go to Britain where he took a course of Economic Studies at the University of Glasgow. In the late fifties he returned to Kenya and entered the Shell Oil Company in some executive capacity. For some years, he has been in Nakuru, owning a respectable firm as Chartered Accountant.

His novel, *Land of Sunshine* (1259), has been translated into Russian.

Goh, Gaston Demand
vid. *Demand Goh, Gaston*

Gologo, Mamadou   Mali

Born about 1924 in Koulikoro, region Bamako, Mali, Mamadou Gologo had his secondary education at the famous Ecole William Ponty at Gorée, Senegal, and then studied Medicine in Dakar. He later became Director of the newspaper "L'Essor" in Bamako, Mali, and Minister of Information of the Mali Republic. When the regime of Modibo Keita was overthrown on November 19, 1968, Mamadou Gologo was also put into prison. Released in 1970 he became a medical doctor at the hospital Gabriel Touré in Bamako.

His autobiographical novel, *Le rescapé de l'Ethylos* (484), is the outspoken and candidly didactic presentation of an acute case of alcoholism, a vice attacked as "the heritage of colonialism". Mamadou Gologo's only volume of poetry, *Mon coeur est un volcan* (483), was published in Moscow.

"In this autobiography the narrator is not only a symbol of a generation brutally pushed from the traditional environment into the modern world, but a person strongly individualized who has his own personal problems" (Bernard Mouralis).

"The picture is living, precise, sincere and testifies an intense sensibility which often turns into passion" (Robert Pageard).

Gonçalves, António Aurélio   Cape Verde Islands

Born on the Cape Verde island São Vicente, António Aurélio Gonçalves received his higher education at the University of Lisbon in Portugal. He then returned to the Cape Verde Islands where he taught History and Philosophy at the Liceu Gil Eanes on the island São Vicente.

His short stories, O enterro de nhâ Candinha Sena (485) and Pródiga (486), have been widely anthologized.

"With all of his innovating freshness, Gonçalves does not betray the revolution in Cape Verdean letters ... In spite of their brevity, his works ... rank among the most important of the new literary production in Cabo Verde" (Norman Araujo).

Portrait on Plate VI.

Gqoba, William Wellington   South Africa

Born in 1840 near Gaga, Cape Province, South Africa, into the Ngqika clan, William Wellington Gqoba attended the elementary mission school at Tyumie, then was sent to Lovedale in 1853. At Lovedale he learned the trade of wagonmaking, a job he pursued for the next ten years. He was held in high esteem for his knowledge of English, and in the late 1860's, the Reverend Tiyo Soga invited him to teach at Emgwali. He later went to Kingwilliamstown, where he taught until 1873. Then he became a pastor of the Native Church at Rabula, a position he held for four years. When in 1877 the ninth and last Kaffir war, which was to initiate the formal annexation of Xhosaland to the Colony, broke out, Gqoba left for Peelton, and assisted in preaching at the church there. He was also employed for a time as a translator at the Native Registry Office in Kimberley. He then returned to Lovedale as an assistant in the translation classes.

From 1884 to his death, William Wellington Gqoba was the editor of "Isigidimi samaXhosa" (The Xhosa Messenger), a monthly journal written in the vernacular, to which he was also a frequent contributor. Among his works are *ImBali yaseMbo* (History of the North-Eastern Peoples), an historical account of the scattering of the tribes under Shaka's reign, and two long didactic poems, *The Discussion between the Christian and the Pagan* (850 lines), and *Great Discussion on Education* (1,150 lines), both of which are allegorial debates in Xhosa language.

William Wellington Gqoba died on April 26, 1888, and "Isigidimi" died with him. Many articles of his were never published during his lifetime, but some were collected by Walter B. Rubusana and published in his anthology "Zemk' inkomo magwalandini", Lovedale 1906.

"Gqoba was a prolific writer, and his works fall into two categories — Christian inspiration and folk inspiration. . . . The death of Gqoba and the end of "Isigidimi" mark the close of a period in the history of Xhosa literature . . ." (Albert S. Gérard).

Guerra, Henrique   Angola

Born on July 26, 1937, in Luanda, Angola, Henrique Lopes Guerra, whose African name is Andiki, received a secondary education. In 1962 he was cornet in the militia. In Luanda he had several expositions of his paintings. He was involved in a trial against Angolan students in 1967 and was put into prison in Lisbon.

His stories have been published under the title *A cubata solitária* (1614), and in journals like "Cultura", "Mensagem" "Jornal de Angola", "ABC — Diário de Angola".

"He knows how to dominate a story, a style, a way of telling. He knows how to stick to a subject and how to carry it to its end" (Amândio César).

Gueye, Lamine   Senegal

Born in 1891 at Madine, region Bamako, Mali, Lamine Gueye came from a family from Saint Louis, Senegal. He qualified as a lawyer in Paris in 1921 and in 1924 became Mayor of Saint Louis, Senegal. Some time later he served as a magistrate in Réunion and Martinique. In 1934 and 1936 he unsuccessfully contested the Senegal seat in the French Parliament, and became in 1937 the political director of the Senegalese Federation of the SFIO (French Socialist Party). Political activities ceased during the Vichy régime, but immediately afterwards Gueye became leader of the Bloc Africain and, with Léopold Sédar Senghor was Deputy of Senegal to the French Assembly in 1945.

In 1946 he was re-elected and became Mayor of Dakar. In 1948 Senghor formed his own party, and as a result, in 1951, Gueye lost his seat. In 1958 however, in the face of the strength of RDA (Rassemblement Démocratique Africain, the party of Houphouet-Boigny), Gueye joined with Senghor. After their party UPS (Union Progressiste Sénégalaise) had won all seats in the territorial elections in 1959, Gueye was elected President of the Assembly, a position he held until his death on June 10, 1968.

Lamine Gueye has written an autobiography, *Itinéraire africain* (494).

Guma, Alex La
vid. *La Guma, Alex*

Guma, Enoch Silinga   South Africa

Enoch Silinga Guma was born in June 1896 in Ncembu, Cape Province, South Africa, as the second of nine children. The date of his birth is unknown, because the Special Branch Police confiscated the notebook of his father, which was in the care of his brother Chrysostom Mbuyiselwa Guma in his home in Langa, Cape Town. Enoch Silinga Guma's father, Stephen Guma, was the first preacher of the immigrant Pondos in Ncembu, where he was sent to from his home Etyeni in 1893 by the Reverend Godfrey Callaway.

Enoch Silinga Guma passed Standards I to IV at Ncembu and Standards V and VI at St. Cuthvert's School under the Principal, Reverend R. A. Scott. He was then trained as a teacher at St. Matthew's College, Keiskammahoek, from 1914 to 1916, where his father had to pay two pounds extra, because the boy had stomach troubles and had to be fed on mealies. In 1917 Enoch Silinga Guma taught at St. Mary's Mbinja School, two to three miles away from his home Ncembu, where he was the only teacher. A year later, in 1918, Enoch Silinga Guma died during an influenza epidemy, a great blow to his father, who had hoped that he could help to educate his younger brothers.

The novel *U-Nomalizo okanye izinto zalomhlaba ngamagingiqiwu* (1615), written while training as a teacher and published posthumously in 1918, is a moral love story, in which the heroine, Nomalizo, who is courted by two young suitors, Mxabaniso, a bad boy, and Bangela, a good boy, finally decides for the good boy and marries him. The book was translated from Xhosa into English and Swahili under the titles *Nomalizo, or, The Things of Life Are Sheer Vanity* (1615 a), and *Nomalizo au mambo ya maisha haya ni ubatili mtupu* (1615 b).

In the preface of the 1918 edition the Reverend Godfrey Callaway claimed that the book gives "just the very conditions of life which now prevail when the old jostles with the new. To my delight, I found that the old was not treated with contempt and that the new was not treated without discrimination."

uHadi Waseluhlangeni
vid. *uHadi Waseluhlangeni* (p. 385)

Born about 1909 in Fonéko-Dibilo, district Téra, Niger, Boubou Hama, a Songhai, went to school in Téra, then from 1917 to 1924 in Dori (Upper Volta), and from 1924 to 1926 in Wagadugu. In 1926 he was admitted to the famous Ecole William Ponty at Gorée, Senegal. In 1929 he started teaching in Niamey, Niger.

Boubou Hama was an early member of the Rassemblement Démocratique Africain (RDA) and of its local section, the Parti Progressiste Nigérien (PPN), led by Hamami Diori. In 1956 Boubou Hama became President of the PPN and was elected to the Niamey Municipal Council. In 1957, when the more radical Union Démocratique Nigérienne UDN won a majority, Boubou Hama joined Hamami Diori in leading the opposition. In December 1958 he was elected for the PPN — now called the Union pour la Communauté Franco-Africaine (UCFA) — to the Assembly, where it formed the Government, and was immediately afterwards made President of the Assembly, a position that he has held ever since. It is his particular concern to unite the chiefs and the people with the regime.

His autobiography in three volumes, *Kotia-Nima* (495), received the Grand Prix de l'Afrique Noire in 1971. He also published quite a number of historical works: *Histoire du Niger*, Paris 1965, *Enquête sur les fondements et la genèse de l'unité africaine*, Paris 1966, *Histoire du Gobir et de Sokoto*, Paris 1967, *L'histoire traditionnelle d'une peuple: les Zarma-Songhay*, Paris 1967, *Recherche sur l'histoire des Touareg sahariens et soudanais*, Paris 1967, *Contribution à la connaissance de l'histoire des Peul*, Paris 1968, et *Essai d'analyse de l'éducation africaine*, Paris 1968.

Hamed bin Muhammed el Murjebi (Tippu Tib)   Tanzania

Born about 1830 in Zanzibar, Hamed bin Muhammed el Murjebi who became known later as Tippu Tib, began trading as a young man for his father, a merchant from Tabora (in Tanganyika). During the 1860's he struck out for himself in a series of wide-ranging ventures into Bemba and Lungu country at the southern end of Lake Tanganyika. Moving northward, the enterprising merchant prince combined trading and raiding, finally securing through a questionable claim of blood relationship a chieftaincy among the Tetela people in the Lomani area, in what is now roughly the centre of Zaire.

By 1875 he had proceeded on the Lualaba to Kasongo which became his headquarters. Here he reigned as a paramount chief among the Bantu people, extended his authority downstream into the rain forest and in 1883 was already established at Stanley Falls. By 1890 Tippu Tib was pre-eminent; he left the Congo in the same year on a trip to Zanzibar, never to return.

In 1887 Stanley managed to persuade Tippu Tib to become governor of the eastern region of the Congo, but Tippu Tib could not control all the Arabs, however, and after he departed for Zanzibar in 1890, relations quickly deteriorated. When Tippu Tib died in Zanzibar on June 14, 1905, his territories had already been incorporated into the Congo Independent State for over a decade (Robert W. July).

His autobiography, *Autobiographie des Arabers Schech Hamed bin Muhammed el Murjebi, genannt Tippu Tip* (1260), was published in Swahili and German, later in Swahili and English under the title *Maisha ya Hamed bin Muhammed el Murjebi yaani Tippu Tip kwa maneno yake mwenyewe* (1261).

Portrait on Plate II.

Hayford, Gladys May Casely
vid. *Casely Hayford, Gladys May*

Hayford, Joseph Ephraim Casely
vid. *Casely Hayford, Joseph Ephraim*

Hazoumé, Paul   Dahomey

Born on April 16th, 1890, in Porto Novo, Dahomey, Paul Hazoumé went to St. Joseph's Elementary School in Porto Novo
and from 1907 to 1910 to the Ecole Normale William Ponty in
Saint-Louis, Senegal, to be trained as a teacher. He became an
elementary school teacher, working with interruptions in Widah,
Abomey and Cotonou. In 1931 he travelled to Paris for the
Colonial Exhibition. The years 1938 to 1939 saw him again in
Paris, where he had joined the Africa department of the Musée
de l'Homme. In 1947 he was elected councillor of the "Union
française" in France, an office he held till 1958, when he retired
and returned to Cotonou. But several trips and missions took
him again to France. Hazoumé is a French citizen.

Hazoumé has always been interested in his people's traditions. His first work *Le pacte du sang au Dahomey*, Paris 1937,
is an ethnological study of Dahomean customs. His only novel
Doguicimi (496) describes life and customs at King Gezo's
court in Abomey, presenting a true picture of the heroic past
of ancient Dahomey.

Portrait on Plate VII.

Head, Bessie   South Africa

Born in 1937 in Pietermaritzburg, Natal, South Africa, Bessie
Head worked as an elementary school teacher and a journalist.
She lives now in Francistown in Botswana.

Her first novel, *When Rain Clouds Gather* (1625), is set
in Botswana and depicts the struggle of people to find their
own way of life after centuries of white domination.

Her second novel, "Maru", London 1971, is again set in Botswana and is essentially a love story.

Bessie Head "has a good style and is a superb story-teller.
She writes with laudable calm, and has remarkable ability to
get inside her characters" (Joe Chukwuemeka Brown).

Henshaw, James Ene   Nigeria

Born on August 29, 1924, in Calabar, South Eastern State, Nigeria, James Ene Ewa Henshaw was the youngest of nine sons. His father was an Efik prince and a member of the Legislative Council of Nigeria. After the death of his father, he was brought up by his eldest brother, the late Dr. Lawrence Eken Richard Henshaw. He was educated at the Sacred Heart Primary School in Calabar, and Christ the King College in Onitsha. In 1943 he entered the National University of Ireland in Dublin to study medicine. He qualified as a doctor in 1949 and specialised as a Chest Physician. Back home, he was appointed a Senior Consultant in Tuberculosis for the Government of Eastern Nigeria Port Hartcourt. He was the first Controller of Medical Services in the South Eastern State of Nigeria, and is still practicing as a medical consultant to the Ministry of Health in the Chest Clinic in Calabar.

Henshaw's first play, *This is Our Chance* (498), was first performed by the Association of Students of African Descent, in Dublin at Mespil Hall, in December 1948. This play, "directed against tribal feuds and prejudices and parental obsession about their off-springs marrying into other tribes or clans", was followed by *Jewels of the Shrine*, a one act play, which "calls for respect for old age and care for the aged", and which won the Henry Carr Memorial Prize for the best one act play in the All Nigeria Festival of the Arts in 1952. *A Man of Character*, a two act play, "is directed against bribery and corruption and its usual accompaniment, blackmail". It has been mentioned in "Nigeria 10", an official publication by the Federal Military Government marking the tenth anniversary of Nigeria's independence. All three plays have been published in one volume with the title of the first play, *This is Our Chance*. His second book of plays, *Children of the Goddess, and other Plays* (499), contains, besides the title play which directs "attention to the impact of the missionaries on the African", two other one act plays, of these *Companion for a Chief* is directed against an "unhappy custom connected with

Léopold Sédar Senghor

Birago Diop

PLATE V

Alioune Diop

Sembene Ousmane

Keita Fodeba

Camara Laye

PLATE VI

Yambo Ouologuem

António Aurélio Gonçalves

the death of some African king", and *Magic in the Blood* is "a humorous onslaught on persons who seek undue advantage by claiming royal privileges".

His third published book is *Medicine for Love* (500). The three act comedy is a satire on "'democratic elections' as practised in some places", and was first produced by the West African Drama Group in London 1956. His fourth book, *Dinner for Promotion* (501), is a four act comedy "on the manœuvres of some 'employees' to get themselves to the top at all cost". It was first produced in an abridged form by Prof. Axworthy in the Arts Theatre, Ibadan University. Another play, *Enough is Enough,* a three act play on the Nigerian civil war, has just been produced by the Emotan Drama Group in Benin City, but is not published yet.

James Ene Henshaw "wants to reconcile the African traditional system to the other system of the Western world by dwelling on what is essentially good in each and thus produce harmonious music. The dramatic situation in his seven plays is usually the same. There is a simple conflict between tradition and modernism, then the conflict suddenly assumes enormous proportions and after a great display of passion the situation is miraculously resolved with modernism triumphing, although with an admixture of what is considered good in tradition. After this, everybody lives happily thereafter" (Oyin Ogunba).

Higo, Aig   Nigeria

Born on June 22, 1932 in Otuo, Western State, Nigeria, Aigboje Higo — this is his full name — received his education at St. Andrew's College in Oyo, at University College, Ibadan, and at the University of Leeds, England. He was Senior English Master of St. Andrew's College in Oyo, Principal of the Anglican Grammar School in Otuo, and is now Managing Director of Heinemann Educational Books (Nigeria) Limited, in Ibadan.

Aig Higo's poetry, which was published in journals like "The

Horn", "Poetry and Audience", "Transition" and "Black Orpheus", and in anthologies like *A Book of African Verse* (A 86) and *Modern Poetry from Africa* (A 75), won him the Prof. Mahoud Poetry Prize of the University of Ibadan in 1958.

Hoh, Israel Kafu   Ghana

Born on May 12, 1912, in Afiadenyigba near Keta, Volta Region, Ghana, Israel Kafu Hoh is the son of an evangelist. He was educated at the Evangelical Presbyterian Infant and Junior School in Afiadenyigba from 1917 to 1922, and at the Evangelical Presbyterian Senior School in Keta from 1923 to 1927, both of which were former Bremen Mission Schools. From 1928 to 1931 he attended the Presbyterian Teachers' Training College in Akropong and in 1932 the Evangelical Presbyterian Seminary in Ho. He holds a teacher's certificate and a diploma in Advanced English. In 1933 he began his teaching career, working successively in the towns of Amedzofe, Keta, Peli, Keta again, and Anloga. In his spare time he acted as bandmaster, choir-leader and boy scout. In 1945 he became a Head Teacher, and in 1953 he was transferred to the administration as Assistant Education Officer at Abor, Anloga and Dabala.

Hoh's first poem, *Henabaeta*, was written in 1929. Since then he published *Prodigal Brothers* (504), a play for schools, and *Srokuda* (505), a small volume in Ewe. Poems and articles have been published in "Présence Africaine", "Ghana Teachers' Journal" and broadcast by Radio Ghana.

Honwana, Luis Bernardo   Mozambique

Born in 1942 in Lourenço Marques, Mozambique, Luis Bernardo Honwana worked, after high school, as a journalist on the daily newspaper "Diário de Moçambique" in Lourenço Marques. In

December 1964 he was arrested by the Portuguese authorities and put into prison.

Luis Bernardo Honwana wrote a number of short stories which were published in journals like "Black Orpheus", "Présence Africaine", and "The Classic" in English and French translations, and which were collected in the volume, *Nós matamos o ção tinhoso* (1630), translated into English under the title *We killed Mangy-Dog and Other Stories* (1630 b).

"One recent contribution is very good, the stories of Luis Bernardo Honwana, who without any preachment recreates convincingly the moods of the passive but tenacious African of Mozambique in *Nos matámos o ção tinhoso* (We have killed Old Nick)" (Gerald M. Moser).

Horatio-Jones, Edward Babatunde Bankolé   Nigeria

Born on January 9, 1930, in Lagos, Nigeria, Edward Babatunde Bankolé Horatio-Jones descends, on his father's side, from a Yoruba family spread from Abeokuta in Nigeria to Freetown in Sierra Leone, and on his mother's side, from the family Manga-Bell, of Cameroon, whose head, King Bell, signed the "contracts" with the German representatives in 1884.

Babatunde Horatio-Jones went to school in Sierra Leone. He left for London in 1943 to study Literature and Philosophy at London University. In 1951 he went to Paris where, in 1957, he studied at the Ecole Normale Supérieure, from 1958 to 1959 at the Institut des Hautes Etudes, and from 1959 to 1960 at the Ecole Photo et Cinéma. In 1961 he moved to Germany, from 1962 to 1964 he studied stage production with Piscator in West-Berlin and at the same time at the Theater am Schiffbauerdamm (Brecht's theatre) in East-Berlin. In 1964 he returned to Nigeria to produce films, and in 1972, as lecturer at Queen's College, New York, he was just ready to leave.

Babatunde Horatio-Jones writes poetry in French, prose in English, and he started to write some fragments of plays in

German, but apparently none of his novels, plays or films were finished. However, poems of his, and chapters of his dense and rhythmic prose appeared in anthologies as "Schwarzer Orpheus" (A 53), "Das junge Afrika" (A 52), "Afrika erzählt" (A 50), and "Das Schlangenorakel" (A 54).

Horton, James Africanus Beale   Sierra Leone

Born in 1835 in Sierra Leone, the son of an Ibo recaptive, James Africanus Beale Horton was educated at C.M.S. (Christian Missionary Society) grammar school in Freetown and Fourah Bay College. He eventually studied Medicine at the University of Edinburgh, Scotland. When he returned to West Africa in 1859, he came as a medical officer in the British army, serving for over twenty years in various stations along the West Coast. He retired in 1880 with the rank of Surgeon-Major and returned to Sierra Leone, where he busied himself chiefly in the promotion of commercial ventures. He became interested in the Gold Coast mines and argued for a railroad construction. In 1883 he founded the Commercial Bank of West Africa in Freetown, but the enterprise was obliged to close down again on account of Horton's death a few months after its opening.

Horton believed in the importance of Western culture to the development of a modern West Africa, but he also believed, that social improvement must end in the establishment of free nations in West Africa. He expressed his ideas in extensive writings, the most important of which are *West African Countries and Peoples, British and Native* (508), and *Letters to the Political Condition of the Gold Coast Since the Exchange of Territory Between the English and Dutch Governments* ... (509). Part of his essays were collected in *Africanus Horton: The Dawn of Nationalism in Modern Africa* (510).

Hutchinson, Alfred   South Africa

Born in March 1924 in Hectorspruit, Eastern Transvaal, South
Africa, Alfred Hutchinson is, on the paternal side, the grandson of a Swazi chief, and, on the maternal side, the grandson
of an Englishman. After attending St. Peter's Secondary School
in Rosettenville he attended Fort Hare College where he obtained a B. A. and a teacher's certificate. He taught for a while
at a high school in Johannesburg. Later he studied Law at the
University of the Witwatersrand. Hutchinson was among the
accused in the treason trial of 1958, but was released and made
his way to Ghana via Nyasaland and Tanganyika. Since 1964
he has been a teacher in London, England.

Hutchinson published *Road to Ghana* (1633), which describes his escape to West Africa and which was translated into
seven languages, a play, *The Rain Killers* (1634), and a radio
play, *Fusane's Trial* (1635).

Road to Ghana "penetrates our life, forces itself into our
privacy and digs out unforgettable traces" (Afrique).

On *The Rain Killers:* "Alfred Hutchinson has built a dull
drama which is as thin in texture as it is frail in artistry" (Bernth
Lindfors).

Ijimere, Obotunde   Nigeria

Obotunde Ijimere is the pseudonym for Ulli Beier, a German-
born writer, who is currently director of the Institute of African
Studies at the University of Ife, Nigeria.

Beier, who had his education in Germany and Britain, went
to Nigeria in 1950, together with his wife, Susanne Wenger.
Both became closely involved with Yoruba culture, Susanne
Wenger as an artist, Ulli Beier as a scholar and writer. As a
member of the Extra-Mural Department of the University College Ibadan, he refused a house on the University compound
and preferred living among the people of Ilobu and Oshogbo.
As a writer he produced, besides numerous articles in many

journals, several books on African art: *The Story of Sacred Wood Carvings from One Small Yoruba Town,* Lagos 1957, *A Year of Sacred Festivals in One Yoruba Town,* Lagos 1959, *Art in Nigeria,* Ibadan 1960, *African Mud Sculpture,* Cambridge 1963, *Yemi Bisiri,* Ibadan 1963, *Aşiru,* Oshogbo 1965, and *Contemporary Art in Africa,* London 1968. In 1957 he founded, together with Janheinz Jahn, the journal "Black Orpheus", and remained its editor until 1967. He edited several anthologies of creative or critical texts, such as *An Introduction to African Literature* (S 13), *Black Orpheus* (A 10), *Political Spider* (A 11), *Three Nigerian Plays* (AW 124) and — together with Gerald Moore — *Modern Poetry from Africa* (A 75). His collections of oral Yoruba poetry include *Yoruba Poetry,* Ibadan 1959, together with Bakare Gbadamosi, *The Moon Cannot Fight,* Ibadan 1964, *Ijala,* Port Moresby 1967, and *Yoruba Poetry,* Cambridge 1970.

As a creative writer Ulli Beier used the pen-name Obotunde Ijimere. He first became interested in popular Yoruba theatre in 1953, when he met playwright-producer Kolawole Ogunmola. Beier remained an enthusiastic supporter of Ogunmola ever since. In 1961 he began to work closely with another Yoruba playwright, Duro Ladipo, with whom he founded the Mbari Mbayo Club in Oshogbo. Beier encouraged Ladipo to expand the range of popular Yoruba theatre. Moving away from the conventional social satire of Ogunmola and Ogunde, Ladipo wrote his historical tragedies, among them "Oba Koso" which Beier helped to reproduce for the Berlin Festival in 1964. His close involvement with the Duro Ladipo theatre group led him to write four plays for this group: *The Imprisonment of Obatala* (532), *Everyman* (532), *Woyengi* (532) and *Born with the Fire on his Head* (AW 124). Ladipo translated *Everyman* into Yoruba as *Eda* (530) and toured Germany and Austria with that play in 1965. Ladipo has also performed free adaptations of *The Imprisonment of Obatala* and *Born With the Fire on His Head.*

In 1963 Beier got involved with another group called "Theatre Express", which was based in Lagos and directed by

Segun Oluşola. This group produced a wide range of plays in English. They concentrated on sketches which required only three to four characters. They became well known with Segun Sofowote's "Sailor Boy in Town" (1084) and Wale Ogunyemi's "Business Headache" (828). Beier made special translations of two plays by Friedrich Dürrenmatt for this company and, using his pen-name Obotunde Ijimere he wrote a farce, *The Fall of Man* (531) which was performed by the "Theatre Express" group in Oshogbo and Lagos. Beier also adapted a one act play, *The Suitcase* (533) by Salazar Bondi and a story, *The Bed* (534) by Samuel Selvon, for this group. *The Suitcase* was included in the "Theatre Express" programme in the Travesse theatre in Edinburgh in 1967.

Ike, Vincent Chukwuemeka   Nigeria

Born on April 28, 1931, in Ndikelionwu near Awka, East Central State, Nigeria, Vincent Chukwuemeka Ike went to Government College in Umuahia, University College, Ibadan, and to Stanford University, Stanford, California, USA, where he obtained his M. A. He was a teacher at the Elementary School in Amichi, near Nnewi, Nigeria, from August 1950 to September 1951, at the Elementary Training Centre in Irete, near Owerri, from June to September 1963 and at the Girl's Secondary School in Nkwerre, near Orlu, from June 1955 to December 1956. In 1957 Ike became Administration Assistant and Assistant Registrar of the University of Ibadan, in October 1960 he became Deputy Registrar of the University of Nigeria, Nsukka, and in March 1963 Registrar of that university. He gave up his post in September 1971 to become Registrar of the West African Examinations Council in August 1971. This council has jurisdiction over Nigeria, Ghana, Gambia and Sierra Leone.

Vincent Chukwuemeka Ike is a member of the Society of Nigerian Authors and a patron of the Writers' Club of the University of Nigeria Nsukka, of the Student Christian Movement at the University of Nigeria and of the Nsukka Social Welfare Council. He also is State Headquarters Commissioner (East Central State) of the "Boy Scouts of Nigeria", Editorial Adviser of "The Nigerian Christian", a monthly newspaper of the "Christian Council of Nigeria" and Director of the "Daily Times of Nigeria".

Ike is the author of two novels. *Toads for Supper* (536) is about undergraduate life at the University of Southern Nigeria before independence.

"It is refreshing to read someone who, though he belongs to the old school of 'simplicity', does not regard style as the end but as a means to it" (Obi B. Egbuna).

In his second novel, *The Naked Gods* (537), Ike makes use of his inside view as registrar into University politics, telling a satirical story of corruption and power struggle at a Nigerian university.

Ikelle-Matiba, Jean   Cameroon

Born on April 26, 1936, in Song near Ndong, district Sanaga Maritime, Cameroon, as son of a medical doctor, Jean Ikelle-Matiba had his elementary and secondary education in Edea, Duala and Sakbajema. From 1957 to 1963 he studied Law and Social Science in Paris, and he got his doctor's degree in Law in 1962. In 1963 he went to Germany as a representative of the Society of African Culture and became Assistant Director of the Evangelische Akademie at Iserlohn, Germany. From 1965 to 1966 he was Advisor for African Students at the University of Frankfurt-on-Main. After his marriage in 1967 he finally settled in Germany.

In 1967 he became General Secretary of the Comité des Amis de l'Académie Internationale de Culture in Mainz, Germany, and a member of the Board of Directors of its journal "Aeropag". He contributed articles, mostly on politics and international relations, to quite a number of journals in Germany and France, like "Afrika", "Présence Africaine", "Mélanges", "Afrika Bulletin", "Echo d'Afrique". A selection of his poems was published in 1968 in "Journal of the New African Literature and the Arts".

His novel, *Cette Afrique-là* (538), which received the Grand Prix de l'Afrique Noire d'Expression Française in 1963, presents the memories of an old Cameroonian: his education at the time of German colonialism and his reactions to the French take-over. It also appeared in German under the title *Adler und Lilie in Kamerun* (538 a).

"*Cette Afrique-là* possesses two main qualities. It is an expression of high morals and it is written with simplicity . . . It shows how a man who is deeply rooted in life, can remain honorable in all circumstances" (Robert Pageard).

Imoukhuede, Mabel
vid. *Segun, Mabel*

Ikiddeh, Ime   Nigeria

Born on April 11, 1938, in Uyo, South-Eastern State, Nigeria, Ikiddeh studied at Legon University, Ghana, then started his postgraduate studies in English at the University of Leeds, Great Britain. He visited the United States and returned in 1966 to teach English and African Literature at Legon University. Since September 1970 he has been teaching African and Commonwealth Literature at the University of Ife, Nigeria.

Besides writing plays and poetry and compiling anthologies of African literature, Ikiddeh devoted himself to Ibibio folk literature and popular fiction in Ghana.

Irele, Abiola   Nigeria

Born on May 22, 1936, at Ꝋra near Benin, Mid Western State, Nigeria, Abiola Irele grew up in Lagos where his father was working. From 1941 to 1948 he went to a Catholic primary school. In 1949 he entered St. Gregory's College, a Catholic secondary school, and left in 1954 after passing his Cambridge School Certificate. In October 1955 he entered the Ibadan branch of the Nigerian College to do his Advanced Level Certificate which he passed in June 1957. In October 1957 he entered the University College, Ibadan, to read English Honours and did his finals in 1960.

After leaving the University College he worked for three months at the Nigerian Broadcasting Corporation, then left for France to study at the Sorbonne, Paris, preparing a French teacher's diploma. In 1966 he received his doctorate with a thesis on the poetical work of Aimé Césaire.

After a short stay as Visiting Professor at the University of Dar es Salaam, Tanzania, Abiola Irele taught French at the University of Lagos and, from 1967 to 1969, at the University of Ghana at Legon near Accra. In summer and autumn 1968 he read German at the Goethe Institute at Brilon, Germany. In 1969 he was appointed Research Fellow at the Institute of African Studies of the University of Ife, Nigeria. In October 1972 he left Ife to take up an appointment as Senior Lecturer in French at the University of Ibadan.

While he was a student at University College, Ibadan, Irele wrote poetry and was editor of the student journal "The Horn". He acted in theatrical productions and took the part of the village schoolmaster in the premiere of Wole Soyinka's "The Lion and the Jewel". In Paris he collaborated with and contributed to "Présence Africaine". Since 1965 Irele has been co-editor of "Black Orpheus". His critical studies and treatises have appeared in many journals such as "Transition", "Présence Africaine", "The Journal of Modern African Studies", "Black Orpheus", "Odù", "Afrika Forum", "Dakar-Matin", and many others. His anthology, *Lectures africaines* (A 46), introduces African writing in French to University students. Since 1972 he has been engaged in the management of the Ethiope Publishing House in Benin City.

Jabavu, Davidson Don Tengo   South Africa

Born in 1885 at Healdtown, Cape Province, South Africa, Davidson Don Tengo Jabavu, eldest son of John Tengo Jabavu and father of Noni Jabavu, was educated at the mission schools of Lovedale and Marija, Lesotho. When his father failed to enroll him in the all-White Dale College at King William's Town, he was sent to Britain, in 1903, to pursue his education. He enrolled at London University and graduated with a B. A. degree in English in 1912. He also studied journalism, in his father's footsteps. From England he travelled to America where he visited Tuskegee Institute, founded by Booker T. Washington, and Hampton University, to learn about Negro higher education in the United States. He returned to England in 1913 and obtained his teacher's diploma at Birmingham University.

In 1915 he returned to South Africa and was appointed the first lecturer at the Native College at Fort Hare (now Fort Hare University) which was founded by his father. From 1916 to 1944 he was lecturer in Bantu languages, teaching Xhosa, Zulu, Sotho and Tswana, as well as English, Latin and History.

After his father's death in 1921, Davidson Don Tengo Jabavu and his brother Macaulay Jabavu carried on the work of "Imvo Zabantsundu", a Xhosa newspaper his father had founded in 1884.

After his retirement from Fort Hare in 1944, Jabavu received the degree of Doctor of Philosophy (honoris causa) from Rhodes University. He was honoured by the Royal African Society with a Bronze Medal for outstanding service, and a coronation medal from Queen Elizabeth II.

Davidson Don Tengo Jabavu died on August 3, 1959.

Jabavu wrote several descriptions of his travels in Xhosa, which first appeared in "Imvo", and were later published by the Lovedale Press, such as *E-Jerusalem* (1636), *E-Amerika* (1637), *E-Indiya nase-East Afrika*, Lovedale 1951(?) He is also the author of *The Black Problem*, Lovedale 1920, *The Life of John Tengo Jabavu*, Lovedale 1922, *The Segregation Fallacy* (1928), *"Native Disabilities" in South Africa*, Lovedale 1932, *Imbumba yamaNyama*, Lovedale 1952, and two works in Xhosa, *Izithuko* (1638) and *IziDungulwana* (1639). Two scholarly works are *Bantu Literature: Classification and Reviews* (SA 391), and *The Influence of English on Bantu Literature* (SA 392).

Jabavu, John Tengo   South Africa

Born in January 1859 at Healdtown, Cape Province, South Africa, John Tengo Jabavu, a Xhosa, was sent to school in Healdtown, where he became eloquent in English and Xhosa. He qualified as a teacher and, in 1866, went to Somerset East to teach, while being an apprentice in a printer's office. In 1881 he passed on to Lovedale Mission School for higher education, and was invited to edit the Lovedale newspaper "Isigidimi sama-Xhosa" for a period of three years. In 1883 he passed his matriculation at the University of South Africa, Cape Town. In 1884 his contract with "Isigidimi" ran out, and Jabavu decided to strike out on his own. He founded "Imvo Zabantsundu" (Native Opinion) at King William's Town, the first newspaper edited by a black South African.

Failing to enter his first son Davidson into Dale College at King William's Town, Jabavu became one of the foremost figures in fighting for higher education for black South Africans. In 1916 his dream came true when he opened the Native College at Fort (now Fort Hare University). His son Davidson Don Tengo Jabavu was appointed the first lecturer on the college staff.

John Tengo Jabavu died on September 10, 1921, at Fort Hare.

Jabavu, Noni   South Africa

Born around 1920 in Eastern Cape Province, South Africa,
Nontando Jabavu — this is her full name — is the daughter of
D. D. T. Jabavu, Professor of Latin and Bantu languages at Fort
Hare University. She attended day school at Lovedale Missionary Institution near her home, then went to England at the
age of fourteen to attend The Mount School, a girls' public
school in York. She wanted to be a journalist, following in the
steps of her paternal grandfather, John Tengo Jabavu, but her
parents and her English guardians pressed her to study medicine. Her compromise was to study music at the Royal Academy
of Music in London in 1939. At the beginning of World War II
she broke off her studies and trained as a sound woman.

Noni Jabavu has broadcast many talks on the BBC in London, and has appeared on television. She is the author of two
autobiographical narratives, *Drawn in Colour* (1640), and *The
Ochre People* (1641).

"*The Ochre People*... deals mainly with Noni's bourgeois
family ... Very few people could make long family lineages or
complex Xhosa salutations interesting. Fewer still could hold an
audience through a couple of hundred pages of chit-chat about
her westernised relations" (Nicholas Bennett).

Jacinto, António   Angola

António Jacinto de Amiral Martins was born in 1924 in Luanda,
Angola. He uses as a writer only his first two names and sometimes the pen-name Orlando Távora. He is a fervent and
militant nationalist. He collaborated in political and cultural
organizations. In 1961 he was arrested because of his political
activities and sentenced to fourteen years of detention. He is
still serving time in the prison of Tarrafal on the Cape Verde
island St. Jago.

His poems have been published in anthologies like "Antologia da poesia negra de expressão portuguesa" (A 4), "Literatura

africana de expressão portuguesa" (A 5), and "La poésie africaine d'expression portugaise" (A 6), in journals like "Présence
Africaine", and in his volume, *Colectânea de poemas* (1642).

"He was one of the most influential animators of the literary
circles in Angola" (Mário de Andrade).

Joachim, Paulin   Dahomey

Born on September 20, 1931 in Cotonou, Dahomey, Paulin
Joachim went to school in Dahomey and Gabon. In 1950 he left
for Lyon, France, to enrol at the law faculty, but had to give
up his studies for lack of funds. He looked for work in Paris and
became the secretary of the surrealistic poet Philippe Soupault.
He collaborated with several student journals. From 1956 to
1957 he was studying for the journalist's diploma. From 1958
to 1960 Joachim was political editor of "France-Soir", from
1960 to 1970 the editor in chief of "Bingo". Since 1971 Paulin
Joachim has been manager of "Décennie 2", Paris, an illustrated
journal of modern Africa. Paulin Joachim is a French citizen.

Paulin Joachim's first published work was a small volume of
poetry, *Un nègre raconte* (546). This was followed by another
collection of poems, *Anti-grâce* (547). Besides these he has published essays and poems in "Présence africaine".

Jolaoso, Mabel
vid. *Segun, Mabel*

Jolobe, James J. R.   South Africa

Born on July 25, 1902, in Indwe, Cape Province, South Africa,
James James Ranisi Jolobe, a Xhosa, the son of a church minister,

went to primary school in Matatiele, East Griqualand, and to Patterson High School in Port Elizabeth. He was trained as a teacher at St. Matthew's College near Keiskammahoek and went to teach in Mount Frere, Transkei, and various other schools in the Cape Province. In 1926 he enrolled at Fort Hare College to become a minister. In September 1937 he was invited, together with Samuel K. Mqhayi, as a Xhosa representative to the African Authors' Conference held in Johannesburg. From 1938 to 1952 Jolobe taught at the Lovedale Bible School, from 1952 to 1959 he was a staff member of the Lovedale Training School teaching mainly English and School Method. During this time he was part-time minister in the Knox Bokwe Presbyterian Church at Ntselamanzi, near Lovedale, and in the Dorringloin Presbyterian Church at Fort Beaufort.

In 1960 Jolobe was called to the St. Patrick's Presbyterian Church in the African township of Port Elisabeth, New Brighton. He remained there until he retired in December 1970. During this period he assisted in producing school books for primary schools — textbooks on health, geography and a series of readers under the name of "Uhitya", working together with L. N. Nyembezi. On his retirement he was asked by Fort Hare University to serve on a committee which is editing a Xhosa-Xhosa, Xhosa-English and Xhosa-Afrikaans dictionary. Jolobe is helping now in the Lovedale Press.

Jolobe received various literary awards. In 1936, *Thuthula,* one of four poems he had translated from the original Xhosa, won him the first prize in the May Esther Bedford Competition. In 1952 he was awarded the Vilakazi Memorial Prize for Nguni writers. In 1953 he won the first prize in a competition organized by the Afrikaanse Pers-Boekhandel in Johannesburg. And in 1957, he received the Margaret Wrong prize and medal "for outstanding services to literature in South Africa".

Jolobe's first work was the short novel *U-Zagula* (1644), which describes "the terribly negative influence that the belief in magic had and still has on the social structure of Xhosa society" (S. Z. Qangule). It was followed by *Umyezo* (1645), a collection of poems, four of which were later translated by the author and published under the title *Thuthula* (1645 a) and *Poems of an African* (1645 b). Jolobe wrote a Xhosa translation of Booker T. Washington's "Up from Slavery" in 1951, and an adaptation of Aesop's fables in 1953. He published a collection of poems about the little town of Alice near Lovedale, *Izicengcelezo zaseDikeni* (1646), a play, *Amathunzi obomi; umdlalo wokulinganiswa* (1647) and the novel *Elundini loThukela* (1648). In 1959 he produced a new collection of poems, *Ilitha* (1649), and a translation of Rider Haggard's "King Solomon's Mines". He contributed, besides, a paper on the problems encountered by African writers at the African Authors' Conference that was held at Atteridgville (Pretoria) from July 7—9, 1959.

"The publication of *Omyezo* in 1936 was a landmark in the history of written Xhosa poetry" (Albert S. Gérard).

Jones, Eldred Duromisi   Sierra Leone

Eldred Duromisi Jones was born on January 6, 1925, in Freetown, Sierra Leone. He went to Sierra Leone Grammar School from 1938 to 1942, was teaching for two years and went then to Fourah Bay College from 1944 to 1947, where he received his B. A. degree in General Studies. For another year he taught, then returned to Fourah Bay College in 1948, got his diploma in Education in 1949, and went back to teaching at the Sierra Leone Grammar School. In 1950 Jones moved to Oxford to study English Language and Literature at Corpus Christi College and did his B. A. in 1953. From 1953 to 1962 he was a lecturer in the English Department at Fourah Bay College, from 1962 to 1964 a senior lecturer there, and in 1964 he was appointed Professor and Head of the Department of English Language and Literature at Fourah Bay College.

In 1960 a Fulbright Research Fellowship and a Smith Mundt Grant enabled Jones to continue his studies at the Folger Shakespeare Library in Washington, U.S.A. Two years later, in 1962, Jones got his Ph. D. at the University of Durham.

Paul Hazoumé

Jean Pliya

PLATE VII

Bernard Binlin Dadié

Ahmadou Kourouma

Efua Theodora Sutherland

Ayi Kwei Armah

PLATE VIII

Kofi Awoonor

Cameron Duodu

In the years 1962, 1964, 1968 and 1969 Jones received Folger Research Fellowships, the result being his treatises, *The Elizabethan Image of Africa* and *Othello's Countrymen: A Study of Africa in the Elizabethan and Jacobean Drama*. At the same time Eldred D. Jones was a visiting professor at the University of Leeds, England, and the University of British Columbia, Canada. From 1970 to 1971 he was a Commonwealth Fellow at the University of Toronto, Canada.

Eldred Duromisi Jones has written many scholarly works on African languages and literature. He is also the editor of "African Literature Today", London. He writes short stories and poetry, does educational broadcasts for Radio Sierra Leone and has directed and acted in many of the leading amateur productions in Sierra Leone.

Jordan, Archibald Campbell   South Africa

Born on October 30, 1906, at Mbokothwana Mission, Tsolo district, Transkei, Cape Province, South Africa, Archibald Campbell Jordan, a Xhosa, is the son of a minister of the Church of England. He attended the primary school of his home town until 1921. After studying at the St. Cuthbert School, he obtained an Andrew Smith bursary, which enabled him to proceed to Lovedale School, where he got his junior certificate. He was trained as a teacher at St. John's College, Umtata. He entered Fort Hare College with another scholarship, and continued his studies at the University of South Africa, Pretoria. There he obtained his education diploma in 1932, and his B. A. in 1934. Later he was a teacher for ten years at the Bantu High School in Kroonstadt, Orange Free State. He became an executive member and later president of the African Teachers' Association. He continued his studies at the University of South Africa and obtained his M. A. in 1942. At the beginning of 1945, he was appointed lecturer in Bantu languages at Fort Hare College. The following year, in 1946, he accepted a similar position at the

University of Cape Town. In 1961 he was awarded a Carnegie travel grant to visit universities in the United States and Great Britain, and to investigate the latest developments in African languages and literatures. He was refused a passport by the South African authorities, but left the country illegally and went to the University of California, Los Angeles, USA, where he remained for two years. In 1963 he went to the University of Wisconsin as a fellow at the Institute for Research in the Humanities, and in 1964 he was appointed as a professor of African Languages and Literature, a post he held until his death on October 20, 1968, in Madison.

Jordan published a novel in Xhosa. *Ingqumbo yeminyanya* (1651), which treats "the theme of modern education versus traditional belief, and the theme of individual love and Christian marriage versus traditional custom and polygamy" (Albert S. Gérard). He also produced a *Xhosa Manual*. He obtained a Ph. D. degree in 1964 for his thesis *A Phonological and Grammatical Study of Literary Xhosa*. The results of his research into the early history of Xhosa writing were published in the journal "Africa South" (later, "Africa South in Exile"). Poems were published in the newspaper "Imvo Zabantsundu" in 1936, and in "Ikhwezi lomso" in 1958. They were in Xhosa, some accompanied by English translations prepared by Jordan himself.

"*Ingqumbo yeminyanya* has burst into South African Bantu-language literary scene, and has immediately been recognized as being a great tragedy, the creation of a master mind" (Daniel P. Kunene).

"The atmosphere of the novel is . . . one of objectivity bordering on starkness" (Harold Scheub).

Jordan is "a Xhosa novelist of note and the best authority on the history of early Xhosa literature" (Albert S. Gérard).

Kachingwe, Aubrey   Malawi

Born on November 27, 1926, in Blantyre, Malawi, Aubrey
Kachingwe had his early education in Malawi and further education in Tanzania. In 1950 he took up work with the "East
African Standard" group in Nairobi, Kenya. In 1954 he re-
turned to Blantyre, Malawi, and worked as a Public Relations
Officer. The next year he left for England where he studied
Journalism and worked for the "Daily Herald". For a time he
worked in the Department of Information in Malawi (then
Nyasaland). He returned to London in 1963 where he worked
in the African Service and News Department of the BBC. Later
he was attached to the Ghana Broadcasting Corporation in
Accra, Ghana. On his return to Malawi he joined the Malawi
Broadcasting Corporation as Director of News.

Kachingwe has now entered the world of business and commerce in Malawi and finds "the new challenge equally thrilling
and rewarding".

Kachingwe has published many short stories in European and
American journals. His novel, entitled *No Easy Task* (1654),
deals with the struggle for independence in a British Central
African colony as seen through the eyes of the journalist-nar-
rator, Jo Jozenzi.

"The plot has immense potential but it is precisely here that
the author has failed to weave a coherent pattern and produce
a powerful novel" (Bankole Timothy).

"Mr. Kachingwe writes in an easy style with a remarkable
power to create lively and dramatic scenes, such as the fight
in a night club" (S. O. Anozie).

Kadima-Nzuji, Dieudonné   Zaire

Born in 1947 at Banzyville on the Ubangi in Equator Province,
Zaire, as the brother of Clémentine Nzuji, Dieudonné Kadima-
Nzuji studied Philosophy and Literature at the University of
Lovanium in Kinshasa.

Dieudonné Kadima-Nzuji has published two volumes of poetry, *Les Ressacs* (1170), and *Préludes à la terre,* Kinshasa 1971. In 1969 Dieudonné Kadima-Nzuji received the third prize for poetry at the National L. S. Senghor Competition and the Silver Medal of Merit in Arts, Sciences and Literature.

"Because of its symbolism, this poetry is not always seizable" (Théophile Ayimpam).

Kagame, Alexis   Rwanda

Born in 1912 in Kiyanza near Buriza, Rwanda, Alexis Kagame studied Philosophy and Theology at the seminary in Kabgayi. In 1941 he became a Catholic priest and editor in chief of the journal "Kinya-Mateka". He obtained his doctorate at the Gregorian University in Rome with the thesis *La Philosophie Bantu-Rwandaise de l'Etre,* Brussels 1956. He works at the Catholic Mission in Butare, Rwanda.

Kagame wrote most of his poetical work in Kinyarwanda, and most of his scholarly work in French. His poetry includes, the didacto-historical epic poem *Isokó y'ámäjyambere* (1269), and *Indyohesha-birayi* (1270), a humorous poem on pork. *Umulirimbiyi wa nyili-ibiremwa* (1271) is a long epic, which depicts the gospel and chapters of the church history in verses. The whole work is divided into eighteen books, each book again being divided into songs. Part I and II have been translated into French by the author under the title *La divine pastorale* (1271 a) and *La naissance de l'univers* (1271 a), part III to XVIII have not yet been published.

Kagame also collected the oral literature of his people. *Icara nkumare irungu* (Sit down, that I pass the time), Kabgayi 1947, is a collection of poems on the famine following World War II. *Iyo wiliwe nta rungu* (Where you pass the day, there is no boring), Kabgayi 1949, is a collection of humoristic poems from the 18th century to today. *Imigani y'imigenurano* (Wise proverbs), Kabgayi 1950, is a collection of 1730 Rwandian proverbs.

His scholarly works include: *La poésie dynastique au Rwanda*, Brussels 1951; *Les institutions politiques du Rwanda précolonial*, Brussels 1952; *Les organisations socio-familiales de l'ancien Rwanda*, Brussels 1954; *La notion de génération appliqué à la généalogie dynastique et à l'historie du Rwanda*, Brussels 1959; *L'historie des armées-bovines dans l'ancien Rwanda*, Brussels 1961; *Les milices du Rwanda précolonial*, Brussels 1963; *La language du Rwanda et du Burundi expliquée aux autochtones*, Kabgayi 1960; *Introduction à la conjugation du verbe rwandais*, Butare 1962; *Le colonialism face à la doctrine missionnaire, à l'heure du Vatican II*, Butare 1963; *Le Rwanda 1900—1950*, Namur 1950; *Histoire du Rwanda*, Leverville s. a. Scholarly works in Kinyarwanda are: *Inganji Karinga*, 2 volumes, Kabgayi 1959, a history of Rwanda and *Umwaduko w'Abazungu muli Afrika yo hagati*, Kabgayi 1947, relating as the title says, "The arrival of the Europeans in Central Africa".

Portrait on Plate XIV.

Kalungano
vid. *Santos, Marcelino dos*

Kamera, William   Tanzania

Born on April 18, 1942, at Mwika Moshi, district Kilimanjaro, Tanzania, William Kamera was educated at Ilboru Secondary School in Arusha where he studied for his Cambridge School Certificate. In 1965 he entered the University of East Africa at Dar es Salaam and graduated in Literature, Linguistics and Education. While at college, he was a member of the Literature Panel of the Ministry of Education, and after obtaining his degree he was appointed tutorial assistant. In 1969 he started graduate studies in English at Cornell University, USA.

In 1964 Kamera won the First Prize in a Poetry Competition organized by the East African Literature Bureau and sponsored by the Rockefeller Foundation. He has also been editor of "Darlite", the student magazine at the University at Dar es Salaam, and a member of the University Theatre Group.

Poems by William Kamera have appeared in "Darlite" and "Transition" and in the anthology "Poems from East Africa", ed. by David Cook and David Rubadiri, London 1971.

Kane, Cheikh Hamidou   Senegal

Born on April 3, 1928, in Matam, River Region, Senegal, Cheikh Hamidou Kane, until the age of ten, spoke only Fulfulde, the language of the Fulani, and learned the suras of the Koran by heart. In 1938 he began his elementary education in French. Three years later he travelled to the Cape Verde Islands, then he was sent to Dakar for secondary education. In 1952 he came to Paris, France, to study Law at the Sorbonne. His diary of this period formed the basis for his novel *L'aventure ambiguë* (556). In 1957 he continued his studies at the Ecole Nationale de la France d'Outre-Mer, which he left in 1959 with degrees (licencié) in Law and Philosophy, to return to Senegal.

On August 5, 1959, he arrived at Dakar. He became attaché in the Ministry for Development, and in March 1960 he was appointed Governor of the Region of Thiès. In 1962 he assumed the office of Chef du Cabinet in the Ministry for Development and Planning. After the failure of the attempted coup d'état of Prime Minister Mamadou Dia, Cheikh Hamidou Kane had no political functions until September 1963, when he became a functionary of UNICEF in Lagos, Nigeria. In 1966 he was transferred to Abidjan, Ivory Coast, where he has been holding the position of Director of UNICEF ever since.

For his only literary work, his novel, *L'aventure ambiguë* (556), in English *Ambiguous Adventure* (556 a), he was awarded the Grand Prix littéraire d'Afrique noire d'expression française in 1962.

"This novel is the story of Samba Diallo's search for a compromise between traditional Islam and the materialist philosophy of Europa ... Each word, each phrase has its meaning and adds to the whole meaning" (Anthony Brench).

"His tone is new and seducing. And ... unpretentious" (Paulin Joachim).

Kanza, Thomas R.   Zaire

Born in 1933 in Boende, Equator Province, Zaire, Thomas Rudolphe Kanza, son of Daniel Kanza who, in 1960, was Vice-President of the ABAKO Party of Kasavubu and, in 1963, Mayor of Léopoldville, received his education at the Catholic University Lovanium in Léopoldville and was, in 1956, the first African student of Belgian Congo to obtain a degree in Pedagogy and Psychology. He continued his studies in Bruges, Belgium, and at Harvard University, Cambridge, Massachusetts, USA.

In 1958 he returned to Belgium to work for the Common Market. When the Congo became independent, Kanza returned to Leopoldville and soon represented his country at the United Nations in New York, where he remained even after Lumumba, whom he supported, was overthrown. In April 1962 he became Congo's representative in London, for England and the Commonwealth. During the Katanga crisis, Kanza assisted Adoula's central government. When Tschombe became Prime Minister, Kanza was called back home. But soon he disagreed with Tschombe, joined the rebel forces and became Minister of Foreign Affairs of the Mulele group. Stationed at Nairobi he tried to unite the different sections.

Kanza has continued his studies in England. He wrote a thesis on the history of the Congo before independence at the London School of Oriental and African Studies. He is now a Research Fellow at Oxford University.

His book, *Congo 196?*, Brussels 1962, complains that the West mistook Lumumba for a communist. The French edition of his book, *Conflicts in the Congo*, Penguin 1971, was confiscated at the publishing house Maspero in Paris by the French police. His novel, *Sans rancune* (1172), emphasizes the contradiction of behaviour of Europeans in the Congo and at home in Belgium. In spite of controversial treatment the hero remains "without rancour" towards his European guardians.

Kariuki, Joseph Elijah   Kenya

Joseph E. Kariuki was born on August 25, 1931, in Banana Hill, Kenya and educated at Alliance High School from 1945 to 1949, Makerere University from 1950 to 1954 and King's College, Cambridge, from 1960 to 1962 where he got his M. A. in English. He was a teacher then at Alliance High School from 1955 to 1956, and at Kangaru School from 1957 to 1960.

In 1963 Kariuki became Training Officer of the Kenya Shell Co. He held this post till 1965 when be became Deputy Principal, and in 1966, Principal, of the Kenya Institute of Administration. In 1968 he joined the Chief Training Section of the U.N. Economic Commission for Africa in Addis Ababa. Since 1969 Kariuki has been Director-General of the Centre Africain de Formation et de Recherche Administratives pour le Développement, in Tanger, Morocco.

Joseph E. Kariuki is the author of a five page poem, *Ode to Mzee* (1276) "The poem succeeds because Kariuki has used a rigid form to evaluate with intensity the poetic meaning of a supreme moment in Kenyatta's history and the life of Kenya" (O. R. Dathorne).

Kariuki, Josiah Mwangi   Kenya

Born in 1929 in the Rift Valley, Kenya, Josiah Mwangi Kariuki was educated at Karima Secondary School, Kerugoya Secondary School, and King's College at Budo in Uganda. He studied Economics, Political Science and Journalism through correspondence courses. He was put in detention during the Emergency, from 1953 to 1960. In 1960 he opened his own secretarial business. From 1961 to 1963 he was Private Secretary to Jomo Kenyatta. In 1963 he was elected a member for Aberdare in the House of Representatives, belonging to the Kenya African National Union (KANU), the governing party.

His autobiographical book, *"Mau Mau" Detainee* (1277), relates his experiences in detention camps during the years 1953 to 1960.

Kassam, Amin   Kenya

Born on November 19, 1948, in Mombasa, Coastal Province, Kenya, Amin Kassam was once assistant editor of "Busara". His work has been published in several East African magazines. His poetry has been published in the anthologies "Drum Beat" (AE 166) and "Poems from East Africa", ed. by David Cook and David Rubadiri, London 1971, and has been broadcast over Radio Uganda, Voice of Kenya, and the BBC. Short stories have appeared in "Busara" and the "Journal of the New African Literature and the Arts".

Kaunda, Kenneth   Zambia

Kenneth David Kaunda was born in 1924 at a Church of Scotland Mission near Chinsali, Northern Province, Zambia. He is the son of an ordained priest from Malawi who had become a teacher. His mother was the first African woman teacher in the territory. Kenneth Kaunda was brought up among the Bemba people. He received his primary education locally and his secondary education at Munali Secondary School.

He qualified as a teacher and in 1943 returned to teach at the Mission. For two years he taught in Tanzania, then was employed by the Welfare Office in Salisbury, Rhodesia. In 1949 he returned to Northern Rhodesia to act as interpreter for Sir Stewart Gore-Brown. He founded a branch of the ANC (African National Congress) in Chinsali and became Organizing Secretary in the Northern Province in 1952. Soon after he became Secretary-General of the whole party. In 1953 the federation with Southern Rhodesia and Nyasaland was imposed. Kaunda opposed it and was sentenced to two months imprisonment for possessing banned documents. In 1957 he visited England and then undertook a long tour of India. In 1958 Kaunda was elected leader of the break-away movement which considered the ANC course too moderate. In 1959 he was rusticated, then sent to prison on the charge of having held an illegal meeting. In January 1960, after nine months of imprisonment, he was released and immediately became President of the new United National Independence Party (UNIP).

After the elections of 1962, Kaunda's UNIP formed a coalition government with his rival Nkumbula's ANC. On October 24, 1964, Northern Rhodesia won its independence. The country was renamed Zambia and Kaunda became President, a position he has held ever since.

His autobiography, *Zambia Shall Be Free* (1661) has been translated into several languages.

Kayira, Legson   Malawi

In his book, *I Will Try* (1662), Legson Kayira writes: "I do not have the slightest idea when I was born". And he does not tell the name of his birthplace which is near Nthalire, Karonga district, Northern Region, Malawi. About 1946 he first went to a Church of Scotland Mission School three miles from his home, then to Wenya School, eight miles from his village. There he dropped his names Didimu and Chalangani to adopt an English sounding name, Legson. In 1954 he entered the senior primary school at Nthalire. He received his secondary education at Livingstonia

Secondary School, from where he began his journey in October 1958. Driven by his ambition to learn, he walked North, leaving his Tumbuka area. He walked and worked his way through Tanganyika to Kampala, Uganda. On September 25, 1960, he arrived in Khartoum. With the help of the American Vice-Consul and with monies collected for him in America, he finally arrived at Skagit Valley College in Mount Vernon, Washington, USA, where he had been granted a scholarship.

He graduated from the University of Washington, then continued his studies at St. Catherine's College in Cambridge, England. He is living and working in England.

After his autobiography he has written three novels. *The Looming Shadow* (1663) is about a feud between villagers in Northern Malawi. *Jingala* (1664) is set in the same area, while *The Civil Servant*, London 1971, depicts urban life in Central Africa.

"Legson Kayira's narrative is shatteringly frank and unpretentious" (Alfred Hutchinson).

The Looming Shadow is "a tale of scalding malice ... it leaves no room for romanticism" (Ezekiel Mphahlele).

Portrait on Plate XVI.

Kayper-Mensah, Albert William　　　　　　Ghana

Born on November 21, 1923, in Takoradi, Western Region, Ghana, Albert William Kayper-Mensah had his education at Mfantsipim School, Cape Coast, the Wesley Teacher Training College in Kumasi, and Achimota College near Accra. From 1946 to 1949 he studied at Queen's College, Cambridge, England, and from 1949 to 1950 at the University of London. In 1950 he returned to Ghana to teach Biology at the Wesley College in Kumasi.

Albert William Kayper-Mensah left the educational service in 1957 to enter the diplomatic service. In 1958 he was sent to London to work there at the Ghana Embassy. In 1961 he was transferred to the Ghana Embassy in Bonn, Germany, in 1965 retransferred to London, and in 1968 retransferred to Bonn where he works as Cultural Counsellor.

His poetry has appeared in anthologies like "A Book of African Verse" (A 86), "Christ erscheint am Kongo" (A 100), "Voices of Ghana" (AW 149), and "New World Writing", USA, 1959, ind in journals like "Afrika heute", "Ghanean Times", "Neues Afrika", "Okyeame", "Zeitschrift für Kulturaustausch", etc. In 1970 his poems were collected in the volume *The Dark Wanderer* (566). In 1957 Albert Kayper-Mensah received the Margaret Wrong Prize, and in 1954 the first prize of the British Council for his radio play *Hearts that Had Loved*.

"Proverb technique in Akan oral literature fascinated me; and now, the more it inspires my writing, the more African I feel my writing is" (Albert William Kayper-Mensah).

Keita Fodeba
vid. *Fodeba, Keita*

Kenyatta, Jomo   Kenya

Born probably around 1893 in Ichaweri, Kenya, Jomo Kenyatta received, under the name of Kamau wa Ngengi, some education at the Church of Scotland mission in Kikuyu. Some time later he was employed in Nairobi as an inspector of water supplies and there was given the nickname "Kenyatta" because of a beaded belt he then wore. From 1920 he was active in Kenyan politics, first as a member of the East African Association and then as General Secretary of the Kikuyu Central Association (K.C.A.). He published a Kikuyu newspaper "Muigwithania". In 1929 he went to England as a member of the delegation which petitioned the government for the Kikuyu to found and run their own independent schools. In 1931 he again went to England. He studied English at the Quaker College in Woodbrooke, Selly Oak, then moved to London. From 1933 to 1936 he worked at the School of Oriental and African Studies as an Assistant in Phonetics. In 1936 he took a post-graduate degree in Anthropology at the London School of Economics under Professor B. Malinowski. For some time he studied at Moscow University.

Shortly after his return to Kenya in 1946 he was appointed Principal of the independent Teachers Training College, but found that the K.C.A. had been proscribed while he, as a politician, was shown the cold shoulder by the administration. On October 22, 1952, he was detained and on November 18 charged with being behind the Mau Mau violence. On April 8, 1953, he was convicted and sentenced to seven years imprisonment. Released in April 1959 he was restricted to a remote village in Northern Kenya. In the following years his release became a virulent issue in the political struggle for independence. When Kenya gained independence at the end of 1963, Jomo Kenyatta was elected Prime Minister. In 1964 Kenya became a republic and Kenyatta combined the offices of Prime Minister and President. He and his party, the KANU (Kenya African National Union) are still leading the country.

Kenyatta wrote *Facing Mount Kenya: the Tribal Life of Gikuyu*, London 1938. It is a detailed study of the customs of the Kikuyu, written so as to show how tribal life was disrupted by the intrusion of the white man. Another anthropological work is *My People of Kikuyu, and, The Life of Chief Wangombe*, London 1942. His speeches are collected in *Harambee! The Prime Minister of Kenya's speeches 1963—1964 from the attainment of internal self-government to the threshold of the Kenya Republic*, edited by Anthony Cullen, Nairobi, London, New York 1964. *Jomo Kenyatta, Suffering Without Bitterness*, Nairobi 1968, is a collection of documents concerning Kenyatta's political career.

Kgositsile, Keorapetse William   South Africa

Born on September 19, 1938, in Johannesburg, South Africa, Keorapetse William Kgositsile had both his primary and his secondary education in Johannesburg. He worked on the staff of "New Age", Cape Town, and "Spearhead Magazine", Tanzania. Since 1962 he has been at the New School for Social Research, New York, USA.

Kgositsile's poems and essays appeared in many periodicals in Africa and the United States. His first volume of poetry, *Spirits Unchained* (1670), won him the second Conrad Kent Rivers Memorial Fund Award. His second volume of poetry is entitled *For Melba* (1671), and the third *My Name is Afrika*, New York 1971.

Khaketla, Bennett Makalo   Lesotho

Born in 1913 into a peasant family in the district of Qacha's Nek, Lesotho, Bennett Makalo Khaketla qualified locally as a teacher. Subsequently, he studied privately and obtained a B.A. degree in Political Science and the Sotho language from the University of South Africa, Pretoria. He first worked as a typist, but in 1946, he was appointed to the Basutoland High School in Maseru. After being dismissed because of a reduction in staff at the Maseru high school in 1949, Khaketla worked briefly for the British administration in Lesotho, then left for South Africa, where he resumed his teaching activities.

In 1952 Khaketla returned home. This was the year when the Basutoland African Congress was founded as the first modern nationalist party, and Khaketla turned to politics. In 1955 the Basutoland African Congress sponsored the publication of "Mohlabani" (The Warrior) under his editorship. The first issue of the paper marked the beginning of the agitational phase of the Sotho nationalist movement. The first elections held in Lesotho in January 1960 led to the victory of the Basutoland

African Congress (BCP). Khaketla was elected to the legislative council, from where he was elected a member of the Executive Council, with responsibility for Health and Education. But dissensions arose, and he resigned in December 1960. In April 1961, Khaketla, together with some other ex-Congress members, launched a new party, the Basutoland Freedom party. In January 1963 this party merged with Chief Matete's Marema-Tlou party, and Khaketla became the vice-president of the new movement. The party split in 1964, and in the elections of 1965 Khaketla ran as an independent candidate, but lost. He was subsequently appointed chairman of the university's senate and a member of King Moshesh II's Privy Council.

Khaketla's first work is *Moshoeshoe le baruti* (1674), "a drama that is little more than a sequence of historical events presented in the form of dialogues. It deals with the arrival of the French missionaries in Lesotho" (Albert S. Gérard). His first novel, *Meokho ea thabo* (1675) treats the marriage theme. A boy, Moeketsi, does not want to marry the girl his family has chosen for him, but, in a lucky coincidence, his individually chosen love, turns out to be the same girl his family had wanted for him. *Lipshamathe* (1676) is a collection of poems. It is of peculiar interest because of its preface, in which Khaketla discusses some of the technical problems with which modern Sotho poetry has to grapple. *Tholoana tsa sethepu* (1677) is a story about polygamy. As deputy he produced his second drama, *Bulane* (1678), which was to be followed by his second novel, *Mosali a nkhola* (1679).

"Khaketla is the most important author inside Lesotho" (Albert S. Gérard).

Khumalo, Philios Mtshane   Rhodesia

Khumalo was born on February 28, 1925, at Ntabazindura Tribal Trust Land, Rhodesia. His father is the son of Mtshane Khumalo, a military leader under Lobengula, King of the

Matabele (ca. 1836—1894), his mother the daughter of Chief Mgandane Dhodlo, also a military leader under Lobengula. Khumalo obtained his B.A. degree at Rome University, Lesotho, and is now Headmaster of David Livingstone Memorial Secondary School at Heany Junction, Rhodesia.

Khumalo is the author of a narrative in Shona, *Umuzi kawakhiwa kanye* (1684).

Kigundu, Clement   Uganda

Born on June 3, 1928, at Kalungo, Masaka district, Uganda, Clement Kigundu was educated in his home area. After primary school from 1938 to 1942, he was at Bukalasa Seminary and Katigonde Seminary. From 1959 to 1960 he was Curator in Bikira Parish, and from 1961 to 1962 Parish Priest at the Kyamuliibwa Parish. From 1962 he was Assistant Editor, and from 1966, Editor of the journal "Munno" (Your Friend), an activity only interrupted from 1968 to 1971 for studies at Duquesne University, Pennsylvania, USA.

Kigundu's publications, religious tracts and works of local importance, all written in Luganda, include *Omulabe wa Buganda* (Enemy of Buganda), Kisubi 1961, *Buganda Kyeki* (What is Buganda), Kisubi 1965, and six others.

Kimenye, Barbara   Uganda

Barbara Kimenye states: "the details of my career as a writer and my age, unless I were a 90 year old genius, have no bearing on the situation" and refuses to disclose her personal data. Known is only, that she worked as private secretary for the Government of the Kabaka of Buganda. She was later a journalist for the newspaper "Uganda Nation", which has ceased publication. She lives in Nairobi, Kenya.

Barbara Kimenye's works include two volumes of stories, *Kalasanda* (1288), and *Kalasanda Revisited* (1289), and seven children's books.

Kalasanda "is charming collection of eight interconnected stories about life in Kalasanda ... Miss Kimenye's description glistens with a warm and delicate sympathy and a twinkling sense of humour" (Bernth Lindfors).

"*Kalasanda* is not so much 'a typical village in Buganda' as a creation of Mrs. Kimenye's very lively, but still very kizungu (European), imagination. We expect something better than this from the Oxford University Press" (F. B. Welbourn).

Kiyingi, Wycliffe   Uganda

Born in 1932 in Uganda, Wycliffe Kiyingi was educated at King's College, Budo, then taught at a local school, Aggrey Memorial. He later went to Makerere University, Kampala, Uganda.

When he was at King's College, Wycliffe Kiyingi became interested in drama, and in Aggrey Memorial School he introduced theatre and acting to the students. Many drama societies in and around Kampala today were founded by former students of his. He was instrumental in the initiation of the Schools' Drama Festival, the fore-runner of the present Youth Drama Festival, a popular event among schools and clubs throughout the country.

Wycliffe Kiyingi has written many plays in his language, Luganda. Most of these have been performed by the Uganda state company, "Theatre Limited", both on the radio and in the National Theatre, Kampala. His play *Gwossussa Myanyi* has been published by Macmillan in East Africa.

Ki-Zerbo, Joseph   Upper Volta

Joseph Ki-Zerbo was born in June 1922 at Toma near Koudougou, district Black Volta, Upper Volta. His father, Alfred

Zerbo, arrived from Dâ, in the Tougan district, with the missionaries and married Thérèse Ki from Toma, from one of the Royal Houses of the Samogo. He was responsible for introducing Christianity to Toma.

At the age of eleven, Josef Ki-Zerbo went to the mission school in Wagadugu, and three years later to another mission school near Bamako, Mali. At the age of 18, in 1940, he entered a seminary at Bobo-Diulasso, Upper Volta. But as the priesthood was not to his liking, he had to study again for a teaching diploma. In 1946 one of the White Fathers recruited Ki-Zerbo to work on "Afrique Nouvelle", then just about to be launched in Dakar, Senegal. At the age of 25, he left the magazine to study for the Baccalauréat and to work as a clerk on the railway in Dakar. In 1949 he took the two parts of the Bac and worked as Maître d'Internat, supervising discipline in a boarding school in Bamako, Mali. With a scholarship to France he studied History at the Sorbonne in Paris and obtained a Degree in 1952. For the next two years he prepared a thesis on "French Penetration in the Countries of the Upper Volta", and continued until he became an agrégé — he and the physicist Abdou Moumouni being the first Africans to attain this degree since Senghor fifteen years earlier.

In Paris he helped to found the Association of Catholic Students in France, and the Volta Students Association. He taught for two years in Lycées in Paris and Orléans, having married Jacqueline Coulibaly, a trained teacher from Segu, Mali. Together they went to teach in Dakar at the Lycée Van Vollenhoven and in 1958, after Guinea's Declaration of Independence, went to work in Guinea, at the Lycée Donka in Conakry.

In 1959 he applied for a job in Upper Volta, but was refused by the Yameogo regime, already firmly in power, but as too many Voltaic people were scandalised that the first Voltaic agrégé should be refused employment, he was eventually given a job in the Lycée.

For the next five years Joseph Ki-Zerbo lived quietly in Wagadugu, working at the school and writing a complete history of Black Africa. In 1962 and 1963 he took a sabbatical year to travel widely in African countries. As by 1965 the Yameogo regime had lost all sympathy, Ki-Zerbo and his wife, now Headmistress of the Girls' Lycée in Wagadugu, decided to help organise the general strike scheduled for January 3, 1966, which led to the overthrow of the regime and brought Colonel Lamizana into power. Joseph Ki-Zerbo has become Director of Education and Director of Youth and Sports.

Besides many articles on African history and culture published in "Présence Africaine" and other journals, he wrote an African History for schools: *Le monde africain noir*, Paris 1963.

Koffi, Raphaël Atta
vid. *Atta Koffi, Raphaël*

Komey, Ellis Avitey   Ghana

Born in 1934 at Labadi, an area of Accra, Ghana, Ellis Ayitey Komey was educated at the Methodist Senior Boys' School, Accra Academy, and the University of London. He spent sixteen years of his life in England, during which, for six years, he was editor of the international black magazine "Flamingo". He is now the Managing Director of "Ludeco", an organization dealing with publishing, public relations and tourism in Accra.

His short stories and poems appeared in anthologies and journals like "Flamingo" and "West African Review". With Ezekiel Mphahlele he compiled the anthology *Modern African Stories* (A 64).

Konadu, Samuel Asare   Ghana

Born in 1932 in Asamang, district Kumasi North, Ashanti Region, Ghana, Samuel Asare Konadu attended local schools and later Abuakwa State College in the Southeast of Ghana. In 1951 he became a government reporter for the Gold Coast Information Service and the Gold Coast Broadcasting Service. He was also reporting for several government newspapers. In 1956 he studied journalism in London and Strasbourg on a UNESCO fellowship. Back home he joined the Ghana News Agency, which had been started by the government after independence. He left the Ghana News Agency in 1963, and joined the oil firm BP. In 1966 Konadu founded the publishing house "Anowuo Educational Publications".

Konadu is the author of *The Wizard of Asamang* (575), *The Lawyer who Bungled his Life* (576), *Come back Dora!* (577), *Shadow of Wealth* (578), *A Woman in her Prime* (579), *Night Watchers of Korlebu* (580), and *Ordained by the Oracle* (581).

"*A Woman in her Prime* is an impressive, short, first novel ... (Konadu) has written a heart-warming, interesting novel which brings to life the feelings and emotions of village life in West Africa with elegance and charm" (M. N.).

"There are discursive passages which occasionally threaten to destroy the reality the novel creates. Yet at his best Konadu uses his background materials to create life rather than simply describe it in the novel" (Douglas Killam).

"This is a short novel but there is a compelling simplicity and authenticity about the world he describes, and we will anticipate with interest subsequent works of this young writer" (Cécile McHardy).

Koné, Maurice   Ivory Coast

Born in December 1932 at Buake, Central District, Ivory Coast, of a Lebanese father and a Senufo mother, Maurice Koné went to primary school in Buake and got his Certificat d'Etudes Primaires in 1961. He had no other schooling, but educated himself privately. He tried several professions (driver, me-

chanic, plumber, amateur boxer, butcher) before he entered the
civil service at the mayor's office at Buake.

Maurice Koné was awarded the Prix des Poètes Ivoiriens de
langue française in 1963, and in 1967 the Prix Notre-Dame
de Lourdes.

Koné writes mainly poetry. Three volumes of poems were
published in the early sixties: *La guirlande des verbes* (582), *Au
bout du petit matin* (583) and *Au seuil du crépuscule* (585). His
novel, *Le jeune homme de Bouaké* (584), is autobiographical.

Kourouma, Ahmadou   Ivory Coast

Ahmadou Kourouma was born in 1940 in the Malinke area,
Northern District, Ivory Coast. He received his secondary
education in Bamako, Mali, but was expelled because of a strike.
He did his military service in Ivory Coast. During this time he
refused to suppress a riot and found himself transferred to
Saigon, Indochina, which was in a state of war. Three years later
he could continue his education, first at Lyon, then at Paris.
Since 1965 he has been working as actuary in Algiers.

His novel, *Les Soleils des Indépendances* (591), is at the same
time an epic of the unity of man and nature and a satire on
recent African politics. Poetry and parody, humour and tragedy
merge in a realistic story which has all the flavour and rhythm
of traditional storytelling. The novel was awarded the Prix de
la Francité in 1968.

"It is true, this novel has caused very little notice in the Press
and this is a great injustice ... There has never been given in our
literature a fairer image of the African soul ... The admirable
lies in the meeting of the realism of the description with the
symbolism of the significations ... Kourouma writes in a language which is wholly his own. While up to now the African
writers worked hard at never leaving the traditional literary
perfectionism, killing within themselves all genuine originality,
all authenticity, forcing themselves to write like an honest acad-

emician, Kourouma has dared to use the French language in an African way. Kourouma does not hesitate to speak Malinke in French" (Mohamadou Kane).

Portrait on Plate VII.

Kuimba, Giles   Rhodesia

Giles Kuimba was born on October 5, 1936 in the Charter District, Rhodesia. When he was a baby his father died. Kuimba was educated at the Primary School at Daramombe Mission, then at Goromonzo Secondary School, where he passed the Cambridge School Examination with distinction. He continued at St. Augustine's Training College in Penhalonga for his Primary Teachers' Higher Certificate.

Kuimba has been a teacher, an editor and a radio producer and announcer. He is now a freelance writer.

Giles Kuimba has published two novels in Shona, *Gehena harina moto* (1689) and *Tambaoga mwana'ngu* (1690).

Kunene, Raymond Mazisi   South Africa

Raymond Mazisi Kunene was born on May 12, 1930, in Durban, Natal, South Africa. He obtained an M. A. degree from Natal University in 1959 with his thesis, *An Analytical Survey of Zulu Poetry Both Traditional and Modern* (SA 396). In 1959 he came to London on a fellowship to complete his Doctorate in Philosophy at London University, but became involved in political activities and had to leave his studies. He is the official representative of the African National Congress in London.

Kunene is greatly inspired by the traditional Zulu poets, especially of Magolwane, court poet of King Shaka, and of Benedict Wallet Vilakazi. His collection of poems, *Zulu Poems,*

London 1970, reflects his rooting in the Zulu language and culture. Idioms and metaphors are transmuted from the Zulu heroic literature into the English language. Articles and poems of his were published in "The New African", "Présence Africaine", and "Transatlantic Review".

Kunene "is a poet, the secret of whose charming and touching verse is its simplicity, clarity and originality ... apt lyrical associations interspersed with images from the sonorous world of the Zulu heroic epic" (Mofolo Bulane).

Kuo, François Sengat
vid. *Sengat-Kuo, François*

Kuoh, François Sengat
vid. *Sengat-Kuo, François*

Kuoh Moukouri, Jacques   Cameroon

Born on June 6, 1909, at Akwa, an area of Duala, Cameroon, Jacques Kuoh Moukouri had his primary education in his home town and his secondary education at the Ecole Supérieure in Yaunde. He left the school in 1926 to become a scribe and interpreter in the administration and served mostly in Yaunde and Duala. From 1950 to 1953 he was Parliamentary Attaché at the Cabinet Aujoula in Paris.

At the end of 1953 he returned to Cameroon to be appointed Head of Administration at Obala near Yaunde. In October 1954 he was called to Paris again, but only for the period of office of Prime Minister Mendès-France, until April 1955. Back in Cameroon, he was appointed in 1957 Administrateur de la France d'Outre-Mer and became Premier Adjoint of the Chef de Région, first at Kribi, then in Duala. In 1958 he became Private Secretary in the Ministry of Economics. In 1959 he was appointed Préfet of the district Nyong et Sanaga whose capital is Yaunde.

Jacques Kuoh Moukouri has described his career before and after independence in his autobiographical book *Doigts noirs* (598).

"In spite of some weaknesses, this report makes us feel unpleasantly all the depersonalisations which the author had to suffer to become the writer- interpreter that he was. *Doigts noirs* is an interesting contribution to the history of Cameroon" (René Philombe).

"You find a harvest of events that have been lived through and which merit being transferred to posterity in spite of the chaotic style and the more than doubtable French of the author" (G. Ngango).

Kyei, Kojo Gyinaye   Ghana

Born in 1932 in Ghana, Kojo Gyinaye Kyei was educated in America and is an architect by profession. In summer 1968 he exhibited his paintings in London. He is also a wood sculptor.

His first volume of poetry, *The Lone Voice*, Accra 1969, contains "a variety of light-hearted poetry, humorous, and quaintly sniggering and the poetry of dead seriousness and doubt" (Kofi Awoonor).

Ladipo, Duro   Nigeria

Born on December 18, 1931, in Oshogbo, Western State, Nigeria, as the grandson of a famous drummer, Duro Ladipo was a member of the school choir at the age of nine. At the age of fifteen, while he was still at school in Otan, he wrote his first play, *Naaman the Leper*. When he became a pupil-teacher, he followed his former headmaster, Mr. Alex Peters, to Kaduna, in order to continue with his dramatic work. At the U.N.A. School in Kaduna, at the age of twenty-six, he produced Shakespeare's "As You Like It". His *Easter Cantata* performed at All Saints Church, Oshogbo, in 1961 aroused considerable controversy even in the press, because Ladipo introduced drums into the church. As a result of this experience, he began to perform his religious compositions outside the church: in schools, on television and — at the invitation of the Nigerian Arts Council — at the Lagos Museum.

In 1962 Duro Lapido was one of the founding members of the Mbari Mbayo Club in Oshogbo. At first his plays did not differ much from the type of play performed by Hubert Ogunde and his numerous imitators. But Ulli Beier suggested to him to use historical themes and to study traditional drumming and classical Yoruba poetry in order to do justice to his theme. Duro Ladipo subsequently resigned from teaching and formed, in 1963, his own group, the "Duro Ladipo Players". He created a new style, breaking away from the rather deadening influence of Yoruba church music. He gained new territory with two historical plays, *Oba Moro* and *Oba Koso* — both published together with his play *Oba Waja* in the volume *Three Yoruba Plays* (608). *Oba Koso* achieved real success at the Berlin Theatre Festival in 1964 and again at the Commonwealth Festival in Britain in 1965. *Oba Koso* and *Eda*, Ibadan 1970, were both taken on a continental tour in 1965.

In his play *Moremi* (611), Duro Ladipo has delved deeper into Yoruba history and has been more liberal with his historical material. Besides English adaptations by Ulli Beier, bilingual editions in Yoruba and English, together with long play recordings were made at the University of Ibadan by Robert L. Awujoola and R. G. Armstrong: *Selections from Oba kò so* (609), *Oba kò so* (610), and *Edá*, Ibadan 1970.

"Duro Ladipo is a man of the theater who learned his art by practising it . . . Since he is a musician, composer, and man of the dance, as well as a playwright, actor, and director, his work contains all aspects of traditional African theater, drama, poetry, dance, music, and mime, all intermingled. His is not a literary drama, but one that uses dialog, action, movement, dance and other stylized forms to express its meaning. It is highly sophisticated in idiom, and it is drama created directly for the theater, for performance and presentation" (Herbert L. Shore). --

"*Oba Waja* demonstrated the strength and adaptability of Yoruba drama" (Adrian A. Roscoe).

"*Moremi* shows a fine insight into the workings of Yoruba religion. On stage it is a moving drama which depends heavily on its rich poetic texture and on the beauty of the music" (Ulli Beier).

Portrait on Plate X.

La Guma, Alex   South Africa

Born on February 20, 1925, in Cape Town, South Africa, Alex La Guma is the son of Jimmy La Guma, the President of the South African Coloured People's Congress and member of the Central Committee of the Communist Party. Alex La Guma completed his formal education at the Trafalgar High School and Cape Technical College, both in Cape Town. Later he worked as a clerk, factory hand, book-keeper and journalist. In 1946 he joined the Young Communist League, later the Communist Party until it was banned in 1950. In 1955 he helped to organize the Congress of People which met in Kliptown, Johannesburg, and adopted a Freedom Charter. As an outcome La Guma was arrested for treason with 155 others in December 1956. During the state of emergency following the Sharpeville massacre he was detained for five months. Between 1956 and 1962 he contributed to the progressive paper "New Age". In 1961, when Verwoord proclaimed the South African Republic, Alex La Guma was arrested again. In 1962 he was placed under house arrest for 24 hours a day for five years. He and his wife were detained under the 90-day regulations. He left South Africa as a refugee in September 1966 and now lives with his family in exile in London.

Alex La Guma has written many short stories which have appeared in journals in Africa, Europe and the United States, like "Black Orpheus", "Flamingo", "The New African" etc., and three novels. *A Walk in the Night* (1692) shows the murderous atmosphere in the black urban areas of South Africa. *And A Threefold Cord* (1693) demonstrates the impossibility to live a normal life in a shanty town. *The Stone Country* (1694) is the world of prison which Alex La Guma has so thoroughly experienced, with its cruel fights for survival. Some of his stories are included in the volume *A Walk in the Night and Other Stories* (1695).

"Alex La Guma did not worry about whether he was creating literature, and so he has done it" (Anthony M. Astrachan).

A Walk in the Night . . . "a picture of such vividness and verisimilitude that one can almost taste and smell the air, the streets, the buildings against which the characters move in sure and full three-dimensional reality" (Robert W. July).

And A Threefold Cord "is essentially a novel of situation; but the private situations of the individual characters run parallel to this. Public and private, with their respective moralities thus intertwine, producing a statement not only of political emergency but also of personal crisis" (Wilfred Cartey).

"In *The Stone Country* La Guma comes closer than ever before to presenting internal development, development in the relationship of human beings and their discovery of one another, in place of a brilliantly precise but entirely external reporting of actions and events" (Gerald Moore).

"La Guma's style is characterized by graphic description, careful evocation of atmosphere and mood, fusion of pathos and humour, colorful dialogue, and occasional surprise endings . . . (His) slumdwelling heroes are victims of their environment and their passions" (Bernth Lindfors).

Portrait on Plate IV.

'Laoye I, John Adetoyese; the Timi of Ede   Nigeria

Prince John Adetoyese 'Laoye I was born in 1899 in Ede, Western State, Nigeria. He was brought up by his maternal uncle who, being a drummer, taught the boy the art of drumming. The young prince received his early education from the Timi's (the king's) clerk, then proceeded to the mission station in Oshogbo for further schooling. In 1911 a missionary couple moved to Ofa and took the prince with them. Back with his family in Ede he attended the Baptist day-school, then the Baptist day-school in Ogbomosho. Not being allowed to continue his formal education he ran away from home to the mission station in Saki and prepared his entry into the Baptist Academy. He entered the academy in August 1916 and stayed there until December 1918. Subsequently he entered King's College in Lagos to study Chemistry as preparation for work in a dispensary. Shortly afterward, in July 1919, he learned dispensing in Lagos.

In 1924 the prince joined the Medical Department of the government. He was posted at the Colonial Hospital in Lagos for two months, before assuming duty in Kano. In 1925 he was transferred to Maiduguri, and in 1929, was transferred again to Benin City via the Colonial Hospital in Lagos. In May 1930 he resumed duty in Warri, and subsequently worked in Sapele, Jos, Lagos, Ibadan, Akure, Ibadan again. With the Timi's death in Ede, John Adetoyese contested for the vacant stool. The contest lasted eleven months, and John Adetoyese won it. He was installed the Timi of Ede on December 13, 1946.

John Adetoyese 'Laoye I is still reigning in Ede. He is a famous drummer and has a famous drum orchestra. He is teaching drumming at the University of Ibadan.

His Highness published his autobiography, entitled *The Story of my Installation,* Ede 1956.

Latino, Juan

Probably born in Guinea in 1516, Juan Latino came to Spain in 1528 at the age of twelve. His mother and he were slaves in the household of Doña Elvira, daughter of Gonzalo Fernández of Cordoba, one of Spain's most famous generals, the "gran Capitán". In 1530 Doña Elvira moved with her household from Baena to Granada; Juan was then fourteen. In Baena he had to fetch the first school books for the third Duke of Sessa, Don Gonzalo Fernández, son of Doña Elvira, who was eight years his junior. He not only fetched the books; he read them, joined in the lessons, and, being much more talented, became his young master's tutor, learning Latin and Greek with him at the Cathedral School and later at the newly founded University of Granada.

Juan was so outstanding at Latin that he renounced his slave-name Juan de Sessa and called himself Juan Latino. In 1546 he got his Bachelor of Arts. Soon he was known throughout the city for his scholarship, but also for his quick wit, pranks and fine voice. He played the organ, lute, guitar "and other strange things", perhaps African ones. The doors of the most elegant houses were open to him, including that of the Duke's estate manager, Don Carlobal, who was a university "licenciate", a councillor and a judge. There the scene occurred which made Juan famous; it was later mentioned by Lope de Vega, and inspired Jiménez de Enciso to write a comedy about it. Juan gave lessons to Don Carlobal's daughter, Doña Ana, and they fell in love with each other. Doña Ana bore him a child, which was christened in 1549 with the name Juana. Juan and Ana got married and had a happy union which produced three other children in 1552, 1556 and 1559.

His academic career was not less successful. In 1556 he graduated at Granada University, and in 1557 became professor there; in 1565 he received the highest honour the University could bestow on him — his Latin address opened the academic year. In 1569 Don John of Austria came to Granada, the subsequent victor of the battle of Lepanto, son of the Emperor

Charles V. He played cards with Juan Latino and Juan's boyhood friend and former master, the Duke of Sessa. Two years later, when Don John won his brillant victory over the Turks, Juan Latino wrote his main work, the *Austrias* (615), which, though written in scholarly form, is like a long African "praise song" for the victor of Lepanto. Works of Juan's appeared in 1573, 1576 and 1585. In 1586, when he was seventy, he gave up his professional chair on health grounds. The date of his death is not quite clear; the years 1606, 1615, 1617, even 1623 are mentioned. His son-in-law, Fuentes, mentions November 20, 1599, as his day of death.

On *Austrias:* "Not a word more nor an idea less, the verses are exact and precise, like fine steel with all the strength yet with all the ductibility and often with inspiration without artifices to give exact tone, measure and softness, but awfully real, the idea of death. The whole book can be summed up as the work of a historian who was also a poet" (Antonio Marin Ocete).

Laye, Camara   Guinea

Born on January 1, 1928, in Kurussa, Guinea, Camara Laye — whose real name is Laye Camara — is the son of a goldsmith. He grew up in his grandmother's compound in Tindican, a "roundé" (area) of Kurussa. He obtained his first education at the Koran school, then at the French school, finally at the Collège Poiret (now Lycée Technique) in Conakry, where he was trained as a mechanic. Through his final examination he won a scholarship to Paris, France, to the Centre-Ecole Automobile where he earned his Certificat d'aptitude professionnelle de l'Automobile, a certificate in car repairing. For eight months he worked at the Simca factories, then at Paris public transport. At the same time he continued studying at evening schools of the Conservatoire National des Arts et Métiers, then at the Ecole technique d'Aéronautique et de Construction automobile to obtain the diploma of Engineering in 1956.

Back in Guinea he worked as an engineer. When Guinea became independent in 1958 Camara Laye was appointed Director of the Centre de Recherches et d'Etudes in the Ministry of Information in Conakry. Since 1964 Camara Laye has been living in exile in Senegal. He is currently a Research Fellow in Islamic Studies at the IFAN Institute (Institut Fondamental de l'Afrique Noire) of the University of Dakar, Senegal.

Camara Laye's first novel, *L'enfant noir* (616), in English *The Dark Child* (616 d), reflects his youth in a traditional society. "Looking back on his childhood from a distance, and having the technical skills European education had to offer, he discovered that these skills had been animated, and had been more closely related to man in his native civilisation" (Janheinz Jahn).

Laye's second novel, *Le regard du roi* (617), in English *The Radiance of the King* (617 b), usually considered an ingenuous allegory about man's search for God, marks the spiritual climax of the anti-colonialist period in African literature. The work reveals the inefficiency of the Western value system when confronted with the African values to which the hero of the novel, a European, is gradually initiated. His third book, *Dramouss* (619), published twelve years later, in English, *A Dream of Africa* (619 b), expresses Camara Laye's disillusionment and his criticism of the development of Guinea. His short stories have appeared in "Black Orpheus", "Présence Africaine", "Paris-Dakar", "Bingo", and other journals and newspapers.

"*L'enfant noir* is an accomplished work which, because of its general perspective and its dramatic structure allows us to apprehend all aspects, whether visible or invisible, of a traditional collectivity" (Bernard Mouralis).

"The rhythmical element adds to the intensity an evocative power, and at the same time keeps the natural diction, the phraseology of the Griot and the pace of Mandingo diction" (Roger Mercier).

"In *The Radiance of the King* Laye ... has written a book which we can read with enjoyment, amusement and keen absorption, but which occupies the mind in such a way that new perceptions keep rising to its surface when the reading is over" (Gerald Moore).

"... it disturbs, it excites, it holds out some promise of a vision that will explain the mystery of our being: but it does not fulfil that promise" (John A. Ramsaran).

"... despite the obvious debt that Laye owes to Kafka, his symbolic novel can also be considered an extended form of the traditional fable and, therefore, to be of African inspiration. A detailed analysis of *Le regard du roi* from this point of view has still to be done, but there are clear indications in the novel that Laye conceived the novel as a synthesis of Kafka and the African folk-tale" (Abiola Irele).

"Laye's vision is a masterful blend of the mythic and the contemporary. In the flight of *Dramouss* and in the tyrant we are afforded both creative and destructive forces, Genesis and Apocalypse. The order is essentially reversed, however, so that we have havoc and death prior to resolution and healing, destruction before creation, Apocalypse before Genesis" (Eric Sellin).

Portrait on Plate VI.

Leshoai, Benjamin Letholoa   South Africa

Born on July 1, 1920, in Bloemfontain, Orange Free State, South Africa, Benjamin Letholoa Leshoai got his teacher's certificate at Healdtown Missionary Institution in 1944. He later studied at Fort Hare University, where he obtained a B.A. in English and Native Administration in 1947. He then taught English at a high school in Pretoria, and was appointed headmaster in 1957. He resigned in 1960 because of a clash with the Department of Bantu Education on a matter of principle. He went to Johannesburg, and became assistant manager of the Union

Artists, promoters of the famous jazz operetta King Kong. In 1963, he left for Zambia and taught English in Ndola. In 1964 he went to the United States and obtained an M.A. degree in Speech and Theatre from the University of Illinois. Returning to Zambia in 1965, he became a lecturer in English at the Mufulira Teacher's College. In 1968 he left for Tanzania where he became lecturer at the Department of Theatre Arts of the University College in Dar es Salaam.

Leshoai's first work, *Masilo's Adventures and Other Stories*, (1705), a collection of traditional tales designed as a school reader, is the first work of creative fiction composed in English by a Sotho writer. It was followed by a short play, *The Wake* (1706), and a collection of three plays, *Wrath of the Ancestors*, 1971.

"He is the first Sotho writer to feel the need to address an international audience directly, and thus to be faced with the crucial dilemma of many African writers today ... Using a Western language, Leshoai has not been able to withstand the temptation of making the story more accessible to the English reader by inserting it into the hackneyed optimistic tradition of European fairy tales" (Albert S. Gérard).

Lima, Santos   Angola

Born about 1935 in Angola, Santos Lima, the son of a low civil servant, spent his childhood in the interior of the country. He had his higher education in Portugal. In 1956 he participated at the First International Congress of Negro Writers and Artists in Paris. He was enlisted in the army, returned to Angola in 1957, became cornet, but deserted the army to join the Liberation Movement in 1961. In 1962 he participated at the Congress of Afro-Asian Writers in Cairo.

His novel, *As sementes da liberdade* (1716), concerned with people and facts, accuses the Portuguese of colonial oppression and shows a world where black and white people suffer under the same system.

"This novel, full of the experience of the writer, with its pains and wounds and sensibilities, extols the sufferings and the revolt of a population yearning for freedom and justice" (Mário da Silva Brito).

Liyong, Taban lo   Uganda

Born in 1938 or 1939 (Taban lo Liyong did not supply specified data) in Gulu, district Acholi, Uganda, Taban lo Liyong was educated at Gulu High School and Sir Samuel Baker School. After graduating from National Teachers College, Kampala, he went to the United States to study Political Science at Howard University and Knoxville College. He received a Master of Fine Arts degree at the writers' workshop at the University of Iowa and was the first African to attend this school. In 1966 he did a graduate course in Washington, D. C. After his return to East Africa in 1968 he was in the Cultural Division of the Institute for Development Studies at the University of Nairobi, doing research work on Lwo and Masai literature. He now has a Tutorial Fellowship and is also lecturer in the English Department.

Liyong has had a rapid output of creative and critical literature in the past three years. His first creative volume was *Fixions & Other Stories* (1295), a collection of short stories, that interlock his American and African experience, but which are mainly African tales retold and transformed. *Eating Chiefs* (1296) is a personal transmutation of Lwo poetry. "My idea has been to create literary works from what anthropologists collected and recorded" (Introduction). *Frantz Fanon's Uneven Ribs*, London 1971, is a collection of poems, that aim at one's prejudices and self-delusion. *The Uniformed Man*, Nairobi 1971, is his most recent individual publication.

The Last Word (SE 365) is a book of literary criticism. The majority of the essays concern African literature, and are a rejection of the philosophy of négritude and related ideas of a special black way of expression. Liyong extended these his views in *Meditations in Limbo*, Nairobi 1970.

Taban lo Liyong has also published articles and verse in "Transition", Kampala, and in the anthologies "Drum Beat", (AE 166) edited by Lennard Okola, and "Faces at Crossroad", edited by the Nairobi University Writers' Workshop, Nairobi 1970.

"Taban has given writers a rude awakening. He is not exemplary himself, but he is prescribing the complex we need to face the competition of the literary world" (Chris L. Wanjala).

Portrait on Plate XV.

Loba, Aké   Ivory Coast

Born on August 15, 1927, in Abobo Baoulé near Abidjan, Ivory Coast, Aké Loba was the last of twelve children. He worked in the fields of his father until he was sent to France in 1945 to learn more about Agriculture. From 1945 to 1947 he worked as a field-hand in Brittany and in the Beauce, later in factories in Paris.

In 1960, when his country became independent, he returned to Ivory Coast to start a new career in the diplomatic service. In 1962 he was attached to the Ivory Coast Embassy in Bonn, Germany, and in 1966 he was at the Embassy in Rome. At present he is in the Ministère d'Etat in Abidjan, Ivory Coast.

Aké Loba is the author of two novels, *Kocoumbo, L'étudiant noir* (621), partly autobiographical, showing the aspirations of Africans travelling to and working in France, and *Les fils de Kouretcha* (622), showing the forces of opposition against the construction of a dam on the river Kouretcha.

For his novel *Kocoumbo*, Aké Loba was awarded the Prix Littéraire de l'Afrique Noire d'expression française.

"Aké Loba is a born writer. He can see and make see. He communicates to the reader what at first sight is the most difficult thing to communicate: the real essence of a singular experience (Guy de Bosschere).

"... Loba jumps from one episode to another, creating an unexpected and unnecessary hiatus in the narrative ... He uses short sentences which follow each other clearly and unambiguously. Unfortunately the effect is often monotonous ... Finally, the Europeans in the novel are with one exception, completely without substance" (Anthony Brench).

Lomami-Tshibamba, Paul   Zaire

Born on July 17, 1914, in Brazzaville, Congo, Paul Lomami-Tshibamba hails from Zaire. His father was a Lulua and his mother a Mugwandi from the area of Libenge. His parents married at the shore of Lake Chad where his father, a soldier in a French "punitive expedition", had met his mother. In 1922 Paul Lomami-Tshibamba came to Kinshasa with his parents. There he had his primary education at the Institute St. Joseph. In 1928 he was admitted to the Collège Saint François Xavier of Bata-Kiéla at the Mayumbe, but had to leave after four years, because he became deaf. Back in Léopoldville, medical treatment bettered his condition, but could not cure him wholly.

He learned typing, entered the Compagnie du Kassai, then became editor of "La Croix du Congo". He left to work at the bureau of the railway of Bas-Congo in Thysville. When this society was taken over by the Otraco company, he entered the service of the General Government. In 1934 he worked at the Public Works Department.

Lomami-Tshibamba contributed to the journal "La Voix du Congolais" and wrote the novel *Ngando* (1174) which was awarded the Literature Prize of the Colonial Fair in Brussels in 1948.

Ngando is the story of a boy who swims in the Stanley Pool and is carried to the underwater spirits by a crocodile. His father hurries to save him, is allowed to take him back under condition that he does not speak a word on the way back. The father fails, and the son is lost forever.

"We must consider Lomami-Tshibamba a great novelist of Black Africa, one of those of whom we have much to learn" (Jean Caillens).

Lopes, Baltasar   Cape Verde Islands

Born in 1907 in Vila da Ribeira Brava on the island São Nicolau of the Cape Verde Islands, Baltasar Lopes, who also used the pen-name Osvaldo Alcantara, has studied Law and Romance Literatures. He became a lawyer and Principal of the Liceu Gil Eanes on the island S. Vicente of the Cape Verde Islands, a position he still holds.

Baltasar Lopes was the founder of the great journal of the Cape Verde Islands, "Claridade" which he edited for thirty-five years, and in which he published his poems and essays. As a philologist, he analysed and described the Cape Verde dialect in his book O *dialecto crioulo de Cabo Verde,* Lisbon, 1957. He collected the Cape Verdean literature in the anthology *Antologia da ficção cabo-verdiana contemporânea* (AW 138). In his novel, *Chiquinho* (623), he shows the great drama of the people of the islands who suffer from draught and hunger and are forced to emigrate to the Americas. In a long cyclical poem, *Romanceiro de São Tomé,* he also hints to the other, more degrading, emigration to the island São Tomé with its exploiting labour conditions.

"*Chiquinho* is a great novel of our modern literature because Baltasar Lopes succeeded in giving into the dramatic history of the islands a dramatic and human intensity which transcends the frame of the islands and wins a large universal significance" (Manuel Ferreira).

"For Baltasar Lopes the poetic form has largely the purpose of exploring the hidden life of the islands, that area of human thought and action which, because of its elusive and intangible quality, escapes the superficial viewer" (Norman Araujo).

Born in 1907 on the island Santo Antão, Cape Verde Islands, Manuel Lopes studied at the University of Coimbra, Portugal. He later lived on the island São Vicente and in the Azores, before settling down in Portugal as a retired telegraph company official.

Already in 1932 he had collaborated with the journal "Claridade", and with the "Almanach Luso-Brasileira de Lembranças". In 1937 he was awarded a prize for his sonnets. He wrote two volumes of poetry, *Poemas de quem ficou* (624) and *Crioulo e otros poemas* (628), a volume of short stories, *O galo que cantou na baía, e outros contos cabo-verdeanos* (626), and two novels, *Chuva braba* (625) and *Os flagelados do vento leste* (627).

"Manuel Lopes, the painter, poet, and novelist . . . rendered the drama of the folk on the island of Santo Antão that is constantly reenacted when the droughts strike" (Gerald M. Moser).

"In depicting (in *Chuva braba*) the grit of his fellow Cape Verdeans, as seen in their fortitudinous reactions to the forms of adversity which assail them in their homespun philosophizing about their suffering, Manuel Lopes does not have any ulterior purpose in mind. Nowhere is there a hint of social reform, although the writer does treat briefly and sparingly the commercial exploitation . . . *Os flagelados do vento leste* is a precious document on the embattled Cape Verdean people, struggling to survive against an inplacable nature" (Norman Araujo).

Lopes da Silva, José   **Cape Verde Islands**

Born in 1872 on the island São Nicolau, Cape Verde Islands, José Lopes da Silva was trained as a teacher. He taught on the Cape Verde Islands and, for some time, in Angola. Then he returned to the island São Vicente where he lived until his death in 1962.

His poetical work is that of a "belated Parnassien" (Gerald M. Moser). He published ten volumes of poetry. Two of them, *Hesperitanas* (631) and *Alma arsinária* (635), consist of more than 400 pages while the others are small: *O berço e a campa* (629), *Jardím des Hespérides (630)*, *Mussolini* (632), *O vandalismo hispano-russo* (633), *Braits* (634), *Saudades da pátria* (636), *Meu preito (637)*, and *Helvétia* (638).

José Lopes da Silva had "a consciousness of a personal role as *the* poet of Cabo Verde; a fundamental detachment from the problems of the archipelago and (an) isolated existence in a dream world of memories and literary evocations" (Norman Araujo).

Lubega, Stephen   Uganda

Born in 1945 in Masaka district, Uganda, Stephen Lubega received his secondary education at Bukalasa Seminary and later joined the National Teacher's College, Kyambogo, where he obtained his teacher's diploma in 1967. Since then he has been teaching English in secondary schools.

Lubega was the first editor of "Student Lines", a literary magazine of the National Teachers' College. Some of his writings have appeared in East African magazines like "Zuka" and "Flamingo", and a number of his poems have been heard over the BBC African Service.

Luthuli, Albert   South Africa

Albert John Luthuli was born in 1898 near Bulawayo, Rhodesia. He spent his early years in the Vryheid district, Natal, South

Africa, and then in the Groutville Reserve. He is the son of a Congregationalist mission interpreter and the nephew of the then elected reigning Chief of the Absemakholweni Zulu tribe. Luthuli was educated at the Groutville mission school, and then proceeded to Adam's College, the American Mission secondary school, where he qualified as a teacher. He stayed on there to teach Zulu History and Literature. Fifteen years later he was asked by the elders of his tribe to fill the vacant position as chief. He accepted after two years and reigned in Groutville for seventeen years.

In 1938 Luthuli travelled to India as a delegate of the Christian Council of South Africa to the International Missionary Council. In 1948 he visited the United States to attend the North American Missionary Conference. He was Chairman of the Congregationalist Churches of the American Board in South Africa, President of the Natal Mission Conference, and Executive Member of the Christian Council of South Africa.

In 1946 Luthuli joined the Native Representative Council and the African National Congress (ANC). He became President of the latter's Natal Provincial Division.

In October 1952 Luthuli was summoned to Pretoria and ordered by the government to resign either from the ANC or from his position as Zulu chief. He refused to do either and consequently was deposed from his position as chief in November 1952. A month later he was elected President-General of the ANC. At the same time he was confined by a government ban to his village for a period of two years. In 1954, as soon as his ban lapsed, he flew to Johannesburg to protest against the Western Area Removal Scheme, by which Africans were forced to leave the suburb of Sophiatown and move to Meadowlands. He was, however, prevented from speaking and served with a further two-year ban. In December 1956 he was arrested on a charge of high treason, but released one year later. In May 1959 he was again banished to his village and banned from all gatherings for five years under the Supression of Communism Act. In March 1960 he was detained under the State of Emergency declared after the massacre in Sharpeville.

Luthuli was awarded the Nobel Peace Prize for 1960 and permitted to travel to Oslo to receive the prize. Back in South Africa he was again confined to his farm in Stanger. He died there on July 21, 1967, reportedly run over by a train.

In his autobiography, *Let My People Go,* (1722), translated into eight languages, Luthuli describes his lifelong nonviolent fight against racial discrimination and injustice in South Africa.

Maddy, Pat Amadu   Sierra Leone

Born on December 27, 1936, in Freetown, Sierra Leone, Pat Amadu Maddy left for France in 1958 and moved to England in 1960. In both countries he studied Literature and Drama. During the 1960's he worked in Britain and Denmark where he produced plays by African writers for the Danish radio. He has also been a producer with Radio Sierra Leone. In 1969 he was responsible for training the Zambian National Dance Group for EXPO '70. He is working as an actor in London and has been in theatre, television and radio productions.

A collection of his plays has appeared under the title *Obasai and Other Plays,* London 1972.

Maimane, Arthur   South Africa

Born in 1932, in South Africa, the son of a minister of the Anglican Church, Arthur Maimane attended St. Peter's Secondary School in Rosettenville. A week following his graduation he began work on a newspaper. His journalistic experience includes work as a cub-reporter, sports editor, feature-writer, sub-editor and layout-man, news editor and political columnist. He soon left South Africa for Tanzania where he was a Reuter's correspondent for East and Central Africa, based in Dar es Salaam. He attended as delegate, the first Conference of African

Writers of English Expression held in June 1962 at Makerere University, Kampala, Uganda. Since 1964 he has been with the BBC, London, working in their newsroom and as a commentator on current affairs.

Some of Maimane's short stories were published in the journal "Transition" and in the anthology "Following the Sun" (AA 173). His radio plays, *The Opportunity* (1746) and *Where the Sun Shines* (1747), were produced by the British Broadcasting Corporation.

Maimo, 'Sankie   Cameroon

'Sankie Maimo was born in Kimbo Town, Nso division, district Bamenda, Western Cameroon. He received his primary education at his home town and his secondary education at the Collège of Sasse in Eastern Cameroon. In 1949 he went to Ibadan University, Nigeria, where he studied English. Later he became a teacher in secondary schools in Western Nigeria.

He returned to Cameroon to be appointed to the Ministry of Health. In 1963 he went to the University of Besançon, France, to study French. From there he returned to take up another appointment in the Ministry of Foreign Affairs in Yaunde.

'Sankie Maimo wrote two plays, *I am Vindicated* (646), *Sov-Mbang, the Sooth-Sayer* (647), in which he interweaves themes of folktale, Biblical story and social satire.

Majara, Simon   Lesotho

Born in 1924 in Thaba-Bosiu, district Maseru, Lesotho, Simon Majara is the author of two novels in Sotho. *O sentse linako* (1750) depicts a boy who runs away from school to enjoy life thoroughly, but finds out, too late, that a good education is the only genuine way to happiness. In *'Makotulo* (1751) "the title heroine is a frivolous and dissatisfied young female, who deserts her husband in the hope of finding excitement and opulence as a prostitute in the Union" (Albert S. Gérard).

Makouta-Mboukou, Jean-Pierre   Congo

Born on July 17, 1929, in Kindamba (Boko), Congo, Jean-Pierre Makouta-Mboukou received his secondary education from 1948 to 1954 at the Collège of Libamba, Cameroon, and from 1955 to 1956 at the Lycée Savorgnan de Brazza in Brazzaville, Congo. Then he went to France where he studied Literature at the University of Grenoble from 1957 to 1960. From 1961 to 1963 he studied at the Sorbonne in Paris and at the Ecole Normale Supérieure of St. Cloud. In 1960 he received his Licence ès Lettres, and in 1961 his Diplôme d'Etudes Supérieures de Lettres Modernes. From 1960 to 1961 he was assistant at the University of Dakar, Senegal, and from 1961 to 1963 in Paris, France. Then he became Assistant Professor at the Centre d'Enseignement Supérieure of Brazzaville, and from 1963 to 1968 he was Deputy of Congo-Brazzaville. In July 1968 he was Plenipotentiary Minister at the Education Conference in Nairobi, Kenya.

On November 21, 1970, his novel, *En quête de la liberté* (1177), was prohibited in Congo-Brazzaville. The author, threatened with arrest, stayed on in Paris where he became appointed Assistant Professor of the Sorbonne. On April 27, 1972, he was elected member of the Board of Directors of the Association des Ecrivains de Langue Française.

Jean-Pierre Makouta-Mboukou published fifteen scholarly articles on Phonetics and Linguistics. His *Introduction à la littérature noire* (N-S 426), includes his reflections on black literature and its tendencies. His short story, *Les initiés* (1176), describes the tragic adventures of an African student in Paris who does not obey the advice of his mother and the Bible. His novel,

En quête de la liberté (1177), is about the spiritual and moral development of an African in search of freedom and hope. His poems, *L'âme bleue,* Yaunde 1971, reflect his involvement with Africa and Christianity.

Malangatana, Valente   Mozambique

Born on June 6, 1936, in Marraçuene, district Lourenço Marques, Mozambique, Goenha Valente Malangatana had no school education. His father was a migrant worker to the gold mines of Johannesburg; his mother sold beads, tattooed and filed teeth. While working as a servant at the Lourenço Marques Club, Valente Malangatana attended night school and began painting "furiously". He was discovered one night by the architect Amançio Guedes who took him into his studio. Since then he has worked both as a decorative artist on architectural schemes and as a painter.

In December 1964 he was arrested for alleged connections to Fremilo. In March 1966 he was released.

In addition to a number of poems which appeared in journals like "Black Orpheus" and in anthologies like "Modern Poetry from Africa" (A 75), he has completed an autobiography.

Malinda, Martial   Congo

Martial Malinda is the pen-name for Sylvain Bemba, born on February 17, 1934, at Sibiti, district Bouenza-Luoéssé, Congo. After finishing his primary and secondary education in 1953 he worked, from 1954 to 1962, as a sports reporter in Brazzaville. In 1955 he also worked on the staff of "Liaison", the journal for the intellectuals of former French Equatorial Africa. He later became Chief Editor of the Agence Congolaise d'Information, the Congolese information service in Brazzaville.

Beginning in 1956 he published short stories in the journal "Petit Journal de Brazzaville". For his short story, *La chambre noire,* he was awarded in 1963 the first prize in the competition organized by the journal "Preuves" in Paris, and his short story, *La mort d'un enfant de la foudre,* won the second prize for short stories organized in 1970 by the journal "Africasia". Sylvain Bemba wrote numerous radio features unter the pseudonym Michel Belvain, and a radio play, *L'Enfer, c'est Orféo,* Paris 1970, which received the third prize at the Concours Théâtral Interafricain in 1969.

Malonga, Jean   Congo

Born on February 2, 1907, in Goma-Tsétsé, near Brazzaville, Jean Malonga entered the school of the missionaries of the Holy Ghost in Brazzaville at the age of ten. In 1920 he was employed by the administration as scribe and interpreter, but fell ill after eight months and was taken back to his village to be cured the traditional way, which lasted ten months. Back in Brazzaville Jean Malonga found employment with the bank and was soon chosen, in 1921, to become Headmaster of the school in Mbamou. But as Malonga was paid only half the salary he had received at the bank, that is 5 Francs instead of 10 Francs he resigned teaching and went back to Brazzaville, this time to find employment with the administration as an apprentice in nursing at the General Hospital. From 1923 to 1925 he worked in Pointe-Noire, but resigned because the authorities refused to make him Caporal (the hospitals at that time being under military rule), as his superiors had proposed. Malonga returned home to his village, but soon found employment again with the Société des Batignolles.

In 1925 Malonga reentered the health service as secretary to the Medical Superintendent in Pointe-Noire. In 1938 he was the winner in a nursing competition, but refused to go to Cameroon for another training as was offered to him.

In 1942 Jean Malonga continued his education. He got his Certificat d'études and entered the P.P.C. (Parti Progressiste Congolais), directed by Félix Tchicaya, in 1947.

In 1948 Malonga was elected Conseiller-Représentatif of the Middle-Congo. The same year he became a member of the Grand Conseil of A.E.F. (Afrique Equatoriale Française) and Senator of Middle Congo. In this function he was in Paris at the Palais du Luxemburg from 1948 to 1955, then returned home and entered the General Hospital in Brazzaville again, this time as staff manager.

When in 1958 broadcasting was introduced in A.E.F., Malonga received training in Paris and became Director of the National Broadcasting on his return to the Congo. In 1966 Jean Malonga retired from the field of public and political affairs.

Jean Malonga published his first article in 1929 in "L'Etoile de A.E.F.", which won him much attention, but his literary ambitions were really wakened only while, being Senator in Paris, he was influenced by Alioune Diop, editor of "Présence Africaine". The result was *Coeur d'Aryenne* (1179), a sentimental love story between a white girl and a black boy, in which Malonga takes a strong anticolonialistic stand. This novel was followed by *La Légende de M'Pfoumou Ma Mazono* (1180), the enterprise to depict the history of a tribe in a novel. A short story, *La Légende de Lafoulakary* appeared in "A.E.F.-Nouvelles", when Malonga was its chief editor.

Mangoaela, Zakea D.   Lesotho

Born in 1883 at Hohobeng, near Palmietfontein, Cape Province, South Africa, of Christian parents, Zakea D. Mangoaela entered school in 1889 in Masitise, Lesotho, where his parents had moved shortly after his birth. He passed the Standard IV examination in 1895, but had to wait until July 1897 to enrol in the Mountain School, because he was too young. He received his teacher's certificate in 1902 and wanted to go on to Lovedale, but couldn't do so because of lack of funds.

In 1903 Mangoaela was appointed teacher and preacher in a backward area of the Maluti Mountains in Lesotho. It was there he wrote a series of three graded Sotho readers, *Lipaliso tsa Sesotho,* long in use in Sotho schools. In 1907 Mangoaela was appointed to the school at Koeneng where Everitt Lechesa Segoete was pastor, and began writing articles and stories for "Leselinyana". In Koeneng Zakea Mangoaele married Berenice Sekokotoana, whose father Bethuel Sekokotoana was the author of several religious tracts.

In 1910 Mangoaela went to Morija to assist Reverend S. Duby in the Book Depot and in the Bible School. He kept the books of the Printing House, did some translation work, and supervised the printing of the journal "Leselinyana". There he wrote *Tsoelopele ea Lesotho* (The Progress of Lesotho) in 1911, an account of the progress of the country under European influence. His only contribution to creative literature is *Har'a libatana le linyamat'sane (1767),* a collection of fifty-four hunting stories. His next volume did not come out until 1921. It was *Lithoko tsa marena a Basotho* (Praises of the Sotho Chiefs), the first collection of Southern Sotho praises to be printed in book form.

"It *(Lithoko tsa marena a Basotho)* was a great step forward in reducing this genre to writing, thereby preserving it and assuring its transmission to later generations. It is on this publication that many a Mosotho poet and writer has had to depend" (Mofolo Bulane).

During those years, Mangoaela also worked with Edouard Jacottet on the *Grammar of the Sesuto Language,* which was edited by C. M. Doke in Johannesburg in 1917. In 1937 he was appointed a member of the Regional Literature Committee for Sotho. From 1954 to 1958 he was the editor of "Leselinyana".

Zakea D. Mangoaela died on October 25, 1963.

Marangwanda, John Weakley   Rhodesia

Born in September 1924 at Katena Kraal, Chiweshe Tribal Trust Land, Mazoe, Rhodesia, Marangwanda went to Howard Mis-

sion School in the Mazoe-District and from 1947 to 1950 to
Goromonzi Secondary School. He holds a Cambridge School
Certificate. He was a teacher at Howard Mission School in 1951,
and in Queque from 1952 to 1953. He was then employed by
an industrial firm in Salisbury. Marangwanda is now working
as Supervisor in the Distribution Department of Air Rhodesia.

Marangwanda is the author of a novel in Shona, *Kumazivan-
dadzoka* (1774).

Mariano, Gabriel   Cape Verde Islands

José Gabriel Lopes da Silva was born in April 1928 in Vila da
Ribeira Brava on the island São Nicolau of the Cape Verde
Islands. All of his writings were published under the pen-name
Gabriel Mariano. He received his secondary education at the
Liceu of the island São Vicente and later studied Law at the
university in Lisbon, Portugal. He has worked as a lawyer
and a civil servant in Lisbon, on the island São Tomé, and also
in the Cape Verde Islands and in Mozambique.

Gabriel Mariano wrote poetry in Portuguese and in Crioulo,
the language of the Cape Verde Islands. His poetry was published in "Claridade" and other local journals like "Cabo
Verde" and, in French translation, in "Présence Africaine" and
"Europa". Some poems were included in the anthologies "Modernos poetos caboverdianos" (AW 130) and "Antologia da
poesia negra de expressão portuguesa" (A 4). He also published
a short story, O *rapaz doente* (649).

In his poems in Crioulo "Mariano has sought to rivet further
attention on the rich folkloric life of the islands, featuring here
local themes and tales of Santiago... In his short stories
Mariano scrutinizes the effects of poverty on the lives of his
fellow islanders. O *rapaz doente* (The Sick Boy) ... is the story
of a boy named Júlio who catches a dreaded disease on São
Tomé and is refused admission to the local hospital because of
the contagious nature of his sickness" (Norman Araujo).

Marshall, Bill   Ghana

Born on May 16, 1936, in Mampong, district Akuapem, Eastern
Region, Ghana, William Okyere Marshall is the son of parents
from Larteh. After his secondary education in Accra where he
was brought up, he worked for a short time at the Ministry of
Education and some years as a laboratory technician at the
Medical Research Institute in Accra. Then he left for the United
Kingdom to study English and Drama at the Guildhall School
of Music in London. During this period he acted in a number of
plays.

In 1965 Bill Marshall was invited to the Mac Dowell Colony
in the United States where he wrote his play, *The Son of
Umbele*.

Some time after the coup of 1966 in Ghana Bill Marshall
returned to his native country and joined the Television Service
of the Ghana Broadcasting Corporation, producing and directing drama. He still holds this position today.

Bill Marshall has written several plays for both the Ghana
Broadcasting Corporation radio and television. He is the creator
of the "infamous" character, Tuli Blanco, in a popular series,
"The Blanko Diary" which appears in a local weekly. Of his
plays, *A Matter of Class, Midnight Strangers, No Time For
Tears, Strange Neighbours, A Rose in My Town*, and others, only
Stranger to Innocence and *A Shadow of an Eagle* have appeared
in print, both in one volume from Ghana Publishing Corporation in 1969.

Martins, Ovídio de Sousa   Cape Verde Islands

Born on September, 17, 1928, on the island São Vicente Cape,
Verde Islands, Ovídio de Sousa Martins studied in Lisbon and
is still living there.

He has published a volume of poetry, *Caminhada* (651),
and a short story, *Tutchinha* (652).

"Ovídio Martins, in his volume *Tutchinha,* reveals himself to us as a narrator awake to the reality around him and as a subtle analyst of the human sentiments which move his people in the climate of his islands ..." (Amândio César).

"The poem *The Hour* by Ovídio Martins ... shows the definite position taken and the degree of spiritual maturity reached by the group of the 'new generation'" (Onesimo da Silveira).

Martinson, Andrews Pardon Adu   Ghana

Born on February 17, 1900, at Nkwatia, near Abetifi, Ghana, Andrews Pardon Adu Martinson grew up at Aburi. From 1906 to 1912 he went to school at Kumasi, from 1913 to 1916 to Akropong Middle School, from 1916 to 1918 to Akropong Training College, and from 1919 to 1920 to the Theological Seminary at Abetifi.

He then was a teacher, from 1920 to 1928 in Kumasi, 1928 at Adukrum, from 1929 to 1934 at the Teacher Training College at Akropong, from 1935 to 1937 at Kumasi, from 1938 to 1939 at Anum, from 1940 to 1942 at Aburi, from 1943 to 1945 at Apapem, from 1945 to 1948 at Amanokrom, from 1949 to 1953 at Awisa, from 1953 to 1958 at Larteh. From 1953 to 1958 he was at the same time Supervisor of Schools. From 1960 to 1961 he taught at the Theological Seminary at Abetifi. In 1962 he joined the editorial staff of the Presbyterian Book Depot and the Waterville Publishing House in Accra.

His story *Adwowa Dwontofo* (653), written in Akuapem-Twi, was published in 1964.

Masegabio, Philippe   Zaire

Born on July 14, 1944, in Bosu-Manzi near Lisala, province Equateur, Zaire, Philippe Masegabio studied Romance Philology at the University Lovanium. He published a volume of poetry, *Somme première* (1182).

"The merit of the poet consists in having given to those words a soul in which tenderness, irony and humour are neighbours" (Dieudonné Kadima-Nzuji).

Masiye, Andreya Sylvester   Zambia

Born on December 30, 1922, at Chamata Village, Chipata, Eastern Province, Zambia, Andreya Masiye, who also spells his first name Andereya, Anderea, and Andrea, was educated at Msoro Mission and Munali High School in Zambia. He then went to Kenya, to the East African Army Education Centre (EAAEC), where he edited a bilingual weekly for East African soldiers. He also worked at the radio in Kenya and Tanganyika. He was at the Army College in Egypt and at the Army School of Education at Bodin, in Great Britain. His last rank in the Army was Warrant Officer A 1.

After his return to Zambia he worked as a journalist and became famous for his radio series "Kubvulumvulu" (Whirl-wind). From 1964 to 1966 he was Deputy Head of Administration of the Zambia Broadcasting Corporation (ZBC), from 1967 to 1968 Permanent Secretary in the Ministry of Information and Postal Services, from 1968 to 1970 Permanent Secretary for Defence in the Office of the President, and from 1970 to 1971 Minister of State for Information, Broadcasting and Tourism. Since 1971 he has been Zambia's High Commissioner to Nigeria, in Lagos.

Andreya Sylvester Masiye published two volumes of short stories, one in Nyanja, *Tsoka Ndi Mwai* (1785), and one in English, *The Lonely Village* (1784), a collection of broadcast talks on the African way of life, *Kubvulumvulu,* London 1959, and a novel, *Before Dawn* (1786), dealing with cultural conflicts in a headman's village in the Chiparamba valley of Eastern Zambia.

Massaki, André   Angola

Born on February 25, 1923, at Kikaka near Lembe in the Province Maquela de Zombo, Angola, André Massaki grew up in Congo-Kinshasa. From 1932 to 1937 he had his primary education at Matadi, then from 1937 to 1939 at the B.M.S. Mission at Ngombe-Lutete near Thysville. From 1939 to 1941 he was pupil-teacher at Ngombe-Lutete and from 1941 to 1942 at Matadi; from 1942 to 1956 he was clerk at several commercial enterprises in Matadi and Kinshasa; from 1956 to 1962 he was working as editor in the publishing houses Envol and Sikama in Kinshasa. Since March 15, 1963, he has been editor and director of the journal "Moyo".

On December 23, 1956, he founded a society of mutual assistance which in 1960, after the independence of Congo Kinshasa, became a liberation movement for Angola: the Democratic Party of Angola (P.D.A.). André Massaki was the President of this Party from the beginning up to the elections of December 13, 1964, when he refused to run for office again. But he remained its Honorary President. In 1961 he was a delegate of his party to Europe. He is also President of the National Council of the F.N.L.A. (Frente Nacional de Libertação de Angola), the main tool of the G.R.A.E. (Revolutionary Government of Angola in Exile).

Besides his political activities, André Massaki is a public secretary who helps everybody who is in need of his help, he is a radio announcer for Protestant programs, and he is a lay evangelist in different Protestant churches at the request of the minister.

Beside his mother-tongue Kikongo, Massaki speaks the languages Kituba, Lingala and French which he studied from 1968 to 1970 at Lausanne, Switzerland. He can read Portuguese but has no practice to speak it. He is learning English at the evening school of the American Embassy in Kinshasa.

André Massaki wrote several pamphlets on Christian instruction. His two volumes of stories, *Mwan'a nsiona* (1183) and *Nzambi muna nkia kanda kvwilu?* (1184), deal with Christian problems. They were written in Kikongo and have been translated into Lingala and Kituba.

Massida, Denise-Esmeralda

Denise-Esmeralda Massida is a French poet from Corsica, delegate to Ivory Coast and Francophone Countries of the Société des Poètes et Artistes de France. Her poetry is inspired by her stay in West Africa.

Matiba, Jean Ikelle
vid. *Ikelle-Matiba, Jean*

Matip, Benjamin   Cameroon

Benjamin Matip was born on May 15, 1932, in Son-Mandeng near Eséka, district Nyong et Kélé, Cameroon. He had his primary education at the mission school in Eséka, his secondary education at Lycée Leclerc in Yaunde. He then studied Law at the university in Paris, France. He is a lawyer, the Doyen of the Conseil National Provisoire du Barreau of Cameroon in Duala.

His novel, *Afrique, nous t'ignorons!* (655), shows the anti-colonial attitude of the young generation in a Cameroon village in 1939. In his collection of short stories, *A la belle étoile* (656), he ironically introduces modern concepts into a subject matter taken from oral tales. His play, *Le jugement suprème* (657), has only been partly published in the journal "Abbia". His book, *Heurts et malheurs des rapports Europe-Afrique Noire dans l'histoire moderne*, Paris 1959 is a political treatise.

"The youth which is described to us by Benjamin Matip does

213

not live anymore in an oasis of exotical charm ... but in a world of effort and struggle ... The tone is powerful and never falls into sermon" (David Diop).

Matsepe, Oliver Kgadime   South Africa

Born on March 26, 1932, at Brakfontein, also known as Chief Hlakudi Location, in the Nebo area Transvaal, South Africa, as son of a policeman, Oliver Kgadime Matsepe was educated at the Phokwane United Christian School in Nebo, where he passed his Standard VI in 1949. He proceeded to Botshabelo High School, a German missionary school, and passed his Standard IX in 1953. From 1954 to 1955 he was at Kilnerton High School where he passed his matriculation.

From 1956 to 1963 Oliver Kgadime Matsepe was employed by the Magistrate of Nebo, District Middelburg, Transvaal. With his savings he started a general dealer's business at Chief Boleu Matsepe's farm in Eensgevonden, but as his shop was burgled twice with all soft goods stolen, Matsepe was obliged to start from scratch and seek employment again with the Magistrate in Nebo.

Oliver Kgadime Matsepe has published five books in Northern Sotho: *Sebata-kgomo* (1796), *Kgorong ya mošate* (1797), *Lesita-phiri* (1798), *Megokgo ya bjoko* (1799), and *Molodi wa mogami* (1800). In 1964 he was awarded the Samuel-Mqhayi-Prize by the South African Government.

Matshikiza, Todd   South Africa

Born around 1920 in Queenstown, Cape Province, South Africa, Todd Matshikiza went to St. Peter's School in Rosettenville and to a teachers' training college. He worked as a teacher, waiter, clerk, assistant in a book shop and at a hair dresser's. He was a journalist and for some time he was assistant news-editor and art-critic of the Sunday paper "Post".

Brought up in a musical family, Matshikiza was mainly a musician and composer. Among his many choral and orchestral works the musicals, "King Kong" and "Makubane", the latter for which Alan Paton wrote the words, have reached outstanding fame.

In 1960 Matshikiza emigrated to London. In 1964 he went to Zambia, to work for the broadcasting company in Lusaka. He died in March 1968 in Zambia.

Matshikiza's only novel, *Chocolates for my Wife* (1802), which makes use of his experiences in South Africa and England, was banned in South Africa in 1961, probably because "Matshikiza laughs at the policeman even while he fears him; and the danger is that he may provoke laughter in several quarters, which is much worse.

Todd Matshikiza is at his best when he relates anecdotes from his South African experiences. His writing then shows something of what we were used to seeing in his journalism in South Africa: jazzy staccato, the sound of whip-cracks and a characteristic, sudden and outrageous twist of prose to suit his needs. All these are produced by the cross-currents of jazz, the literature of jazz, Negro literature and the South African experience that runs in the writer's veins" (Ezekiel Mphahlele).

Matta, Joaquim Dias Cordeiro da   Angola

Born on December 25, 1857, in Cabiri, at Rio Bengo, district Luanda, Angola, Joaquim Dias Cordeiro da Matta was a sales clerk in Luanda in 1873. Later he had his own business in Barra do Cuanza. He owned a small boat for the transport of building material from Barra do Cuanza to Luanda, and was Commander of the first division of the district of Calumbo. He died in Luanda on March 2, 1894.

He wrote love poetry when he was young, *Delirios* (1904), then his interest concentrated on Luanda folklore. He collected over 700 proverbs in Kimbundu, *Philosophia popular em provérbios angolenses*, Lisbon 1891. The following year he produced a Kimbundu grammar, and in 1893 a Kimbundu dictionary, in the writing of these works he was assisted by the Swiss missionary Héli Chatelain. His work was dedicated to his fellow countrymen "as an incitement to the study of Kimbundu and Angolan traditions". He collaborated with many journals, such as "O Mercantil", "O Pharol do Povo", "O Futuro d'Angola" and "O Polícia Africano".

Matthews, James   South Africa

Born in 1929 in Cape Town, Cape Province, South Africa, James Matthews is the eldest son of a poor family with many children. As a school boy he had to sell newspapers. He went to a secondary school. He was a messenger, journalist, collaborating with the journals "Africa South" and "Drum", and is at present a receptionist.

James Matthews' short stories have been published in anthologies and journals in Africa, Europe and USA. Four of them are contained in the anthology "Quartet" (AA 195), fifteen of his short stories were united in a volume which was published in Swedish, "Azikwelwa" (1805). Also in Sweden, and only there, appeared his novel, *Mary, Billy, Cyril, John och Joseph* (1806).

Maunick, Edouard J.   Mauritius

Born on September 23, 1931, on the Isle of Mauritius, Edouard Joseph Marc Maunick was a librarian at the Municipal Library in Port-Louis. He lives now in Paris, working with Coopération Radiophonique.

Maunick has published four volumes of verse: *Ces oiseaux du sang* (1307), *Les manèges de la mer* (1308), *Mascaret ou Le livre de la mer et de la mort* (1309), and *Fusillez-moi* (1310).

"He writes with an authority that puts him in the forefront of a new generation of Negro poets writing in French" (Ellen Conroy Kennedy).

Portrait on Plate XVI.

Maxwell, Highbred   Nigeria

Highbred Maxwell is no author but an Onitsha market publisher. He gave his name to be used as a pen-name by quite a number of different, mostly very young Onitsha market writers. He wanted his name to be a kind of trademark for the texts of his printing press. The publishing house was called Students' Own Bookshop.

The different "novels", though having different authors, centre round one subject, the relations between boys and girls, and they give strategic and moral advice, as reflected in titles like *Our Modern Ladies (!) Characters Towards Boys* (661), *Public Opinion on Lovers* (662), *Wonders Shall Never End* (663), *Forget Me Not* (664), *Guides For Engagement*, Onitsha 1960.

Mazrui, Ali A.   Kenya

Ali Al'Amin Mazrui was born in 1933 in Mombasa, Coast Province, Kenya. He was educated at the Government Boys School, Mombasa, at Huddersfield College of Technology, Yorkshire, England, and at the University of Manchester. He obtained an M. A. at Columbia University, New York, USA, and a Ph. D. at Nuffield College, Oxford, England. He has also been a Rockefeller Foundation Fellow and Visiting Professorial Scholar at the Universities of Chicago and of California in Los Angeles, at Harvard at Cambridge, Massachusetts, at Singapore, and at the Indian School of International Studies in New Delhi, India. In 1965 he was appointed Professor and Head of the Department of Political Science at Makerere University College, Kampala, Uganda.

Ali A. Mazrui has published many essays in journals like "Transition", "Black Orpheus", "Présence Africaine" etc. His essays have been collected in several volumes, *The Anglo-African Commonwealth*, Oxford 1967, *On Heroes and Uhuru-Worship*, London 1967, *Towards a Pax Africana*, London 1967, *Violence and Thought*, London 1969. His novel, *The Trial of Christopher Okigbo*, London 1971, takes place in After-Africa, a paradise where Africans go when they die.

"The book is entertaining to read, and in places witty" (Kaye Whiteman).

M'Bague, Louis-Marie Pouka
vid. *Pouka-M'Bague, Louis-Marie*

M'Baye, Annette   Senegal

Born on December 15, 1926, in Sokone, region Sine-Saloum, Senegal, Annette M'Baye d'Erneville had her primary and secondary education at the Institution-Saint-Joseph-de-Cluny in Saint-Louis. From 1942 to 1945 she studied at the Ecole Normale d'Institutrices in Rufisque. From 1945 to 1946 she was General Superintendent at the Ecole Normale in Rufisque. The following year, from 1946 to 1947, she had the same post at the Collège Ahmet Fall in Saint-Louis. She then went to Paris to further her studies. She attended Lycée Jules Ferry in Paris from 1947 to 1948, and the Ecole Normale des Batignolles in Paris from 1948 to 1950. During the latter half of her studies, from 1949 to 1950, she was also a teacher in Montrouge, Seine. In 1955 she studied at OCORA (Office de Coopération radiophonique), Paris, and from 1957 to 1958 she was a teacher in her home town Sokone, Senegal, at the same time being headmistress of the school in Diourbel.

Annette M'Baye (also spelt Mbaye) then entered journalism. She worked as reporter for the magazine "Elle", then as freelance journalist for "Bingo" and "La Vie Africaine".

In 1960 Annette M'Baye became commissary of the Regional Information in Diourbel, and in 1963, assistant to the head of the Regional Centres of Information. The same year she founded and edited the women's magazine "Awa", which she still edits. She is simultaneously Programme Director of Radio Senegal and works as a freelance journalist for "Jeune Afrique" and "Soleil".

Annette M'Baye is a member of the Associations nationales des Journalistes Sénégalais, and member of the Senegalese section of the Société Africaine de Culture.

She has published *Poèmes africains* (667), and *Kaddu* (668), which was awarded a prize in 1964 by Poètes Sénégalais de Langue Française. Her story, *La bague de cuivre et d'argent,* won her a prize by "Jeune Afrique". A novel, *La vaine pâture,* and poems for children, *Chanson pour Laïty,* are in preparation.

Mbiti, John Samuel   Kenya

Born on November 30, 1931, in Kitui, Eastern Province, Kenya, John Samuel Mbiti had his first education at mission schools in his home town. From 1950 to 1955 he studied History, English, Geography and Sociology, but also Art and Theology at Makerere University, Kampala, Uganda. From 1954 to 1957, after his B. A., he went to the Providence Barrington Bible College in Providence, Rhode Island, USA, to continue his theological education. He preached in American churches. On his way back home, he travelled through Europe. In 1958 he worked as missionary among his Kamba people, then from 1959 to 1960, continued his studies, at Selly Oak College in Birmingham, England, and from 1961 to 1962 at Westminster College, Cambridge, England. In 1965 he became Lecturer for the New Testament and African traditional religions at the Department of Religious Studies of Makerere University, Kampala, Uganda. From 1966 to 1967 he was Visiting Professor at the University of Hamburg, Germany. Since 1968 he has been Professor of Religious Studies at Makerere.

John Samuel Mbiti's three major books deal with religion: *African Religions and Philosophy*, London 1969, *Concepts of God in Africa*, London 1970, and *New Testament Eschatology in an African Background*, London 1971. He retold traditional stories of his Kamba people in Kamba language, *Mŭtŭnga na ngewa yake* (1311), and he wrote a volume of poetry in English, *Poems of Nature and Faith* (1312). "John Mbiti's poems show a deep religious zeal; he has a great yearning for his God but expresses himself through objects of the earth" (Chris W. Wanjala).

Mboukou, Jean-Pierre Makouta
vid. *Makouta-Mboukou, Jean-Pierre*

Mbumua, William Eteki'a   Cameroon

Born on October 20, 1933, in Duala, Cameroon, William Eteki'a Mbumua had his primary education in Cameroon. In 1947 he left for France for his secondary and university education. In 1957 he became Licencié en Droit, and in 1959 Diplomé d'Etudes Supérieures in Political Science. The same year he left the Ecole Nationale de la France d'Outre-Mer as administrator.

In 1960 Mbumua was Préfet of the district Sanaga-Maritime. In June 1961 he was appointed Minister of National Education,

Culture, Sport and Youth, and held this post till January 1968. From 1962 to 1969 he was a member of the political bureau of the Union Nationale Camerounaise.

In 1962 Mbumua was a member of the Executive Council of UNESCO, and became its Vice President in 1966. In 1966 he was chosen President of the 15th session of the general conference of UNESCO.

Mbumua's volume, *Un certain humanism*, Yaunde 1971, collects some of his speeches and papers "as contribution to the triumph of a new humanism".

Medou Mvomo, Rémy   Cameroon

Born on December 25, 1938, at Nkpwang, near Sangmelima, district Dja et Lobo, Cameroon, Rémy Medou Mvomo received his primary and secondary education in France. Four years thereof he spent in the Massif Central. In 1963 he began his studies at the Faculty of Law of the University of Yaunde, Cameroon, but he dropped them to become a journalist.

His novel, *Afrika Ba'a* (692), set in southern Cameroon, is the story of a young man going to town and returning to his village. His second novel, *Mon amour en noir et blanc*, Yaunde 1971, centres around an interracial love story in the Massif Central of France.

Menga, Guy   Congo

Born in 1935 at Mankonongo, a village on the river Foulakari, district Pool, south of Brazzaville, Congo, Gaston Guy Birouta-Menga — this is his full name — had his primary and secondary education at Brazzaville, from 1945 to 1951 in the catholic school of St. Joseph, from 1951 to 1956 in the Lycée Catholique Cheminade.

From 1956 to 1961 he was assistant teacher. From 1961 to 1962 he was trained in journalism at OCORA (Office de Coopération Radiophonique), Paris, and worked with Radiodiffusion Congolaise in Brazzaville after his return. After his second course at OCORA, from 1963 to 1964, he directed programmes of Radiodiffusion Télévision Congolais, to become Director of this station in 1967. He has been working there since 1968 as Animator or Director of Programmes.

His play, *La marmite de Koko-Mbala* (1186), was presented at the First Festival of the Negro Arts in Dakar, 1966. His second play, *L'oracle* (1188), got the Grand Prix du Concours Théâtral Interafricain 1967/68 and was performed in the Studio des Champs-Elysées, Paris, in January 1969. His novel, *La palabre stérile* (1187), received the Grand Prix de l'Afrique Noire in 1969. A new play, *Okouele,* had its premiere in Brazzaville in March 1971.

Portrait on Plate XIV.

Menkiti, Ifeanyi   Nigeria

Born in 1940 in Onitsha, East Central State, Nigeria, Ifeanyi Menkiti attended Christ the King College, Onitsha. In 1964 he took a B. A. degree in Literature and Philosophy at Pomona College, Claremont, California, USA. His thesis on the poetry of Ezra Pound won the F. S. Jennings Distinguished Senior Thesis Award. In 1965 he took an M. A. degree in Journalism from Columbia University in New York City, and in 1968 an M. A. in Philosophy from New York University. In 1972 he is completing a Ph. D. in Philosophy at Harvard University, Cambridge, Massachusetts.

Ifeanyi Menkiti has taught African Literature at Bryant and Stratton Junior College in Boston from 1969 to 1971, at Northwestern University, Evanston, Illinois, in summer 1969, and at the University of Massachusetts in Boston from 1971 to 1972.

Menkiti's poetry has been published in many journals like

"Transition", "Nigeria Magazine", "African Arts", "Pan African Journal", "Sewanee Review", "Evergreen Review", "Chelsea", "Stony Brook", "Bitterroot", "Journal of Black Poetry", "Liberator", and others, and has been anthologized in "Contemporary African Literature", New York 1972, "The Word Is Here", New York 1972, and "Open Poetry", New York 1972. A collection of his poetry, *Affirmations,* was published in Chicago in 1971.

Mensah, Albert W. Kayper
vid. *Kayper-Mensah, Albert William*

Mezu, Sebastian Okechukwu   Nigeria

Born on April 30, 1941, at Ezeogba near Emekuku, Owerri Province, East Central State, Nigeria, Mezu went to Christ the King School, Amaimo near Ikeduri from 1947 to 1948, and to Our Lady of Mount Carmel School, Emekuku near Owerri, from 1949 to 1952. Because of a double promotion he spent only six of the normal eight years in Elementary School, then went to Holy Ghost Junior Scholasticate, Ihiala, from 1953 to 1956, and to Holy Ghost Secondary School, Owerri, from 1957 to 1958, where he got his West African (Cambridge) School Certificate in 1958. Mezu continued at the Holy Family College, Abak, in 1959 and got his Cambridge University Higher School Certificate in 1960.

In 1961 Mezu enrolled with the College of Arts and Sciences Georgetown University, Washington D. C., to study French and Philosophy, obtaining his B. A. degree in 1964. He continued his studies at Graduate School of Arts and Sciences, the Johns Hopkins University, Baltimore, Maryland, from 1964 to 1967, obtaining his M. A. in French and Spanish in 1966. At the same time he did a correspondence course in Law at La Salle

Extension University Law School, Chicago, Illinois, and got his LL.B. (Bachelor of Law) in 1966. He left for Paris the same year to complete research for his Ph.D. at the Ecole Pratique des Hautes Etudes, Sorbonne, as part of a Johns Hopkins University Doctoral Programme. He got his Ph.D. in 1967 at the Johns Hopkins University, Baltimore, Maryland, with a thesis on Léopold Sédar Senghor.

During the Nigerian Civil War Mezu held various posts in the Biafran Government. He was the co-founder and Deputy Director of the Biafra Historical Research Centre, Representative to Ivory Coast and Chargé d'affaires in Ghana and French-speaking West Africa, and also a Biafran delegate to various peace talks in Niamey and Addis Abeba.

Sebastian Okechukwu Mezu is now Associate Professor, French Department, State University of New York in Buffalo, USA. In December 1969 he founded the publishing house Black Academy Press in Buffalo, in which, until summer 1972, twenty-two African and Afro-American essayistic books appeared. He is editor and publisher of the "Black Academy Review", a quarterly of the black world, the first issue of which came out in spring 1970.

Mezu, who speaks Igbo, English, French, Spanish, and German, is known both as a scholarly and a creative writer. He has contributed to various journals such as "Abbia", "The Conch", "Journal of the New African Literature and the Arts", "France-Eurafrique", and "Afrique Littéraire et Artistique". He is the author of an extensive study of Senghor's works, *Léopold Sédar Senghor et la défense et illustration de la civilisation noire* (1006), translated also into English under the title, *The Literary Works of Senghor*, London 1971.

His creative writing includes a volume of poetry, *The Tropical Dawn* (671), and a novel on the Biafran War, *Behind the Rising Sun*, London 1971. This novel opens the post-war period of Nigerian literature. In its precise observation of the political afflictions of Biafran functionaries in Europe and of the sufferings and the beliefs of peoples and soldiers on both fighting sides, Mezu's novel demonstrates that neither corruption nor humanity

Ama Ata Aidoo

Abioseh Nicol

PLATE IX

Raymond Sarif Easmon

Amos Tutuola

Wole Soyinka

Duro Lapido

PLATE X

Kola Ogunmola

John Pepper Clark

could be found in one party alone. *Behind the Rising Sun* is a contribution to inter-Nigerian understanding and reconciliation.

Portrait on Plate XI.

Mikanza, Norbert   Zaire

Born on April 19, 1944, in Mbelo, district Bandundu, Zaire, Norbert Mikanza was educated in Kinzambi and Kikwit, where he had specialized in literature at the Institut Saint Jean-Bosco. He left in 1964 and went to Belgium to study Literature and History. Back in Zaire he taught French and History at the Institut Saint Jean-Bosco. In October 1969 he founded an amateur theatre group " Le théâtre du Petit Nègre", which devoted itself to the propagation of the new African theatre. Norbert Mikanza is now Director of the Théâtre National Congolais, which he founded.

He is co-author of the play *Pas de feu pour les antilopes*, Kinshasa 1970, with Paul Mushiete.

Misipo, Dualla   Cameroon

According to his autobiographical text, *Der Junge aus Duala* (680), written in German, and printed in Frankfurt-on-Main in 1930, Dualla Misipo was born about the beginning of this century in Duala, Cameroon, where he went to a German school. He then continued his education at Giessen, Germany, where he graduated and became a medical doctor. When the Nazis took over in Germany, Dr. Misipo left for Paris, France, where he worked in hospitals and gave private lessons in German. Dr. Misipo, recently very ill, did not want to supply his biographical data, and would prefer not to be included in this volume. His narrative, *Korrongo* (681), written in German, is based on an epic legend about the Waganna empire, supposedly having spread from the Benue valley from the 12th to the 14th century.

Mncwango, Leon(h)ard L. J. South Africa

Born on October 28, 1926, at Thokazi, near Nongoma, Natal, South Africa, Leon(h)ard Litha Jotham Mncwango — this is his full name, the initials being derived from his father's and his mother's name — left his birth place in 1933, a day after his father's death, to live with his maternal grandmother at Mapopoma, some thirty miles away. There, in 1934, he attended primary school for about six months. He was then sent to Christ King School, now renamed Nkosiyethu, at Nongoma, where he found a sponsor in the Reverend Erasmus Betz who paid his school fees under the condition that he learned Latin. In 1942 Mncwango left Christ King School and proceeded to Impumelelo Higher Primary, some thirty miles from Nongoma, but left again after a year, at the instigation of the Reverend Betz, to continue at Inkamana High School, formerly St. Joseph's College. After two years he was transferred to St. Francis' High School in Mariannhill, Natal, where he matriculated in 1948.

In 1949 Mncwango went to Pius XII College, now a university, in Lesotho, to study for the Bachelor of Arts degree. In December that same year he left for Durban. He registered with the University of Natal and found employment with the timber merchants. After four months he found a post as a clerk with the Bantu Administration in Durban, but in 1951 was transferred to another department where he was assistant librarian, a job he kept over fourteen years. Mncwango is now teaching at Thokazi Bantu School at Toggekry, Natal.

In the field of drama Mncwango "has contributed more than any single playwright in this field" (D. B. Z. Ntuli). His first drama, *Manhla iyokwendela egodini* (1831), written while at college in Lesotho and meant to impress a lady student, is a love tragedy, in which both the girl and the rival die, while the suitor, who caused their death, becomes insane. *Kusasa umgcwabo wakho nami* (1832) deals with tuberculosis among the Africans in the urban areas and the slums of South Africa. *Ngenzeni?* (1833) depicts life during the times of Shaka, the great Zulu king, and has been prescribed as a school book ever since its publication. Besides these plays in his mother tongue Zulu Mncwango has produced two books in English, which have not yet been published.

Modisane, Bloke   South Africa

Born on August 28, 1923, in Sophiatown, Johannesburg, William Modisane — this is his real name — saw during his childhood one of his sisters die of starvation and his father battered to death. After a primary and some years of secondary education he was reporter, feature writer, theatre and music critic for "Drum" publications, a white-owned magazine sympathetic to Africans. As an actor, he appeared in a number of productions which included the play "No Good Friday" and the secretly made film "Come Back Africa" on African locations. In 1959 he left South Africa for England, as a refugee via Rhodesia. In England he has appeared in a number of stage and television productions which include "The Blacks" at the Royal Court Theatre and "Waiting for Wenda" on BBC. In the spring of 1963 he undertook a lecture tour of America on African music and literature.

Bloke Modisane has written many articles for "Drum" and the "Golden City Post". His short story, *The Situation,* won the first prize of the Mbari competition and of the Alban Writers Club. His book, *Blame Me On History* (1836), is the reconstruction of his life seen from a point in time that saw the destruction of his home town and his decision soon after to leave South Africa. His short story, *The Dignity of Begging,* has been widely anthologized.

"The handwriting on the wall of a horrible, immediate catastrophy speaks out of every page of *Blame Me on History*" (G. Pracher).

Portrait on Plate III.

Modupe, Prince   Guinea

Born in about 1903 in, then, French Guinea as the son of a Yoruba merchant and a Susu princess, Prince Modupe went to America, via Sierra Leone, and settled down in Los Angeles, where he married. After the publication of his autobiographical novel, *I Was a Savage* (682), American title, *A Royal African,* written in English and presented by Elspeth Huxley, he did not write any further works and could not be traced.

Mofolo, Thomas   Lesotho

Born on December 22, 1876, (as the parish register of Hermone shows and not in August 1877 as he himself believes) in Khojane, province Mafeteng, Lesotho, Thomas Mokopu Mofolo, the son of Christian parents, was baptised on September 30, 1877. In 1880 his parents moved to the fertile Qomoqomong valley, Quthing district, where Mofolo herded his father's cattle and attended elementary school when he could. His teacher was Everitt Lechesa Segoete, who was later to appear in one of his novels. Mofolo then attended school in Matatiele, then left for Morija, where he became a houseboy in the service of the Reverend Alfred Casalis, who was the head of the Bible School, the printing press and the Book Depot. He entered the Bible School in 1894, and the Teacher Training College in 1896, but had to leave after two years when his money ran out. He was able to return though and resume his studies on credit. He obtained a teacher's certificate in 1898, and started working for the

Reverend Casalis at the printing press and the Book Depot in 1899. But at the end of the year, the Anglo-Boer war put an end to the publishing activities of the mission. Mofolo left Morija and went to Leloaleng, Quthing district, where he was trained as a carpenter at the Leloaleng Technical School for two years. He then entered teaching, first at Leloaleng, then at the Bensonvale Institution, Cape Province, and subsequently at the Maseru mission school, Lesotho. In 1904 he returned to Morija as secretary to the Reverend Casalis and proofreader for the press.

While working at the printing press, Mofolo was strongly encouraged by the missionaries to write. He produced "an absolutely original work of imagination", his novel *Moeti oa bochabela* (1842), first serialized in the newspaper "Leselinyana" and translated also into English under the title *The Traveller of the East* (1842 a). It is a Christian tract, a quest story set in Lesotho, in which the hero, Fekesi, wanders from the darkness of Africa to the light of the Christian faith.

Mofolo next embarked on a second novel, which, according to Le Livre d'or de la mission du Lessouto, Paris 1912, was to have the title *L'Ange déchu* (The Fallen Angel, Sotho title unknown), but which was never published.

Mofolo's second published novel was *Pitseng* (1843), the name of a village in the Leribe district. It was also serialized in "Leselinyana" before it appeared in book form. *Pitseng* is a love story between two teachers, in which Mofolo, contrary to his earlier identification with Christian ideals, strongly emphasizes the contrast between this ideal and actual behaviour among Christians, both black and white. One of the chief characters, in the book, the Reverend Katse, is a portrait of Mofolo's teacher Everitt Lechesa Segoete.

Around 1909 Mofolo travelled through Natal on bicycle to gather material for his third novel, *Chaka* (1844), translated also into English under the title *Chaka, an Historical Romance* (1844 b). "At Mogungundlovu, the capital of the former Zulu nation (today Pietermaritzburg), Mofolo was welcomed and fêted, an ox was slaughtered in his honour, and a hut for him was erected by order of the Chief" (Daniel Kunene/Ronald Kirsch). Mofolo visited Shaka's grave and observed the ceremonies of the Zulu people. The manuscript was submitted in 1911 or 1912, but rejected by the missionaries. It was finally published in 1925.

Chaka recounts historical events in the life of the great Zulu king and founder of the Zulu nation, but Mofolo interprets Shaka's life from an essentially ethical view. Shaka's development from innocence to evil and crime is directed and dictated by Isanusi, a witch-doctor and the personified principle of evil.

After a brief stay in South Africa, Mofolo went to Lealui in Barotseland, Zambia, but had to return to South Africa because of the bad climate. He worked a short time on the Rand, and in 1912 settled in northern Lesotho as a labour recruiting agent for the Eckstein Group of the Central Mining Rand mines. He also took over the management of a thirty-mile postal route between Teyateyaneng and Ficksburg, Orange Free State, until the end of World War I. In 1916 he purchased a government portable steam engine and milling plant to relieve Sotho women from the heavy task of pounding their corn. His wife died, and he remarried in 1918.

After the war, Mofolo turned to politics. He became a member of the Basutoland Progressive Association.

In 1922 Mofolo left the Eckstein Group to become an independent labour agent, recruiting workers for the Rand mines and for the Natal farms and sugar plantations. In November 1925 he opened a new branch in Teyateyaneng with his brother Ben Mofolo in charge; but Ben gave up the business in 1927. In the same year, Mofolo's second wife died. He closed his recruiting agency and sold his mill. In 1928 he bought a store in Bokong, in the Maluti Mountains. He married for the third and last time in 1933. He sold his store in 1937, and left the mountains where the high altitude was harmful to his health. He settled in Port Elizabeth, but, wishing to be nearer to his people, bought a farm from a white farmer at Matatiele, Griqualand East, not far from the Lesotho border. But the transaction was invalidated under the Bantu Land Act of 1913, according to which a black South African could buy only land bordering another black South African's land. "Mofolo's property was just touching another African's land, and so Mofolo took the case to court. But he lost not only his case, but his health and wealth besides" (Daniel Kunene/Ronald Kirsch). He tried, unsuccessfully, to run a tea-room in Matatiele, and in 1940 returned to Lesotho. Sir Patrick Duncan, the then governor general, awarded him a pension of £ 3 per months, which he received until Sir Patrick's death in 1943. In 1941 he suffered a stroke that left him speechless for several months. Thomas Mofolo died on September 8, 1948, in Teyateyaneng.

On *Moeti oa bochabela:* "It was a new product — not a history, but a novel describing native life in ancient days" (F. H. Dutton). "*Moeti oa boachabela* is interesting in that it shows the merging of Sotho beliefs and Christian thought" (P.-D. Beuchat).

On *Pitseng:* "Although Mofolo fails, as he was bound to do, to provide a convincing picture of the ideal syncretism he advocates, this novel has more realistic subtlety than the previous one, because it is based on something that was fast becoming fundamental in the African mind: a clear perception of the antinomy between Christian theory and Christian practice" (Albert S. Gérard).

"*Chaka,* a genuine masterpiece of insight and composition, and perhaps the first major African contribution to world literature" (Albert S. Gérard).

"Mofolo's book is in many points remarkable, and differs luckily from certain very European productions, whose authors, in black Africa, could usefully take lectures thereof in poetry, culture and humanity" (Luc Decaunes).

Moiloa, James Jantjies   South Africa

Moiloa was born on June 6, 1916, in the district of Wepener in the Province of Orange Free State, South Africa, and started his primary education at Jammerdrift about three miles from Wepener along the Caledon River. Here he passed his Standard IV in 1924 whilst the exam was still conducted externally under the Native Education Department. As this school didn't go beyond Standard IV Moiloa worked on a farm minding the herd for two years, then went to Wepener to work as a kitchen boy for a Mrs. Robinson "who later became sympathetic and allowed me to attend school whilst working, though under ought (bad) conditions" (In a letter to Janheinz Jahn on March 12, 1971). In 1932 he passed the Standard VI, continued to work for another two years, then, in 1935 took up J.C. at the Bloemfontein Bantu High School. He passed the examination in 1938, being one of the first students to complete J.C. in Bloemfontein. Moiloa then proceeded to the Thabanchu Moroka Missionary Institution, where he completed his Teachers' Training in 1940, being one of the first to obtain a first class at this institution.

J.J. Moiloa started teaching at Brandfort in 1941 and stayed there till 1951. During this time he was busy with his Matric and later with his B.A. degree for which he studied privately at the University of South Africa. In 1952 Moiloa became a teacher at the Bantu High School in Bloemfontein, and in 1958 he passed his B.A. while still a teacher. In 1966 he was appointed Principal of the Secondary School in Bloemfontein, being the first African at this post. In 1970 Moiloa was appointed Assistant Speech Aide at the University of the Orange Free State in Bloemfontein, also here being the first African to be appointed at a European University in the Orange Free State.

James Jantjies Moiloa has written several books in his mother tongue Southern Sotho and is still busy writing. Besides essays he published a volume of humorous short stories, *Dipale le metlae* (1851), a volume of poems praising animals, birds and insects, *Mohahlaula dithota* (1852), a play, *Jaa o siele Motswalle* (1954), and two novels, *Paka-Mahlomola* (1853) and *Mehla e a fetoha*. Besides his creative work he is engaged in translating school textbooks.

Mondlane, Eduardo   Mozambique

Born on July 20, 1924, in Chibuto, district Gaza, Mozambique, Eduardo Chivambo Mondlane was educated at a Swiss Calvinist and an American Methodist mission school. Between his 15th and 22nd years he lived in Lourenço Marques. At 24 he left for South Africa to attend high school, later enrolled at the University of the Witwatersrand in Johannesburg, but had to leave in 1949 at the instigation of the Malan government. Back in Mozambique he received a scholarship for one year's study in Lisbon. At 31 he left for the United States. He obtained his Ph. D. in Sociology at Northwestern University, Evanston, Illinois, and found employment at the United Nations, doing research work. In 1961 he became Assistant Professor at Syracuse University, New York.

In 1962 Mondlane returned to Africa, and helped to found FRELIMO (Frente de Libertaçao de Moçambique), whose president he became.

Eduardo Mondlane was killed on February 3, 1969, in Dar es Salaam, Tanzania, by a bomb, sent to him by mail.

Mondlane wrote *Le mouvement de libération au Mozambique*, Présence Africaine, no. 53. His autobiographical narrative, *Schitlangu, der Sohn des Häuptlings* (1866), was published only in German translation. *The Struggle for Mozambique*, Harmondsworth, England 1969, which has also been published in German translation under the title *Kampf um Mozambique*, Frankfurt am Main 1970, is a description of the national liberation struggle from the point of view of FRELIMO. His biography, *Eduardo Mondlane*, has anonymously been published by Panaf Books, London 1972.

Mongita, Albert   Zaire

Born on May 8, 1916, in Irebu, province Equateur, Zaire, Albert Mongita came to Kinshasa, when he was one year old. He went six years to a primary school, two years to a professional school and five years to the middle school Institut St. Joseph. After school he stayed there and taught for five years. He left to become employed by the post administration. In 1949 he joined Radio Congo Belge as editor and announcer. He wrote several sketches, which made him well known among his audience. Mongita became more and more interested in theatre. He founded a theatre troupe, "La ligue folklorique congolaise", and wrote several plays in French, one of which, *Mangengenge* (1190) was published. *Soko Stanley te* was performed in Léopoldville at the fiftieth anniversary of Stanley's death in 1954. *Lifoco* was first performed on November 12, 1955, in the presence of the Governor General.

Mongo, Pabé   Cameroon

Born on June 6, 1948, at Dume, district Haut Nyong, Cameroon, Pascal Bekolo-Mongo — this is his real name — had his first education at his home town at the Ecole Saint-Jean Bosco of the Catholic mission, and at the Collège de la Salle. In 1967, he joined, as a novice, the Frères des Ecoles Chrétiennes at Efok, near Obala, district Lekié. In 1969, he took the First Vow and entered the Scolasticat of Mvolyé, near Yaunde. After founding a "Club Littéraire", he left the monastery in 1970.

His play, *Innocente Assima,* a comedy in four acts, was published in 1971 by CLE, Yaunde.

Moningi, Oscar   Zaire

Born on April 1, 1930, in Lisala, Equator province, Zaire, Oscar Moningi received his secondary education at the Institut Saint-Joseph in Kinshasa. He is employed in the administration of SONECA (Société nationale des Editeurs, Compositeurs et Auteurs) in Kinshasa.

Oscar Moningi was awarded the Sebastian Ngonso Prize for his small volume of poetry, *Complainte bantou* (1193).

Moore, Bai T. Liberia

Born in 1916 in Dimeh, Vai area, 22 miles north-west of Monrovia, Liberia, Bai Tamia Moore received his higher education at the Virginia Union University in Richmond, Virginia, USA. In 1941 he returned to Liberia as an expert in Agriculture. As a civil servant he held different positions in the administration, was temporarirly on the staff of the UNESCO education programme of Liberia, and was appointed Undersecretary for Cultural Affairs in the Liberian Government, a position he still holds.

Bai Tamia Moore has travelled widely. From 1954 to 1955 he was in India on a UNESCO fellowship and afterwards visited the Middle East. In 1958 he survived a plane crash in Guinea, and had to stay in hospital for some time. In 1959 he revisited the United States going to California, Minnesota, Virginia. From January to March 1962 he visited West Germany and Berlin. Since then he has been representative of his country on numerous international conferences and festivals, 1966 in Dakar, 1969 in Algiers, 1970 in Ife, etc.

Bai Tamia Moore wrote a volume of poetry, *Ebony Dust* (684), and a novel, *Murder in the Cassava Patch* (685), about a man who has been cheated by a girl. An essay, *Categories of Traditional Liberian Songs* was included in the anthology "Liberian Writing", Tübingen 1970.

"The author's extensive travels in America, where he was educated, Europe and Asia have contributed a variety of experiences which are reflected in his work" (Rosina Robinson).

Mopeli-Paulus, Atwell Sidwell   South Africa

Born in 1913 in Witzieshoek, a Sotho reserve in the Orange
Free State, South Africa, Atwell Sidwell Mopeli-Paulus is a
descendent of the Sotho King Moshesh and linked to the royal
family of Lesotho. He was educated at Edendale, Natal, and
at the Witwatersrand University, where he studied Medicine
for some time. He holds a certificate as an art teacher in non-
European schools. During World War II he served with the
Cape Corps in East Africa and Egypt. After the war he settled
in Johannesburg, where he was employed in a law office. In
1967 Mopeli-Paulus was confined to a place in the Northern
Transvaal.

Mopeli-Paulus is the author of three collections of poems in
Southern Sotho, *Ho tsamaea ke ho bona: lithothokiso* (1870),
Lilahloane oa batho (1871), and *Liretlo* (1872), and a story,
Moshweshwe moshwaila (1875). Two novels in English, *Blanket
Boy's Moon* (1873) and *Turn to the Dark* (1874) were told by
him and written down by Peter Lanham and Miriam Basner
respectively.

Blanket Boy's Moon tells the story of Monare, a present day
Sotho, who leaves Lesotho to go to Johannesburg. There he
gets involved in the temptations of modern city life. Engaged
in a ritual murder he is caught by the police and sentenced to
death. "The story of Monare, very simply told, but carefully
constructed, enables the author to touch on most of the problems
of South African society, and it is a grim picture that arises
from the novel" (Albert S. Gérard).

Turn to the Dark tells the story of Lesiba, a young Sotho,
who is expelled from school because he has taken part in a school
rebellion. He settles in his village in Lesotho and integrates
into customary life. His tragedy begins when he is engaged in
ritual murder and can't combine the demands of the two worlds
he was initiated in, the white man's conceptions and his Christian belief and his African beliefs and customs.

"Mopeli-Paulus has been able to bring into focus the central
dilemma facing Africa and its tragic meaning for the African"
(Albert S. Gérard).

Mopila, Francisco José   Zaire

Born on December 24, 1915, at Lebu, near Lake Albert, Eastern
Province, Zaire, Francisco José Mopila, an Azande, became
assistant to a Spanish medical doctor, working in that area, and
accompanied him to Spain, in 1948, to spend the holidays with
him. With this fact ends his autobiography *Memorias de un
congolés* (1194), written in Spanish. His further whereabouts
could not be traced.

Motsamai, Edward   Lesotho

Born in 1870 at Masite, district Maseru, Lesotho, Edward
Motsamai, a Sotho attended the Bible School at Morija, from
which he graduated with honours in 1886. He went to the
Teacher Training College and took his teacher's certificate in
1888. From 1889 to 1892 he taught both at the Bible School
and at the Mountain School. In 1893 he started preparing for
the ministry, but owing to ill-health and the loss of his voice,
he had to give up his studies from 1896 to 1899. He worked
for a while at the Morija Book Depot and later resumed his
studies. He was ordained in 1900. Sickness forced him to give
up the ministry, but in 1901 the synod assigned him to a post at
Letsunyane in the Maluti Mountains, where he recovered fully.
Edward Motsamai died in July 1959.

Motsamai is the author of one of the earliest printed books
by a Sotho writer, *Majoe a mahlano a molatsoana* (Five Pebbles
from the Brook), Morija 1907, a collection of five meditations
previously written for the newspaper "Leselinyana" and composed "with the purpose of putting Christian youth on guard
against the seductions of sin and paganism" (Livre d'or). His
only contribution to creative writing is *Mehla ea malimo* (1884),
a collection of eighteen stories, most of which Motsamai collected from the mouths of the old men of Lesotho. Motsmai then
returned to religious writing with *Kereke* (The Church), Morija

1925. His last book was a biographical account of Chief Mos-hesh, *Morena Moshoeshoe mar'a Mokhachane* (Chief Moshesh, Son of Mokhachane), Morija 1942.

Moukouri, Jacques Kuoh
vid. *Kuoh Moukouri, Jacques*

Mphahlele, Ezekiel   South Africa

Born on December 17, 1919, in Pretoria, South Africa, in the sub-urb of Marabastad, Ezekiel Mphahlele entered school for the first time at the age of thirteen. He obtained his elementary educa-tion in Pretoria and his high school education in Johannesburg. From 1939 to 1940 he was trained as a teacher at Adams Col-lege, Natal, an institution run by the American Board of Mis-sions. From 1941 to 1945 he worked as a clerk, shorthand typist and instructor to the blind at an institute near Johannesburg. At the same time he continued his education. From 1941 to 1942 he prepared for his Matriculation Certificate at the University of South Africa, Pretoria, after correspondence courses. From 1945 to 1952 he taught English and Afrikaans at Orlando High School, Johannesburg, and again studied by correspondence at the University of South Africa. He obtained his B. A. in English, Psychology and African Affairs in 1949. In 1952 he was banned from teaching by the South African Government as a result of a campaign which he had run as general secretary of the Teachers' Association against the "Bantu Education", a system which aimed at lowering education standards for Africans. In 1955 he received a B. A. degree in English Literature, again after correspondence studies at the University of South Africa.

After a number of odd jobs Mphahlele joined "Drum" maga-zine, Johannesburg, in 1955 as fiction editor, sub-editor and political reporter. He held the job until 1957. At the same time he prepared his M. A. at the University of South Africa and obtained the degree in 1956 with the thesis *The Non-European Character in English Fiction.*

In 1957 Mphahlele exiled himself to Nigeria, where he taught English at C.M.S. (Church Missionary Society) Grammar School in Lagos, and English Literature to adults under the University of Ibadan extension system. He became an editor and contributor to the literary journal "Black Orpheus", helped establish Mbari Writers' and Artists' Club and became its first president. In 1961 he became director of the African Programme for the Congress for Cultural Freedom (now International Association for Cultural Freedom), Paris, toured Africa and helped establish creative centres and writers' workshops in Nigeria and Kenya.

In 1965 Mphahlele joined the University College in Nairobi, Kenya, as lecturer in English Literature. The following year saw him in the United States, where he was a teaching fellow in the English Department of the University of Denver, Denver, Colorado, while studying for the Ph. D. in the creative writing programme. In 1968 he obtained his Ph. D. degree for the novel *The Wanderers* (1900), submitted in lieu of a dissertation. From 1968 to 1970 he taught in the English Department of the University of Zambia, Lusaka, Zambia, and directed the African Literature courses. Since 1970 he is back at the University of Denver as Associate Professor in the Department of English. He is also associate editor of "Africa Today" published at the University of Denver.

Mphahlele first published *Man Must Live, and other Stories* (1896). This was followed by his autobiography, *Down Second Avenue* (1897), a book, which is "at the same time a witness and an artistic realization, moving, well written, true" (Mercer Cook). It was translated into eight languages. The stories *The Living and Dead, and other Stories* (1898) were published by the journal "Black Orpheus" as special publication. *The African Image* (London 1962) is a collection of essays centering round race and colour, négritude and literature, nationalism and the African personality. *In Corner B* (1899) is a collection of short stories. The novel *The Wanderers* (1900) was awarded first prize as the best African novel for 1968/69 by the magazine "African Arts/Arts Afrique", Los Angeles, California, USA. Mphahlele edited the anthology *African Writing Today* (A 76) and co-edited the anthology *Modern African Stories* (A 64). Articles on African cultures and literatures have appeared in "Présence Africaine", "Black Orpheus", "Afrique", "Foreign Affairs" and "The New African".

Portrait on Plate III.

Mqhayi, Samuel Edward Krune   South Africa

Born on December 1, 1875, at Gqamahashe in the Tyumie Valley, Cape Province, South Africa, as son of a preacher, Samuel Edward Krune Mqhayi was sent to school at Evergreen at the age of six. When he was nine, his family moved, on account of a famine, to Kentani near Butterworth in the Transkei, where they settled close to the homestead of the boy's great-uncle, Chief Nzanzana. Here he acquired a remarkable knowledge of Xhosa life, language and history, while he attended school intermittently, being mostly occupied with herding cattle. In 1891 his sister took him to Lovedale. Though the missionaries opposed the circumcision, Mqhayi secretly underwent the rites and was circumcised on March 6, 1894. He was ready to accept being chased from school, but the authorities pardoned him after a while and allowed him to return.

After training as a teacher in Lovedale, Mqhayi taught for a time in East London, but found teaching uninteresting and soon left. He contributed to "Izwi Labantu", a newspaper that was founded in 1897 by Nathaniel Cyril Mhala, and later became one of its editors. After an interval in Kentani, Mqhayi resumed his work on "Izwi Labantu", but the journal had to stop publication for lack of funds and because of differences of opinion among the editors. Mqhayi went back to East London

Chinua Achebe

Gabriel Okara

PLATE XI

Christopher Okigbo

Sebastian Okechukwu Mezu

Ferdinand Oyono

Mongo Beti

PLATE XII

Francis Bebey

René Philombe

as a teacher, and assisted John Tengo Jabavu in editing "Imvo Zabantsundu" until Jabavu's death in 1921.

In 1922 Mqhayi was invited to teach at Lovedale, but he could not come to an agreement with the missionaries as to how Xhosa history should be taught, and he desisted, but kept up, as he says in his autobiography, friendly relations. In 1936 Mqhayi took part in the Conference of Bantu Authors convened at Florida, Transvaal, by R. H. W. Shepherd, director of the Lovedale Press.

In the late twenties Mqhayi had settled on Tilana's Hill, near Berlin, Ciskei, Cape Province, on a plot, that was allotted to him by the government to build up a model farm. He renamed the place Ntab'ozuko (Mountain of Glory). He acted as secretary to the Ndlambe chief until he died on July 29, 1945.

Mqhayi's first original work was *Ityala lama-wele* (1905), a legal dispute between twins over who is the elder and therefore entitled to their father's inheritance. *U-Bombi bom-Fundisi u John Knox Bokwe* (1906) is a biography of the Reverend Bokwe. *Imihobe nemibengo, yokufundwa ezikolweni* (1907) is a collection of poems for children. His second important work of prose is *U-Don Jadu* (1908), a picture of an ideal South African society, the first Xhosa utopia. This book won him the first prize in the first May Esther Bedford Competition in 1935. This was followed two years later by a collection of eight cantos on Chief Hintza, *U-Mhlekazi U-Hintza* (Hintza the Great), Lovedale 1937. At the same time, he was writing his autobiography, which was first published in German, in Diedrich Westermann's collection, *Afrikaner erzählen ihr Leben* (A 115), before it appeared in Xhosa under the title *U-Mqhayi waseNtab'Ozuko* (Mqhayi of the Mountain of Glory), Lovedale 1939. His last volume was one more collection of poems, entitled *I-nzuzo* (1910).

"It was perhaps as a poet that Mqhayi was chiefly valued by the Xhosa audience, not least because he had completely mastered the form and the spirit of the traditional praise poem (izibongo) while adapting it to modern circumstances and topics" (Albert S. Gérard).

Portrait on Plate III.

Mtshali, Oswald South Africa

Born in 1940 in Vryheid, Natal, South Africa, where he matriculated, Oswald Joseph Mtshali came to Johannesburg at the age of eighteen. He wanted to enroll at the University of Witwatersrand, but was refused because of the separate universities legislation. He works as a messenger and lives in Soweto, a "Bantu location" near Johannesburg.

Mtshali published a volume of poetry, *Sounds of a Cowhide Drum*, Johannesburg 1971.

Muhammed Said Abdulla Tanzania

Born on April 25, 1918, in Zanzibar, Muhammed Said Abdulla went to Primary School from 1928 to 1934 and to Secondary School from 1935 to 1938. He passed his Senior Cambridge Examination in 1936. In 1938 he joined the Health Department to learn the profession of a Sanitary Inspector. He worked then as Sanitary Inspector until 1948. From 1948 to 1958 Muhammed Said Abdulla was editor of "Zanzibari", and assistant editor of "Al-Falaq", "Al-Mahda" and "Africa Kwetu". From 1958 to 1968 he was employed by the Agriculture Department to edit the magazine "Mkuliuea".

Muhammed Said Abdulla has published two novels in Swahili, *Mzimu wa watu wa kale* (1322) and *Kisima cha Giningi* (1323).

Mulaisho, Dominic Zambia

Born in 1933 at Mkando, Zambia, Dominic Mulaisho was educated at Chalimbana Teachers' College and the University College of Rhodesia and Nyasaland, where he studied Economics, History and English. Since 1965 he has been Permanent Secretary in the Office of the President, in the Ministry of

Education and in various other ministries. When Zambia nationalized 51 per cent of the holdings in the country's copper mines, the Mining Development Corporation was established, whose Chairman Mulaisho became in 1971.

Mulaisho is the author of a novel, *The Tongue of the Dumb*, London 1971.

Mulikita, Fwanyanga M.   Zambia

Born in 1928 at Sefula, Mongu, Barotse Province, Zambia, Fwanyanga Matale Mulikita received his primary education in Mongu. In 1945 he came to Munali, Lusaka, for his secondary education. In 1949 he passed the Cambridge School Certificate with distinctions in General Science and English Literature. He worked in the High Court as clerk-interpreter for two years before proceeding to Fort Hare University College, South Africa, where in 1954 he did his B. A., majoring in English and Psychology. He taught at Mongu Secondary School from 1954 to 1956, then joined the Municipality of Kitwe as Welfare Officer.

In 1957 Mulikita returned to the teaching profession, teaching at Kitwe Teacher Training College. In 1958 he obtained a Certificate in Freelance Journalism. From 1959 to 1960 he studied for an M. A. in Psychology at Stanford University, California, USA. In 1961 he opened the Chalimbana Secondary School in Zambia as Headmaster. In 1964 he left again for America to take up a course in Diplomacy and International Relations at Columbia University, New York. The same year, after Zambia's Independence, Mulikita was appointed first Ambassador of Zambia to the United Nations. In 1966 he returned to Zambia as Permanent Secretary, Ministry of Education. In March 1968 he became Permanent Secretary in the Ministry of Foreign Affairs. At the end of that year he was appointed Minister for Luapula Province. In September 1969 he was appointed Minister of Labour and Social Services and since 1971 he has been first Minister of Health and now Minister of Power, Transport and Works.

Mulikita's first work was a narrative in Lozi, *Batili ki mwanaka* (1923). After nearly ten years of silence, a play in English, *Shaka Zulu* (1924), followed, as did a collection of short stories, *A Point of No Return* (1925).

Munonye, John   Nigeria

Born in 1929 at Akokwa, East Central State, Nigeria, as the fourth of seven children, John Munonye was educated at St. Barnabas Primary School, Akokwa, Christ the King College, Onitsha from 1943 to 1947, and at University College, Ibadan from 1948 to 1952, where he read Latin, Greek and History and obtained his B. A. From 1952 to 1953 Munonye studied at the Institute of Education, University of London.

Since 1954 Munonye has been employed by the Ministry of Education, Nigeria, in various capacities. Currently he is Principal of the Advanced Teacher Training College, Owerri, Nigeria.

John Munonye is the author of three novels: *The Only Son* (687), *Obi* (688) and *Oil Man of Obange*, London 1971.

Mushiete, Paul   Zaire

Born on November 19, 1934, in Kinshasa, Zaire, Paul Mushiete was, from 1940 to 1952, six years at primary and six years at secondary schools in Kinshasa. From 1953 to 1959 he was at Leuven, Belgium, to study Psychology, Pedagogy, Political Science, and Social Economy.

Back in Kinshasa, he was appointed to different governmental positions. He was a member of the Conseil Monétaire of the Congolese Republic, ambassador of his country to Paris, Minister of National Economy and Finance, and Minister of National Education and Culture. On July 2, 1971, he was appointed Postmaster General, a post he held until February 21, 1972.

Paul Mushiete is co-author of the play *Pas de feu pour les antilopes*, Kinshasa 1970, which he wrote with Norbert L. Mikanza, and editor of several anthologies: *La littérature française africaine* (A 77), *Anthologie des écrivains congolais* (AC 151), and *Kongolesische Märchen*, Cologne 1971. His essay on Congolese literature, *La littérature congolaise*, was published in the journal "Le Flambeau", Brussels.

Mutwa, Vusamazulu Credo   South Africa

Vusamazulu Credo Mutwa was born around 1921 in Natal, South Africa, out of wedlock to Allan Mutwa, who, according to African custom, accepted the illegitimate child. His father was a former Catholic catechist from the Embo district. His mother was the descendant of a long line of Zulu medicine-men and custodians of tribal lore and customs. His parents parted shortly after Vusamazulu's birth, because his mother refused to convert to Christianity. Mutwa was educated by his maternal grandfather, a medicine-man, and carrying the bags for him, the boy learned some of the older man's secrets.

In 1928 Vusamazulu was taken to Transvaal by his father. They lived on a farm beyond Potchefstroom, where his father was a labourer. After twenty years on different farms the father found employment in one of the Johannesburg mines as a carpenter. Mutwa himself found employment in 1954 in a curio shop in Johannesburg and has been working there ever since.

When he visited his mother and grandfather in Zululand after thirty years of absence, he renounced Christianity at their command, and underwent the Ceremony of Purification, in order to begin training as a medicine-man. He also prepared himself to assume the post of custodian of tribal lore and customs in the event of his grandfather's death.

In fulfillment of an oath Mutwa wrote three books on Zulu customs and beliefs, *Indaba, My Children* (1935), *Africa is My Witness* (1936), and *My People, My Africa,* (1937).

Mveng, Engelbert   Cameroon

Born on May 9, 1930, in Enam-Ngal, division of Ngulmakong, district Ntem, Cameroon, Engelbert Mveng received his education at the Petit Séminaire in Akono and the Grand Séminaire in Otélé. After his novitiate in Djuma, Congo-Léopoldville, now Zaire, Mveng studied at the Faculty of Philosophy and Literature in Namur, Belgium, the Faculté St.-Albert (the Philosophical Faculty) of the University of Louvain, Belgium, and in de Vals-Chantilly, France, obtaining a Licence en philosophie scolastique at the two latter universities. He then studied Philosophy at the Faculté de Fourvière, Lyon, France, became a Licencié en Théologie and rounded up his studies at the Faculté de Lettres of the Sorbonne, Paris, and in Lyon, with a Doctorat ès Lettres. With the thesis, *Les Sources grecques de l'histoire négro-africain, depuis Homère jusqu'à Strabon,* Engelbert Mveng received a Doctorat d'Etat in Paris in 1970.

From 1958 to 1960 Mveng was a teacher at the Collège Libermann, Dakar, Senegal. He was in the preparatory committee of the First World Festival of Negro Arts in Dakar, in 1966. He is President of the Art Section of the African Cultural Society, Paris, Consulting Expert to UNESCO, a member of the International Association of Writers in the French Language (ANEMOM), Paris, and a member of the Egyptological Foundation Reine Elisabeth, Belgium. Père Engelbert Mveng is a Professor at the Federal University of Cameroon, Yaunde, and Director of Cultural Affairs of the Federal Republic of Cameroon. He is also the founder of the Atelier Art Nègre, Yaunde.

In 1964 Engelbert Mveng was chosen Lauréat by the Académie Française for his *Histoire du Cameroun,* Paris 1963.

Père Mveng's interests are wide-ranged. Besides his comprehensive *Histoire du Cameroun,* he has published many articles on history and archaeology in various journals. His *Dossier culturel pan-african*, Paris 1966, is a concise introduction into all matters African, his *Guide Bibliographique du Monde Noir*, Yaunde 1971, an ambitious enterprise to list a representative choice of Africana. His interest in art is documented with *L'art d'Afrique Noire*, Paris 1964, and *Art Nègre, art chrétien*, Rome 1969. Engelbert Mveng is an artist himself, who illustrates some of his books, and paints and designs new African decorations for mass vestments. His contribution to creative literature is *Si quelqu'un*, Paris 1962, a way of the cross, illustrated by himself, *Mon amour, pour toi*, Paris 1964, and *Lève-toi, amie, viens* (69ì), two collections of poetry, illustrated by the author.

Mvomo, Rémy Medou
vid. *Medou Mvomo, Rémy*

Naigiziki, Saverio   Rwanda

Saverio Naigiziki was born on September 9, 1915, in Mwulire, Busanga, Rwanda, into the tribe of the Hutus. He received his first schooling from the White Sisters in Save, then continued at the Catholic Seminary in Kabgayi, but was told, as the result of his disobedience, that he was not fit to become a priest. He never got over this disappointment. Naigiziki became a teacher in a mission school, then worked as a printer's assistant and finally as a translator of school textbooks. One day he left Save and his family and tried his hand at business in Nyanza, the then capital of Rwanda, but was lending money too generously to his friends, and having the choice at the next cash audit between trial and flight, he choose the latter, travelling to Tanganyika, from where he was sent back to Rwanda, and escaping again to Uganda, where he stayed with fellow countrymen. It was during this time that he wrote most of his book *Escapade ruandaise* (1327).

In the meantime a missionary friend was able to rehabilitate him. His book won the Prix de Littérature de la Foire Coloniale de Bruxelles in 1949 and the money helped to pay his debts.

In 1950 Naigiziki was working as a bank clerk in Goma, in 1951 he found employment with the research institute Irsac in Astrida, Rwanda. He wrote several sociological and political studies in collaboration with this institute and, in 1954, his play, *L'Optimiste* (1328), which was presented and acted by his colleagues. The theme, a marriage between a Hutu farmer and a Tutsi girl, did not appeal to the Mwami, the King of Rwanda — a Tutsi himself — and there were no further performances. It was only in August 1954, a UNO delegation visited Rwanda, that the Belgian administration asked for this play to be performed publicly.

In 1958 Naigiziki was sent to Elisabethville, now Kisangani, by Irsac to do an editing job. He seized the opportunity to enrol at the University of Elisabethville, and also became secretary and editor of the periodical "Jeune Afrique".

In 1959 Naigiziki returned to Rwanda to become President of the Fonds Mutara and vice delegate and chief candidate in the Territory of Nyanza. In 1960 he became Chef de Bureau in the Service des Affaires Economiques in Usumbura, Burundi. A year later he was back in Rwanda as Secrétaire Permanent of the Assemblée Législative in Kigali. When, in 1963, Fonds Mutara was merging with Trib/Instance in Butare, Naigiziki became a teacher at the Seminary in Save, Butare, where he still is today.

Ndao, Cheik   Senegal

Born on August 3, 1933, in Dignona, Casamance, Senegal, from parents who came from Saloum and belonged to the family of the princes of Ndoucouman, Cheik Sidi Ahmed Ndao is of Mandingo, Serer, and Wolof descent. He received his education at the Collège de Hann in Dakar, then, until 1954, at

Lycée at Béziers in France. From 1960 to 1964 he studied at the University of Grenoble, then, from 1964 to 1965 at the University of Swansea, Wales.

Back in Senegal, he became a teacher at the famous Ecole William Ponty in Thiès. Later he went to the United States. After a professorship at the Oakland City College, Oakland City, Indiana, he is, since 1971, teaching French at the French Department of the De Paw University at Greencastle, Indiana, USA.

Cheik Ndao writes in French, Wolof, and English. His first volume of poetry, *Kaïrée* (696), was awarded the prize for Senegalese poets in French (Prix des poètes sénégalais de langue française). His play, *L'exil d'Albouri* (697), was awarded the first prize of theatre at the Pan-African Festival in Algiers 1969. Albouri, a Wolof king, prefers exile instead of surrender to the French. *La décision* (697), another play, dramatizes a race riot in the United States. In his last volume of poetry, *Mogariennes*, Paris 1970, he sings of African and French towns.

"*L'Exil d'Albouri* does not present a very new conflict, but here it has a powerful prominence by its authenticity, its colourful folklore and its permanent actuality" (Claude Baignières).

Ndawo, Henry Masila   South Africa

Born on March 29, 1883, at Bethesda, near Matatiele, Griqualand East, Cape Province, South Africa, Henry Masila Ndawo was educated at the primary school of his district and got his teacher's certificate at Bensonnoale in the Herschel district. He taught for a while in Matatiele. Henry Masila Ndawo was killed in a railway accident in 1949.

Ndawo belonged to the Hlubi tribe, which had left its original habitat in Natal as the result of Shaka's wars, and had settled among the Xhosa, but he "wrote the Xhosa language as if he was born and bred among the Ngqika tribes" (James J. R. Jolobe).

Ndawo's first work is a novel, *Uhambo luka Gqoboka* (1953), "an imaginative progress of a Native from heathenism to Christianity, through much struggle with wild beasts and men, and with the elements" (I. Schapera).

Inxenye yen-Tsomi zase-Zweni (Selections of Folktales), Mariannhill 1920, is a book-length collection of popular tales in Xhosa. *Izibongo zenkosi zamaHlubi nezamaBaca* (Praise poems of the Hlubi and the Bhaca), Mariannhill 1925, and *Iziduko zamaHlubi* (Clan names of the Hlubi), Lovedale 1939, are the result of a visit to the great Hlubi chief Langalibalele, which inspired him to compile the traditional praise poems of the Hlubi chiefs. His next novel *U-Nolishwa* (1954) "shows less ambition and greater skill than *Gqoboka*" (Albert S. Gérard).

His third and last novel is *U-Nomathamsanqa no Sigebenga* (1955), "an allegorical story of mankind led astray, but redeemed by the eldest son of an African chief" (Albert S. Gérard).

UMshweshwe, published posthumously in Lovedale in 1951, is a historical sketch of the famous Sotho chief Moshesh.

"In his books you find pleasing Xhosa not usually met with among people born in the region of the country in which he spent all his life. ... In his novels here and there you find verse of a high standard leaning more to lyrical poetry marked by touching pathos. In his poems he has caught the traditional spirit which he seeks to convey through them. It is clear that he was not only gifted in prose writing but also in poetry and from his writing generally one can sense that he was a patriot" (James J. R. Jolobe).

N'Debeka, Maxime   Congo

Born on March 10, 1944, in Brazzaville, Congo, Maxime N'Debeka received his secondary education at the Collège Chaminade, which he left to enter the military service. He was sent to military schools in France and the Soviet Union to study electronics. After his return to Congo, he left the army to be appointed General Director of Culture and Arts.

He wrote a volume of poetry, *Soleils neufs* (1197), and a play, *Le président* (1198).

"Maxime Ndebeka ... repeats in his poems over and over that this unique self, that he is, is only a product of the society and the history in which he lives ... The wrath and the revolt which appear as a basic shout to the play, are of poetical essence" (Henri Lopez).

Ndedi-Penda, Patrice   Cameroon

Born in 1945 at Yabassi, district Nkam, Cameroon, Patrice Ndedi-Penda received his primary and secondary education in Duala and then moved to Paris, France, where he obtained his Baccalauréat. He has studied Philosophy and Psychology at the Faculty of Arts and Human Sciences at Nanterre.

Patrice Ndedi-Penda was granted the "Prix des Auditeur" in the inter-African competition of the O.R.T.F. (Office de Radiodiffusion et Télévision Française) in 1969 for his play, *Le fusil*, Paris 1971. His novel, *La nasse*, Yaunde 1972, is about lovers who have to separate because the girl has been promised to a rich man.

Nditsouna, Francesco
vid. *Sengat-Kuo, François*

N'Dintsouna, Francesco
vid. *Sengat-Kuo, François*

Ndzaagap, Timothée   Cameroon

Born in November 1949 in Mbâhpouot (Bagam) near Galim, district Bamboutos, Cameroon, Timothée Ndzaagap entered the elementary school of the protestant mission in his village in 1956. In 1959 he changed to the Central School Jules Ferry in Mbouda, the Capital of the district of Baboutos. In 1963 he entered the Collège de la Réunification in Baoussam, and in 1967 he finished his studies with the diploma of an Assistant Teacher at the E.N.I.A. (Ecole Normale d'Instituteurs-Adjoints).

He had just entered the Collège of Menoua district, Dschang, when he left it to found, with his friend and former teacher, Patrice Kayo, a journal called "Echo des Sports". Ndzaagap became its director and local delegate of the A.P.E.C. (Association Nationale des Poètes et Ecrivains Camerounais).

On February 22, 1970, his house was searched and Ndzaagap accused of subversion. On March, 1970, he founded a new journal, "Le Perroquet", the first issue of which was immediately seized. Ndzaagap was again charged with subversion, and put into prison on July 22, 1970, to be acquitted after a detention of seven months and ten days by the Temporary Military Tribunal on March 2, 1971. He returned to his village until he was called to Yaunde by the General Secretary of A.P.E.C. to join the staff of the journal "Cameroun Littéraire".

Ndzaagap published a play, *La fille du roi a menti,* Yaunde 1972. His poems, stories, and articles have appeared in "La Nouvelle Revue Française", "Jeune Afrique", "Floréal", "Le Cameroun Littéraire", "Bingo", "Essor des Jeunes", "Ozila", etc. In spring 1972 he received the first prize in poetry by African authors for his poem, *La Blessure,* from the Concours International de la Francophonie.

Nénékhaly-Camara, Condetto   Guinea

Born on September 10, 1930, in Beyla, Province Beyla, Guinea, Condetto Nénékhaly-Camara attended schools in Guinea, Dahomey, Senegal and France. He holds diplomas in Literature from the Institut des Hautes Etudes in Dakar and from the Institut d'Ethnologie in Paris. From 1955 to 1958 he was on the staff of "Présence Africaine" in Paris. For a long time he was representative of the FEANF (Fédération des Etudiants d'Afrique Noire en France). He rose finally to Guinea's Minister for Scientific Research. Nénékhaly-Camara died in August 1972.

Condetto Nénékhaly-Camara has published a volume of poetry, *Lagunes* (701), and two plays, *Continent-Afrique suivi de Amazoulou* (702). *Continent-Afrique* is a visionary allegory about African history. *Amazoulou* is a play about Chaka, the hero of the Zulu people.

"Two prospective visions ... of an Africa totally liberated, fraternal and solidary with the other peoples who are engaged to construct a new society and new type of man" (Mário de Andrade).

Neto, Agostinho   Angola

Born on September 21, 1922, at Icolu-i-Bengu (Icolo e Bengo) near Luanda, Angola, António Agostinho Neto was educated to secondary level at Luanda. From 1944 to 1947 he worked in the Angola health services and played a considerable part in building up a cultural society in Luanda — political organizations were forbidden — which became increasingly nationalist in tone. In 1947 he went to study Medicine in Coimbra, Portugal, and published a series of poems giving voice to the sufferings of his poeple. In 1952 he was imprisoned for taking part in demonstrations. Freed, he was imprisoned again from February 1955 to June 1957. In 1958 he qualified as a doctor and was one of the founders of the Anti-Colonial Movement (M. A. C.), centred in Lisbon.

In 1959 he returned to Angola. He worked in his birth place as a medical doctor until he was arrested in June 1960. At the time of his arrest the people of his own village staged a demonstration which was brutally suppressed and the village itself burnt. This was the beginning of the 1961 resurrection.

Agostinho Neto was transferred to Lisbon, then to the Cape Verde Island Santo Antão, then to Lisbon again. In August 1962 he escaped, and went to Kinshasa to make peace between Holden Roberto (FNLA) and Mário de Andrade (MPLA). He soon became the leader of MPLA (Movimento Popular de Libertação de Angola), and is directing and organizing the guerrilla warfare in eastern Angola.

Agostinho Neto's poetry was published in three anthologies, *Colectânea de poemas* (1967), *Con occhi asciutti* (1968 a), in Portuguese and Italian, and *Očiju bez suza* (1968 b), in Portuguese and Serbo-Croatian.

"In the best of his poems about Africa, he is at pains to reveal his own situation as he glimpses it in the lives of other Africans" (U. S. Merwin).

Portrait on Plate XIII.

Nganthojeff, Job   Cameroon

Job Nganthojeff is the pen-name of Thomas Ngandjon, born on March 24, 1936, in Bandeng, district Mifi, Cameroon. In 1960, just before the independence of the country, he was private secretary to Pierre Kandem Ninyum, the Minister of Health. He belongs to the editorial board of the journal "Le Cameroun Littéraire".

Job Nganthojeff has published poetry in "Le Cameroun Littéraire" and in his volume *Mélange* (703).

Ngcobo, Moses John   South Africa

Born on November 28, 1928, in Durban, Natal, South Africa, Moses John Ngcobo, a Zulu, was trained as a teacher and

studied privately for his B. A. He soon gave up teaching in order
to devote his life entirely to writing. His first novel in Zulu,
Inkungu maZulu (1975), was awarded a prize by the South
African Academy for Arts and Sciences in 1961. It was followed
by *Wo he bantu* (1976), and *Ukufika kosuku* (1977).

Ngoh, John Emmanuel Akwo   Cameroon

Born about 1940 in Kombone, district Kumba, in Western
Cameroon, John Emmanuel Akwo Ngoh was educated at the
Government and the Basel Mission Schools in Kumba and in
1956 at the Kombone Native Administration School, where he
got his School Leaving Certificate. In 1957 he moved to Onitsha,
Nigeria, where he was at the New Bethel College. In 1958 he
changed to the Catholic Trinity High School in Oguta. There
he started writing in his free time, poems like *Influenza and
the Love of God,* or *Trinity High School.* His novel *Florence
in the River of Temptations* (705) is a typical "Onitsha novel".

Ngugi, James   Kenya

Born on January 5, 1938, in Limuru, Central Province, near
Nairobi, Kenya, James Thiong'o Ngugi — this is his full name —
comes from a polygamous family, and has many brothers and
sisters. In 1946 his mother sent him to a mission school, in 1947
to a Kikuyu school at Karinga, where he was educated until
1955, except for the period from 1948 to 1950 when there were
no lessons because of Mau Mau. In 1955 he entered Alliance
High School, and in 1959 Makerere College in Kampala,
Uganda. After graduating from Makerere in 1964, he worked on
Nairobi's "Daily Nation" for several months before he left
to do graduate work at the University of Leeds, England. Back
in Africa in 1967, Ngugi became a special lecturer in English

at Nairobi's University College until the students' strike in January 1969, when he resigned in protest. He accepted the position of a Visiting Professor at Northwestern University, Evanston, Illinois, USA, in 1970.

As a student in Makerere he already edited the journal "Penpoint", and he was editor of the journal "Zuka", from 1967 to 1969. His creative work includes three novels, *Weep Not, Child* (1337), *The River Between* (1338), *A Grain of Wheat* (1339), and a play, *The Black Hermit* (1340).

"*Weep Not, Child,* the first English-language novel to be written by an East African writer, received awards from both the 1966 Dakar Festival of Negro Arts and the East African Literature Bureau. *Weep Not, Child* is divided into two parts: the first deals with the period just before the Emergency, the second with the Emergency itself in the life of a Kenyan family" (Ime Ikiddeh).

"*Weep Not, Child* is also an autobiographical novel, and its weaknessess come from the need to make it at once a book about the Mau Mau rebellion and yet also a book written out of immediate and personal experience" (John Reed).

"Ngugi records Njoroge's tragedy in a simple but expressive prose which, even at its most impassioned, is never shrill" (Bernth Lindfors).

"The novel consists of too many unrelated essays and stories; things just do not dovetail" (Taban lo Liyong).

"The book is too dream-like. We long for someone to get a headache, or drop something, or just yawn. We begin to wish the hero would kiss that girl . . . Perhaps this is just the way Ngugi writes — the dream-novel, with its psychological, not eventful, structure, is certainly the modern thing" (M. M. Carlin).

"This novel announces without doubt an important literary career" (Abiola Irele).

James Ngugi's second novel, *The River Between,* again raises issues of vital importance. "The conflict centres on circumcision, especially female circumcision, and it is seen as a struggle for the very soul of the people" (M. M. Carlin).

"... formal as a ballet with predictable characters and predictable interactions and relationships ... The characters involved are almost stereotypes" (Margaret Amosu).

"... in *The River Between*, nature is at center stage, playing an active role, influencing a character's feelings and thoughts in a way only human beings do in most European and American novels ... All this is very exciting to me as a writer, because it suggests new ways of telling a story, new relationships of character and setting" (William Melvin Kelley).

James Ngugi's third novel, *A Grain of Wheat,* "is longer and more ambitious than his two earlier works. (It) is set on the eve of Kenya's achievement of independence. Uhuru has become a reality but not quite the panacea that was half optimistically expected and half uneasily hoped for ... (It) is remarkable for approaching the theme ... in terms of the minute conflicts that actually make up life ... The characters are ... people with a recognizable identity as individuals, living their lives and facing their problems in a vividly caught environment" (Derek Elders).

"*A Grain of Wheat* is hard, sober and serious. It is free from pretentious contrivances and smug judgements. The issues it raises are painful: the very foundations of Uhuru, and hope for the future are questioned" (Primila Lewis).

"Ngugi's handling of his present material, as compared with his earlier works, shows great dexterity and the maturity he himself has attained since the undergraduate days of his earlier novels ... If *A Grain of Wheat* were James Ngugi's first novel, nobody would quarrel with his choice of subject matter, but because his earlier novels deal with the same problems I begin to wonder whether there is anything else he can write about other than the Emergency, the Independent school movement and the detention of Jomo Kenyatta" (Clem Abiaziem Okafor).

James Ngugi's first play, *The Black Hermit,* written for the Uganda National Theatre as part of the Independence celebrations in 1962, is written in a "Poetic diction". The play "touches upon a number of issues which are immediate enough to the East African world, but not one of these issues — the claims of tribe, nation, ideology, religion, family and sexual love — is properly explored or developed in the manner we are entitled to expect of a full-length play" (Gerald Moore).

Portrait on Plate XV.

Niane, Djibril Tamsir   Guinea

Djibril Tamsir Niane was born on January 9, 1932, in Conakry, Guinea. He was educated at the Institut des Hautes Etudes in Dakar, Senegal, and at the University of Bordeaux, France, where he obtained his licence ès lettres in History and Literature in 1958 and his diplôme d'études supérieures d'histoire in 1959.

Back home at the end of 1959 Niane became a teacher of History at the Lycée classique in Conakry and shortly afterwards headmaster of the Lycée technique. From 1960 to 1961 he was headmaster at the Lycée classique. In 1961 he was appointed Directeur de l'Enseignement du 2e degrée in the Ministry of National Education. In 1964 he was appointed professor of History at the Institut Polytechnique in Conakry. Since 1967 he has been a member of the Conseil Supérieur de l'Enseignement, and since 1968 he has been Dean of the Faculty of Social Sciences at the Institut Polytechnique in Conakry.

Simultaneously Niane collaborates with the National Institute of Research and Documentation and contributes to the radio series "Tribune de l'Histoire". He is also engaged in theatre, directing university drama groups and collaborating with the Federal Troup in Conakry.

As a historian Niane has specialised on the medieval African empires, particularly the Massina empire and the Mandingo people. His knowledge of their history is woven into the historical novel *Soundjata ou L'Epopée mandingue* (707) — translated also into English under the title *Soundiata. An Epic of Old Mali* (707 b) — and into the play *Sikasso ou La dernière citadelle,* Honfleur 1971. The latter volume also contains *Chaka,* a play in two acts about the great Zulu king. His scholarly works include *Recherches sur l'empire du Mali,* Conakry 1959 to

1960, and, in collaboration with Jean Suret-Canale, *Histoire de l'Afrique occidentale,* Paris 1961.

On *Soundjata:* "Niane, in completing the recital of the griot [the West African minstrel], has preserved his naiveté, his greatness and his fascination" (Robert Pageard).

Niang, Lamine   Senegal

Born in 1923 in Saint-Louis, Senegal, Lamine Niang is a diplomé des Cours Gougaud (P.T.T.) and a bachelor of literature. For some time he was an assistant teacher at the Lycée Corneille in Rouen, France. In 1957 Niang founded the Association des Travailleurs Noirs en Normandie (Association of Black Workers in Normandy). In 1968 Niang was chosen Lauréat by "Amitiés poétiques" in Marocco. The following year, he was one of Senegal's official delegates to the First Pan-African Festival in Algiers, and in 1971 he was the delegate of the Senegalese Government to the Conférence Inter-Etatique du Cafrad in Tanger. Lamine Niang is now Conseiller at the Senegalese Embassy in Rabat, Morocco.

Lamine Niang published a volume of poetry, *Négristique* (708), the introduction of which was written by Léopold Sédar Senghor.

"This poetry is poetic right down to its vocabulary. Lamine Niang takes the words like in a dice-boy, shakes them and throws them on the table, on the page, where they arrange freely in mysterious attractive powers and correspondences. One has the impression of a certain shifting between the word and its common meaning, of a certain chance; but a lucky chance, that produces, here, the emotional short-circuit" (Léopold Sédar Senghor).

Nicol, Abioseh   Sierra Leone

Born in 1924 in Freetown, Sierra Leone, Davidson Abioseh
Nicol — this is his full name — spent the first nine years of his
life in Nigeria where his father was teaching Pharmacy. Then
he was at the Prince of Wales School in Freetown, Sierra Leone.
In 1943 he was given a scholarship to Christ's College, Cambridge, England, where he studied Medicine. He was assistant
doctor at a hospital in London. He returned to Cambridge as
College Supervisor in Medicine and Natural Science.

From 1952 to 1954 he was lecturer for Medicine and Bio-
chemistry at the University College, Ibadan, Nigeria, then was
an honorary medical officer in Nigeria, a senior pathologist
in the Sierra Leone medical service, a pathology consultant to
the Sierra Leone Government, a member of its Public Service
Commission, and Director of the National Bank of Sierra
Leone. In the capacity of guest lecturer, Dr. Davidson Nicol
has been to the United States (Yale University, Mayo Clinic,
and UNESCO conference), Germany, and Ghana. In 1960 he
was appointed Principal of Fourah Bay College in Freetown,
Sierra Leone, and 1966 Vice-Chancellor of the entire University
of Sierra Leone, which united Fourah Bay College and Njala
University College.

In 1967 Dr. Davidson Nicol retired from all functions to
dedicate himself to his private studies. But soon he was Ambassador of Sierra Leone to the United Nations in New York. In
1971 he was appointed Sierra Leone's Ambassador to London.
In summer 1972 Nicol returned to the United Nations as Executive Director of the United Nations Institute for Training and
Research (Unitar).

Dr. Davidson Nicol outlined his personal views in *Africa:
A Subjective View*, London 1964. His creative work is a volume
of short stories *The Truly Married Woman* (709), in which are
included also the *Two African Tales* (710). As creative writer
he uses the name Abioseh Nicol.

"Abioseh Nicol is one of Africa's most talented short story
writers" (Bernth Lindfors).

"The world of work and play — and frequently the world of children — is his subject" (Robert P. Cobb).

"The English are seen very much as they would see themselves, the Africans more often than not, as the white man would see them" (Christine Obumselu).

"It all looks so simple, so utterly natural; as though Nicol is casually taking a slice of real life and offering it to us in all its workaday detail, all its blending of the tragic and the absurd. Yet the style that allows this effect must possess the translucence of chrystal; and the sensibility behind the style must be one of marvellous richness and iron control" (Adrian A. Roscoe).

Portrait on Plate IX.

Nikiéma, Roger   Upper Volta

Born in 1935 at Konioudou, Upper Volta, Roger Nikiéma was the head of the Information Service of Radio Upper Volta until 1962, when he became its Director. Since the end of 1970 he has been a journalist at the University of Dakar, Senegal.

Roger Nikiéma has written a novel, *Dessein contraire* (712), about a girl being forced to marry a sorcerer, and two short stories which have appeared in one volume, *Deux adorables rivales; Les soleils de la terre*, Yaunde 1971.

Njau, Rebecca   Kenya

Born on December 15, 1932, in Kanyariri, a village near Kikuyu, Central Province, a few miles west of Nairobi, Kenya, Rebecca Njau was educated at Kabete Intermediate School, from 1948 to 1952, at Alliance Girls' High School, Kikuyu, and from 1953 to 1958 at Makerere University College, Kampala, where she got her Diploma in Education. From 1958 to 1959 she was teaching at Alliance Girls' School, Kikuyu, from 1960 to 1962 at Makerere College School, Kampala. In 1964 she founded the Nairobi Girls' Secondary School, Nairobi, and became its headmistress. From 1965 to 1966 she was Kenya representative of the University College Council.

Among other activities — Rebeka Njau as she prefers to spell her name now; she also uses the pseudonym Marina Gashe — has represented her country at women's educational gatherings, including the University Women's Seminar held in East Africa in 1964. She is married to the artist Elimo Njau, under whose influence she discovered her own artistic talent. She is now a textile designer. Her art was first exhibited at Paa-ya-Paa Gallery in Nairobi in 1968. In March 1969 she held her second show at the National Museum in Dar es Salaam, Tanzania. She designed the material for the National Dance Troupe of Tanzania, which attended the Pan-African Festival in Algiers in 1969. In October 1969 she was invited by the Director of Zambia Cultural Services to participate in Zambia's Arts Festival in 1969, with an exhibition of textile design, wall hangings, bed spreads, cushion covers, and dresses and shirts in batik. In 1971 she had another exhibition at the Paa-ya-Paa Gallery in Nairobi.

Rebecca Njau has written several plays, that were produced in Nairobi, Kenya, and at Makerere University, Kampala, Uganda. One, *The Scar* (1341), was printed in Tanzania, and won a drama festival award at the National Theatre in Kampala.

Njoya, Martin   Cameroon

Born in 1944 into a family with a Muslim mother from East Cameroon and a Christian father from West Cameroon. Because of the movements of his parents he had an ever-changing schooling, finally gaining the First School Leaving Certificate from the Baptist Mission School in Soppo, in 1959. From 1960 to 1964 he studied at the Cameroon Protestant College at Bali, district

Bamenda. From 1964 to 1966 he studied in the Arts Department of Cameroon College of Arts, Science and Technology.

He served as a tutor in the Presbyterian Secondary School at Manfe, and then entered the Civil Service as a teacher in the Practising Bilingual College of the Higher Institute of Education in Yaunde. He died on May 31, 1970, in Yaunde, in a car accident.

His poetry was published in the journal "Le Cameroun Littéraire".

Nketia, J. H. Kwabena   Ghana

Born on June 22, 1921, in Mampong, Ashanti, Ghana, as son of a cocoa farmer, J. H. Kwabena Nketia was educated at the Primary and Middle Schools of Mampong from 1928 to 1936. He then went to the Teacher Training College in Akropong, Akuapem, Ghana (1937—40) and got his Teacher's Certificate 'A'. Akropong was already under the influence of Dr. Amu, father of Ghana's musicology, and Nketia started writing music while training as a teacher. When he had finished his training he joined the staff of the Akropong College to teach music and languages.

In 1944 Nketia came to London to assist in the teaching of Twi at the School of Oriental and African Studies. He held this position till 1946, during which time he was able to take his Certificate in Phonetics. The years from 1946 to 1949 Nketia spent at Birkbeck College and Trinity College of Music, both in London and got his B. A. in Music, English and History. On his return in 1949 Nketia worked again as a teacher at the Training College in Akropong. In 1952 he became Acting Principal of this school, but left the same year to join the staff of the Institute of African Studies, University of Ghana, Legon, as Research Fellow. As part of his studies he spent the 1958/59 semester at Columbia University, USA, where he attended courses in Ethnomusicology and Composition, and the 1959 semester at Northwestern University.

From 1959 to 1961 J. H. Kwabena Nketia became Senior Research Fellow, University of Ghana, Legon, in 1962 Associate Professor, in 1963 Professor, and in 1965 Director of the Institute of African Studies. In 1969 Nketia became Professor in the Department of Music at the University of California in Los Angeles, USA.

For his services to Ghana's music J. H. Kwabena Nketia was awarded the Grand Medal of the Government of Ghana in 1968.

Professor Nketia has written many scholarly articles on traditional African music and poetry, mainly Akan. He is an active musician himself, directing the Atenteben orchestra, which consists of students of the School of Music and Drama, University of Ghana. His creative writing is in his mother tongue Twi. He published a collection of short stories from traditional history *Sɛmɔdɛ* (716), a play *Ananwoma* (717), a collection of poems *Anwonsɛm* (718), a collection of narrative poems *Akwansosɛm Bi* (719), and two stories *Kwabena Amoa* (720) and *Wokɔ a, na Wohunu* (721).

Nkonde, I. Braim   Zambia

Born on January 4, 1916, in Old Fife, Eastern Bemba area, Zambia, I. Braim Nkonde was educated at Lubwa Mission in Chinsali, of the Church of Scotland. From 1939 to 1942 he was trained as a teacher at Adam's College, Natal, South Africa. After five years teaching in Zambia he was granted a scholarship at the London University School of Oriental and African Studies where he took a diploma in Bemba. On his return to Zambia he was assigned to the Information Department at Lusaka. Transferred to the African Education Department, he became Headmaster of two schools. In 1951 he was appointed as Manager of the Government Schools in Central Province of Northern Rhodesia.

After twelve years in civil service, I. Braim Nkonde resigned in April 1953 to open a business as grocer and fruiter at Kabwe (formerly Broken Hill).

I. Braim Nkonde wrote several plays in Bemba, one of which, *Supuni alete misoka* (1985), was published.

Nkosi, Lewis   South Africa

Born on December 5, 1936, in Durban, Natal, South Africa, Lewis Nkosi was educated in public schools in Zululand. One year he spent at the M. L. Sultan Technical College in Durban. In 1955 he was editor of the Zulu-English weekly "Ilanga laseNatal" (Natal Sun). From 1956 to 1961 he was collaborator of "Drum" and "Golden City Post" in Johannesburg.

In 1961 Nkosi left South Africa to study journalism at Harvard University, Cambridge, Massachusetts, USA. He then worked for the Radio. From 1964 to 1969 he edited a monthly information service "South Africa — Information and Analysis" for the Congress for Cultural Freedom, Paris. He is living in London as collaborator of numerous papers and journals, like "The Observer", "The Guardian", "New Statesman", "Spectator", "West Africa", "The New African", etc.

Nkosi has published important critical essays on African literature in "Black Orpheus", and in several issues of "Africa Report" (S 99—S 106, SA 409). A collection of his essays, *Home and Exile*, London 1965, includes reflections on apartheid, New York, and African and Afro-American literature.

His play, *The Rhythm of Violence* (1986), was first performed on October 27, 1965, at the J. K. Randle Hall, Lagos, Nigeria. It is the first play to be written in English by a black South African since 1936. Set in Johannesburg in the early sixties, it is concerned with a bomb planted in the City Hall by left-wing students.

"Although the characterization is usually clear and the dialogue sometimes powerful, *The Rhythm of Violence* is too undisciplined in movement and too hysterical in message to be effective drama" (Bernth Lindfors).

Portrait on Plate IV.

Nkrumah, Kwame   Ghana

Born in September 1909 at Nkroful in the Western Region of Ghana as a member of the Nzima tribe, Francis Nwia Kofie Nkrumah, who later called himself Kwame Nkrumah, was a son of a goldsmith and was educated at Catholic mission schools. Later he became a pupil teacher. In 1926 he went to the Government Training College in Accra where he took a teaching diploma and then taught at a variety of schools until in 1935 an uncle helped him to pay his passage to the United States. In 1939 he graduated from Lincoln University with a major in Economics and Sociology, staying on to study Theology. Having obtained post-graduate degrees in Education and Philosophy from the University of Pennsylvania, he was appointed lecturer in Political Science at Lincoln University and, while there, was elected President of the African Students Organization of America and Canada. He contributed to the journal of this organization, "The African Interpreter", which had five issues between February 1943 and Spring 1944.

Coming across the works of Marcus Garvey, he became fired with the idea of Pan-Africanism. In June 1945 he went to London to read Law and write a thesis. Becoming Vice-President of the West African Students Union, he worked closely with George Padmore and in October was one of the joint secretaries of the 5th Pan-African Conference at Manchester, where plans were made to win independence in Africa through the organization of mass parties. As General Secretary of the Working Committee he edited "The New African" in 1946. In 1947 he was asked to become the General Secretary of the UGCC (United Gold Coast Convention), so he set sail for the Gold Coast on November 14, 1947. In February 1948 a boycott of European and Syrian traders led to disturbances which were blamed on the UGCC leaders who were all arrested. Nkrumah was detained in Lawra in the Northern Territories, but released to give evidence, he continued his activities and founded the "Accra Evening News" in September 1948. In June 12, 1949, he broke away from the UGCC and formed his own party,

CPP (Convention People's Party). In January 1950 Nkrumah was detained in James Fort prison. But he won the elections and on February 12, 1950, he was released to become leader of Government Business. In March 1952 his title was changed to Prime Minister. On March 6, 1957, the country became independent and changed its name to Ghana. In April 1960 Nkrumah was elected President of the new republic. He founded the journal "Voice of Africa" which existed until 1965. Nkrumah directed substantial contributions to movements he considered useful to his ultimate goal of a free and united Africa, but he neglected the economic situation of Ghana and suppressed all criticism.

On February 24, 1966, when he was abroad, the Ghana military forces under General Ankrah overthrew his government. Nkrumah was deposed because of "absolutist" government, "abuse of the constitution" and "corruption". He found asylum in Guinea where President Sekou Touré appointed him Co-President. He died in Bucharest on April 27, 1972.

The Autobiography of Kwame Nkrumah (722) has been translated into many languages, along with his other political and politico-philosophical writings: *I Speak of Freedom*, London — New York 1961, *Africa Must Unite*, London — New York 1963, *Consciencism*, London 1964, *Neo-Colonialism, the Last Stage of Imperialism*, London 1965, *Axioms of Kwame Nkrumah*, London 1967, *Challenge of the Congo*, London 1967, *Voice from Ghana*, London 1967, *The Big Lie*, London 1968, *Dark Days in Ghana* (723), *Handbook of Revolutionary Warfare*, London 1968, *The Spectre of Black Power*, London 1968, *The Struggle Continues*, London 1968, *Two Myths*, London 1968, and *The Way Out*, London 1968.

Nokan, Charles   Ivory Coast

Born on December 28, 1936, in Yamoussokro, Central district, Ivory Coast, Charles Nokan received his elementary education at Yamoussokro and Toumodi, his secondary education in France — in Blois and Montargis. He studied Sociology and Philosophy in Poitiers and Paris. He is Licencié in Sociology and he has a Doctor's Degree in Philosophy.

In 1964 he was arrested in Ivory Coast, his writings being considered to be subversive. When released in 1965, he left for France. He is a member of the staff of the journal and publishing house "Présence Africaine", Paris.

His first book, *Le soleil noir point* (727) is a poetical narrative, "the expression of a juvenile romantism in a grandiloquent style" (Robert Pageard).

His second book, *Violent était le vent* (728), "takes up the subject of *Le soleil noir point,* and even the technic is nearly the same. But in this second novel Charles Nokan has put more emphasis on the dramatical development of the novel, thus avoiding the 'poetic' pulverisation which damaged *Le soleil noir point*" (Bernard Mouralis).

On his plays, *Les malheurs de Tchakô* (729) and *Abraha Pokou ou une grande africaine*, Paris 1970, Jacques Howlett writes: "Again Nokan challenges the problematic Africa, the Africa in making, to be reconstructed by those who constitute her living force: the silent people. His challenge is revolutionary."

His poem *La voix grave d'Ophimoï*, added to the small volume of *Abraha Pokou,* includes his *Carnet de Prison,* his memories from prison, fights for revolution and evokes the solidarity of the workers. "This poem is a profession of faith and hope" (Mikel Dufrenne).

Noronha, Rui de   Mozambique

Born on October 29, 1909, in Lourenço Marques, Mozambique, Rui de Noronha spent all his life in his home town. He was in constant conflict with social and racial barriers and had a short and unhappy bohemian life. He died in Lourenço Marques on December 25, 1943.

From his only volume of poetry, *Sonetos* (1988), some verses were published posthumously in journals like "Présence Africaine" and in anthologies like "La poésie africaine d'expression portugaise" (A 9).

"Rui de Noronha ... expresses timidly the conflicts in the colonial society in which he had to live all his life. Sensible to the spectacle of oppression, but alone in his endeavour, he was for a long time the prisoner of his mystical quest" (Mário de Andrade).

"His posthumously published *Sonetos* picture Africa as a sleeping slave who must be recalled to life like Lazarus by the new saviour Progress" (Gerald M. Moser).

Noumé, Etienne B.   Cameroon

Etienne B. Noumé is the pen-name of Etienne NKepndep, born in January 1944 at Bangou, district Nifi, Cameroon. After his elementary education at the Catholic mission school of Banka near Bafang, he studied at the Collège Saint-Paul of Banka. In 1958 he entered the Lycée of Joss in Duala. He left in 1960, but could not find work. In 1963 he came into contact with Patrice Kayo of Bandjoun with whom he read and wrote poetry for six months. In this time he created the collection of poetry which was published in a special issue of the journal "Ozila" in Yaunde, as supplement to Nr. 14.

From 1964 to 1966 Etienne Noumé was at the Ecole Normale d'Instituteurs at Nkongsamba. In 1967 he taught at Garua. In 1968 he had his first mental crisis. In 1969, while teaching at the Ecole Principale at Loum, he had a second mental crisis and burned all his manuscripts except the poems he had sent to Patrice Kayo. The family treated him, but he escaped, never to be seen again. In 1970 his Identity Card was found in Duala, and his family announced his death.

"His poetry reflects the image of a world in prey of madness and fear ... Like Rimbaud he has produced all his work before

being nineteen. The work of Noumé is thin, but highly original"
(Patrice Kayo).

Nsimbi, Michael Bazze   Uganda

Born in 1910 in a village near Masaka, district Masaka, Uganda,
Michael Bazze Nsimbi was educated from 1928 to 1929 at St.
Henry's College, Kisubi, and from 1930 to 1932 at Makerere
College in Kampala where he received his Teaching Diploma.
He taught as Assistant Headmaster at Rubaga Secondary School
from 1933 to 1934, and as Assistant Teacher at the school of
Tabora in Tanganyika from 1934 to 1937. In 1938 he became
Assistant Inspector of Schools in Uganda. In 1938 he rose to
Education Officer and in 1962 to Senior Education Officer in
the Central Inspectorate, a position he kept until 1965.

From 1955 to 1956 he did an Education course at the University of Bristol, England, and from September 1961 to June
1962 he was at Georgetown University, Washington, D.C.,
USA, to assist a professor who was doing research in Luganda.

In 1966 Michael Bazze Nsimbi became Curator of the British
Council in Kampala, and in 1968 Vernacular Language Advisor
to the Uganda Publishing House.

In 1955 Michael Bazze Nsimbi was awarded the Margaret
Wrong Prize for his book *Waggaumbulizi,* a monography on
Luganda place names. In 1960 he was awarded the honour of
M. B. E. (Member of the Order of the British Empire) for his
work on the vernacular.

Michael Bazze Nsimbi wrote all his books in Luganda. *Siwa
Muto Lugero* on Ganda Proverbs, *Mudda Awulira* (1346) on
Exhortations, and *Amannya Amaganda n'Ennono Zaago* col-
lecting legends connected with place names in Buganda.

His collection of stories *Kitagenda ne Kagenda* (1347) and
his two novels *Kagenda ne Banne* (1348) and *Kagenda ne Banne
Bakola ki?* (1349) are written for young readers.

Ntara, Samuel Yosia — Malawi

Samuel Yosia Ntara was born in 1905 in Malawi. He was a teacher at the Kongwe Station School, a mission school of the Dutch Reformed Church Mission, in Dowa.

Both his books were written in his mother tongue Nyanja but published only in English translation. *Man of Africa* (1992) was awarded a prize on its publication in 1934. *Headman's Enterprise* (1993) is a biographical novel about Chief Msyamboza, a historical personality who died in 1926, leaving behind a flourishing village with a mission school and Western innovations, which Ntara slightly idealizes. *Mbiri ya Achewa,* Lusaka and Limbe 1949, is a history of the Chewa tribe.

Ntiru, Richard — Uganda

Born in 1946 near Kisoro, district Kigezi ,in the extreme Southwest of Uganda, Richard Ntiru received his secondary education at Ntare School, Mbarara, district Ankole. In 1968 he entered Makerere University, Kampala, to study literature. He edited the campus newspaper "Makererean", organized the 1969 Makerere Arts Festival, participated in the Makerere Travelling Theatre, and edited the campus journal of creative writing, "Penpoint". Besides a radio play and a few stories, Richard Ntiru has contributed to East African magazines.

Ntiru has had his first book published, a collection of poems, *Tensions,* Nairobi 1971. "It points to the direction creative writing in Africa must take" (Mauri Yambo).

Ntsane, Kem Edward — Lesotho

Born on April 4, 1920, in Kolojane, province Leribe, Lesotho, Kemuel Edward Ntsane, the son of a schoolteacher, had his primary education at Mmamathe near Teyateyaneng, province Berea, then went to the Morija Teacher Training College. After graduating, he first taught in Roma and was later transferred to Maseru High School. In 1947 he left for London, to attend courses on the teaching of English. Sometime after his return, he gave up teaching and entered the civil service. In the mid-sixties, he followed a course in journalism in Kitwe, Zambia, but had to give up because of ill health.

Ntsane is the author of the volume of poetry, '*Musa-pelo* (2002), which, fifteen years later, was followed by a second volume under the same title (2004). He also published the novel, *Masoabi, ngoan'a Mosotho 'a Kajeno* (2003), two short novels, *Nna, Sajene Kokobela, C.I.D.* (2005) and *Makumane*, Johannesburg 1961, *Bana ba Roma*, Morija 1954, a book for juvenile readers, and *Bao batho* (2006). All his works are in Sotho.

"Important is Ntsane's introduction of humorous and satirical elements into written Sotho poetry" (Albert S. Gérard).

Ntsikana   South Africa

Ntsikana was born around 1783 as son of Gabo and his second wife into Chief Ngqika's tribe in the Tyumie Valley, Cape Province, South Africa. In his youth he heard the preachings of Dr. Johannes Theodosius van der Kemp (1747–1811), a Dutchman, who had wandered for several months between the Tyumie and the Buffalo rivers to teach Christianity to the Xhosa. When van der Kemp left on account of impending tribal war, Ntsikana was educated according to custom. In 1816 the Reverend Joseph Williams of the London Missionary Society took up residence in Chief Ngqika's territory, and Ntsikana learned more of the Christian faith. After William's death in 1818, Ntsikana set up his own "school" at Makanzara and taught his followers to give up heathen dances and traditional face-painting. He composed a number of hymns in Xhosa, which were learned by heart, because neither he nor his followers could read or write. They were transmitted orally till the mission in Lovedale was founded, where they were transcribed.

Ntsikana must have died about the end of 1820.

Ntsiko, Jonas
vid. *uHadi Waseluhlangeni*

Ntuli, Denteronomy Bhekinkozi Zeblon   South Africa

Born on May 8, 1940, in Eshowe, Zululand, South Africa, Deuteronomy Bhekinkozi Zeblon Ntuli got his secondary education at Ndaleni High School, his Matric at the Catholic Mission School at Mariannhill near Durban, Natal, and his B. A. at the University of Zululand.

From 1964 to 1967 he was a radio announcer, and presently he is a lecturer in Zulu at the University of South Africa in Zululand.

Besides a critical survey written in English, *A Brief Survey of Modern Literature in the South African Bantu Languages: Zulu,* and published in the journal "Limi" in 1968, all his works are written in Zulu. He wrote two novels, *uBheka* (2013) and *Ngiyoze ngimthole* (I will find him), Johannesburg 1970, two volumes of short stories, *Izikhwili* (2015) and *Imicibisholo* (2016), two volumes of poetry, *Amangwevu* (2014) and *Imvunge yemvelo* (The harmony of nature), Johannesburg 1972, and a play, *Indandatho yesethembiso* (The engagement ring), Johannesburg 1971.

Nunes, António   Cape Verde Islands

Born in 1917 on the island St. Jago of the Cape Verde Islands, António Nunes was a poet who participated in the Portuguese movement of neo-realism. He died in 1951 in Portugal. "Like Aguinaldo Fonseca, António Nunes is forced to seek his salvation in continental Portugal. He discovers there, however, only misery and a tragic death from mental illness in 1951" (Norman Araujo).

António Nunes has published two volumes of poetry, *Devaneios* (735) and *Poemas de longe* (736). His poems have also been printed in journals like "Vértice" and "Cabo Verde" and in the anthology "Modernos autores portugueses", Lisbon 1942.

"His Capeverdianism, barring an initial Classical temptation, sings out on every page of verse — and to such an extent that he reverses the desire of escape, feeling *saudades* for the islands as he longs, from afar, for the moment when he may return to them. As far as the African aspect is concerned, he cultivates it more substantially and more artistically than Fonseca. His poetic worth is in every way greater" (Norman Araujo).

Nwankwo, Nkem — Nigeria

Born on June 12, 1936, in Nawfia-Awka, East Central State, Nigeria, Nkem Nwankwo was educated at King's College, Lagos, and University College, Ibadan, where he studied English from 1959 to 1962. For many years he taught English at the Ibadan Grammar School. Since the Nigerian civil war he has been working for the "Daily Times" in Lagos.

In 1962 Nkem Nwankwo was awarded the short story prize of the Lagos Branch of the Nigerian Arts Council for his story *The Gambler*. This event marked the beginning of his career as a writer. He wrote books for children, *Tales out of School* (744), and *More Tales Out of School* (746). His novel *Danda* (745), introduced the genre of the picaresque novel into Nigeria and was later transformed into a successful play (747).

"The profile of *Danda* is too sketchy for the book to be entirely successful. Yet Nwankwo's gift for dramatic dialogue, his ability to capture atmosphere and idiom, as well as his warmth and talent for sketching humorous scenes . . ." (Thomas Cassirer).

"*Danda* is in some ways a disjointed novel. Some of the chapters read as though they had been written as short stories and later linked, and Danda's escapades are often episodic, with little connection between them. But Danda himself is a vibrant and memorable character, and Nwankwo's energetic prose can bring to immediate life, in a few sentences, a whole environment" (Margaret Laurence).

Nwankwo, Victor   Nigeria

Victor Nwankwo was born in 1945 in Ajalli, East Central State, Nigeria. He obtained an honours degree in Civil Engineering from the University of Nigeria, Nsukka, in 1971. He is Editor-in-Chief of "Nsukka Engineer" and Associate Editor of the publishing house Nwankwo-Ifejika & Co, Enugu.

Nwankwo's novel *The Path to Udima,* was published only in a German translation, *Der Weg nach Udima* (748). A story, *The End of the Road,* appeared in the anthology "The Insider", Enugu 1971.

Nwanodi, Okogbule
vid. *Wonodi, Okogbule*

Nwapa, Flora   Nigeria

Born on January 18, 1931, in Oguta, Oguta Division, East Central State, Nigeria, Flora Nwapa went to C.M.S. School in Oguta, Archdeacon Crowther's Memorial School in Elelenwa near Port Harcourt from 1945 to 1948, and to C.M.S. Girls

School, Lagos, from 1949 to 1950. She did a post secondary year at Queen's School in Lagos in 1951, spent the years from 1953 to 1957 at University College, Ibadan, and from 1957 to 1958 at the University of Edinburgh, Scotland, where she got her diploma in Education.

Back in Nigeria, Flora Nwapa became Education Officer in Calabar, in 1959. From 1959 to 1962 she taught English and Geography at Queen's School in Enugu, and from 1962 to 1964 she was Administration Officer at the University of Lagos. In 1964 Flora Nwapa became Assistant Registrar (Public Relations) of the University of Lagos. The year 1967 saw her home during the crisis, and she was employed in the Transport Directorate in Biafra for a period of nine months.

At present Flora Nwapa is Commissioner for Health and Social Welfare, East Central State. She is married to Gogo Nwakuche.

With her novel *Efuru* (750) Flora Nwapa is the first woman writer to use the Ibo village as her scene.

"The style is quiet, simple and slow, perhaps too slow for most readers: but it is a style designed to reflect the life it describes. It (the novel) is an impressive beginning" (D. W.).

"I like this writer's style and way of writing very much, especially because of the artistic merits of oral literature which one feels when reading her text . . . the language is quite near to the material which it describes. The flavour and the beauty of Ibo language are, in spite of a faultless English, always present in the reader" (Mbella Sonne Dipoko).

"In *Efuru* therefore, there seems to be a gap between intention and realization, and we must surely attribute this to Flora Nwapa's failure to think out her themes deeply, and to devise adequate techniques with which to convey them. Add to these deficiencies her pedestrian style . . ." (Eustace Palmer).

Flora Nwapa's second Novel *Idu* (751), also set in a small Nigerian town, centres round the question, of whether children are the only happiness on earth. Her latest work is a collection of short stories *This is Lagos and other Stories,* Enugu 1971, in which she recaptures the frustrations of modern Nigerian city-women.

Nwogu, Matthew Chinke   Nigeria

Born in 1927 in Umuahia-Ibeku, East Central State, Nigeria, Matthew Chinke Nwogu received a secondary education. After training at a nursing school he was appointed health inspector in Kaduna. His manuscript *West African Elephant* (752) was awarded the Margaret Wrong Prize in 1955. The book was published only in a German translation, *Der Elefant Goza* (752 a).

Nxumalo, Otty E. H. Mandla   South Africa

Born on August 23, 1938, in Louwsburg, Natal, South Africa, Otty Ezrom Howard Mandlakayise Nxumalo studied at the University of South Africa, where he got his B. A. He also received a Lower Primary Teacher's Certificate and a Diploma in Journalism and Short Story Writing. He is employed as Circuit Inspector of Schools in the Department of Education and Culture of the KwaZulu Government Service, Zululand.

Nxumalo has published two novelettes, *Ikusasa Alaziwa* (2017) and *Ngisinga Empumalanga* (2019), and two volumes of poetry, *Ikhwezi* (2018) and *Umzwangedwa,* all in his mother tongue Zulu.

Nyabongo, Akiki   Uganda

Born in 1907 in Kabalore, district Toro, Uganda, Prince Akiki Nyabongo descends from a long line of Toro kings. He was educated at Mengo High School, Kampala, Uganda, King's College, Buddo, Uganda, and at Clark College High School in the United States of America. He continued at the Caman Theological Seminary, USA, at Howard University, USA, and Yale

University, USA. Nyabongo left then for England where he took up his studies at Oxford University as a Rhodes Scholar. In 1939 he got his B. Litt, and in 1940 his Ph. D., both at Oxford.

Akiki Nyabongo taught at Alabama State College, North Carolina Agriculture and Technical College, Winston-Salern State Teachers' College, and at Langston University.

In 1956 Akiki Nyabongo was recalled from the United States to help his country in negotiations for a new agreement between the British Government and the Kingdom of Toro. Shortly before Uganda's Independence Nyabongo was assigned by the Prime Minister of Uganda to a friendship mission to East Asian countries. After Independence he was elected to the Toro Kingdom Assembly and appointed President of the Town and Country Planning Board of Uganda. He is a member of the Committee for Ancient and Historical Monuments, the Toro Kingdom Land Board, the Education Committee, the Kasese Town Board, and Chairman of the National Disablement Advisory Council of Uganda.

Besides his political ambitions Nyabongo is engaged in many other activities. He is a member of the Authors and Composers of Great Britain and Ireland. He is a member of the International Institute of Afro-American Studies in Mexiko, the Simeto African Studies, the American College and University Professors Association, and editor of the "African Magazine". He is also a member of the Italian Anthropological Society and the Japanese African Society.

Akiki Nyabongo is the author of *The Story of an African Chief* (1350) — American title *Africa Answers Back* — a novel about the devastating intrusion of the Europeans into Uganda. This book was recommended by the Book of the Month Club.

Nyembezi, Sibusiso   South Africa

Born on December 6, 1919, in Babanango, Zululand, South Africa, into the Zulu tribe, as son of a minister of the Methodist

Church, Cyril Lincoln Sibusiso Nyembezi received his primary education and teacher training in Natal. After matriculating by private studies he went to the South African Native College (later the University of Fort Hare) for a B. A. degree, and to the University of the Witwatersrand in Johannesburg for his M. A., which he received for a thesis entitled *Zulu Proverbs* (published by Lovedale Press in 1954). After teaching in secondary schools in Natal for five years Nyembezi joined the staff of the Department of Bantu Languages of the University of the Witwatersrand as Language Assistant. He worked under C. M. Doke. In 1954 he was appointed to the Chair of Bantu Languages at the University College of Fort Hare, Cape Province. He resigned in 1959 and joined the publishing firm Shuter and Shooter in Pietermaritzburg as Book Editor.

Nyembezi's first work is *Mntanami! Mntanami!* (2020), a story of a young boy leaving home and getting into trouble in Johannesburg. His next novel, *Inkinsela yaseMgungundlovu* (2021), generally considered his best novel, "deals with a cunning rogue who cheats naive villagers disguised as a rich tycoon from the big city" (Albert S. Gérard).

Ubudoda abukhulelwa (2022) "is the edifying story of an orphan boy who manages to overcome the adversities of life" (Albert S. Gérard).

Apart from creative fiction Nyembezi has compiled several Zulu grammars and manuals and anthologies of Zulu poetry. In collaboration with G. R. Dent he compiled the *Compact Zulu Dictionary*, 1959, and *Scholars' Zulu Dictionary*. In 1958 he published a collection of praises of Zulu and Swazi kings entitled *Izibongo Zamakhosi*, in 1966 a book of traditional lore and customs, *Inqolobane Yesizwe*. Nyembezi also translated Alan Paton's "Cry the Beloved Country" into Zulu under the title *Lafa Elihle Kakhulu*, 1957. His *Review of Zulu Literature* is one of the most valuable sources of information on the subject.

Nyunaï, Jean-Paul   Cameroon

Born on July 26, 1932, in Yaunde, Cameroon, as son of the
first Cameroonian geometrician, Jean-Paul Nyunaï had his
primary education in Yaunde and his secondary education in
Tarbes (Hautes Pyrénées), France, Cahors (Lot), and Pau (Bas-
ses Pyrénées). In 1947 Nyunaï went to Paris to study Law and
Literature simultaneously. There he became acquainted with
Alioune Diop, Aimé Césaire, René Maran and was made a
member of the editorial committee of "Présence Africaine" by
Alioune Diop. He was Cameroon's official delegate to the "First
Congress of Black Writers and Artists" in Paris in 1956. From
1964 to 1970 Nyunaï was the legal and financial advisor to the
German insurance company "Allianz" in Paris, then returned
to Cameroon, to become staff manager of Renault in Duala.

Jean-Paul Nyunaï is married to Princess Duala Bell, whose
ancestors signed the protectorate treaty with the Germans in
1884, an historical event that Nyunaï chose for a doctor's
thesis (1971).

Jean-Paul Nyunaï produced a volume of poetry, *Piments sang*
(756). This was followed by *La nuit de ma vie* (755).

"*La nuit de ma vie* is a slender book of lyrics, sprung from
the first (and ultimately unrequited) love of a sensitive and
very young man. Boy meets girl, boy loves girl, boy loses girl;
an old story, pieced together here through poems in many
moods — joyful (some with an amusing wordplay reminiscent
of Jacques Prévert), nostalgic, meditative, impassioned, anguish-
ed, embittered. Nyunaï's poems are unpretentious, often touching. One forgives occasional overdramatizations ("L'amour
d'une femme est un amour qui tue") as natural to the poet's age
and situation" (Ellen Conroy Kennedy).

In 1964 followed another small volume of poetry, *Chansons
pour Ngo-lima* (757), and in 1971 a play, *La chute d'Uli*,
published in Duala.

Nzekwu, Onuora   Nigeria

Born on February 19, 1928, in Kafanchan, Benue Plateau State,
Nigeria, Onuora Nzekwu attended the Catholic School in Ka-
fanchan from 1934 to 1939, the Catholic School in Kano from
1939 to 1941 and Holy Trinity School in Onitsha in 1942. He
trained as a teacher at the St. Anthony's Elementary Teacher's
College in Onitsha in 1943 and at the St. Charles' Higher
Elementary Teachers College in Onitsha from 1944 to 1946. He
obtained the Teachers' Higher Elementary Certificate in 1946.
He taught at Mount St. Mary's Teacher Training College,
Oturkpo from 1947 to 1950, at St. Charles' Teacher Training
College, Onitsha, in 1951, at St. Mary's Practising School in
Onitsha in 1952 and at the Lagos City College in Yaba from
1953 to 1955.

In 1956 Nzekwu joined the staff of "Nigeria Magazine" as
Editorial Assistant, becoming subsequently Sub-Assistant Editor
and Assistant Editor. In 1961 he received a six months Rockefeller Foundation Fellowship to study American Methods of
Magazine Production. In 1962 he was promoted Editor of
"Nigeria Magazine". In 1964 he obtained a UNESCO Fellowship to study Copyright Administration. In 1966 he was transferred to the Eastern Region Public Service. He returned to
the Federal Public Service in 1970 as Senior Information Officer and is now a Deputy Director with the Federal Ministry
of Information in Lagos.

Onuora Nzekwu's first novel, *Wand of Noble Wood* (759),
centres around the tragic conflict of a couple educated in
Western civilization failing to lift the curse from the bride who
finally commits suicide. His second novel, *Blade Among the
Boys* (760), is about the problems of becoming a Catholic priest
out of an African family, who considers the production of
children essential to human life. *Highlife for Lizards* (762),
Nzekwu's third novel, concerns a woman of great spirit and
independence. Onuora Nzekwu is co-author, with Michael
Crowder, of a collection of short stories for schools, *Eze Goes
to School* (761).

"*Wand of Noble Wood* is, in the first place, a description of tribal Ibo customs, reported with such detail and exactness that would have delighted Malinowski" (Kaye Whiteman).

"*Blade Among the Boys* ... poses the power of traditional African values and practices against Western 'enlightenment', and concludes that the individual who chooses the latter and flouts the former does so at his own peril" (Robert July).

"*Blade Among the Boys* has a dramatic knot and the untangling is ably done. The dialogues are sometimes incoherent, but in other moments, especially in the disputes, they spark of fire" (Kaye Whiteman).

"*Highlife for Lizards*, is the most successful of Nzekwu's writing. His picture of Agom is more fully drawn than anything else he has done, and local beliefs and rituals are handled with greater insight and sympathy than is shown in his previous novels" (Margaret Laurence).

Nzouankeu, Jacques Muriel   Cameroon

Jacques Muriel Nzouankeu was born in 1938 in Manjo near Nkongsamba, district Moungo, Cameroon. He received his elementary education at Protestant mission schools in Ndoungue and Duala, his secondary education in Nkongsamba and at the Lycée in Duala. In 1963 he obtained a diploma from the Ecole d'Administration, in 1964 his Baccalauréat, and in 1965 his Licence of Law. He also holds a diploma from the Institut des Hautes Etudes d'Outre-Mer and the title of Administrateur Civil Principal. Since 1965 he has been a high functionary of the Penalties Administration of the Republic of Cameroon.

Jacques Muriel Nzouankeu wrote short stories which have been published partly in the journal "Abbia" and collected in the volume *Le souffle des ancêtres* (764). His play, *L'agent spécial* (763), a comedy about a young civil servant being seduced into corruption, has been published by "Abbia".

Nzuji, Clémentine   Zaire

Born on January 21, 1944, in the Kasai Province of Zaire, Clémentine Nzuji was educated at the Lycée du Sacré-Coeur in Léopoldville, now Kinshasa. After her studies at the University of Lovanium in Kinshasa she was in charge of the library of that University. When the Faculty of Arts was moved to Lubumbashi in 1971, Clémentine Faik-Nzuji — this is her name after her marriage — was also transferred.

From 1964 to 1966. Clémentine Nzuji was editor of the literary journal "Le Cahier de la Pléiade du Congo". Her work includes several volumes of poetry: *Murmures* (1201), *Le Temps des amants* (1202), *Kasala* (1203), *Lianes*, Kinshasa 1971, and a study of Luba proverbs, *Enigmes Luba, Nshinga*, Kinshasa 1970. In 1969, Clémentine Nzuji received in Kinshasa the first prize of Poetry, from the hands of President Senghor.

"A movement from darkness to light, from emotional chaos to full bloom, from images of death and misery towards images of life which has to be grasped . . ." (Maurice Hambursin).

Portrait on Plate XIV.

Nzuji, Dieudonné Kadima
vid. *Kadima-Nzuji, Dieudonné*

Obiechina, Emmanuel N.   Nigeria

Born on September 20, 1933, in Nkpor, East Central State, Nigeria, Emmanuel Nwanonye Obiechina graduated from the University of Ibadan in 1961. He obtained a doctoral degree from the Cambridge University, England, in 1966 with the thesis *Cultural Change and the Novel in English in West Africa*. Obiechina is at present lecturer in English at the University of Nigeria, Nsukka, Nigeria.

Obiechina published *Literature for the Masses,* Enugu 1971, a study of the popular "Onitsha-Literature" in Nigeria. Essays, book reviews and short stories have appeared in "Présence Africaine", "African Literature Today", "African Forum", "The Voice", and "The Conch".

Oculi, Okello   Uganda

Born in 1942 at Dokolo County, district Lango, Uganda, Okello Oculi was educated at Soroti College, St. Peter's College, Tororo, and St. Mary's College, Kisubi, before reading Political Science at Makerere University, Kampala. He then attended a post-graduate course at the University of Essex. A columnist for the Uganda newspaper "The People", he has also been news editor for "The Makererean".

Oculi wrote the verse tale *Orphan* (1351), a series of free-verse monologues, in which an orphan boy is seated at a crosscroads lamenting the death of his mother. This symbol of Africa torn from its ancient traditions gives the author opportunity to express his views on contemporary Africa. His second work is a novel, *Prostitute* (1352).

"The poem *(Orphan)* is not, as he modestly suggests, a 'village opera', but an orchestration of voices telling a story of alienation and the pangs of loss" (James Stewart).

"Vivid writing, abounding with images of fruitfulness" (Anim Kassam).

"Energetic imagination and impressive eloquence" (Bernth Lindfors).

"One is told a story *(Prostitute),* not allowed to experience it, and this removes much of its interest" (Anim Kassam).

Odinga, Oginga   Kenya

Born in 1912 at Sakwa Location, Nyanza province, Kenya, Ajuma Oginga Odinga, the son of an overseer on a plantation, was educated at Maseno Secondary School, at Alliance High School and at Makerere College, Uganda, where he graduated with a Diploma of Education in 1939. From 1940 to 1942 he taught Mathematics at the Church Missionary School in Maseno, Kenya, and from 1943 to 1946 served as headmaster of the Veterinary School there. In 1947 he founded the Luo Thrift and Trading Corporation, a construction and printing business, serving first as its secretary and then as its managing director.

In 1948 he came in touch with Jomo Kenyatta and accepted a seat on the Central Committee of the Kenya African Union (KAU), building up its Nyanza branch into one of the strongest in the territory. In 1952 Kenyatta was arrested for his alleged connection with the Mau Mau and KAU was banned. Odinga went to India on a study tour for two months, and from his return until 1957 he served as the President of the Luo Union. In May 1957 he was elected to the Kenya Legislative Council for Central Nyanza, and then elected Chairman of the African Elected Members Organization. In 1959 he founded, with Tom Mboya, the Kenya Independence Movement. In January 1960 he took part in the Constitutional Conference in London. In May 1960 he became Vice-President of the newly founded Kenya African National Union (KANU).

After Kenya's independence in 1963 Odinga became Minister for the Interior, but when Kenya was proclaimed a republic in 1964, he was already transferred to the more representative post of Vice-President. In March 1966 he lost his post as Vice-President of KANU, and in April he resigned as Vice-President and founded the Kenya Peoples Union (KPU), a left-wing radical party, which was opposed to the government. In 1968 Odinga's passport was withdrawn. Suspected of being guilty of the death of Tom Mboya, and after bloody disturbances in the Luo country, KPU was prohibited and Odinga put into prison. After eighteen months of detention he was freed in March 1971.

He called upon his supporters to return to KANU, and in September 1971 his own return to the ruling party was allowed.

Odinga is the author of the autobiography *Not Yet Uhuru* (1358).

Odunjo, Joseph Folahan   Nigeria

Born in 1904 in Abeokuta, Western State, Nigeria, as son of Chief Odunjo, the Ekerin of Ibara, Joseph Folahan Odunjo was educated at St. Augustine's Catholic Primary School, Abeokuta, from 1914 to 1920, then at the Catholic Teacher's Training College, Ibadan, from 1920 to 1924, and at the Institute of Education, London University, from 1946 to 1947. Odunjo was appointed Headmaster of St. Augustine's Catholic School, Abeokuta, in 1924 and held this position till 1939. From 1940 to 1946 he was Headmaster of St. Paul's Catholic School, Ebute Metta, Lagos, and from 1948 to 1949, Supervising Teacher of Abeokuta and Colony. Simultaneously, from 1945 to 1950, Odunjo was Senior Tutor at St. Gregory's College, Lagos. The year 1951 Odunjo spent as Senior Tutor at St. Leo's Teacher Training College in his native town Abeokuta. In 1952 Odunja decided to enter higher administration and was appointed Minister of Lands and Labour, Western Nigeria, which he stayed till 1956. From 1957 to 1963 he was Executive Director of Agriculture in the Western Nigeria Development Corporation. From 1963 to 1972 Odunjo was President of the Ibadan Catholic Diocesan Council.

Joseph Folahan Odunjo received several honours. In 1952 he was created Chief Lemo of Ibara by His Highness the Olubara Lalubu II, Head Chief of Ibara, in 1968 he became Oluwo of Iro and in 1969 he was installed as the Asiwaju of Egbas by Oba Alaiyeluwa Gbadebo II, the Alake of Egbaland. In 1966 Pope Paul chose Chief Odunjo as Knight of the Order of St. Gregory.

Chief Odunjo writes in Yoruba. In 1945 he published *Ijinle Majemu Laarin Egba ati Egbado,* an historical sketch in poems. This was followed by a play, *Agbalowōmeri bālè Jòntolo*

(789), a collection of poems, *Akójopò ewì aládùn* (790), and the novels *Kuye* (791), *Omo òkú òrun* (792) and *Kadara ati egbon re* (793). Besides these works Chief Odunjo has written six bible expositions, two Yoruba textbooks for secondary schools and a collection of church hymns in Yoruba.

Ofori, Henry   Ghana

Born in 1925 in Ghana, Henry Ofori graduated from Achimota College in 1949, then lived in a small rural town in the forest belt. From 1951 to 1955 he taught Physics at the Government Secondary Technical School at Takoradi. Ofori has written a twice-weekly column for the "Ghanaian Times" for more than ten years. He is working now in the Ghana Information Service in Accra.

Ofori's book, *Tales from Dodora Forest*, was published by Waterville Press, Accra. A one-act play, *The Literary Society*, appeared in "Plays from Black Africa" (A 68).

Ogali, A. Ogali   Nigeria

Ogali Agu Ogali was born on October 27, 1935, in Item, Bende Division, East Central State, Nigeria. He had his early primary education at Item Methodist Central School and his secondary education at the Hope Waddell Training Institution in Calabar from 1943 to 1949. Between March 31, 1950, and December 11, 1954, he worked in the United Fruit Company in Calabar, first as an account clerk, beach clerk, cashier and finally as a store-keeper. Between January 15, 1955, and June 30, 1959, he taught at Methodist schools at Nneato, Uturu, Ovim and Alayi, all in East Central State. From 1959 to 1961 he did a two year course in the Ghana School of Journalism in Accra, Ghana. Back in Nigeria, he became a Senior Reporter in the then Eastern Nigerian Information Service, publisher of "Nigerian Outlook" in Enugu. In 1962/63 he was posted as a representative of the Information Service to Port Harcourt, then to Kaduna.

From 1963 to 1965 he did a course in cinematography in London, England. On his return to Nigeria, he worked for the Eastern Nigerian Broadcasting Corporation as sub-editor. He is still sub-editor in the East Central State Broadcasting Service, Enugu.

Ogali A. Ogali is the author of many cheap books, dramas like *Veronica My Daughter* (796), *Adelabu* (799), *Mr. Rabbit Is Dead* (800), and *Patrice Lumumba* (804), "novels" like *Long, Long Ago* (797), *Okeke the Magician* (801), *Eddy, the Coal-City Boy* (802), and *Caroline the One Guinea Girl* (803), and books which give advice and opinion like *No Heaven for the Priest*, Enugu 1971.

Ogieriaikhi Emwinma
vid. *Ogieiriaixi, Evinma*

Ogieiriaixi, Evinma   Nigeria

Evinma Ogieiriaixi was born on April 15, 1936, in Benin, Mid Western State, Nigeria, as a descendant of Oba Osemwede of Benin (1816—47). He is thus related to the present Oba of Benin, Oba Akenzua II.

After his primary school education in schools in and around Benin, Evinma Ogieiriaixi attended Saint Patrick's College in Asaba, Mid Western State, from 1951 to 1955. He passed his three GCE Advanced Level Papers on his own in 1957 and gained admission to the University of Ibadan, but could not enrol for lack of funds. He therefore found employment as Executive Officer in the, then, Western Region in order to finance his university education. He then studied History of Philosophy, Economics and Ethics and graduated in London in 1961. After that he registered with London University for his Master's degree in Metaphysics, but had to give up his studies "when in 1963, at the creation of the Midwest State, my talent as a playwright was incessantly called upon by my drama-loving Edos". His first play, *My Wife or My Wives?* (806), dealing with the problem of introducing monogamy, and published under the old spelling of his name Emwinma Ogieriaikhi, was the first modern play staged in Midwestern Nigeria on the creation of that state. Together with this play was published another one, *The Marriage Couldn't Continue,* which treats the fashion of changing the wife with changing educational standards.

Evinma Ogieiriaixi founded the "New Era Drama Group", the "Benin Theatre Group", and the "Olokun Club", all in Benin.

In 1967 Ogieiriaixi was asked by the University of Lagos to train as a Linguist at the University of Ibadan, so that he could initiate Edo Studies at the University of Lagos. He accepted the chance and is today a Linguist at the School of African and Asian Studies, University of Lagos, Nigeria.

Ogot, Grace   Kenya

Born on May, 15, 1930, at Butere near Kisumu, district Central Nyanza, Kenya, Grace Emily Okinyi Ogot — this is her full name — had her first education at Maseno Junior School, Ng'iya Girls' School, and Butere Girls' High School. After being trained at the Nursing Training Hospital at Mengo, near Kampala, Uganda, from 1949 to 1953, she went to England to the St. Thomas Hospital for Mothers and Babies in London. From 1958 to 1959 she was a Midwifery Tutor and Nursing Sister at Maseno Hospital. In 1959 she married Bethwell A. Ogot, who was then lecturer of History at Makarere College, Kampala, Uganda. With her husband she went to England, and was, from 1960 to 1961, a radio announcer with B.B.C. in London.

From 1961 to 1962 she was Community Development Officer and Principal of the Women's Training Centre at Kisumu,

Kenya, from 1963 to 1964 nursing sister at the Makerere University College in Kampala, Uganda, and from 1964 to 1965 Public Relations Officer for the Air India Corporation of East Africa in Nairobi, Kenya. In the following years she continued her many activities, being member of the Maendeleo ya Wanawake Organization of Women, member of the Executive Committee of the Kenya Council of Women, regular contributor to "Voice of Kenya" Radio and Television, columnist of "View Point" in the "East African Standard", proprietress of Lindy's of Nairobi, and member of the Board of Governors of the Nairobi Girls' Secondary School.

Grace Ogot wrote a novel, *The Promised Land* (1359), which deals with the Luo migration from Uganda to the Eastern shore of Lake Victoria, and a volume of short stories, *Land Without Thunder* (1360). "*The Promised Land* is a disappointment in view of the considerable promise Miss Ogot has shown in her earlier published short stories" (Charles R. Larsen).

"The fault is not the simplicity of the story but the author's attempt to present it as a complex situation" (Shiraz Dossa).

"Grace Ogot is a very good writer of short stories ... she manages to write from the inside of traditional Luo society, so that it comes to life in a wholly new way" (F. B. Welbourn).

Ogunde, Hubert   Nigeria

Born in 1916 in Ososa, Ijebu-Ode, Western State, Nigeria, Hubert Ogunde had his elementary education at the Wasimi African School which he left in 1931 to be appointed a school teacher. He taught at school for nine years and furthered his education by means of postal tuition from Bennett College, England. In 1940 he joined the Nigerian Police Force and was stationed in Lagos where he rose to second class constable.

By his father, Jeremiah Ogunde, a catechist, organist and choirmaster, Hubert Ogunde had been taught to play the organ.

So, while a teacher, he served as choirmaster to several churches and composed anthems for their harvest thanksgiving festivals. While in Lagos he left the Baptist Church for the Church of the Lord, an African Protestant sect, on whose request in 1943 he composed a Service of Songs into which he injected some drama. The result was the *Garden of Eden,* his first play which had its premiere at the Glover Memorial Hall, Lagos, in 1944.

In 1945 he resigned from the Police Force to become a professional actor-producer and founded the "Ogunde Concert Party". Beset by the problem of losing his actresses in rapid succession to prospective husbands, he decided in 1946 to become a polygamist and marry from among the best actresses in his troupe in order to keep the Concert Party alive.

Hubert Ogunde has made twelve grammophone records and produced more than two dozen plays including his *Strike and Hunger,* banned from their areas of jurisdiction in 1945 by the Kano and Jos Native Administrations for fear it would incite workers against their employers, his *Bread and Bullets,* depicting the Enugu coalmine shooting banned from Northern Nigeria in 1949, and his *Yoruba Ronu* (817) for which his Concert Party was banned from performing in the Western Region in 1965. Despite these set-backs, his Concert Party waxes with a troupe of sixteen professional actors, his six wives, and eight stage hands.

Most of his plays are in Yoruba language and are part of the repertoire of the Yoruba folk opera. Besides *Yoruba Ronu* (817) his most successful plays are: *O Tito Koro* (818), *Aropin n't'enia* (819), and *Ologbo Dudu* (820).

"Ogunde's style is characterised by 'the opening glee, the slapstick, the slightly monotonous high life tunes" (James Morel Gibbs).

"A natural showman, he believes that the function of theatre is to entertain and that to succeed you must give the public what they want. His most enjoyable recipe is a mixture of social satire, slapstick humour and sex appeal. During the recent political troubles (1966) he came out with courageous topical plays which caused him to be banned from the Western Region,

but which greatly enhanced his already immense popularity"
(Ulli Beier).

Ogunmola, Kola   Nigeria

Elijah Kolawole Ogunmola was born on November 11, 1925,
in Okemesi, Ekiti Division, Western State, Nigeria. He became
a primary school teacher before he founded, in 1948, his own
theatre troupe, the "Kola Ogunmola Players", in which he has
been working as director, playwright and actor. He received
a six months grant from Rockefeller Foundation to study at the
Drama Department of the University of Ibadan.

His more than twelve plays are Yoruba folk-operas. Among
the best known are *They Were Enemies*, involving the betrayal
of a friend, *Agbaraj' agbara* (The Reign of the Mighty), produced at the University of Ibadan Arts Theatre in 1962. *Ife owo*
(823), about a man who gives in to the greedy demands of his
second wife and suffers accordingly, was printed in 1965. Ogunmola's dramatized version of Amos Tutuola's "Palm-Wine
Drinkard", *Omuti, Apa Kini* (824) was also published in a
bilingual edition, together with a long play record, by the
Institute of African Studies in Ibadan, under the title *The
Palmwine Drinkard* (825).

In 1970 Kola Ogunmola had a stroke and was reported dead.
But this proved false. Ogunmola has now recovered and had an
overwhelming come back in Oshogbo in May 1972. One arm
is still paralyzed, but he acts on with all his vigour and freshness.

"In a few years his group matured into a professional, adult
company, touring the Western Region of Nigeria with little
moral song-and-dance plays, in a style entirely his own. Although entirely self-taught, Ogunmola is a superb actor, and an
accomplished composer and director" (G. J. Axworthy).

Portrait on Plate X.

Ogunyemi, Wale   Nigeria

Born on August 12, 1939, in Igbajo, Western State, Nigeria, Wale Ogunyemi was educated in Ibadan. He is a playwright and actor. Introduced to drama in 1962 when television began in Nigeria, he joined the now defunct Nigerian Theatre Group and shortly thereafter, in 1962, led this group. For two years he worked with the N.B.C. Television in Lagos. During the 1966/67 session he entered the Drama School in Ibadan and also joined Wole Soyinka's group "1960 Masks". Furthermore, he had eighteen months training with the University of Ibadan Theatre Arts Company. Presently, Wale Ogunyemi is a Research Assistant at the Institute of African Studies, University of Ibadan, Nigeria.

Wale Ogunyemi's first play, *Business Headache* (828), is a humorous story about two deceived deceivers. His second play, *The Scheme* (829), deals with the might of African gods and was one of the set books for the West African School Certificate Examination in Ghana. *Be Mighty, Be Mine* (830) is based on a mythical fight between the gods Ogun and Shango over Ogun's wife Oya. *Aàrè Akogun* (831) is a Yoruba adaptation of Shakespeare's Macbeth, *Esu Elegbara*, Orisun Acting Edition 1960, is based on a Yoruba creation myth, *Ijaye War*, Orisun Acting Edition 1970, puts the Ijaye War of the 19th century into verse, and *Obaluaye*, a Yoruba musical drama translated into English, was performed at the Second All Nigeria Festival of the Arts in Ibadan in December 1971 by the University of Ife. His most recent and ambitious play, *Kiriji*, yet unpublished, an epic on the Ekiti Parapo war, a Yoruba tribal war in the 19th century, was presented at the Second All Nigeria Festival of the Arts in Ibadan in 1971 by the Department of Theatre Arts, University of Ibadan. This play also revived the popular "Theatre on Wheels" which was suspended by the School of Drama of the University of Ibadan during the Nigerian Civil War.

Apart from the published plays, Wale Ogunyemi wrote an average of one play in two weeks for the Orisun Theatre television series for two years while Wole Soyinka was in detention. One of these plays, *The Vow*, won him a special 1971 African Arts Prize donated by the University of California, Los Angeles, California, USA. In April 1972 his play, *Sign of the Rainbow*, won him a B.B.C. African Theatre Prize, organized by the World Service of the B.B.C. in London. *Poor Little Bird* and *Obatala and Ojiya* were performed by the Fisk University Black Studies Department, Nashville, Tennessee, USA in spring 1972.

Wale Ogunyemi is also a known actor. Among other roles, he has taken part in the performance of Wole Soyinka's play *Kongi's Harvest* at the First Festival of Negro Arts in Dakar, Senegal, in 1966. In 1967 he performed at the University World Theatre Festival in Nancy, France, in 1969 he took part in the performance of Kola Ogunmola's "The Palmwine Drinkard" at the First Pan-African Festival of the Arts in Algiers, and in 1970 he played in Wole Soyinka's "Madmen and Specialists" in a production of the Theatre Arts Company at the Eugene O'Neill Memorial Theatre Center in Connecticut, USA.

Okai, John   Ghana

Born in 1941 in Accra, Ghana, John Okai was educated at Gambaga Native Authority School, Nalerigu Middle Boys' School — both in Northern Ghana near the junction of the Morago and the White Volta — Methodist Middle Boys' School in Accra and the Accra High School before going to Moscow, where he got an M. A. (Litt.) degree from the Gorky Literary Institute in 1967.

In 1968 he was elected a fellow of the Royal Society of Arts in London. He has read his poetry over radio and television and to live audiences in Europe and Africa.

In 1969 he was invited to the Pan-African Cultural Festival in Algiers, where he gave a reading of his works.

Okai's poems have appeared in journals such as "The New African", "African Arts", "The Legon Observer", "The Ahisco

Magazine", "Okyeame", "The Atlantic Monthly", "The Acro-
polis", "The Surrey Guardian", "Literary Cavalcade", "Slant
X", and "The New American Review". They have been translated into several languages including German and Russian.
After *Flowerfall* (838) in 1969, he had a new collection of poems
published, *The Oath of the Fontomfrom and Other Poems*, New
York 1971.

Having spent a year in Ghana after leaving the Soviet Union,
John Okai was awarded a post-graduate scholarship by the
University of Ghana for further work at the University of
London.

Flowerfall "is a poem of three parts, of subtle sensuous
imaginary gradually increasing in intensity towards the final
climax. Its deep impressionistic effect is gained by the sound of
it, which can best be appreciated without attempting a close
examination of each phrase" (J. D.).

Okara, Gabriel   Nigeria

Born on April 24, 1921, in Bumodi, Niger Delta, Rivers State,
Nigeria, Gabriel Imomotimi Gbaingbain Okara, an Ijaw, is
the son of Chief Sampson G. Okara. He was educated at
Government College, Umuahia, and trained as a book-binder.
In 1956 he read a course in Journalism at Northwestern Uni-
versity, Evanston, Illinois, USA. In 1963 he visited Germany
on an invitation of the Bavarian Academy of Fine Arts.
Throughout most of the past two decades, Okara was employed
in Enugu as Information Officer for the Eastern Nigerian
Government Service. During part of 1969, he toured the United
States with Chinua Achebe. In 1972 he became Director of the
Rivers State Publishing House in Port Harcourt, Nigeria.

Gabriel Okara has translated a great deal of the folklore and
the poetry of his Ijaw heritage. He became known by his poetry
which appeared in numerous magazines, in particular in "Black
Orpheus", and was widely anthologized and translated. In

1953 he won an award at the Nigerian Arts Festival. His short story, *The Crooks,* was translated into many languages.

Okara's only novel, *The Voice* (839), is about a man who "read too much book" and who asks for truth in a traditional and then in a modernized society. The novel is written in a special language, full of rhythmic repetitions, Ijaw imagery and a grammar which tries to keep the flavour of Ijaw structure.

"Much of *The Voice* seems to be a poem in the form of a novel. ... Okara's images have vitality because in addition to being symbolic, they are firmly rooted in the reality of his own Ijaw culture ... The language of the book is rich in literal translations of Ijaw idiom, skillfully handled to present various characterizations of African life" (Wilfred Cartey).

"... is a fascinating experiment — but also a gallant failure" (Ulli Beier).

"Although it is set within a tribal society, *The Voice* contains a voice which reaches out. Okolo, essentially, is a man anywhere who must continue to question every establishment which becomes rigid and which surrounds itself with bulwarks of pretence" (Margaret Laurence).

"*The Voice* is an important attempt to solve a problem facing the development of West African prose. In so far as it steers a middle course between the realism of western fiction and the fantasy of traditional African modes ... it appears to offer a satisfying synthesis ... It suggests a form that could be handed on" (Adrian A. Roscoe).

Portrait on Plate XI.

Okigbo, Christopher   Nigeria

Born on August 16, 1932, in Ojoto, near Onitsha, East Central State, Nigeria, Christopher Okigbo was educated at Government College in Umuahia, then studied Classics at Ibadan University. After obtaining his degree in 1956, he acted as Private Secretary to Nigeria's Federal Minister of Research and Information in Lagos for the following two years. From 1958 to 1960 he taught Latin at the Boys' Secondary School at Fiditi near Ibadan. In 1960 he went home to Ojoto for a visit, then joined the Pioneer Library staff of the University of Nigeria at Nsukka. From there he moved to the library on the Enugu campus, then became the West Africa representative of Cambridge University Press and West African editor of "Transition" magazine, as well as an editor of Mbari Publications, Ibadan.

In 1965 Okigbo attended the Commonwealth Arts Festival in London and read two poems, *Lament of the Drums,* and *Dance of the Painted Maidens* to the accompaniment of drums. In 1966 the First Festival of Negro Arts in Dakar awarded him its First Prize for Poetry, which, however, he declined, saying "There is no such thing as Negro art".

Christopher Okigbo, a Major in the Biafran army, was killed in action in October 1967.

Christopher Okigbo published three volumes of poetry, *Heavensgate* (843), *Limits* (844), and *Distances* (845). A critical evaluation of Okigbo's work has been written by Sunday O. Anozie, *Christopher Okigbo,* London 1971.

"There is a basic narrative element in Okigbo's poetic style which clothes the archetypes of his experience" (Joel A. Adedeji).

"The poetry is abstract, Delphic, written almost in a personal code and in need of explanation and annotation . . ." (K. W.).

"Okigbo's art is pure motion because he does not presume and force himself over the ordeal, but suffers it and summons at the end all his energy to resume and carry us all on to continous illuminations all along the way to death" (Paul Theroux).

"Christopher Okigbo has a mystical grasp of words, and evokes out of them a universe of images and even thoughts. But the thoughts are disconnected — and the images, though often succeeding in forming a pattern, fall short of forming coherence" (Ali A. Mazrui).

"Okigbo may be considered as one of those African creative writers and artists with an acute sense of form within formlessness" (Sunday Anozie).

"Okigbo transmutes all experience into ceremony" (Ronald Dathorne).

"The whole of *Limits* is strangely prophetic of the Nigerian civil war" (Michael J. Etherton).

"I believe that writing poetry is a necessary part of my being alive, which is why I have written nothing else" (Christopher Okigbo).

Portrait on Plate XI.

Oko, Akomaye   Nigeria

Born in 1943 at Ibong, near Obudu, South Eastern State, Nigeria, Akomaye Oko enrolled, after his secondary studies, at Ahmadu Bello University, Zaria, in 1965. During the crisis of 1966 he transferred to Nsukka University where he graduated in English in 1971.

Akomaye Oko is President of the Writer's Club of the University of Nsukka. His poetry has been published in German, in the anthology "Gedichte aus Biafra" (AW 133), and in the anthology "Nsukka Harvest", Nsukka 1972.

Okpaku, Joseph   Nigeria

Born on March 24, 1943, in Lokoja, West Central State, Nigeria, Joseph Okpaku is of rather mixed origin, his father, a postmaster, coming from Ora, a group close to the Bini, his mother, a midwife, the daughter of a Ga father and a mother from Itsekiri in the Niger Delta. Okpaku grew up in Sapele and attended the Sapele Government School, later called Sapele Township School, from 1948 to 1955. In September 1955 he gained admission, one year prematurely, to the Government College at Ughelli — one of the five public boarding schools in the country. From 1960 to 1962 he read Mathematics, Physics, and Chemistry at Ughelli. In 1962 he won a fellowship of the African Scholarship Program of American Universities to study Civil Engineering at Northwestern University in Evanston, Illinois. From 1962 to 1965 he studied at Northwestern and obtained his B. S. in Civil Engineering. He then worked as an Efficiency Analyst for Bemis Brothers, Inc. in Minneapolis, Minnesota, but soon took up his studies again. In September 1965 he entered Stanford University and obtained an M. S. degree in Structural Engineering the following June.

All the while he was pursuing his technical career, he had a loving eye on the arts. In 1960 he had already won the second prize in the state-wide essay competition of the then Western Region in Nigeria. In 1966 he started his own literary magazine "Journal of the New African Literature and the Arts". The same year he began his doctorate in theatre history and dramatic literature at Stanford University. Two years later, in November 1968, Okpaku passed his Ph. D. with distinction.

Joseph Okpaku is a vivid essay-writer, who has published many unconventional and critical essays on African literature and culture. He is also a playwright. *Born Astride the Grave* (861), a wholly "un-African" play, set in America, with the universal theme of youngsters searching their way, was produced at Stanford in 1966. *Virtues of Adultery* (863) won the second prize of the BBC African Drama Competition in 1967. *Under the Iroko Tree* (864), a short novel, was published in the Literary Review in 1968, and *The Virtues of Adultery* and *The Silhouette of God* (865) in 1969, both being produced at Stanford.

In 1967 Okpaku received a grant to tour Africa and Europe. He lectured in Lagos, at Makerere College in Kampala and the University College in Dar es Salaam. In early 1969, he conducted a course in contemporary African literature at Stanford University. In 1969 he received a fellowship to study at the University of Warsaw in Poland, but returned the same year to establish the New York office of his "The Third Press — Joseph Okpaku Publishing Company", which had been started in 1968. The Third Press devotes itself to black studies in the widest sense: African and Afro-American, creative and critical.

Oladiti, F. O. Nigeria

Born about 1944 at Ibokun near Ilesha, Western State, Nigeria, F. O. Oladiti had his primary and secondary education at Ilesha. In 1964 he joined the "Ayinle Concert Party". In 1968 he formed his own troupe, the "Omobokun Concert Party". So far he has produced nine plays in Yoruba which had their first performances at the Lisabi Hall, Ebute Metta, near Lagos, or in the Obokungbusi Hall at Ilesha. So far, his plays have not been published.

Olisah, Sunday Okenwa Nigeria

Born in 1936 in Nnewi near Onitsha, East Central State, Nigeria, Sunday Okenwa Olisah, who used for some of his works the pen-name "Master of Life", "Strong Man of the Pen" or "Money Master", was one of the most prolific "Onitsha"-writers. He died on December 12, 1964.

His writing includes "Onitsha-novels" like *No Condition is Permanent* (872), *The World is Hard* (873), *Dangerous Man* (874), *Money Palaver* (877), *Story About Mammy-Water* (878), *Man Has No Rest In His Life* (879), *The Life in the Prison Yard* (880), *My Wives Are In Love With My Servants* (884), quite a number of "Onitsha-plays" like *Dangerous Man Vagabond Versus Princess* (875), *Half-Educated Messenger* (876), *Elizabeth My Lover* (881), *My Seven Daughters Are After Young Boys* (882), *My Wife — About Husband and Wife Who Hate Themselves* (883), and some mixtures of advices, historical stories and comments like *Drunkards Believe Bar As Heaven*, 1959, *Man Suffers*, 1960, *The Life Story and Death of Mr. Lumumba*, 1964, *Money Hard to Get But Easy to Spend*, 1965, *How Lumumba Suffered in Life and Died in Katanga*, 1966, *Guides For Engagement*, no year, *How to Know Who Loves You and Hates You*, no year, *Money Hard But Some Women Don't Know*, no year, and *Trust No-Body In Time Because Human Being Is Trickish*, no year.

Olusola, Segun   Nigeria

Born in 1936 in Iperu, Remo division, Western State, Nigeria,
Segun Olusola was educated at the Remo Secondary School,
Shagamu. After completion in 1953 he went into professional
broadcasting. He was features producer for Radio Nigeria until
1959 when he joined the WNTV (Western Nigeria Television),
Ibadan, as Nigeria's first television producer. In 1960 he was
awarded a six-month grant by the U. S. Government to participate in an international seminar on Radio-TV Organization
and Production at Syracuse University, New York. In 1964 he
left Ibadan for the NTS (Nigerian Television Service), Lagos,
where he was Manager of Production Services. He is now
Programme Director.

His active interest in theatre dates back to 1958 when he
co-founded an amateur drama group "Players of the Dawn".
He has produced European and African plays, among the latter
Christina Ama Ata Aidoo's "Dilemma of a Ghost" in 1965,
Wole Soyinka's "My Father's Burden" in 1961, and "Trials of
Brother Jero" in 1965, Duro Ladipo's "Crucifixion" in 1962,
Kola Ogunmola's "The Palmwine Drinkard" in 1964, Chris
Olude's "The Avenger" in 1964, and J. P. Clark's "Song of a
Goat" and "Masquerade" in 1965. *Iya Abiku* is a TV original
Olusola did in 1965.

Papers and reports Segun Olusola produced include *Five
Years of Nigerian Television Development*, 1964, *Television and
the Nigerian Village*, 1964, *TV and the Village Audience*, 1965,
and *Television and the Arts — the African Experience*, 1965.

Omotoso, Kole   Nigeria

Kole Omotoso was born on April 21, 1943, in Akure, Western
State, Nigeria, the second of three children. His father died in
1948, and his mother did not marry again. He went to Oyemekun Grammar School in 1957 and left with the equivalent of

the General Certificate of Education (G.C.E.) in 1961. In 1962 he went to King's College Lagos. In 1963 he taught English, History and Geography at Oyemekun Grammar School for seven months. In 1964 he got admission to the English Department of the University of Ibadan but changed to read Arabic instead. After graduating in June 1968 he taught English, French and Arabic at Ansar-ud-Deen Grammar School in Ikare for just over a year. In September 1969 he came to Britain on a Commonwealth Universities Commission grant to do a Ph. D. thesis on the controversial issue of drama in Arabic literature. He has just completed the thesis (June 1972).

Kole Omotoso is the author of *The Edifice*, London 1971, "a novel about a black student in a white man's country and a white woman in a black man's country".

Onyeama, Dillibe   Nigeria

Born on January 6, 1951, in Enugu, East Central State, Nigeria, Charles Dillibe Ejifor Onyeama is the son of a distinguished African judge at the International Court at The Hague. He studied at a British preparatory school for five years after arriving in the United Kingdom in 1959. He then entered Eton where he stayed for four years, obtaining seven "O" Level Passes. He is widely travelled and has visited Denmark, Italy, Germany, Belgium and Holland; since moving to Britain he has also revisited Africa four times.

Onyeama is at present studying Journalism at a Fleet Street writers' school in London.

His book, *Nigger at Eton*, London 1972, is an autobiographical report of his education in the world's most famous college.

Opoku, Amankwa Andrew   Ghana

Born on November 25, 1912, in Bechem, district Ahafo, Ashanti, Ghana, of an Aburi family, Amankwa Andrew Opoku, the son of a Presbyterian minister, grew up in Bompata, Ashanti. His father died in 1920, and the family moved back to Aburi, where he attended the middle school, going on to Nsaba and the Presbyterian Teachers' College at Akropong, where he was trained as a teacher and catechist. He started teaching in 1935, and taught at middle schools in Anum, Abetifi and Aburi. In 1945, he went back to the Training College for a year's special course, and taught for 18 months. Then he worked in the timber industry in Twifu. In 1948 he was appointed Headmaster of the primary school in Akwasiho, going on to the middle school in Mpraeso. From 1951 to 1956 he was Twi editor in the Vernacular Literature Bureau in Accra. In 1956 he joined the Ghana Broadcasting System.

The works of Amankwa Andrew Opoku, a play, *Odehuro* (904), and a story, *Mo Ahenewa* (905), are written in Akuapem-Twi.

Osadebay, Dennis Chukude   Nigeria

Born on June 29, 1911, in Asaba, Mid Western State, Nigeria, Dennis Chukude Osadebay was educated at Asaba Government School, Sacred Heart School in Calabar and at Hope Waddell Institute in the same town. Starting work in 1930, he became a Customs Officer in Calabar, Port Harcourt and the then British part of the Cameroons. In 1944 he was a founder member of the NCNC (National Council of Nigeria and the Cameroons) to whose Central Committee he continued to belong all the time, except for the four years from 1945 to 1949 when he read Law in London. In 1949 he was called to the Bar. Returning to Nigeria, he headed a firm of solicitors in Aba and became legal advisor to the NCNC. In 1951 he was elected a Member of the Western Region House of Assembly and from there to the Federal House of Representatives in Lagos. In 1954 he gave up his double membership and concentrated on the leadership of the NCNC Opposition in the Western Region until the post was taken over by Adelabu in 1956. Becoming Opposition Leader again in March 1958, when Adelabu was killed in a car accident, he was elected Deputy Speaker in 1958. In 1960, when Azikiwe was appointed Governor-General of Nigeria, he was made President of the Senate.

In August 1963, with the creation of the Mid-West State, Dennis Chukude Osadebay became its Prime Minister. At the Military Coup on January 15, 1966, he was deposed and consequently alleged to have amassed some 200.000 pounds during his tenure of office. This money was tied up in landed property, bank accounts and shares in companies. In April 1968 he was sentenced to repay 104.000 to the Government of the Mid Western State, and in October 1968, all his property in this state was confiscated. He then withdrew into private life. In November 1971, an edict, taking effect from October 1, 1967, stopped the payment of all pensions to him.

His poetry, all written between 1930 and 1950, has a strong nationalistic fervour and has been collected in a volume *Africa Sings* (910). In 1965 an admirer, Nosike Ikpo, wrote a political pamphlet in his favour, *Osadenism the Philosophy of Humanism,* Benin City 1965.

Africa Sings, published in 1952, was the first volume of poetry in English from Nigeria. "The inferiority syndrome, that most devastating result of colonialism, is here in all its glory" (Adrian A. Roscoe).

Osorio, Ernesto Cochat   Angola

Born on June 15, 1917, in Luanda, Angola, of a Portuguese father and a French mother, Ernesto Cochat Osorio spent twenty-seven years in Portugal, before he settled in Angola as a medical

Agostinho Neto

Mario António

PLATE XIII

Oscar Bento Ribas

Castro Soromenho

Alexis Kagame

Tchicaya U Tam'si

PLATE XIV

Guy Menga

Clémentine Nzuji

doctor. He published three volumes of poetry, *Calema* (2025), *Cidade* (2027), and *Biografia da noite* (2029), and two books of stories, *Capim Verde* (2026) and *O homen do chapéu* (2028).

Ouane, Ibrahima-Mamadou   Mali

Born on July 10, 1908, in Bandiagara, Mopti region, Mali, Ibrahima-Mamadou Ouane attended the Ecole Terrasson de Fougères in Bamako. There he studied Arabian, Islamic Law and Theology. He is a member of the Office International de Culture.

He published two volumes of stories, *Fâdimâtâ, la princesse du désert, suivi du Drame de Deguembéré* (921), stories from the Islamic part of Africa, the Sahara and the camel nomads of the Tuareg, and *Les filles de la reine Cléopâtre* (923). A volume of poetry is entitled *Le collier de coquillages* (922). Essays are *L'énigma du Macina*, Monte-Carlo 1952.

Ouologuem, Yambo   Mali

Born on August 22, 1940, in Bandiagara, Mopti region, Mali, Yambo Ouologuem is the only son of a land owner and school inspector. After his primary education in his home town, and his secondary education at the Lycée Terrasson-de-Fougères in Bamako, he left for Paris in 1960 to continue his education at the famous Lycée Henry IV. From 1964 to 1966 he taught at the Lycée de Charenton in Paris. He gave up teaching in order to continue his studies. He got diplomas in Literature, Philosophy, and English.

In 1968 Yambo Ouologuem was awarded the distinguished Prix Renaudot for his first novel, *Le Devoir de Violence* (925), which immediately was translated into other languages, into English as *Bound for Violence*. It is a historical novel reaching up to the present day, contradicting a decade of African novels which were glorifying the African past. Also by him is *Les mille et une bibles du sexe* (926), supposedly written by one Utto Rodolph and published in his own Editions Dauphin.

"Yambo Ouologuem is a small, mercurial man, with a mocking sense of humour and a scathing intellect, which make him a supreme conversationalist. *The Pilgrims of Copernaum,* his next novel, now completed, has 250 characters from five continents covering a time span from before Abraham to 1971" (West Africa, August 13, 1971).

"*Le Devoir de Violence* ... a work of very first value as to the importance of the subject, as to the brilliant ability with which the author organizes his story and masters his style" (Sully Faik).

"The novel of Ouologuem can be considered as a gigantic requiem for the Negro, the privileged victim of both forms of violence (traditional violence and colonial violence), and as a baroque painting of prayers and of 'miserere nobis, Deus'" (Sunday O. Anozie).

"Ouologuem is one of those people who need little sleep — three hours a night he says. When the inspiration takes him, he is capable of sitting at his typewriter writing furiously for 24 hours at a time" ("West Africa", December 14, 1968).

"... The text reproduced on the left comes from a novel by a Malian writer first published in Paris in 1968, the text on the right, which anyone could conclude was a close but stylish version of the same passages, comes from a novel by Graham Greene in 1934 ... The asserted African-ness of *Le Devoir de Violence* has recently, as it happens, been challenged elsewere ..." ("Times Literary Supplement", May 5, 1972).

"... when I asked my friend Mohamed-Salah Dembri his opinion of this brilliant novel, he was less enthusiastic and said flatly that *Le Devoir de Violence* was no more than an imitation of André Schwarz-Bart's 'Le Dernier des Justes', published in 1959 by the same house and awarded the Prix Goncourt ..." (Eric Sellin, Fall 1971).

Portrait on Plate VI.

Ousmane, Sembene   Senegal

Born on January 8, 1923, at Ziguinchor, Casamance, Senegal, Sembene Ousmane — Sembene being the family name — is essentially a self-educated writer. After only a few years of primary education, he became a fisherman like his father. At the age of twelve he was taught to be a mason. He disliked it and became a mechanic. At the outbreak of World War II he was drafted into the French army and saw fighting in Italy and Germany. Demobilized at Baden-Baden, Germany, he returned to Senegal in 1947 when there was the strike of the railway workers. In order to further his literary ambitions he returned to France, where he worked as a docker for ten years in Marseille. There he became a trade-union leader. During this time he started writing. In 1957 he settled down in Dakar, but continued to travel widely.

Besides his career as a writer, Sembene Ousmane, after studying at the Moscow Film School, established himself as the most prominent African film director. In 1963 he produced the short feature, *Borom Sarret,* in 1966 *La Noire de . . .,* his first full-length film, which won him several prizes, and, after *Véhi Ciosane,* in 1968, his first full-length colour film, *Manda-Bi* (in French "Le Mandat"), which received a prize at the Venice Film Festival in 1969. In 1971 he produced *E Mitai* (God of Thunder), a film set in Casamance during World War II, when France was press-ganging the athletically-built Diolas of Casamance into her colonial armed forces, to be shipped as cannon fodder to Europe. This film is the only one not based on novels or short stories which Sembene Ousmane had published before.

Sembene Ousmane's first novel, *Le Docker Noir* (927), in which a white woman embezzles the manuscript of a black dockworker's novel in order to publish it in her own name, failed to express his message. His second novel, *O pays, mon beau peuple* (928), about a man educated in Europe who returns home with his white wife, and tries to bring progress to his people, but whose ideas are resisted by both traditionalists and colonialism, was translated into many languages, as was his next novel, *Les bouts de bois de Dieu* (929), about the strike of the railway workers in Senegal in 1947 *(God's Bits of Wood)*. His novel, *L'harmattan* (931), was to be the first volume of a trilogy dealing with problems of cultural conflict, but has so far been followed only by two short novels, or long stories, both in one volume, *Véhi-Ciosane ou Blanche-Genèse, suivi du Mandat* (932), which he used as texts for his films. Other texts for his films are included in his volume of short stories, *Voltaïque* (930).

"*(O pays mon beau peuple)* cannot be called a successful novel, taken all in all. But there is much in it that is worth our attention and the author shows ability and promise" (Ulli Beier).

On *God's Bits of Wood:* "Ousmane captures expertly the contrast between bush and 'bidonville' Africa and the European colonials" (James Fernandez).

"In *Voltaïque* and *Véhi-Ciosane, suivi du Mandat,* Sembene Ousmane describes certain aspects of modern African society. The glance he casts is merciless, and it is not wrong to state that he has created true literature of licidity" (Bernard Mouralis).

Portrait on Plate V.

Owono, Joseph   Cameroon

Born on December 17, 1921, in Menguemé, district Nyong et Sô, Cameroon, Joseph Nkoudou Owono finished his education in Yaunde with the Diploma of the Ecole Supérieure d'Agriculture in 1943.

From 1943 to 1957 he did research work in Agriculture. From 1957 to 1959 he held various offices in the Ministry of Agriculture and Finance. In 1959 he was trained at the Ministry of Foreign Affairs in France, and then attached to the French diplomatic representations in Washington and New York. In 1960, with the Independence of Cameroon, he became Director of the American Section in the Ministry of Foreign Affairs in Yaunde, and then was sent to the 15th Session of the United Nations as head of the Cameroonian Delegation.

Since 1961 Joseph Nkoudou Owono has served his country as Ambassador, from 1961 to 1962 in Monrovia, Liberia, from 1962 to 1965 in Cairo, United Arab Republic, from 1965 to 1970 as ambassador to the United States, to Canada and to the United Nations as Head of Delegation or Permanent Representative. Since 1970 he has been ambassador in Moscow, the Soviet Union.

He wrote a sociological study, *Le mariage dotal au Cameroun Français*, 1954, and a novel *Tante Bella* (936), which was the first novel to be published locally in Cameroon.

Oyono, Ferdinand   Cameroon

Born on September 14, 1929, in Ngulemakong, district Ntem, Cameroon, Ferdinand Léopold Oyono entered the Ecole Régionale in Ebolowa in 1939. His mother, a practicing Catholic, separated from her baptised, but polygamous husband, earned her living as a travelling tailoress. The boy had his secondary education at the Lycée Général Leclerc in Yaunde, and was then sent by his father to France, where he matriculated at the Lycée in Provins (Seine et Marne) in 1950. He studied Law and Political Economy at the Sorbonne, and at the Ecole Nationale d'Administration, Paris. He passed his period of probation at the French Embassy in Rome, Italy.

Back in Cameroon he was appointed director of the Bureau d'Etudes in Yaunde, then, in 1960, he was attached to the Cameroonian Embassy in Paris. From 1960 to 1961 he was Cameroon's delegate to UNO, and from 1961 to 1962 he was Cameroon's ambassador to Guinea, Ghana, Mali and Morocco. He served his country in many special missions and good-will tours. From 1962 to 1965 he was Cameroon's ambassador to Liberia, and from 1965 to 1969, to the Benelux countries and the Common Market. Since 1969 he has been ambassador to France, Italy, Tunisia, Morocco and Algeria, with residence in Paris.

Oyono holds high decorations from Cameroon, France, and Belgium.

Ferdinand Oyono has written three novels. In *Une Vie de Boy* (941), translated into English under the title *Houseboy* (941 c), he ridicules the world of the colonialists as seen through the eyes of the houseboy Tundi. "Neither Africans nor Europeans have any individual characteristics. They have the stock reactions of people in any colonial society" (Anthony Brench).

"The caricatural humour of Oyono catches a small society, mean and conventional, against which he likes to void his anticolonialistic scorn" (Simon Battestini).

"This is a very compelling novel, beautiful in its simplicity, gripping, humorous, frank and painfully true of life" (Kunle Akinsemoyin).

His second novel, *Le vieux nègre et la medaille* (942), also translated into English, under the title, *The Old Man and the Medal* (942 c), is written in the same anticolonialistic spirit. It depicts the tragic story of an old man who lost his sons and his land to the French colonialists and is rewarded for his services with a medal, the decoration of which brings him only pain and shame. "A raw and merciless light strips blank the contradiction between the sweet words of the white people and their real behaviour" (David Diop).

His third novel, *Chemin d'Europe* (943), tells the story of an African who gains his selfconfidence through his experiences in Europe. "Again Oyono has demonstrated his capability to set up an intrigue with a rather dramatic sense of discipline. The solid architecture of his books enforces his sense of biting comic, his taste of realistic and percussive detail, and his art to treat all important scenes with brio" (Gerald Moore).

Portrait on Plate XII.

Oyônô-Mbia, Guillaume   Cameroon

Born in 1939 in Mvoutessi near Sangmélima, district Dja et Lobo, Cameroon, Guillaume Oyônô-Mbia had his early education at the Collège Evangélique de Libamba, where he passed his Baccalauréat, and where he taught French, English, and German. "French I learnt at school and English at about 16 mostly by myself through magazines collected by my mother from the missionaries. I was taught German by my grandfather. He used to tell me lots of stories in German."

In 1964 Guillaume Oyônô-Mbia went to London, and from 1964 to 1969 he studied English and French at the University of Keele, Staffordshire, England, where he graduated. At present Oyônô-Mbia is Assistant Head of the Department of English at Cameroon's Federal University in Yaunde.

Guillaume Oyônô-Mbia wrote his plays in French, and re-wrote them himself in English. *Trois prétendants, un mari* (945), a comedy about the marriage of a girl, is performed at the end of the school year by almost every school in Cameroon. The English version *Three Suitors; One Husband* (946) is in the same way successful in English-speaking West Cameroon. His second play, first written in English, *Until Further Notice* (946), deals with the same set of persons and their deception with the new ways of young people. Its French version *Jusqu'à nouvel avis* (947) was awarded the El-Hadj-Ahmadou-Ahidjo Prize. After a radio play in English *His Excellency's Special Train* (948) which he transformed into a stage play in French *Le train spécial de son Excellence,* he wrote the play *Notre fille ne se mariera pas!,* Paris 1971. Short stories in French, collected in two small volumes *Chroniques de Mvoutessi 1,* and *Chroniques de Mvoutessi 2,* both Yaunde 1971.

Three Suitors: One husband, a play, in which African customs are overcome by Western ways of life, is a comedy in the spirit of Molière.

Palangyo, Peter   Tanzania

Born on August 17, 1939, in Arusha, Tanzania, Peter Palangyo
received his elementary education in his home town and his
secondary education at Old Moshi Secondary School in Moshi,
Kilimanjaro, Tanganyika.

Peter Palangyo has attended the following Universities:
Makerere University in Kampala, Uganda, where he received a
diploma in Education, St. Olaf College in Minnesota, USA,
where he studied Biology, the University of Minnesota in Minneapolis, the University of Iowa in Iowa City, and the State
University of New York in Buffalo, where he finished his Ph. D.
in Literature in spring 1972, before returning to Tanzania to
teach at the University of Dar-es-Salaam.

Before his academic career he was teaching Biology at the Old
Moshi Secondary School, and was Headmaster at the High
Schools of Lyamungu and Tambaza in Tanzania, and Principal
of one of Dar-es-Salaam's leading day schools H. H. The Aga
Khan Boys' Secondary School.

Peter Palangyo's first novel, *Dying in the Sun* (1372), shows
a man who for days and nights questions his relationship with
his father, and gives a deep inside view of African rural life
and thinking.

Portrait on Plate XV.

Parkes, Frank Kobina   Ghana

Born in 1932 in Korle Bu, an area of Accra, Ghana, Frank
Kobina Parkes completed his secondary education in Accra.
He was a reporter for the "Daily Graphic", Accra, editor at
Radio Ghana, then editor of two short-lived local newspapers.
He is President of the Ghanaian writer's association, and has
been living in London since 1964, editing "The Dawn", the
journal of the Convention Peoples Party.

Parkes has published a volume of verse, *Songs from the Wil-
derness* (949).

"The poetry of Frank Parkes is at its best in its quieter moments" (O. R. Dathorne).

"There is vision, and depth of feeling, and a creative as well as a precise use of words ... This is a varied talent, and still a young one. Nor is it a talent whose interest depends at all on it being a Ghanaian talent, since it is a universal one" (P. W.).

"Mr. Parkes is one of the best poets writing on Africa and the world, in our days" (Mbella Sonne Dipoko).

p'Bitek, Okot   Uganda

Born in 1931 at Gulu, district Acholi, Northern Uganda, Okot p'Bitek was educated first at Gulu High School and later at one of the most high-flying of Ugandan schools, King's College, Budo. He went on to read Education at Bristol, England, Law at Aberystwyth and Social Anthropology at Oxford. Returning to Uganda, he lectured at the University College at Makerere, Kampala. This academic versatility was matched by considerable athletic skill: among other achievements, he played football for Uganda. A drummer and dancer, he founded an annual festival of African arts at Gulu. For a while he was Director of the National Cultural Centre in Kampala. After spending the academic year of 1969/70 as a fellow of the International Writing Program at the University of Iowa, Iowa City, USA, Okot p'Bitek returned to his residence in Kisumu, Kenya. In 1971 he became a Research Fellow at the Institute of African Studies and part-time Lecturer in Sociology and Literature at the University of Nairobi.

Okot p'Bitek's first creative work, the novel *Lak Tar Miyo kinyero wi lobo* (1373), was written in Lwo, his first long poem, *Song of Lawino* (1374), he translated himself from his own language, Acholi, into English. In this genre he had found his line, and produced two more songs of this kind, *Song of Ocol* (1375), and *Song of a Prisoner*, New York 1971.

"Okot is explosive, elusive ... many obvious words rush into the mind: dynamic, awkward, witty ... the talent for irony and satire, the clearly brilliant gift, the quality of the 'enfant terrible'" (Edward Blishen).

"*Song of Lawino* is a song of angry protest ... The problem of 'African imitating European' is certainly not new, but p'Bitek's analysis is a fresh, dispassionate — and therefore reliable — appraisal ..." (Akin Osunbunmi).

"Transition has presented the poet with painful problems. Rhyme, assonance and tonal variations, the chief ornaments of the original text, are lost. The sharp, chopping consonants of Lwo speech must give way to the relatively softer and more sibillant ones of English. But Okot p'Bitek has found a clean, simple and dignified language for his poem" (Gerald Moore).

Portrait on Plate XV.

Penda, Patrice Ndedi
vid. *Ndedi-Penda, Patrice*

Peters, Lenrie   Gambia

Born in 1932 in Bathurst, Gambia, of Sierra Leonian parents, Lenrie Peters received his basic education in Bathurst and moved in 1949 to Sierra Leone, where he obtained a Higher School Certificate from Prince of Wales School, Freetown. In 1952 he left for England to study at the Cambridge Technical College, but soon changed to Trinity College, Cambridge, to study Medicine. After qualifying as a doctor, Dr. Peters went on to specialize in surgery at a hospital in Guildford, England. He has now returned to Gambia.

Peters, who was also trained as a singer, has participated in BBC programmes, in "Calling West Africa", and was Chairman of its "Africa Forum".

Lenrie Peters has published two volumes of verse and a novel. His poetry has appeared in both African and British journals. His first volume, *Poems* (950), was published by Mbari. "What characterises Peters' poems is the wonder he feels at suddenly discovering he is among the living and capable of loving — the wonder of the discovery and the wish to share it. ... More than anything else, Peters asks dignity of men and exemplifies this by writing with dignity" (Paul Theroux).

"Peters is good at vignettes" (Melvin B. Tolson).

His second work was the novel *The Second Round* (951). "Peters shows a talent for working weird and wonderful materials into the fabric of his story ... But he fails to knit his materials together tightly, and, weakened by false starts and loose ends, the fabric loses pattern and design" (Bernth Lindfors).

"His is the true storyteller's art: frightfully compelling, grotesquely real. In *The Second Round,* he has outreached a whole generation of young African novelists" (Charles R. Larson).

"Lenrie Peters has ably demonstrated that in his first novel his true forte is the half-world of tragedy and joy, where lives are lived and where death encroaches lightly like a song" (O. R. Dathorne).

His most recent book is *Satellites* (952), a book of verse. "His language acquires a simplicity which one could say is totally out of character and almost startling" (Ama Ata Aidoo).

Philips, Femi   Nigeria

Born in 1942 at Awe, Afijio division, Western State, Nigeria, Femi Philips, son of the Are Onilu of Lagos, had his primary education at St. Anthony's Catholic School in Awe, then went to Lagos and attended the Cosmopolitan Evening College. In 1963 he founded the USA Pat-Boone-Fan Club and became its president. The same year he joined the "Ogunde Concert Party" and toured West Africa with this group. With broader experience he decided to have his own theatre, and thus, in 1966, founded "Osumare Theatre", which he later named "Osumare National Theatre". His first public performance took place at the palace of the Oba of Lagos, with a play entitled *Oba Alahusa*. Since then he has produced many plays in Yoruba, among them *Aiye Fotito Pamo, Awe-Oladokun, Sogidi, Igbehin-Osika, Olofin Oduduwa*, and *Iku Akogun*.

Femi Philips is also a musician. He has had records made by Philips West African Records and by Badejo.

Philombe, René   Cameroon

Born about 1930 in Ngaundere, district Adamaua, Cameroon, René Philombe — this is the pen-name for Philippe-Louis Ombedé — is the son of an Interpreter of the French Colonial Administration, who had been transferred there from his home in Batchenga, District Lékié, near Yaunde. He received his primary education at different schools, his secondary education partly in Dschang in 1944. In 1945 he was at the Ecole Primaire Supérieure in Yaunde and on the staff of a school journal "L'Appel du Tam-tam".

From 1947 to 1949 he was Secretary to the Native Court of Saa, District Lékié, and founded there a cultural association. From 1950 to 1957 he got more and more involved in politics as partisan to the U.P.C. (Union des Populations du Cameroun). In 1957 he was stricken with Poliomyelitis, the consequences of which he is still bearing courageously.

In 1959 he founded two weeklies, one in French, "La Voix du Citoyen", the other in Ewondo "Bébéla-Ebug". Because of this he got into difficulties and was sent to prison and his health deteriorated. But he was elected Treasurer of the Union of Cameroonian Journalists (U.N.J.C.). On January 23, 1960, he founded, with friends, the National Association of Poets and Writers of Cameroon (A.P.E.C.) of which he still is General Secretary.

In 1962 he interrupted his journalistic activities and returned to his home town Batchenga, where he founded an Association of Farmers and Workers. In September 1963 he was arrested and condemned to six months imprisonment for subversion.

Starting in 1964 he spent all his time in literary activity. He founded "Le Cameroun Littéraire", mouthpiece of the A.P.E.C., and he published his first collection of short stories, *Lettres de ma cambuse* (954), for which he was awarded the Prix Mottard of the French Academy. In the same year he received two more prizes, the First International Prize for Short Story of the International Centre of French Arts and Thinking, and the First Prize for Cameroonian Poets from the Society of Poets and Artists of France for his collection of poems, *Hallalis et Chansons Nègres*.

In 1966 his first novel was published, *Sola ma Chérie* (955), the story of a young girl who, when her parents married her to a rich man, flees back to her first poor husband whom she had married secretly and who could not pay the bride price.

In 1967 René Philombe's house was searched and legal proceedings were begun against him, but in 1968 the President of the Republic nominated him to the jury, formed to award the El Hadj Ahmadou Ahidjo-Prize for Literature, Arts, and Science. In 1969 René Philombe founded the theatre company "Les Compagnons de la Comédie".

His second novel, *Un sorcier Blanc à Zangali* (956), the story of a European missionary of the first generation who refuses to be the tool of colonialism, appeared in 1970. In the same year René Philombe founded the journal "Ozila" and was elected Director of the journal "Le Cameroun Littéraire". His new collection of short stories, *Histoires queue-de-chat*, Yaunde 1971, contains stories of critical realism. His play, *Les époux célibataires*, Yaunde 1971, had its premiere on June 16, 1971, at Yaunde, and was performed by "Les Compagnons de la Comédie" at the French Cultural Centre.

Portrait on Plate XII.

Phiri, Desmond Dudwa   Malawi

Born on February 23, 1931, in the Mzimba district in the
northern region of Malawi, Desmond Dudwa Phiri passed out
of the Blantyre Secondary School in 1949 with the Government Junior Certificate, Thereafter he studied by correspondence for the London General Certificate of Education and the
Bachelor of Science (Economics) degree. The latter he took in
1959. From 1961 to 1962 he was sent to the London School of
Economics by the Tanganyika Government of which he was a
civil servant. In London he took the Diploma in Economic and
Social Administration.

His studies went parallel to a career as a civil servant. From
1950 to 1952 he was working in what is now Zambia (then
Northern Rhodesia). From 1952 to 1964 he was a civil servant
in what is now Tanzania (then Tanganyika), to return home to
what is now Malawi (then Nyasaland) on the eve of independence. From October 1966 to September 1969 he was First Secretary in the Malawi Embassy in Bonn, Germany. Since 1969 he
has been back home, now working in the Office of the President
and Cabinet Economic Planning Unit.

Desmond Dudwa Phiri wrote in English and in his mother
tongue Tumbuka. In 1961 the East African Literature Bureau
published his *Hints to Private Students.* In 1964 his play, *The
Chief's Bride* (2040), was performed and printed in 1968. All his
other creative work is in Tumbuka, consisting of four short
novels, *Mankhwala pa nchito* (2036), *Kanakazi kayaya* (2037),
Kumsika wa vyawaka (2038), and *Ulanda ma Mavunika* (2039).

Pieterse, Cosmo   Namibia

Born in 1930 in Namibia, Cosmo Pieterse graduated at Cape
Town University, South Africa. He taught in South Africa for
eleven years before going to teach in London. He is now Associate Professor in the Department of English, State University
of Ohio, USA.

Pieterse co-edited and contributed to *Protest and Conflict in African Literature* (S 115). He edited *Ten One-Act Plays* (A 83), compiled *Seven South African Poets,* London 1970, *Five African Plays,* London 1972 and *Short African Plays,* London 1972. The latter includes a play of his, *Ballad of the Cells.*

Plaatje, Solomon T. South Africa

Born in 1877 at Boshof, Orange Free State, South Africa, into the Rolong tribe, Solomon Tshekiso Plaatje attended Pniel Missionary School in Barkly West, an outpost of the Lutheran Church. He passed Standard IV, his highest formal education. After leaving school in 1890 he was teaching for some time, then, in 1893, he went to Kimberley and found employment as a postman. In his spare time he learned Dutch, French, German, Sotho, Zulu and Xhosa. In 1899 he became an interpreter in the Magistrate's Office in Mafeteng, and soon afterwards he was appointed interpreter to the Court of Summary Jurisdiction under Lord Edward Cecil. In Mafeteng Plaatje acquired his thorough knowledge of the Tswana language. When the Anglo-Boer War broke out in 1899, Plaatje enlisted as a signal man in the service of the British Government, and served as a war correspondent during the siege of Mafeking.

After the war, Plaatje settled in Kimberley and established the "Koranta ea Becoana" (The Tswana Gazette), a newspaper that was printed in Tswana and English and whose editor he was from 1901 to its end in 1908.

In January 1912, at the very first meeting of the South African Native National Congress Solomon Tshekiso Plaatje was elected its first Secretary-General, and he helped to draft its constitution. In the same year he began publication of "Tsala ea Batho" (The Friend of the People). The newspaper was widely read in the Tswana speaking population of Transvaal, the Orange Free State, and in the diamond mines of Kimberley, but Plaatje had soon to stop publication, because his Congress duties took up too much time.

In 1914 Plaatje was — with John L. Dube, Walter B. Rubusana, Thomas M. Mapikela, Saul Msana — in the delegation that went to London to protest against the Land Act of 1913, which aimed at establishing segregation in land ownership and occupation. The protest was ignored, the delegation returned to South Africa, but Plaatje stayed in Britain, touring the country and holding speeches in which he pleaded for the position of the Africans in his country. When he ran out of money he wrote articles for various journals. In 1915 he published his *Native Life in South Africa, Before and Since the European War and the Boer Rebellion*, London 1916. In London he met Prof. Daniel Jones of the Linguistics Department of the University of London, and they collaborated on the *Sechuana Phonetic Reader*, published in 1916.

That same year, Plaatje published his famous *Sechuana Proverbs, with Literal Translations and Their European Equivalents*, London 1916, a collection of over 700 proverbs.

In 1919 Plaatje was in an unofficial delegation that represented the Africans at the Versailles Peace Conference, but neither his nor another unofficial delegation led by General Hertzog and Dr. D. F. Malan, representing the Afrikaners, was acknowledged.

While the deputation returned to South Africa, Plaatje attended the first Pan-African Congress organized by the American Negro William Edward Burghardt Du Bois. From France, he travelled to Canada and the United States giving speeches on the situation of his people in South Africa. He returned to South Africa and devoted himself to temperance movements and to the improvement of the welfare of the African population of Kimberley. In 1928 he was given property to live on by the people of Kimberley in appreciation of his outstanding public service.

In December 1930 Plaatje made a final protest against the South African Government, condemning the Pass Laws. Two years later, on June 19, 1932, Solomon Tshekiso Plaatje died.

James Ngugi

Okot p'Bitek

PLATE XV

Taban lo Liyong

Peter Palangyo

Jean-Joseph Rabearivelo

Jacques Rabemananjara

PLATE XVI

Legson Kayira

Edouard Maunick

Plaatje's only contribution to creative writing is a novel, *Mhudi, an Epic of South African Native Life a Hundred Years Ago* (2043), the first historical novel of modern African literature in English. It is a love story between two young Rolong, embedded in the bloody aftermath that followed the death of the great Zulu king Shaka and which brought the rise of Mzilikazi.

"Solomon T. Plaatje, whose mother tongue was Tswana, was fully aware of the importance of English, both because there was yet no tradition of creative writing in Tswana, and because he was so fully immersed in the all-African struggle for recognition" (Albert S. Gérard).

He also translated Shakespeare's "Comedy of Errors" into Tswana entitled *Diphóshóphóshó*, 1930, and "Julius Caesar" entitled *Dintshontsho tsa Bo-Juliuse Kesara,* which was published posthumously in 1937.

Pliya, Jean   Dahomey

Born on July 21, 1931, in Djougou, Northwestern District, Dahomey, Jean Pliya entered the public school of Cotonou in 1940 and continued in Whydah. In 1949 he passed his Brevet Elémentaire at the Ecole Primaire Supérieure Victor Ballot in Porto-Novo, Dahomey, then went to Dabou, Ivory Coast, for his Baccalauréat, which he received in 1952. He left for Dakar, Senegal, and obtained his Propédeutique at the university there, then went to Toulouse, France, where he got his Licence d'Histoire-Géographie in 1955, the Diplôme d'Etudes Supérieures and a certificate enabling him to teach at secondary schools in 1957. He taught then at the secondary school in Porto-Novo.

Pliya's political career began in March 1959, when he became Secretary General of the Liberation Movement M.L.N. He held this office till November 1960. In 1963 he became the Secretary of Information of the P.D.U. (Partie Démocratique Dahoméen) and represented his party in the government from 1964 to 1965.

From 1961 to 1963 he was also Director in the Ministry of Education and Culture, then became Minister for Information and Tourism in 1963. From January 1964 to December 1965 he was Representative of Abomey and First Secretary of the National Assembly of Dahomey.

Going back to teaching, Pliya taught at the Lycée Technique in Cotonou, then in Lyon, France, from where he returned to become a professor of geography at the University of Bénin in Lome, Togo.

Jean Pliya's literary production comprises fiction, plays and school manuals of history and geography. His first work, a short story, *L'arbre fétiche,* won him the Grand Prix de la Nouvelle Africaine 1963, donated by the journal "Preuves" and afterwards published in its May issue 1964. Three other short stories, *L'homme qui avait tout donné, La voiture rouge* and *Le gardien de nuit,* were published successively by the journals "Afrique", "L'Afrique littéraire" and "Présence africaine". His first play, *Kondo le Requin* (957), was just as successful. It won the Special Prize of the Dahomean Society of Banks in 1967, the Grand Prix de Littérature d'Afrique Noire the same year, and the Second Prize at the Concours radiophonique de l'O.R.T.F. in 1968. With his second play, *La secrétaire particulière,* published in 1970 in Cotonou, a satire on African bureaucracy, Pliya self-consciously turned away from the conflicts of the clash of cultures, depicted in his other works, to face modern political problems.

Portrait on Plate VII.

Pouka-M'Bague, Louis-Marie   Cameroon

Louis-Marie Pouka-M'Bague was born on August 15, 1910, in Khan, district Sanaga Maritime, Cameroon. In 1919 he entered the Catholic Mission School in Edea. Five years later he was admitted to the Seminary St. Joseph in Yaunde where he remained until 1931. At this time he was employed by the administration as scribe and interpreter. In 1953 he was awarded the title of an Officer of the Academy of Cameroon.

In 1931 Louis-Marie Pouka-M'Bague began to write for Cameroonian newspapers, which brought him, in 1935, an award in a journalists competition. In 1946 he began to write poetry, and he has since published seven small pamphlets of poetry: *Rires et sanglots*, 1947, *Les amours illusoires*, 1948, *Les rêveries tumultueuses* (958), *L'innombrable symphonie* (959), *A Son Excellence Ahmadou Ahidjo* (960), *Réflexions à l'occasion d'un anniversaire* (961), *Fusées 1964* (962), *Nouvelle entrevue d'outre-tombe ou Rehabilitation de Ruben Um Nyobe* (963) and *Ce siècle est triste* (964). Other works are his satire, *Hitler ou la chute de l'hydre*, 1948, *Paroles de sagesse*, Yaunde 1958, and *Les étapes vers l'indépendance du Cameroun*, 1959. Most of these writings have been published by the author himself.

Prudencio, Eustache   Dahomey

Born on September 20, 1924, at Bopa (Mono), Dahomey, Eustache Prudencio had his secondary education at the Lycée Victor Ballot in Porto-Novo. From 1944 to 1947 he was a student at the Ecole Normale William Ponty at Sébikotane near Dakar, Senegal. From 1947 to 1961 Eustache Prudencio was headmaster of different schools in Senegal, most of the time at the school of Djourbel. This activity was interrupted by one year of political activity at home: from 1957 to 1958 he was appointed Chef du Cabinet of the Ministry of the Interior of Dahomey.

Eustache Prudencio finally returned to Dahomey in 1961, to teach literature at the Lycée Technique Coulibaly in Cotonou. In 1962 he was appointed Superintendent of Primary Education, a position which he held at first at Mono, from 1962 to 1968 at Whydah, and since 1968 in Cotonou.

From 1964 to 1965 he was elected member of the Municipal Council of Whydah, and in 1968 he was running for President and won 5,6 % of the votes.

Eustache Prudencio had articles published in daily papers and journals like "Afrique Nouvelle", "Paris-Dakar", "L'Educateur", and his works include educational books like *Les rois d'Abomey*, Dakar, 1957, *Vade mecum des instituteurs*, Porto-Novo 1965, *Pédagogie vivante*, Cotonou 1967, and three volumes of poetry: *Vents du lac* (965), *Ombres et soleils* (966), and *Violence de la race* (967).

"Eustache Prudencio, a new voice in the concert of voices which speak through the world of the eternity of Man" (Lamine Diakhaté).

Rabearivelo, Jean-Joseph   Madagascar

Born on March 4, 1903, in Tananarive, Madagascar, and not in 1904 as he tried to make believe for wanting to appear younger, Jean-Joseph Rabearivelo was the son of a noble mother who later married a tailor. He was the only child of his mother Rabozivelo, who, originating from Ambatofotsy, a suburb of Tananarive, and belonging to the Andriana (noble) caste of the Zanadralambo (the sons of Ralambo), was related to most of the notables of the capital. She was, like most of the high society of Merina, a Protestant.

Jean-Joseph Rabearivelo was educated by his uncle, a Catholic who sent him, when he was five years old, to the Ecole des Frères des Ecoles Chrétiennes at Andohalo, then to the Collège Saint-Michel in Amparibe, from where he was expelled when he was thirteen years old. Then, in 1914 and 1915, he attended the public school of Faravohitra but only for a few months.

The next three or four years he was secretary and interpreter of the head of the Canton of Ambatolampy, 70 kilometres from Tananarive. In 1919 he returned to Tananarive and worked subsequently as errand-boy for a dealer in old iron, designer of lace for Mrs. Anna Gouverneur, and clerk at the Union Club, where he was in charge of the library enabling him to read much. Being without work for some time, he flung himself into literature, writing poetry under pseudonyms like Amance Valmond and Jean Osmé and collaborating at journals like "Journal de Madagascar". When the international revue "Anthropos" accepted an article of his on the poetry in Madagascar in 1923, he was proud and decided on a career in literature. In 1923 or 1924 he became proof-reader at the printing press of the Imerina, a job for which he was paid only from 1926 and which he kept until his death.

In 1926 he married Mary Razafitrimo, a photographer's daughter, who bore him one son and four daughters. When one of the daughters, Voahangy, died in 1933, Rabearivelo was desperate. Often he would visit the countryside: Ambatofotsy, the village of his family, and Ambohimanga, Ambatoharanana, Amboatany. Nothing could diminish his sorrow, not even the birth of another daughter in 1936, whom he named Velomboahangy, i. e. "Voahangy is reborn".

Rabearivelo's salary was too small to support his family and to pay for his books and stamps. He attempted to find work in the administration, but in vain, because he had not passed the examinations. On June 20, 1937, he received the final refusal, on June 22, 1937, Rabearivelo committed suicide by poisoning himself.

Jean-Joseph Rabearivelo wrote many collections of poetry in Malagasy and French: *La coupe de cendres* (1381), *Presquesonges* (1382), *Sylves* (1383), *Volumes* (1384), *Enfants d'Orphée* (1385), *Imaitsoanala — Fille d'oiseau — Cantate* (1386), *Traduit de la nuit* (1387), *Chants pour Abéone* (1388), *Vieilles chansons des pays d'Imerina* (1389), *Lova* (1390), *Des stances oubliées* (1391). His works were all printed in Tananarive during his life time, except one which was printed in Mauritius. It was only thirty years after his death when a selection appeared in Paris (1394). Another selection appeared in an English translation under the title *24 Poems* (1392).

"Rabearivelo appears in the first place as the singer of the Hova highlands. It seems that he wanted this, and that he believed in it as his real vocation" (Jean-Jaques Rabemananjara).

"*Flûtistes* (a poem from the volume *Presque-songes*) is the most beautiful and the most original expression of that cosmic pessimism which is one of the basic elements of his inspiration" (Albert Gérard).

"Unconsciously Rabearivelo transformed life into a simple meditation over death, a death he called between a mediocre life and the consolations which gave him his dreams and his Chimeras" (Gabriel Razafintsambaina).

"Rabearivelo's world is a world of extreme strangeness and also of extreme loneliness. We seem to be let in for an experience we cannot share with others and the cosmos we see is full of 'paths deserted by goats, and roads frequented by silence'. A recurring image is that of 'birds that have become strangers and cannot recognize their nests' . . . Rabearivelo's poems are clear and precise visions of a strange and personal world. In his life he has destroyed and dismembered reality. And out of the fragments he has built a new mythical world; it is a world of death and frustration, but also transcended by a sad beauty of its own" (Ulli Beier).

Portrait on Plate XVI.

Rabemananjara, Jacques   Madagascar

Born on July 23, 1913, in Maroansetra, province Tamatave, Madagascar, Jacques Rabemananjara was educated at the seminary of Sainte-Marie and later at the seminary of Tananarive. He published his first verse in "Revue des Jeunes de Madagascar", a journal which he had founded and whose editor he was until it was banned for too-nationalistic tendencies. In 1936 he left for France to study at the Sorbonne. In 1939 he represented Madagascar at the 150th anniversary of the French Revolution, then was drafted to the French Army. Back home in 1946, he was elected to the French National Assembly as member of the MDRM (Mouvement Démocratique de la Rénovation Malgache), whose secretary he became a little later. But before he left for France, the Resurrection took place and Rabemananjara was jailed in 1947 and sentenced to life imprisonment. He was in detention in Tananarive, on Lava Island at the North-West Coast of Madagascar, and in Marseille. In 1956 he was granted amnesty, and went to Paris. He was a co-editor of "Présence Africaine", and he took part at the First Congress of Black Writers and Artists in Paris in 1956. He returned home in 1960, and became Minister for Economics in the first Malagasy cabinet. On August 26, 1965, he was appointed Minister for Development and Agriculture, and from 1971 to May 18, 1972, he was Minister for Foreign and Social Affairs.

Rabemananjara has so far published five volumes of poetry, three plays, and two political essays. His first work was a collection of poems, *Sur les marches du soir* (1395), "a royal song dedicated to the 'millenial rites' of Love" (René Depestre). His second work of lyrics was *Rites millénaires* (1397): "Love here is decision, is freedom" (Eliane Boucquey-de Schutter). "His verses have the rhythm of the waves of the Indian Ocean which die smoothly on sandless beaches" (François Savarolles). *Antsa* (1398) "is no declaration of war against France. If Jacques Rabemananjara agrees to be a French poet he agrees to be one of us" (François Mauriac). Léopold Sédar Senghor called this poem "phrases of a solemn harmony like the step of gods and princes". His last poems appeared in 1961, entitled *Antidote* (1401).

Rabemananjara's plays are *Les dieux malgaches* (1396), the tragedy of a Malagasy king, who commits suicide over the corpse of his beloved, a princess, who was taken as hostage. "Form and verse are in classical French, the young poet obeys strictly the Alexandrian" (Erica de Bary); *Les boutriers de l'aurore* (1400), a symbolic tragedy of the first Malayan immigrants who settled in Madagascar, and *Agapes des dieux* (1402), a love tragedy between Prince Ratrimo and the daughter of Prince Ratany, who both commit suicide by drowning themselves in the sacred lake. "By the number of dead in the last act, it resembles Shakespeare" (Robert Cornevin).

His political essays are *Un Malgache vous parle*, Paris 1956, and *Nationalisme et problèmes malgaches*, Paris 1958.

Portrait on Plate XVI.

Rabetsimandranto, Fidélis Justin   Madagascar

Born in October 1907 in Mananjara, province Tananarive, Madagascar, Fidélis Justin Rabetsimandranto was educated at Collège Saint-Michel and got his Certificat d'Aptitude à l'Enseignement (Teacher's Diploma) in 1925. He is a teacher and editor of "Ny feon' ny Mariana", an important Catholic journal.

In 1926 he published his first collection of poems in Malagasy, *Fehezam-boninkazo*, reedited in 1960 (1407), in which he hammered himself a language swinging in dance and marching rhythms. Since then he has written about fifteen novels and novelettes, and six plays — one of which, *Kabary taloha sy ankehitriny*, was highly appreciated. Among his works are the following collections of poems: *Bouquets de rêves* (1405), *La nymphe dorée ou Fleur d'Andraikibe* (1406), and *Trimofoloalina* (1407) which was given an award by the Conseil Municipal de Tananarive in 1959.

Raditladi, Leetile Disang   Botswana

Born on July 13, 1910, at Serowe, district Ngwato now Botswana, Leetile Disang Raditladi received his primary education at Tiger Kloof Institution of the London Missionary Society. He got his secondary education at Lovedale Institute, Alice, Cape Colony, South Africa, and spent one year at Fort Hare University in South Africa.

In 1936 Leetile Disang Raditladi had to leave college because Chief Ishekedi Kgama framed him in his divorce case against his first wife. "This supposed civil case which was a breach of justice suddenly became a political case against me and my father Disang. He demanded our banishment by the British Government which danced to his music. This incident gave birth to my book *Motswasele II* (2047)", writes Raditladi. "Reading their injustice to me, the British Government offered me employment." Thus from 1938 to 1948 he was employed by the Government of the Bechuanaland Protectorate, then by the Botswana tribe as Tribal Secretary from 1948 to 1953.

In 1959 Leetile Disang Raditladi became Tribal Authority in various districts in the Bammangwato country, a position he still holds.

On Botswana Day, September 30, 1971, Raditladi was awarded the Presidential Order of Meritorious Service by President Seretse Kgama, Raditladi's second cousin on his father's as well as mother's side.

Raditladi wrote all his books in Tswana language, three plays *Motswasele II* (2047), *Dinšhontšho tsa loratô* (2048), and *Sekgoma I* (2050), and a volume of poetry *Sefalana sa menate* (2049).

Rajemisa-Raolison, Régis   Madagascar

Born on May 8, 1913, in Antsirana, province Diégo-Suarez, Madagascar, Régis Rajemisa-Raolison had his first schooling at the then Ecole Officielle in Ambinanindrano, which he entered in 1921. In 1922 he continued at the Ecole des Frères in Betafo and Antsirabe, and from 1923 to 1924 at the school of the Frères des Ecoles Chrétiennes in Ambositra and Andohalo. From 1923 to 1931 he was educated at the Petit Séminaire of Ambohipo. After secondary school he obtained his teacher's diploma and entered the teaching profession.

Régis Rajemisa-Raolison is still a teacher. He is also a member of the Malagasian Academy and a renowned grammarian. During the years 1935/36 he founded the "Revue des Jeunes de Madagascar" together with Jacques Rabemananjara. In 1952 Rajemisa-Raolison was President of the Malagasian Union of Poets and Writers.

Régis Rajemisa-Raolison published his first volume, a long poem, in 1948: *Les fleurs de l'île rouge* (1410). This was followed by *Mba Olombanona* in 1951, and the novel *Kilalaon' afo* (1411) both in Malagasy. Besides his literary ambitions Rajemisa-Raolison is engaged in studies on his mother tongue. He published a dictionary of Malagasian synonyms, *Vakoka,* and a Malagasian grammar.

Ranaivo, Flavien   Madagascar

Born on March 13, 1914, in Arivonimamo, some forty kilometres West of Tananarive, Madagascar, Flavien Ranaivo studied in Madagascar and in France. He has diplomas of the Ecole Nationale de la France d'Outre-Mer, the Certificat des Sciences Sociales d'Outre-Mer, the Certificat d'Etudes Supérieures de Maîtrise de Préhistoire et d'Archéologie de l'Océan Indien, and a diploma of the Film Studies in Gennevilliers, France.

His career began in 1938 as an editor in the Civil Cabinet of the Gouvernement Général, interrupted by military service from 1939 to 1940. From 1941 to 1943 he was Assistant Postmaster of Antsirabe, and from 1943 to 1945 he served voluntarily in the forces of Free France as a secretary in the regimental staff. From 1945 to 1950 he was Director of the Press in the General Information Service and edited the journal "Vaovao frantsaymalagasy" and "Informations de Madagascar". From 1950 to 1952 he was at the Ecole Nationale de la France d'Outre-Mer and a member in the Cabinet of the Secretary of State for France-Overseas, and from 1952 to 1955 he was again Director of the Malagasy section of the General Information Service. From 1955 to 1956 he worked at the Overseas Social Sciences, and from 1956 to 1959 he was Representative of the Madagascar Students at the Présidence du Conseil of the French Republic in the Office for Overseas Students. Since 1959 he has been Director of the Tourist Office of Madagascar in Tananarive, in addition to which he is President of the Administrative Council of Radio Madagascar. From 1952 to 1960 he was a member of the National Commission of the French Republic to represent the Overseas Territories at UNESCO.

Flavien Ranaivo wrote three volumes of poetry, *L'Ombre et le Vent* (1418), *Mes Chansons de Toujours* (1419), and *Le retour au Bercail* (1420), which brought him high recognition. He was Laureate of the section "Lettres" of the Exposition of Madagascar in 1946, he was awarded the Grand Prix Littéraire of Madagascar in 1955, the Prix Akbaraly in 1965, the Prix Carlier Monceau in 1969. He is a Member of the Académie Malgache, President of the Society for the Library of Madagascar, and member of the Committee of the Alliance Française in Madagascar. Flavien Ranaivo has represented Madagascar at numerous international literary and poetical conferences, and is President of the Film Festival of the Indian Ocean, of the Administrative Council of the Agency Madagascar-Press and the National Information Committee of the World Campaign against Hunger. He has produced numerous films, the most remarkable of which, *Tananarive aux mille visages* was awarded the Diploma of Honour at the 19th Festival of the Films for Tourism in Marseille in 1967.

Flavien Ranaivo received quite a number of decorations: He is Knight of the Legion of Honour, Officer of the National Order of Madagascar, Grand Officer of the Order of the Brilliant Star of the Chinese Republic (Taiwan), Commander of the Order of Merit of Germany, Officer of the Michan El Anouar, Officer of the Academy, Knight of Arts and Letters of the French Republic, Knight of the Black Star of Benin, Officer of the Order of Public Welfare, he has the Medal of Free France and the Medal for the Memory of the War 1939–1945.

Raolison, Régis Rajemisa
vid. *Rajemisa-Raolison, Régis*

Reindorf, Carl Christian   Ghana

Born on May 31, 1834, at Prampram, near Great Ningo, Eastern Region, Ghana, Carl Christian Reindorf is the grandson of John Frederic Reindorf, a Danish Governor in Christiansborg Castle in the middle of the 18th century, who had married a princess of Accra, Okailey of Gbese. At the age of eight, Carl started school together with the children of the European settlement at Osu, an area of Accra. After five years he left with his senior brother to attend the Basel Mission School in Akropong, Akwapim, where the Ga language was being taught for the first time. Studying Ga frustrated him, and he gave up his schooling altogether in favour of trading and commerce at Great Ningo. He amassed much wealth through trading, but his father sent him back to school again, although he was eighteen years of age. He continued his education further in the Basel Mission School as a catechist and rose to become Vice-Principal of the Akropong Theological Seminary. He was ordained on October 13, and stationed at Mayera, 17 miles north of Accra.

Reindorf took part in the wars of 1866 between the Adas and the Awunas, in which he captained the Asafos from Osu as allies of the Adas. Apart from his duties as a chaplain, he served as doctor through his knowledge of African herbs successfully treating many soldiers stricken by malaria and dysentery.

Carl Christian Reindorf died on July 1, 1917.

He published the first history of the Gold Coast, *The History of the Gold Coast and Asante*, Basel 1895, 2nd ed. 1951.

Portrait on Plate II.

Ribas, Oscar Bento   Angola

Born on August 17, 1909, in Luanda, Angola, Oscar Bento Ribas is the son of Arnaldo Gonçalves Ribas, a native of Guarda in Portugal, and Maria da Conceição Bento Faria, a native of Luanda, Angola.

He went to school in the Liceu de Salvador Correia in the city of Luanda. At the age of twenty-one, when he was already a civil servant, he became blind. Before he learned typing he used paper laid in small pleats for orientation in his writing. In his normal work, however, he used to dictate. "I use scribes, normally boys between 15 and 19 years old, of rudimentary education. For more difficult work I had the untiring services of my two brothers Mário and Joaquim. When Joaquim died in 1966, I had to recur to the help of my two nieces", he writes.

Except for a year of holiday in Portugal, Oscar Bento Ribas spent all his life in Angola, mostly in Luanda, but due to his father being frequently transferred during 33 years of government service in Angola as Director of plantations, he obtained a good knowledge of many parts of the country.

Oscar Bento Ribas wrote his first novel, *Nuvens que Passam,* when he was 16 years old — it was published in 1927. His second novel, *O Resgate duma Falta,* written when he was eighteen, came out in 1929. Then, because of his blindness, he stopped writing for nineteen years. In 1948 appeared his short stories, *Flores e Espinhos* (2061). In 1951 his novel *Uanga* (2062) was published, and in 1952 another volume of short stories, *Ecos de minha terra* (2063), of which the story *A Praga* received the Margaret Wrong Prize in 1952.

Oscar Bento Ribas wrote much non-fiction. *Ilundo,* 1952, a monography on African religion in Angola, *Missosso,* three volumes of Angolan folklore published in 1961, 1962, and 1964, *Izomba,* 1965, an essay on associations, and *Alimentação Regional Angolano,* 1971, a study of Angolan alimentation.

Oscar Bento Ribas is a member of many intercultural societies in Brazil, Argentina, Angola, and Portugal, where in recent years he attended many literary and cultural conferences.

Portrait on Plate XIII.

Ribeiro, Emmanuel F.   Rhodesia

Born in 1935 in Enkeldoorn, province Midland, Rhodesia, Emmanuel F. Ribeiro grew up in Gatooma. He did his secondary education at Kutama, Gokomere and Chishawasha. In 1967 he was elected Chairman of the Shona and Ndebele Writers' Association.

His first novel, *Muchadura* (2064), written in Shona, won first prize in the 1964 Literary Competition of the Rhodesia Literature Bureau. His second novel, *Tonderai* (2065), also in Shona, won a prize in the 1966 Literary Competition.

Rifoé, Simon   Cameroon

Born on April 4, 1943, at Eseka, district Nyong et Kélé, Cameroon, Simon Rifoé is the son of a catechist of the Presbyterian Church, who had come from Bafia, district Mbam. After having been educated in Cameroon, he received a special education at the Académie internationale de culture physique in Paris, France. In Cameroon he worked as a teacher of physical education. In 1964 he toured his country on a racing bicycle, an experience which he described in his report, *Le tour du Cameroun en 59 jours* (970).

Rive, Richard   South Africa

Born in 1931 in Cape Town, South Africa, Richard Rive was trained as a teacher at Hewat Training College and at the University of Cape Town. In 1962 the Farfield Foundation, New York, awarded him a grant to study literary life in European and African countries. He was a teacher for Latin and English at the South Peninsula High School in Diep River near Cape Town and is at present doing a post-graduate degree at Oxford University, England.

Richard Rive started short story writing when still at school. After his stories had appeared in more than a score of countries, translated into many languages, and had won several literary awards, they were published in the collection *African Songs* (2066) in 1963. His novel, *Emergency* (2067), partly autobiographical, deals with the more subtle and more ludicrous aspects of the racial situation in South Africa. He has also compiled and anthology, *Modern African Prose* (A 89), and has contributed to the anthology "Quartet, new Voices from South Africa" (AA 195). His play, *Make Like Slaves,* a study of the relationship between a coloured poet and a white girl, won the BBC African Theatre Competition Prize in May 1972.

"Mr. Rive is at his best in telling a story; he has a good eye for a face, a place or an action, and it is this which makes the novel readable" (W. Stevenson).

Portrait on Plate IV.

Robert, Shaaban   Tanzania

Born on January 1, 1909, in Vitambani, region Tanga, Tanzania, Shaaban Robert was educated at schools in Masimbazi and Dar es Salaam from 1922 to 1926. From 1926 to 1944 he was secretary of the Customs Office at Pangani, from 1944 to 1946 secretary of the veterinary station of Longido, from 1946 to 1952 functionary of the local administration in Tanga and later member of the Town Council of Tanga. In 1948 he was a member of the Inter-Territorial Language Committee for East Africa. Besides his professional functions he was a reader for the East African Swahili Committee of which he became a member in 1952 and its chairman in 1961. He was awarded many literary prizes, among them the Margaret Wrong Prize in 1962. Shortly before his death in Tanga on June 20, 1962, he became a Member of the Order of the British Empire.

Shaaban Robert wrote many volumes of poetry and stories in Swahili, and his complete works are published in thirteen volumes so far under the title *Diwani ya Shaaban* (1431–1440). They include his autobiography *Maisha yangu* (1441), his stories in the style of traditional tales, *Kusadikika nchi iliyo angani*

(1442) and *Adili na nduguze* (1443), and all his poetry which contributed to forming Swahili into a modern language. '

"Shaaban Robert is the most important representative of modern Swahili literature" (Mechthild Jungwirth).

"*Maisha yangu* is a clear example of the product of paternalism (colonial). One gets the impression that the story could apply to a 'very naive school boy' in Robert's attitude and relationship with Europeans (who are in the background) in the book. He speaks like some old man giving advice to his children. Thoughts or ideas tend to be disconnected" (John Samuel Mbiti).

Rotimi, Ola   Nigeria

Born on April 13, 1938, in Sapele, Mid Western State, Nigeria, of a Yoruba father and an Ijaw mother, Emmanuel Gladstone Olawale Rotimi — this is his full name — had his primary school education in St. Cyperians's School in Port Harcourt, a then predominantly Ibo city. He received his School Certificate at Methodist Boys' High School in Lagos. From 1959 to 1963 he attended Boston University, USA, where he got his Bachelor's Degree. From 1963 to 1966 he was a Rockefeller Foundation Scholar at Yale University, New Haven, Connecticut, USA. There he was selected for a course in Advanced Playwriting for television, sponsored by the American Broadcasting Company. In 1966 he returned to Nigeria to be a Research Fellow in the Institute of African Studies of the University of Ife.

By virtue of his tribally heterogeneous background he speaks three of Nigeria's major languages, Yoruba, Ibo and Ijaw, an asset to a wider understanding of Nigeria's customs which come into play in character delineation and dialogue. For, apart from being a writer, Ola Rotimi is a Producer for the Ori Olokun Players in Ife. He was the first to produce the English version of Aimé Césaire's *Tragedy of King Christophe* in December 1970. Ola Rotimi often has leading roles in his own plays.

His first plays were staged in America, *To Stir the God of Iron* in 1963 at Boston University, and *Our Husband Has Gone Mad Again* in 1965 at Yale. *Cast the First Stone*, a tragi-comedy, was produced at Ife University in 1968, where all later plays were first to be staged: *The Gods Are Not to Blame* (975) in 1968, *Kurunmi* (973) and *The Prodigal* at the Second Ife Festival of the Arts in 1969.

On *Kurunmi* Ola Oke wrote: "The great asset of this play is its language. Soyinka has shown how powerful the English language could be when based on the kind of structure that is characteristic of Yoruba proverbs. In this sense, Rotimi has followed in the line of Soyinka and come out with an idiom far more effective than anything there is of that type."

For *The Gods are not to Blame* Ola Rotimi was awarded the first Prize by the African Arts Magazine, U.S.A. in December 1969, and for *Our Husband Has Gone Mad Again* the first Prize by the Oxford University Press in January 1970.

Ola Rotimi has contributed short stories and essays on African drama in journals and reviews like "The Bronze", "Interlink", "Nigeria Magazine", and "Sunday Times".

Rowe, Ekundayo   Sierra Leone

Born on July 26, 1937, in Freetown, Sierra Leone, Sylvester Ekundayo Rowe received his primary and secondary education in Sierra Leone. He then went to England and attended the Sound Broadcasting School of the British Broadcasting Corporation (BBC) in London. In Berlin, East Germany, he studied at the Institute of Mass Communication.

He has broadcast widely in West Africa and over BBC in London. In addition to doing both creative and non-creative writing for the radio, he has published articles in newspapers and magazines at home and abroad. At present he is with the United Nations as a writer-producer in the Radio and Visual Services Division, New York, USA.

He has published a volume of short stories, *No Seed for the Soil, and Other Stories* (976).

Rubadiri, David   Malawi

Born on July 19, 1930, at Liule on the Tanzania shore of Lake Nyasa, where his father, a Malawian, was training as a teacher, David Rubadiri spent his childhood there. From 1941 to 1950 he went to King's College in Budo, Uganda. From 1950 to 1951 he was trained at the Domasi Teacher Training School near Zomba in Malawi. Then he studied History and English at Makerere University College, Kampala, Uganda, where he was elected President of the Students Union. In this position he had the opportunity to travel widely. After his degree in 1956 he continued his studies in England, at the University of Bristol.

He returned to Malawi in 1957 to teach English and History at Dedza Secondary School. Having organized a students meeting to be addressed by Dr. Banda, he clashed with the authorities and was transferred to Blantyre as an Education Officer. Because of his political activities he and his wife were arrested on March 6, 1959, and detained in Khami prison. Upon his release he was awarded a scholarship to King's College, Cambridge, England. After his return to Malawi he was appointed Principal of the Soche Hill College in Limbe. He then worked in the Ministry of Education, and in 1964 he was appointed the first Ambassador of Malawi to the United States and the United Nations. For several years he has been teaching at the Extra-Mural Department of Makerere University, Kampala, Uganda, where, since 1971, he has been President of the Commonwealth Literature Association.

David Rubadiri's poetry was widely published in journals like "Transition", "Black Orpheus", "Présence Africaine", "Negro Digest", and in anthologies like "Darkness and Light" (A 90), "Modern Poetry From Africa" (A 75), "Origin East Africa" (AE 158), "Commonwealth Poems of Today" (A 95),

"Poetry From Africa" (A 97), and others. His only novel to date *No Bride Price* (2073), is about the love and life of a young civil servant. "... his characters ... are all very real as are their human situations. *No Bride Price* makes engrossing reading" (Okot p'Bitek).

"Rubadiri has given us a short, compact novel which, nevertheless, manages in a most complex way to touch all the major nerves of a typical contemporary African urban-rural complex ... Written in a language of emotion and intellect, from intimate knowledge of experience" (Pio Zirimu).

Rubusana, Walter B.   South Africa

Born on February 21, 1858, at Mnandi near Somerset East, Cape Province, South Africa, into the Cira clan, Walter B. Rubusana began school at Peelton in 1874. Then he attended Lovedale from 1876 to 1882. He obtained his Teacher's Certificate and worked at Peelton Mission Station assisting the Reverend R. Birt until 1884, when he was ordained a Minister of the Congregational Church of the London Missionary Society.

The greater part of Rubusana's activity was devoted to writing religious articles. In 1905 he also took part in the revision of the Xhosa Bible. But his more important work is his contribution to the preservation of the Xhosa folklore. He collected a vast number of Xhosa proverbs and praise poems, that were printed, together with a glossary and some of Gqoba's unpublished material, in 1906 under the title *Zemk' Inkom Magwalandini* (Away go the cattle, coward), Lovedale 1906. He also wrote a *History of South Africa, from the Native Standpoint,* for which it is said he was awarded an honorary Ph. D. by a Negro college, McKinley University, when he visited the United States. For several years he was also a contributor to "Izwi Labantu" (The Voice of the People), a newspaper founded in 1897 by Nathaniel Cyril Mhala.

In 1909 Rubusana took part in the National Convention that met in Bloemfontein to discuss the forthcoming union of the various South African territories and its consequences for the Africans. In 1910 he was elected as an African candidate to the Provincial Council in Cape Province, representing Thembuland. In 1912 Rubusana presided over the first meeting of the South African Native National Congress, that was newly founded in Bloemfontein, but at the Cape Province elections in 1914, his rival Don Tengo Jabavu managed to split the vote, and Rubusana lost his seat on the Provincial Council.

In 1914 Walter B. Rubusana accompanied the Reverend John L. Dube, Solomon Plaatje and others in a deputation to London to protest against the Land Act of 1913, which aimed at establishing segregation in land ownership and occupation. Though the protest was ignored, Rubusana offered the British foreign minister to recruit black soldiers to assist the South African forces in their fight against the Germans in South-West Africa. The offer was declined on the ground that the British government was "anxious to avoid the employment of its Native citizens in a warfare against Whites".

Walter B. Rubusana died in August 1916.

Ruhumbika, Gabriel   Tanzania

Born in Tanzania in 1938, Gabriel Ruhumbika was educated there and took his B. A. Degree at Makerere University College, Kampala, Uganda. In 1964 he went to France to study at the Sorbonne and to prepare a thesis on African theatre.

His novel, *Village in Uhuru* (1455), shows in its interplay of characters and circumstance, the social and political changes caused by independence in a remote island village.

Sadji, Abdoulaye   Senegal

Born in 1910 in Rufisque, region Cap-Vert, Senegal, as son of a marabou, Abdoulaye Sadji went to the Koran School till his eleventh year. He went to Primary School then, followed up by a secondary education at the Lycée Faidherbe in Saint-Louis-du-Sénégal and the Ecole Normale William Ponty, where he got his teacher's diploma in 1929. He was a teacher for several years, first in the bush, later in Rufisque and Dakar.

Abdoulaye Sadji started writing around 1940. In 1946 his first articles appeared in "Présence africaine". In 1947 he was a member of the editorial committee of this journal. He also collaborated with "Condition humaine", Dakar, and "Bingo", also Dakar. From 1954 Abdoulaye Sadji worked for the broadcasting company of A.O.F. (Afrique Occidentale Française). In 1959 he became School Inspector and held this position till 1961, when he died of alcoholism.

Sadji follows two different literary lines. In his stories he evokes the traditional Africa, in his novels he describes modern African life. The story *Tounka* (980) depicts the migration of a "peuple sans nom" from the northeast of Senegal to the sea. The symbolism indicates already the theme "Rapture between Man and Nature", which is taken up in later novels, especially in *Maimouna, petite fille noire* (981), a love story in which Maimouna, deprived of her beauty by smallpox, and left by her lover, returns to the natural life of her village. In *Nini, mulâtresse du Sénégal* (982) Sadji examines the life of a young mulatress in Saint-Louis. *Modou-Fatim* (984), a short novel, appeared a year before his death.

"He (Sadji) is a moralizer with strong feelings about virtue and evil. He has certain fixed attitudes but, because of the conflict ... between his acceptance of the colonial system, his revolt against it and his Muslim faith, these values have no firm foundations except blind, dogmatic affirmation" (A. C. Brench).

Salifou, André   Niger

Born in 1942 in Niger, André Salifou studied History and was at the Ecole Nationale d'Art Dramatique in Abidjan, Ivory

Coast. He founded several theatre groups of amateurs. His play *Tanimoune*, performed in Algiers in 1969, is a historical drama, Cheikh Omar of Bornu puts Tanimoune on a throne to stop the wars between his vassals. But Tanimoune wants to unite the vassals to found the state Danagaram, shortly before the arrival of the Europeans.

Samkange, Stanlake   Rhodesia

Born in 1922 at Mariga, Chipata, in the Zwimba Tribal Area, Rhodesia, Stanlake Samkange grew up in Bulawayo, where his father was a Methodist minister. After attending the Waddilove Institution and Adams College, he went to Fort Hare University, South Africa, graduating in History. On his return to Rhodesia he took up teaching and became active in politics. He was general Secretary of the African National Congress for many years.

Samkange furthered his studies by reading Education at Indiana University, Bloomington, Indiana, USA. Back in Rhodesia again, he directed a thriving firm of Public Relations Consultants and published a weekly paper for African businessmen. In 1966 he returned to Indiana University to prepare his Ph. D. in History.

Samkange published a novel, *On Trial for My Country* (2076), the story of the British occupation of Rhodesia and the clash between Cecil Rhodes and Lobengula, the Matabele king.

"The author has managed to paint a magnificent picture of a brave nation while giving us a full historical account of the birth of modern Rhodesia" (Benedicta Nwozomudo).

"Stanlake Samkange ... has here written what is both a very readable piece of imaginative writing and an accurate popular historical account of the British occupation of Lobengula's kingdom" (J. D.).

Sancho, Ignatius

Born in 1729 on board a slave ship between Africa and the West Indies, Sancho received baptism at Cartagena, in what is today Columbia, from the hand of the bishop, and the name of Ignatius. A disease of the new climate put an early end to his mother's existence, and his father defeated the miseries of slavery by an act of suicide.

When he was two years old, his master brought him to England, and gave him to three maiden sisters, resident at Greenwich. They named him Sancho, from a fancied resemblance to the "squire of Don Quixote".

Ignatius Sancho was discovered by the Duke of Montagu who "admired in him a native frankness of manner as yet unbroken by servitude, and unrefined by education — he brought him frequently home to the Duchess, indulged his turn for reading with presents of books, and strongly recommended to his mistresses the duty of cultivating a genius of such apparent fertility. His mistresses, however, were inflexible" (Joseph Jekyll).

Ignatius Sancho fled to the Duchess of Montagu, who "at length consented to admit him into her household, where he remained as butler till her death, when he found himself, by her Grace's bequest and his own economy, possessed of seventy pounds in money, and an annuity of thirty".

After his money was spent, he again was looking for employment, and found it in the same household, as butler for the young Duke, until in 1773 repeated attacks of a gout and a constitutional corpulence rendered him incapable of further attendance in the Duke's family. With his wife, a young woman of West Indian origin, he opened a grocery shop and settled down, where mutual and rigid industry decently maintained a numerous family of children.

Thus, after having served the Duke's family for over twenty years, he exchanged letters with many people, including Sterne and the Duchess of Kent, from the backroom of his greengrocery. Unfortunately only a few correspondents are named in his *Letters* (993) which were published posthumously, in 1782, "a work not equalled perhaps in charm and literary merit by any other butler, white or black, before Sancho's days and since" (Vernon Loggins).

Ignatius Sancho died in December 1780.

Portrait on Plate I.

Santo, Alda do Espírito
vid. *Espírito Santo, Alda do*

Santos, Arnaldo   Angola

Born in 1936 in Luanda, Angola, Arnaldo Santos has been a public servant in Angola. He sometimes uses the pen-name Ingo Santos.

Arnaldo Santos wrote poetry and short stories, published in journals like "Cultura", "Jornal de Angola", in anthologies like "Contistas Angolanos" (AA 171), "Novos contos d'Africa" (AA 188), and in a volume, *Dumbe e a bangala* (1510) which he edited with Benúdia and António Cardoso. He has published a volume of poetry, *Fuga* (2078), and a volume of short stories, *Quinaxixe* (2079).

"He is a story teller who perceives the dimension of a story in face of a material ready for testimony ... *Quinaxixe* (is) a document of high value, a book of high interest, a revealing testimony" (Amândio César).

Santos, Marcelino dos   Mozambique

Born on May 20, 1929, in Lumbo near Lourenço Marques, Mozambique, Marcelino dos Santos, son of a railway worker, went to a Lycée in Mozambique and to the University in Lisbon,

Portugal. His articles and his participation at students' demonstrations brought him into conflict with Salazar's political police. In 1951 he studied Sociology at the Sorbonne, Paris.

In 1955 he participated at the Youth Festival in Warsaw, Poland, was invited to China, went to the Youth Festival in Moscow, 1957, and to the Conference of Asian and African Writers in Tashkent in 1958.

In 1959 he was expelled from France. In 1961 he was elected General Secretary of Frelimo. In 1962 he participated at another Asio-African Writers' Conference in Cairo, and in 1964 at the Festival Weeks in West Berlin. He lives in Tanzania, working in the Frelimo Office. Dos Santos also uses the pseudonym Kalungano.

A selection of his poetry was translated into Russian and published in Moscow, *Liliju Mikaja* (2080).

Seboni, Michael Ontefetse Martinus   Botswana

Born on July 12, 1912, in Botswana, Michael Ontefetse Martinus Seboni attended school in St. Matthews, Cape Province. There he passed the Junior Certificate examination. He proceeded to Fort Hare College, where he matriculated. Furthering his studies, he received his B. A. degree from the South African Native College in 1939, and the University Education Diploma in 1942. In 1947 the University of South Africa, Pretoria, Transvaal, awarded him the degree of Master of Education for his thesis, *The Development of Education in the Bechuanaland Protectorate 1824 to 1944.* In 1958 he completed his doctoral studies with a dissertation on the history of the University College of Fort Hare.

Seboni accepted his first teaching assignment in 1940 at the Basutoland High School in Maseru, Lesotho. The following year he assumed duty at St. Matthews High School, Cape Province, and also taught at the St. Matthews Training School. During 1943 he became Principal of the Nigel United Christian Schools, which later developed into the Charterston High School in Nigel. In May 1951 he was appointed Senior Lecturer and Head of the Department of Bantu Languages at the South African Native College at Fort Hare, now Fort Hare University. In 1954 he was transferred to the post of Senior Lecturer in Education at this institution. In 1961 Seboni was promoted to the Chair in Empirical Education. Michael Ontefetse Martinus Seboni died on May 24, 1972.

Seboni published a novel, *Rammône wa Kgalagadi* (2082), a long story, *Kgôsi Isang Pilane* (2083), and a volume of poetry, *Maboko maloba le maabane* (2084), all in his mother tongue Tswana. He also translated Shakespeare's "Henry IV" and "The Merchant of Venice" into Tswana.

Segoete, Everitt Lechesa   Lesotho

Born in 1858 at Morifi, Lesotho, Everitt Lechesa Segoete was named "Lechesa", which means "fire", because the Boers had recently burnt down a few villages. After some time, his father Menoah Segoete moved to Maphutseng, where the boy attended the mission school run by the Reverend D. F. Ellenberger, when he was not herding cattle. When Ellenberger went to teach at Masitise, Segoete followed him, and then went on to Mountain School in Morija, where he obtained his Teacher's Certificate. But instead of teaching he left for the Cape Colony, an adventurous trip that provided him with the material for his novel *Monono ke moholi ke mouoane* (2085). On his return home he worked at the Printing Press in Morija, then left again to work for a newspaper in Aliwal North, Cape Province. There he met his future wife. He returned to Lesotho and became headmaster of the school at Qomoqomong, where his most famous pupil was Thomas Mofolo, who greatly admired his teacher and modelled Moruti Katse in his novel *Pitseng* after him. As Segoete's work was well appreciated he was chosen for the theological seminary in Morija, from where he graduated in 1896. He was ordained in 1899 and sent as minister to Hermone (Mafeteng), then to Koeneng (Leribe), then back to Hermone.

Monono ke moholi ke mouoane is a story of a tribal boy who goes to town. "Considering that the novel as a genre was entirely foreign to the literary tradition of Africa, its structure is certainly remarkable" (Albert S. Gérard). Three years later Segoete published *Raphepheng*, Morija 1913, "a strange hotchpotch of a book, which illustrated the duality that had been observable among Xhosa authors since the middle of the nineteenth century. It is a random collection of traditional lore placed in the mouth of the title character. In the first section, Raphepheng describes and glorifies the customs of the Sotho people of the past and deplores the neglect into which they have fallen among the younger generations" (Albert S. Gérard). Besides these works Segoete has published *Mefiboshethe kapa pheello ea molimo ho moetsalibe*, a collection of religious meditations that had been printed serially in "Leselinyana". *Moea oa bolisa* (The spirit of shepherding), 1913, and *Mohlala oa Jesu Kreste* (The example of Jesus Christ), posthumously published in 1924, are also religious works. Al lhis works are in Sotho.

Everitt Lechesa Segoete died on February 7, 1923, in Hermone.

Segun, Mabel   Nigeria

Born in 1930 in Ondo, Western State, Nigeria, Mabel Segun was educated at the Girls' High School in Lagos from 1942 to 1947, and at University College in Ibadan from 1949 to 1953. She was editor of the "Hansard" in Ibadan, the report of happenings of the Western Nigerian Parliament, and she is now in charge of the overseas publicity in the Information Services of Western Nigeria. A freelance broadcaster and journalist, she has had poems published in "Black Orpheus" and in the anthology "Schwarzer Orpheus" (A 48). She is also the author of narratives for children, *My Father's Daughter* (1001).

Mabel Segun, née Mabel Imoukuede, whose former married name was Mabel Jolaoso has published her works under all these three names.

Seid, Joseph Brahim   Chad

Born in 1927 in Fort-Lamy, Chad, Joseph Brahim Seid had his secondary education at the Collège de la Sainte-Famille in Cairo, Egypt. Then he went to France to study Law at the University of Lyon where he became Licencié. In Paris he took a Doctor's degree in Roman Law and History of Law. After a special training at the Ecole Nationale de la France d'Outre-Mer he was Ambassador of Chad in Paris from 1961 to 1966. Since April 1966 he has been Minister of Justice in Fort-Lamy, Chad.

Un enfant du Tchad (1206) is a partly autobiographical novel, relating the spiritual evolution of a child from Islam to Catholicism. In his collection of stories, *Au Tchad sous les étoiles* (1205), Seid retold oral tales of his country.

Sekese, Azariele M.   Lesotho

Born in 1849 at Tsereoane, district Berea, Lesotho, Azariele M. Sekese was one of the first students to enroll at the Sekolo sa Thabeng (The Besutoland Training College), founded by the Reverend A. Mabille at Morija in 1866. After graduating in 1869, he became a teacher and a catechist at Tlepaneng in 1872. In 1881 he was appointed secretary to Chief Jonathan (Morena Jonathane), a grandson of Moshesh, but soon resigned to teach at Hlotse, Leribe, where he engaged in research on the history of the Sotho people. Dissatisfied with poor wages he gave up teaching and worked in a trade store from 1884 to 1891. Chief Jonathan employed him again as his personal secretary. He served Chief Jonathan for three years, and afterwards acted as intermediary between the chief and the British Assistant Commissioner, Sir Charles Bell, until old age forced him to retire.

Azariele M. Sekese died in 1930.

In the 1880's and early 1890's, Sekese contributed numerous articles about Sotho folklore to "Leselinyana", a monthly paper in Sotho. These were gathered into *Mekhoa ea Basotho le maele le litsomo* (Customs and proverbs of the Basuto), Morija 1893, which was the first collection of its kind ever to have been published in book form by an African. It went through at least four editions under slightly different titles, as Sekese kept enriching it with stories, fables, and praise poems.

His contribution to creative writing is *Bukana ea tsomo tsa pitso ea linonyana le tseko ea Sefofu le Seritsa* (2089), a satirical animal story in Sotho, which he composed, during the 1880's, possibly in collaboration with Job Moteane, one of the first three students who graduated from Morija and one of the first two Sotho ministers. In this book Sekese drew from his experience at Chief Jonathan's court of justice. Although the work was highly popular and was often performed in play form in various schools, it does not seem to have been printed until 1928.

"Sekese's story tells how the birds have called a meeting to protest against the hawk's greed, cruelty, and injustice ... (It) is a satire of a judical system that was basically tribal and feudal. ... The fact that Sekese's partridge solely adresses the conscience of the guilty, and threatens them only with God's justice, without calling for popular rebellion or even for institutional reform, can be considered an illustration both of Protestant inwardness and native reluctance to question traditional institutions as such" (Albert S. Gérard).

Selormey, Francis   Ghana

Born on April 15, 1927, in Keta, Volta region, Ghana, Francis Selormey had his first education in his home town, 1933 at

Keta, from 1934 to 1939 at Ho Primary and Senior School, from 1940 to 1942 at Keta Senior School. From 1943 to 1946 he studied at Saint Augustine's Training College in Cape Coast. In 1947 he taught at a secondary school at Denu, and from 1949 to 1950 at Dzodze. In 1950 he studied Physical Training at Achimota College near Accra. He then taught, from 1951 to 1952, in Aflao, 1953 in Denu, 1954 at St. Francis Training College in Hohoe, then at the Technical College at Kumasi. From 1955 to 1960 he again taught at St. Francis Training College at Hohoe.

From 1960 to 1964 he was Senior Sports Organizer for the Central Region of Ghana, of the erstwhile Central Organization of Sports (COS). In 1965 he resigned and joined the Ghana Film Industry Corporation as a script writer. In 1968 he was appointed by the Government of Ghana as Director of Sports for the Sports Council of Ghana which replaced the COS.

Francis Selormey's novel, *The Narrow Path* (1003), is an autobiographical work of childhood memories. "Aside from a nice chapter on murder by witchcraft, and a couple of references to the family's ancestral guardians, Selormey's childhood is not particularly 'African' in the traditional sense" (Margaret Henry).

"It is rather disappointing that Mr. Selormey does not develop (the) theme of ambiguity in Kofi's father resulting from a sense of psychological failure which could be really tragic, in a man whose life appears to have been dedicated to Christian ideals and education" (Sunday O. Anozie).

"In style and language there is a notable difference between chapters, and one is left with the impression that it is the product of two different authors" (Timothy Bankole).

Sembene Ousmane
vid. *Ousmane, Sembene*

Sengat-Kuo, François   Cameroon

François Sengat-Kuo was born on August 4, 1931, in Duala, Cameroon. He also spells his name Sengat-Kuoh and uses the pen-name Francesco N'Dintsouna, often misspelt N'Ditsouna. He was educated in Cameroon and France, where he was elected President of the National Union of the Cameroonian Students in 1956. In Paris he was one of the animators of "Présence Africaine".

When Cameroon became independent, François Sengat-Kuo was appointed one of the highest diplomats of his country, heading an OCAM (Organisation Commune Africaine et Malgache) delegation to New York and representing the OAU (Organization of African Unity) at the UNO. In 1962 he became Plenipotentiary Minister, in 1968 Deputy General Secretary at the Presidency of the Republic of Cameroon, a position he still holds.

François Sengat-Kuo published his first volume of poetry, *Fleurs de latérite* (698), under his pen-name Francesco N'Dintsouna, and his second volume, *Collier de cauris* (699), under his real name. *Fleurs de latérite,* together with *Heures rouges,* has been republished in Yaunde in 1971.

"The author of *Fleurs de latérite* incarnates the poet of today to whom art is nothing if it is not extended into action" (David Diop).

"Since 1954, Francesco N'Ditsouna has announced himself with *Fleurs de latérite* and *Heures rouges* as a great poet by the phantasy of his vision, the harshness of his images, the vigour and irony of his tone, and especially by the freshness of this interior rhythm of a soul totally engaged in the fight for the gestation of a new Africa" (Thomas Melone).

"With *Collier de cauris* the African political poetry prides itself henceforth on having born the missing voice between the novelists Mongo Béti and Ferdinand Oyono" (Thomas Melone).

Léopold Sédar Senghor was baptised on August 9, 1906. His name was, however, added to the official register on October 9, 1906, and this became his official birth date. His birth place is Joal-la-Portugaise, a village at the Atlantic coast, in the Sine-Saloum region, Senegal. His father, Basile Diogoye Senghor, was a prosperous Serer merchant; his mother was from a Fulani family. At the age of seven, Léopold Sédar Senghor was sent to the school of the Catholic mission in Joal, and one year later, in 1914, to the Fathers of the Holy Ghost at Ngasobil, ten miles north of Joal, also on the Atlantic coast. In 1922 he entered the Collège Libermann in Dakar, later changing to the Lycée Van Vollenhoven in the same city. In 1928 he went to France on a scholarship, to the Lycée Louis-le-Grand in Paris, where he was a fellow student of Georges Pompidou — with whom he has maintained his friendship — Thierry Maulnier, Paul Guth and Henri Queffelec. In 1930 he met Aimé Césaire, and they became friends.

In 1933 Senghor obtained the French citizenship and was the first African to win an "agrégation", qualifying him to teach in a lycée. On the staff of Lycée Descartes in Tours, from 1935 to 1938 he was appointed in 1938 to the Lycée Marcelin-Berthelot in Saint-Maure-des-Fossés, near Paris. Here, along with his teaching, he was able to study African languages at the Ecole des Hautes Etudes. During this period he developed the theory of Négritude, together with Aimé Césaire, with whom he founded in 1934 the journal "L'Etudiant Noir".

In 1939 Senghor was inducted into the army, as a second class soldier in the 23rd, then in the 3rd regiment of Colonial Infantry. On June 20, 1940, he was taken prisoner at Charité-sur-Loire by German troops and for two years was transferred from one prisoner of war camp to the next. Released from Frontstalag 230 because of illness in 1942, he returned to his chair at Lycée Marcelin-Berthelot and joined the anti-nazi resistance group "Front national universitaire".

The Liberation changed his life. He will continue to be a

poet and a writer, but from 1945 on he has been primarily a politician. In 1945 he joined the Bloc Africain and was elected with its leader, Lamine Gueye, as one of the two Deputies for Senegal in the French Constituent Assembly, and he began teaching African languages and cultures at the Ecole de la France d'Outre-mer. He became a member of the SFIO (the French Socialist Party), and when re-elected as a Deputy in 1946, he pressed for greater decentralisation and started his own journal "Condition Humaine". In October 1948 he formed his own party, the Bloc Démocratique Sénégalais (BDS). In 1947 he participated with Alioune Diop in setting up the journal "Présence Africaine" as a common front against cultural colonialism. In 1951, when Senghor's BDS won both seats held by Senegal in the French Chamber of Deputies, Senghor became leader of the IOM (Indépendants d'Outre-Mer), a party in opposition to the RDA (Rassemblement Démocratique Africain) of Félix Houphouet-Boigny. In 1956 Senghor founded the BPS (Bloc Progressiste Sénégalais), in 1957 he merged with the MSA (Mouvement Socialiste Africain) of Lamine Gueye to check the growing strength of the RDA, and in 1958 he joined with all non-RDA leaders to found the PRA (Parti du Regroupement Africain), of which his new UPS (Union Progressiste Sénégalaise) was the local branch. In the referendum of 1958 the UPS voted "oui" — in favour of limited autonomy within the French Community.

Senghor's attempts to form a federation of the French territories in West Africa were unsuccessful. Senegal and Sudan were the only countries to unite as the Mali Federation. Senghor was named President of Parliament in April 1959 and in June 1960 Mali became independent. In August of the same year, however, the Federation dissolved, and Senghor became President of the independent Republic of Senegal, a position he still holds. When on December 17, 1962, Prime Minister Mamadou Dia failed to overthrow Senghor in a coup d'état, Senghor joined the office of Prime Minister to his office as President.

Besides an enormous number of essays and speeches published in many journals and papers all over the world, the prose of

Léopold Sédar Senghor includes the volumes *Nation et Voie Africaine du Socialisme*, Paris 1961, *Liberté I: Négritude et Humanisme* (S 191), with his cultural essays and speeches, *Les Fondements de l'Africanité ou Négritude et Arabité*, Paris 1957, *Négritude et Germanisme*, Tübingen, 1958, *Liberté II: Nation et Voie Africaine du Socialisme*, Paris 1971, with his more political speeches in the years 1946 to 1960.

Senghor's anthology, *Anthologie de la nouvelle poésie nègre et malgache* (A 94), with the preface by Jean-Paul Sartre, was the first important manifestation of the Négritude movement, of which Léopold Sédar Senghor remained the most eminent spokesman and philosopher.

Senghor's poetry is collected in several volumes: *Chants d'Ombre* (1006), *Hosties Noires* (1007), *Chants pour Naëtt* (1008), *Ethiopiques* (1012), *Nocturnes* (1013), all these compiled in the volume *Poèmes* (1017). Three volumes have appeared in English translation: *Selected Poems* (1019), *Prose and Poetry* (1020), and *Nocturnes* (1013 b).

As a President of State and as a Poet and Philosopher, Léopold Sédar Senghor has received many honours, titles, and decorations. In 1968 he was awarded the Peace Prize of the Börsenverein des Deutschen Buchhandels at the Frankfurt Book Fair, an event which caused a student riot. In 1969 he was elected Member of the French Academy.

All over the world critical essays and evaluation have been written on Senghor's works. Here only published books are quoted which deal with Senghor exclusively. A biography with texts is Armand Guibert's *Léopold Sédar Senghor*, Paris 1961, and the small volume with the same title by Roger Mercier and M. and S. Battestini, Paris 1964. Jean Rous' *Léopold Sédar Senghor, un président de l'Afrique nouvelle*, Paris 1967, describes Senghor's political career. Hubert de Leusse, in *Léopold Sédar Senghor l'Africain*, Paris 1967, analyses his poetry, while S. Okechukwu Mezu, *Léopold Sédar Senghor et la défense et illustration de la civilisation noire*, Paris 1968, looks critically at Senghor's philosophy. In English language, S. Okechukwu Mezu introduced and commented Senghor's poetry in *The poetry of L. S. Senghor*, London 1972. Gisela Bonn's book, *Léopold Sédar Senghor, Wegbereiter der Culture Universelle*, Düsseldorf 1968, is an uncritical adoration, Irving Leonard Markovitz, *Léopold Sédar Senghor and the politics of Negritude*, New York 1969, places the man and the movement in the political and historical context.

Ernest Milcent and Monique Sordet, *Léopold Sédar Senghor et la naissance de l'Afrique moderne*, Paris 1969, describes mainly Senghor's political career, while Barend v. D. Van Nierkerk's book, *The African Image (Négritude) in the Work of Léopold Sédar Senghor*, Cape Town 1970, restricts itself to the analysis of Senghor's poetry.

The study by Irmgard Hanf, *Leopold Sedar Senghor, ein afrikanischer Dichter französischer Prägung*, Munich 1972, compares Senghor's poetry with verses of Charles Péguy, Paul Claudel and Saint-John Perse. The most detailed biography is Jacques Louis Hymans, *Léopold Sédar Senghor, an intellectual biography*, Edinburgh 1971, at the end of which there is a review of the major sources for the study of Senghor.

Portrait on Plate V.

Serumaga, Robert   Uganda

Born in 1939 in Uganda, Robert Serumaga went to Trinity College, Dublin, Ireland, from where he graduated in 1965 in Economics. In 1968 he returned to Kampala, Uganda, and became Director of "Theatre Limited". He has been Senior Fellow in Creative Writing at Makerere University for 18 months. He is secretary and treasurer of the Commonwealth Literature Association, which has its headquarters in Kampala, and has also set up "Kiyingi Productions Limited", which runs a private commercial recording studio, and records plays, songs, advertisements, etc.

Serumaga published two plays, *A Play* (1459) and *The Elephants*, Nairobi 1971 and the novel, *Return to the Shadows* (1460). A new play, *Majangwa*, was first presented by "Theatre Limited" at the end of May 1971 at the National Theatre in Kampala.

Sibanda, Amos M. P.   Rhodesia

Born in 1927 at Malole near Wanezi Mission, Filabusi district, province Matabeleland, Rhodesia, Amos M. P. Sibanda is the first child of a large family. After attending primary school at Malole, Amos Sibanda trained as a teacher at Dadaya Mission and later taught there for nine years. In 1963 he was assigned to Mambo Government School, Gwelo, where he trained and qualified as headmaster. In 1965 he was appointed to Chinotimba Government School, Victoria Falls.

Wangikholisa, Gwelo and Salisbury 1968, the author's first novel, was awarded top prize in the 1966 competition of the Rhodesia Literature Bureau. The novel, written in Ndebele, varies the Romeo and Juliet theme, telling of the feud between two neighbouring villages, which is ended by the love between a son and a daughter of the two families concerned.

Sigogo, Ndabezinhle S.   Rhodesia

Ndabezinhle S. Sigogo was born on June 2, 1932, in Filabusi, province Matabeleland, Rhodesia, the son of illiterate parents. His father died when he was six years old, but the boy was sent to school. He passed the Rhodesia Junior Certificate and General Certificate of Education "O" level with four subjects. He is now employed as Ndebele editor with Mambo Press in Bulawayo.

Sigogo published three novels in his mother tongue Ndebele, *USethi Ebukhweni Bakhe* (2101), *Gudlindlu Mntanami* (Rub around the hut, my son, and disappear), Gwelo 1967, and *Aku-lazulu Emhlabeni* (There is no heaven on earth), Gwelo 1970. Poems were published in the anthologies "Imbongi Zalamhla Layizolo" (AA 176) and "Kusile Mbongi Zohlanga" (AA 178).

Silva, José Lopes da
vid. *Lopes da Silva, José*

Silva, María Perpétua Candeias da   Angola

Born near Caconda, district Huíla, Angola, Maria Perpétua Candeias da Silva lived in Vila Mariano Machado, district Benguela, and later in Benguela. She has been teaching languages.

She has published the story *A mulher de duas cores* (2103), for which she received a local literature prize from the Town Council of Sá da Bandeira in 1960. The volume also contains another story, *Falsos trilhos*. The Town Council of Nova Lisboa had already in 1949 honoured her first short story, *Nihova*. Her short story, *O homem enfeitiçado* (2104), was also published locally, as was her only novel, *Navionga, filha de branco* (2105). Her short story, *Escrava*, is included in the anthology, "Novos Contos d'Africa" (AA 188).

"Maria Perpétua Candeias da Silva succeeded in presenting us with her short story *Escrava* an aqua fortis of indigenous rites, a narrative which comes from the closest knowledge and contact with the local population far from urban centres. A remarkable document . . ." (Amândio César).

Silveira, Onésimo da   Cape Verde Islands

Born on February 16, 1935, on the Cape Verde Island São Vicente, Onésimo da Silveira worked as a forced labourer on plantations on the island São Tomé from 1956 to 1959, then went to Angola. Political reasons drove him into exile. In 1966 he went to China, in 1967 to Sweden.

He was a collaborator of the journal "Claridade" (Cape Verde Islands). He published two volumes of poetry in Angola, *Toda a gente fala: Sim, Senhor* (1034), and *Hora grande* (1035), and an essay on Cape Verdean literature, *Consciencialização na literatura caboverdiana* (SW 332) in Lisbon.

"Onésimo Silveira denounces the traditional European acculturation of the islands, calling boldly for Africanization instead . . . Not surprisingly, Silveira lives now in Exile" (Gerald M. Moser).

Sinda, Martial   Congo

Born about 1930 in Mbamou near Kinkala, Pool District, near Brazzaville, Congo, Martial Sinda received his elementary and the beginning of his secondary education at the Pères-du-Saint-Esprit in Brazzaville, then went to France. In spite of financial difficulties he managed to continue his education in Chartre and Paris. In 1956 he married in Brazzaville, then returned to Paris.

His only volume of poetry, *Premier Chant du Départ* (1208), shows "a most vivid sense of rhythm, desolate and proud, sometimes dense with rebellion, sometimes liquid and fresh" (Cristina Brambilla).

Sinxo, Guybon B.   South Africa

Born on October 8, 1902, in Fort Beaufort, Cape Province, South Africa, as son of an interpreter at the magistrate's office, Guybon Budlwana Sinxo received his primary education in his home town and was later trained at St. Matthew's College, Keiskammahoek, where in 1920 he qualified as a teacher. He taught for some years in the Cape Province.

In 1924 Sinxo married Beula Nohle, Samuel Mqhayi's eldest daughter, who died in 1929. For some time he was employed by the Lovedale Press, but he soon left so seek work in Port Elizabeth. As most African writers, he was generally concerned with educational problems. In 1934 he joined the staff of the Johannesburg "Bantu World", where he edited the Xhosa pages until about 1938, when ill health forced him to resign. In 1935 he collaborated with W. G. Bennie in the preparation of the Stewart Xhosa Readers, a series of anthologies for schools which were printed in Lovedale.

Guybon Budlwana Sinxo died on June 14, 1962.

Sinxo wrote in Xhosa and tried his hand at all literary genres. His first novel was *UNomsa* (2106). This was followed by a collection of school plays, *Imfene kaDebeza* (2107), "which dealt with such varied topics as superstitions, countryside life and mentality, the disturbances brought about by men's entanglement in women's affairs, and the like" (Albert S. Gérard). His second novel, *Umfundisi wase-Mtugwasi* (2108), dedicated to his wife, tells the story of a teacher who has to give up his job because he is too poorly paid, but who later enters the ministry in compliance with his father's will, revealed to him in a dream. His third novel, *Umzali wolahleko* (2109), deals with the problem of the moral education of children in the family. His next work, a collection of short stories, *Isakhono somfazi namanye amabalana* (2110), appeared almost seventeen years later. It was followed by a collection of poetry in the form of the traditional praise poem, *Thoba sikutyele amabali emibongo angama — 76* (2111), and three volumes of short stories, *Imbadu (amabali amafutshane) (2112)*, *UNojayiti wam: iimbalana ezingamashumi amabini, incwadi 1.* (2113), and *Isitiya* (2114). He also adapted into Xhosa several popular English novels, such as Anthony Hope's *The Prisoner of Zenda* and H. Rider Haggard's *She*.

Sinxo "describes the prostitution and hooliganism that plague the African township of big cities . . . It is this realism that is Sinxo's chief merit and has earned him an important place in the historical development of Xhosa literature. . . . Sinxo innovated by using in prose fiction the language actually spoken by the people . . . In the light of his later works, it appears that this realism in style was only a prelude to an increasing realism in subject matter, as Sinxo came to concentrate on the demoralization and seaminess of African life in the native locations of such big South African cities as East London, Port Elizabeth, or Johannesburg" (Albert S. Gérard).

Sissoko, Fily Dabo   Mali

Born in 1900 in Bamako, Mali, Fily Dabo Sissoko was educated at the famous Ecole William Ponty in Senegal. He became a delegate to the French National Assembly where, from October 1945 to June 1951, he represented the colonial territories of Sudan-Niger, and from 1951 to 1958 the Sudan (later called Mali). In 1946 he founded the Parti Soudanais Progressiste (PSP) and in 1948 he was Junior Secretary of State for Industry and Commerce in the French Government of Robert Schumann.

When his party was losing ground because of the success of the Union Soudanaise (US), the party of Modibo Keita, Sissoko joined the US for the elections of March 1959, but refused to fuse his party with the US. After the 1962 riots against the introduction of the Mali Franc, Fily Dabo Sissoko was accused of sedition and sentenced to death. The death sentence was changed into rigorous labour on October 8, 1962. Sissoko died in summer 1964 in a Mali prison.

Fily Dabo Sissoko wrote four volumes of poetry, *Crayons et portraits* (1037), *Harmakhis* (1038), *La Savane rouge* (1040), and *Poèmes de l'Afrique noire* (1041), and a novel, *La passion de Djimé* (1039).

"The works of Fily Dabo Sissoko published at the end of his life are rather strange. The best of it, *La Savane rouge*, mixes in a strange way memories, historical documents, and poetical evocations. The basic form is a verse which in reality conceals a beautiful prose" (Robert Pageard).

Born on July 21, 1920, in the district Nyamandhlovu, province Victoria, Rhodesia, Ndabaningi Sithole herded cattle and goats until he was twelve. In 1932 his family moved to Shabani where his father worked in an asbestos mine. Ndabaningi found work as a caddy, kitchenboy, gardener and waiter. From 1933 to 1934 he attended an evening school, from 1935 to 1939 the Dadaya Mission School. From there he proceeded to Waddilove Institution, where he was trained as a teacher. In 1942 he started to teach at a village school, but continued his education by private studies and obtained his Junior Certificate and his B. A. in 1949.

In 1955 Sithole went to the United States to study Theology at the Andover Newton Theological Seminary. He obtained his Bachelor of Divinity three years later, and returned to Rhodesia. In April 1959 he was ordained.

Sithole then combined his ministry with politics. In 1959 he was in the process of setting up branches of the nationalist African National Congress when the government banned the party. The National Democratic Party (NDP) was founded in 1960 as a successor to the Congress and Sithole was elected Treasurer at the first annual meeting in October 1960. He took part as the party's delegate at the constitutional conferences on Southern Rhodesia held in London in December 1960 and in Salisbury in February 1961.

In December 1961 the government banned NDP, citing the violence used by some of its members. Soon afterwards a new nationalist party, the Zimbabwe African People's Union (ZAPU), was founded and Sithole was again a leading officeholder. In September 1962 ZAPU was proscribed, and Sithole, who was attending a conference in Athens at the time, stayed abroad and settled in Dar es Salaam, Tanzania.

In July 1962 a fight broke out over the leadership in ZAPU, and the rebels founded a new party, the Zimbabwe African National Union (ZANU), with Sithole as President. Both parties were banned in August 1964. From July 1964 the government has kept Sithole either in prison, where he was sent for a breach of the Law and Order (Maintenance) Act, in restriction, or in detention.

Already in detention Sithole was tried in February 1969 by the Rhodesian High Court and found guilty of incitement to murder three Rhodesian Ministers. After the verdict Sithole told the court: "I wish publicly to dissociate my name in word, thought, or deed from any subversive activities, any terrorist activities, and from any form of violence." Sithole is still serving time in a prison in Gonokudzinga.

Sitholes first book, *Amandebele kaMzilikazi* (2116) is a historical in Ndebele which depicts the Matabele rebellion against the English in 1898. His second work *African Nationalism* (2117) reflects his political experiences. The book had a second edition in 1968 with extensive changes and additions. Another book, *Obed Mutezo,* was published in Nairobi in 1970. Sithole also wrote many articles for Rhodesian and South African newspapers, such as "The Rhodesian Herald", "The Evening Standard", "The Daily News", "African Mail", "Parade", "The African Weekly", and "The Bantu Mirror".

Socé, Ousmane   Senegal

Ousmane Socé Diop was born on October 31, 1911, in Rufisque, region Cap-Vert, Senegal. As a politician, he used his full name but as a writer only his first names. He began his education at the Koran school. After elementary school he went to the Lycée of Dakar where he received his B. A. in Philosophy. Then he came to the famous Ecole Normale William Ponty at Gorée. He was among the first students sent to France for study. His intention was to study Medicine, but the French authorities distributed scholarships only for the study of Veterinary Medicine, and so he enrolled at the National Veterinary School at Alfort. In 1930 he continued his studies at the Institut de Médicine Vétérinaire Exotique in Paris where he received a diploma. At the same time he took courses at the Faculté des

Lettres and obtained his teaching certificate for French Philology in 1935.

In 1937 he began his work at the Cavalry School at Samur. Then he was transferred to Africa and for some time, directed the Cattle Inspection Service of Senegal.

In 1945 the French Government proclamed elections in all colonies and in 1946 Ousmane Socé Diop was elected Senator of the SFIO (the French Socialist Party). In the same year he was appointed Secretary of the Conseil de la République Française, a position he held until 1948. From 1952 to 1957 he edited the journal "Le Phare du Sénégal" in Rufisque. In 1953 he founded the journal "Bingo" in which his short stories and poems were published.

In 1956 Ousman Socé Diop became a member of the PSAS (Parti Sénégalais de l'Action Socialiste) of Lamine Gueye, and was elected Councillor on March 31, 1957. When the new party UPS (Union Progressiste Sénégalaise), led by Léopold Sédar Senghor, was formed, Ousmane Socé Diop was appointed editor of the party journal "Regroupement". From November 25, 1958, to 1959 he was Deputy of the UPS, from June 1958 to April 1959 Minister of Planning, and from April 1959 to January 1961 Representative of Senegal at the French Community. From February 1959 to July 1960 he was Assistant Secretary of the UPS Party. Then, for a short time he was Mayor of Rufisque. On November 25, 1960, he was appointed Ambassador of Senegal to the United States and the United Nations.

On March 31, 1968, he returned to Senegal because of his increasing blindness. He kept his seat in the Senegalese Assembly, but retired to his home town, Rufisque. Ousmane Socé is the President of the Senegalese section of the International PEN-Club.

As a student in Paris, 1930 to 1935, he participated in the beginnings of the Négritude movement. In 1935 he published his first novel, *Karim* (1043), for which he was awarded the Grand Prix Littéraire des Ecrivains de la Mer et de l'Outre-Mer in 1948. It deals with a group of young Senegalese in Saint-Louis who try to copy their ancestors overdoing each other in extravagance to impress their girls. His second novel, *Mirages de Paris* (1044) is a love story between an African and a French girl in Paris. Both novels reflect a world in which Paris is the brilliant centre and the Senegal only a far off province of France. His *Contes et légendes d'Afrique noire* (1045) retell traditional tales in today's French. His poems, *Rythmes du khalam* (1046), sing of the glory of a French Empire reaching from Waterloo to Dakar, from the Rhine to the Niger.

His speeches at the United Nations were published in the volume *L'Afrique à l'heure de l'indépendance, New York, 1960 to 1963*, Paris 1963.

In *Karim* "the light generous and chivalrous character of the Wolof is sympathetically represented" (Robert Pageard).

Soga, John Henderson   South Africa

Born in 1859 as Tiyo Soga's second son, John Henderson Soga was sent to Scotland at the age of three, and he received his education there, attending the Glasgow High School from 1870 to 1873, and the Dollar Academy from 1873 to 1877. He followed the arts course at Edinburgh University from 1886 to 1890 and received his theological training at the United Presbyterian Divinity Hall from 1890 to 1893. He was ordained in 1893 and returned to South Africa, together with his Scottish wife, Isabella Brown, to found the Mbonde Mission in the Mount Frere district, among the Bhaca.

John Henderson Soga composed hymns, many of which made their way into the Xhosa Presbyterian Hymnbook, *Amaculo ase-Rabe*. In 1910 he started work on a Xhosa translation of Aesop's fables, but the manuscript was never published.

In 1916 Soga was transferred to the Miller Mission, Elliotdale, to succeed his brother, Dr. W. A. Soga, a medical missionary, who had just died there. He went on with his translation work, rendering mostly religious work into Xhosa. But his most important translation work is *U-Hambo lom-Hambi II*, Part II of Bunyan's *Pilgrim's Progress,* which was published in London by the Society for the Promotion of Christian Knowledge in 1927, Part I having been translated by his father Tiyo Soga. Soga also wrote scholarly historical and anthropological works. *The South-Eastern Bantu (Abe-Nguni, Ama-Mbo, Ama-Lala)* was published in Johannesburg in 1930, and *Ama-Xhosa Life and Customs* was printed in Lovedale in 1931. In his preface to the former book, he wrote that his purpose "was to place in the hands of the rising generation of the Bantu something of the history of their peoples, in the hope that it might help them to a clearer perception of who and what they are and to encourage in them a desire for reading and for studying their language."

In 1936 John Henderson Soga retired from the ministry. He spent the remaining years of his life in England with his family. In March 1941 he was killed together with his wife and son during a German air raid on their home in Southampton.

Soga, Tiyo   South Africa

Tiyo Soga was born in 1829 in Gwali, Cape Province, South Africa, a place where, in 1824, the agents of the Church of Scotland had set up their first printing press and whose mission station they had renamed Lovedale in 1826. His father had eight wives and twenty-nine children, and was, according to R. H. W. Shepherd, "the first African to use a plough in his district and the first to make a water-furrow". He was killed by Fingo auxiliaries of the colonial army in 1878.

Tiyo's mother was a Christian and sent her son to school at Gwali under the Reverend William Chalmers, who sent him on to Lovedale for further education. While in Lovedale the War of the Axe broke out, Lovedale was closed, the missionaries were dispersed, and the first principal, the Reverend William Govan, returned to Scotland, taking Tiyo Soga with him in order for the youth to complete his education. From 1846 to 1848 Soga attended the Glasgow Free Church National Seminary. He then returned to South Africa with the Reverend George Brown to do catechismal work at the Umondale Mission in the vicinity of Keiskamahoek. In 1851 he returned to Scotland to prepare for the ministry. He took the arts course at the University of Glasgow, and received his clerical training in the Theological Hall of the United Presbyterian Church. In 1856 he became the first African minister to be ordained in Great Britain. In 1857 he married a Scotswoman, Janet Burnside, and they left together the same year for Africa, where they founded a mission station at Emgwali in the Stutterheim district, among the Ngqika Xhosa.

During that period Soga started writing hymns. He produced among others *Lizalis' indinga lakho* (Fulfil thy promise), *Khangelani nizibone izibele ezingaka* (Open your eyes and behold how great the blessings are), and *Sinesipho esikhulu esisiphiweyo thina* (We have a great gift which was given us). Many of his hymns were incorporated into the Xhosa hymnbooks produced by the Glasgow Missionary Society and other missionary presses.

In the late fifties Tiyo Soga began the translation of Bunyan's "Pilgrim's Progress". He finished the work in 1866, and the book came from the press in 1867 under the title *U-Hambo lomhambi*. The second part was to be translated by Tiyo's son, John Henderson Soga, in 1929.

From the first issue of "Indaba", a monthly magazine from Lovedale, Tiyo Soga was a regular contributor under the pseudonym of UNinjiba Waseluhlangeni (The Dove of the Nation), or simply N.W. Most of his articles were didactic and moralizing, but he also published recordings of oral art, fables, legends, proverbs, praise songs, and genealogies. He was an eager collector of folklore material, but a great deal of his recordings has never been published.

In 1866 Tiyo Soga left Emgwali to establish a new mission north of the Kei, at Tutura, near Butterworth, where he died on August 12, 1871, from acute congestion of the lungs, while still working on the translation of the "Acts of the Apostles" into Xhosa.

Solarin, Tai   Nigeria

Born around 1920 in Western Nigeria, Tai Solarin was in the Royal Air Force in England during World War II. With degrees from London and Manchester, he returned to Nigeria in 1957 to teach at the Molusi Grammar School in Ijebu-Igbo. When the Principal of this School, Awokoya, became Minister of Education in Western Nigeria, Tai Solarin was his successor. But soon he was in disagreement with the Council because of the subject Religion. Tai Solarin resigned and founded his own pioneer school, "Mayflower School", in Ikenne, the birthplace of Obafemi Awolowo. He is still its principal.

For many years he contributed a column to the "Daily Times", Lagos, giving his opinions on all kinds of public matters. A selection of his essays has appeared in the volume *Thinking With You,* Ibadan 1965.

". . . in one essay he is the scourge of corruption or the visionary reformer, in another, a schoolmaster ombudsman, a virulent iconoclast, an idealist, a socialist, a pragmatist, or a humanist. His likes and dislikes are bellowed from the rooftops" (Adrian A. Roscoe).

Sontonga, Mankayi Enoch   South Africa

Mankayi Enoch Sontonga was born in Lovedale, Cape Province, South Africa, in the early 1870's. He was a teacher, at the end of the nineteenth century, in an African township near Johannesburg. He is chiefly known as a composer of songs; he wrote both the music and the words. His songs were very popular, but the best known is *Nkosi sikelel' i-Africa* (God Bless Africa), which he composed in 1897, but which was not sung until 1899, when Sontonga had founded a church choir in the African Presbyterian Church. *Nkosi sikelel' i-Africa* was sung at the first meeting of the South African Native National Congress held on January 8, 1912, in Bloemfontein, immediately following the prayer. The Congress adopted it in 1925 as its national anthem. It is now the official anthem of the Transkei.

Mankayi Enoch Sontonga died in 1904 in Johannesburg.

Though not a member of the Gcaleka tribe, Sontonga wrote in Xhosa. "Sontonga's Tembu origin is a symptom of the way the recruitment area for Xhosa writers began to widen after the annexation of Xhosaland to the Cape Province" (Albert S. Gérard).

Soromenho, Castro   Mozambique

Fernando Monteiro de Castro Soromenho, who signed everything he wrote with his last two family names, was born on January 31, 1910, in Chinde, Zambezia, Mozambique. His father was a district officer for the Portuguese Congo (Cabinda), who later became governor of the Lunda Province, Angola, and his mother was the daughter of a judge in the Supreme Court in Lisbon.

His spent his childhood in Angola, where his parents took him as a baby in 1911. In his sixth year he was sent to Portugal for his education in elementary and secondary school. Returning to Angola in 1925, he remained there until 1937. He was first employed by "Daimang", the Diamond Company of Angola, which operates in the northeastern inland region of Lunda, as a recruiting agent of African labour. From there Castro Soromenho went back to school in Huila, to be trained as a colonial administrator in the Escola Superior Artur de Paiva. Upon completion of his studies he served for many years as a chefe de posto in various interior districts. In 1932 he gathered materials in the Dala district, Lunda, for his study of the circumcision and initiation rites for boys of the Chokwe tribe. Finally he gave up his administrative career and moved to Luanda. Here he became a journalist, joining the staff of the "Diário de Luanda".

Still a journalist, he moved to Lisbon in 1937 and began to edit the weekly "Humanidade", there. He wrote also for

Brazilian publications, such as "Dom Casmurro" in Rio de Janeiro. In 1943 he gave up journalism and turned to publishing. He started his own publishing house, first the Sociedade de Intercâmbio Luso-Brasileiro, then the Ediçoes Sul.

Following his move to Europe and his first stay in Brazil, he had published *Nhári* (2123), his first collection of African stories, and the first of several of his works to be awarded the Prize for Colonial Literature, with which the Portuguese government of the time sought to stimulate overseas writing in Portuguese.

In 1960 life in Lisbon grew unbearable for Soromenho, whose opposition to the ruling dictatorship was well known. When the government prevented further distribution of its titles, his publishing house was ruined and with it his livelihood. Warned of imminent arrest, he fled to France, choosing exile. For the rest of his life he wandered from country to country, from France to the United States, where he taught at the Portuguese Centre of the University of Wisconsin, Madison, and back to France. In Paris he worked as Portuguese and Spanish reader for the publishing house of Gallimard, contributed to the reviews "Présence Africaine" and "Révolution", and did research work for the African Section of the Musée de l'Homme under the direction of Michel Leiris.

In December 1965 Brazilian and Portuguese friends brought him to São Paulo, Brazil, where he could make a meager living by giving sociology courses at the State University in the city and its branch campus in Araraquara.

Castro Soromenho died of a brain hemorrhage in São Paulo on June 18, 1968.

Aside from several other ethnographical studies, he published works of prose fiction, all of which dealt with what he was most familiar with, the Lunda Province, relatively unspoilt by European colonists: two collections of stories, *Rajada e outras histórias* (2125), and *Calenga* (2127), and three novels, *Homens sem caminho* (2126), *Terra morta* (2128), and *Viragem* (2129). The manuscript of *Terra morta* was completed in 1945, but published only in 1949 and then in Brazil. It had been banned in Portugal, because it dealt with the process of "pacification" from inside knowledge. In *Viragem* he described the relations between the African villagers and their traditional chieftains on the one hand, and the Portuguese district officers, their assistants, womenfolk, and native constabulary on the other.

Castro Soromenho's manner of writing underwent a noteworthy change. In his early work the dialogues read like normal Portuguese speech. But in his later works the author shortened the dialogues to achieve a greater veracity, giving the Portuguese reader a more vivid impression of African speech. "The style is always compact, impetuos, virile; and the objectivity and bluntness of the prose make it extraordinarily accessible and expressive" (Franco Nogueira).

Castro Soromenho has undergone "an evolution from an attitude of sympathetic, benevolent paternalism to a humanistic socialism that has abandoned all unscientific feelings of superiority. ... (He) became a realist of the highest order, in the best, rarely recognized Portuguese tradition" (Gerald Moser).

Portrait on Plate XIII.

Sousa Martins, Ovídio de
vid. *Martins, Ovídio de Sousa*

Sousa, Noémia da   Mozambique

Born on September 20, 1927, in Lourenço Marques, Mozambique, Noémia Carolina Abranches de Sousa Soares received her elementary education in Lourenço Marques and her secondary education in Brazil. From 1951 to 1964 she lived in Lisbon, then fled to France into exile.

Noémia da Sousa also used Vera Micaia as a pen-name. She became known for her poetry published in journals and newspapers in Angola, Mozambique, Portugal, Brazil and France, and in "Présence Africaine" and "Europe", and in many anthologies like "Antologia da poesia negra de expressão portuguesa" (A 4), "La poésie africaine d'expression portugaise" (A 6), "Modern Poetry from Africa" and many others.

"Noemia da Sousa ... looks for her African roots and echoes the spirituals which she heard sung by Paul Robeson and Marian Anderson" (Gerald M. Moser).

Soyinka, Wole   Nigeria

Born on July 13, 1934, in Abeokuta, Western State, Nigeria, of Yoruba parents (an Ijebu father and an Egba mother), Akinwande Oluwole Soyinka received his secondary education in Ibadan. While still in school, he submitted short stories to the N.B.C. (Nigerian Broadcasting Corporation). From 1952 to 1954 he attended the University College of Ibadan, then proceeded to Leeds, England, where he obtained an Honours Degree in English. Upon graduation Soyinka had to find work and was employed as a bartender and supply teacher. In 1958 he was accepted as resident playwright by the Royal Court Theatre. During this period he wrote *The Swamp Dwellers* and an early version of *The Lion and the Jewel,* both of which where produced as double-bill by Geoffrey Axworthy in Ibadan in 1959. In 1960 Soyinka obtained a Rockefeller grant and returned to Nigeria to study African dramatic arts. He became a lecturer at the Extra-Mural Department of the University of Ibadan and founded a theatre group, "The 1960 Masks". In October 1962 he joined the staff of the English Department of the University of Ife in Ibadan. In October 1963 Soyinka was appointed to Lagos University as Acting Head of the English Department. In 1964 he founded the theatre group "Orisun Theatre Company".

In October 1965 Soyinka was put into detention and accused of having removed and stolen two tapes from the Ibadan office of the Nigerian Broadcasting Corporation with a speech by the Regional Premier, Chief Akintola. The tape was substituted by another one, calling on Chief Akintola to resign. Though evidence has been given that Soyinka was not the intruder, the judgement was deferred until December 20, 1965, after which Soyinka was released.

In 1966 Soyinka shared with Tom Stoppard the John Whiting drama prize. In 1967 he was appointed Director of the School of Drama, University of Ibadan, but before he could start work he was arrested in August by the Federal Government for alleged pro-Biafran activities. On December 22, 1967, he was moved from Lagos to Kaduna Prison. On December 18, 1968, he was awarded the Jock Campbell Prize for Commonwealth Literature by "The New Statesman" for his novel *The Interpreters* and his poems.

On October 26, 1969, Soyinka was released as part of an Independence Anniversary Amnesty. He reassumed his post as Director of the School of Drama at Ibadan and held it until April 1972 when he resigned.

Wole Soyinka has to his credit eleven plays, a novel and two volumes of poems. His first play was *The Invention* (1057), which was followed by the radio play *Camwood on the Leaves* (1058). *A Dance of the Forests* (1060) was first performed as part of the Nigerian independence festivities. It is a play set among gods, spirits and men and dealing with politics, the relevance of history, art, reality and mythology. "There are moments when the multiplicity of themes creates the feeling that there are a few too many plates spinning in the air — some of them speed by without being properly seen, and some crash down. But these are minor flaws in a work of enormous richness" (Margaret Laurence). *The Lion and the Jewel* (1061) treats the choice of a village beauty between the schoolteacher, a symbol of progress and civilization, and the old Bale, the king of the community, a symbol of tradition, who proves, however, to have a better notion of genuine progress.

The volume *Three Plays* (1062) contains the plays *The Swamp-Dwellers, The Trials of Brother Jero* and *The Strong*

Breed. The theme of *The Swamp-Dwellers* is misfortune, occasioned by nature, both physical and human. *The Trials of Brother Jero* is a comedy about a fraud working as a beach prophet and making a good living by his eloquence. In *The Strong Breed* Soyinka takes up the role of the scapegoat in an African community. "Wole Soyinka constructs an identity between the carrier in traditional Africa and the artist in the literary tradition of modern West Africa ... The artist-carrier is saddled with the weight of human sins and foibles and his task is so help his community achieve a purgation" (Oyin Ogunba). *Before the Blackout* (1064) was an evening of commentary and satirical sketches performed in Ibadan in March 1965. "Without any reservations, some of the finest shorts of modern theatre existing anywhere on stage" (John McDermott).

The Road (1066), "is Soyinka's writing on the nation's wall. He draws a society that is on the road to death and dissolution, a society for which there seems no hope" (Adrian Roscoe). Soyinka developed here one of his favourite ideas, as Eldred Jones observed: "Death on the roads is one of the most frequently recurring motifs in Soyinka's writing". *Kongi's Harvest* (1067) is a satire on modern totalitarian regimes, "a fierce onslaught on West Africa's modern breed of politicians, and especially on Kongi himself, the President of Isma" (Adrian Roscoe). His most recent play is *Madmen and Specialists*, London 1971. An early version was staged in 1970 during the Playwrights Workshop Conference at Waterford, Connecticut, USA. The new version was first performed at Ibadan in March 1971. "An ironic expression of horror at the universal triumph of expediency and power lust which makes dehumanization possible" (Preface).

Soyinka's novel, *The Interpreters* (1065), deals with a group of young intellectuals who are interpreting each other and their society as well. It is a complex composition of traditional values and modern pretensions, of social and political satire, Yoruba religion and Western psychology.

Soyinka's poetry comprises two volumes. *Idanre & Other Poems* (1068) has as towering theme the violence which Ogun, the Yoruba god of iron and war, symbolizes. *A Shuttle in the Crypt,* London 1972, consists of poems written in gaol inspite of the deprivation of reading and writing material in nearly two years of solitary confinement. *Poems from Prison* (1070) is a leaflet of two poems also written in prison.

Soyinka wrote three important critical essays, *From a Common Back Cloth* (S 122), *And after the Narcissist?* (S 202) and *The Writer in an African State* (S 123). He also translated the late Chief Daniel Olorunfemi Fagunwa's novel *Ogboju ode ninu Igbo Irunmale* from the Yoruba into English under the title *The Forest of a Thousand Daemons, a Hunter's Saga* (451 a).

Monographs on Wole Soyinka are: Kay McNeive, *Wole Soyinka, Nigerian Dramatist,* M. A. thesis, University of Kansas 1967; Eldred Jones, *The Writing of Wole Soyinka,* London 1971; Gerald Moore, *Wole Soyinka,* London 1971; and Alain Ricard, *Théâtre et nationalism, Wole Soyinka et LeRoi Jones,* Paris 1972.

Portrait on Plate X.

Sutherland, Efua Theodora   Ghana

Born on June 27, 1924, in Cape Coast, Central Region, Ghana, Efua Theodora Morgue — as was her maiden name — was educated at St. Monica's Training College in Mampong, Ashanti. She studied in Cambridge and London, England. She taught at a secondary school in Takoradi, Ghana, and took interest in writing when teaching at St. Monica's Training College in Mampong.

Her children's book, *Playtime in Africa* (1090), was the first expression of her deep concern for more suitable books to be written for and about African children, and has been followed by two 'rhythm' plays for children *Vulture! Vulture!* (1094) and *Tahinta* (1094).

From 1958 to 1961 she founded a programme of experimental theatre, and, with grants from the Rockefeller Foundation and the Arts Council of Ghana, built the "Ghana Drama Studio" in Accra to house it. Her own plays, *Foriwa* (1093) and *Edufa* (1092), have been performed there.

Since 1963 she has held a research appointment in African Literature and Drama at the Institute of African Studies, University of Ghana, Legon, Accra.

The play *Foriwa* is concerned with the problems of progress and education in a country town in Ghana. *Edufa* has the force of a Greek tragedy. The hero tries to get rid of the curse he unwillingly has inflicted upon his wife. His western education makes him reject the help he could get from African tradition. Faltering between two worlds he is doomed. If the theme of this play has a dramatic forerunner, it is to be found in the "Alkestis" of Euripides.

Portrait on Plate VIII.

Syad, William J. F.   Somalia

Born on September 30, 1930, in Jibuti, French Somalia, William J. F. Syad studied in Arabia and France. At the Sorbonne, Paris, he attended courses in Social Economy and Ethnology. From 1953 to 1955 he was in exile, for political reasons. Then he worked at Radio Djibouti, but in 1960 he had to leave again, for he was a supporter of Somalian unity.

When in 1960 the Somalia Republic was formed, William J. F. Syad became head of the department of Tourism and Culture at the Ministry of Information in Mogadishu. Still in the diplomatic service of his country, he has been on many assignments at Embassies and Consulates General in Brussels, the United States, Canada etc.

His volume of poetry, *Khamsine* (1465), merges Islamic and Western images with a spiritual option for Africa. "His poems have the subtle perfume of the Song of Songs. And the tone of the poems of Tagore. They are natural flowers of a land of poetry, of the land of nard and incense: balmy orchids" (Léopold Sédar Senghor).

Tati-Loutard, Jean-Baptiste   **Congo**

Born on December 15, 1938, in Kovilov district, a village on the Atlantic coast, 15 kilometres from Pointe-Noire, Congo, Jean-Baptiste Tati-Loutard received his elementary education at Ecole St. Jean-Baptiste of Pointe-Noire, his secondary education at Lycée Chaminade of Brazzaville, and his university education from 1961 to 1966 in Bordeaux, France, where he studied Modern Literature and Italian. He obtained his Teacher's Diploma in 1963, his Certificate to teach Italian in 1964. In 1969 he received his Doctorat ès lettres.

In 1966 he had returned home to teach Literature at the Ecole Normale Supérieure d'Afrique Centrale in Brazzaville until 1967 when he became Professor of Literature at the Centre d'Enseignement Supérieur de Brazzaville (C.E.S.B.).

Jean-Baptiste Tati-Loutard has published three volumes of poetry, *Poèmes de la Mer* (1210), *Les Racines Congolaises* (1211), and *L'Envers du Soleil,* Honfleur, Paris 1970. He has two further works in preparation, a volume of poetry, *Les Normes du temps,* and a collection of stories, *La Réussite et l'Echo.*

"To-day there is a crisis of originality among the young African writers which paralyzes their literary vocation. In their fear not to be able to express themselves other than in a European or Asian way they use all their efforts to emphasize their difference, when it would be sufficient to lift the barrier of race to liberate their creativity" (Jean-Baptiste Tati-Loutard).

Tchicaya, Gérald Félix
vid. *Tchicaya U Tam'si*

Tchicaya U Tam'si   Congo

Born on August 25, 1931, in Mpili, district Djoué, near Brazzaville, Congo, Gérald Félix Tchicaya is the son of the Deputy
Jean Félix Tchicaya. He uses as pen-name Tchicaya U Tam'si
meaning "the little bird who sings from home". At the age
of fifteen he went to France and had his secondary education
in Orléans and at the Lycée Janson de Sailly in Paris. After
matriculating he was a farm-hand in the Champagne, drew
plans for a construction firm in Paris, was doorman in a
restaurant and carrier in the Halls of Paris, helped to assort
parcels at post offices. He spent his evenings in Cafés of the
Quartier Latin.

Besides his odd jobs he wrote poetry. In 1957 he was awarded
a literature prize for French Equatorial Africa, and started to
write for the radio.

When the Belgian Congo won its independence, Tchicaya
went to Léopoldville as Chief Editor of a new daily paper,
"Congo", which, because of the disturbances, existed only one
week. He returned to Paris as Cultural Attaché at the Embassy
of Congo-Brazzaville, and since 1960 he has been representing
his country as Permanent Delegate at UNESCO, Paris.

Tchicaya U Tam'si has published six volumes of poetry,
Le mauvais sang (1212), *Feu de Brousse* (1213) which was also
published in English as *Brush Fire* (1213a), *A Triche-Coeur*
(1214), *Epitomé* (1215), *Le Ventre* (1216), and *Arc musical*
(1218). A selection of his poems was published in English,
Selected Poems (1219). His volume, *Légendes africaines*, Paris
1969, is a collection of oral texts.

"The great River Congo flows through U Tam'si's poetry,
swarming with canoes and crocodiles... But many things, I
believe, have helped to shape his poetry: the inspiration of
Césaire, and beyond him the technique and example of the
surrealists; the sculpture, music, dancing and poetry of the
Congo; and not least, his own unique genius" (Gerald Moore).

Portrait on Plate XIV.

Tenreiro, Francisco José   São Tomé

Born on January 20, 1921, in São Tomé, Francisco José Tenreiro received a diploma from the School of Colonial Administration. He joined the staff of the Geographical Institute of the University of Lisbon, Portugal, and collaborated with Prof. Orlando Ribeiro. He then went to London to study at the School of Economics and Political Science. Back in Portugal he was Assistant Professor for Social Geography in the Faculty of Arts, University of Lisbon.

Tenreiro is the author of a collection of poems, *Ilha de nome santo* (1105).

Francisco José Tenreiro died in 1963 in Lisbon.

Themba, Can   South Africa

Born in 1923 in Pretoria, Transvaal, South Africa, Can Dorsay Canadoise Themba or Can Von Themba as he preferred to call himself, was a teacher at the then Western High School on the outskirts of Western Native Township, Johannesburg, where he taught Literature, Poetry Appreciation and History. He received a scholarship, left the school and went back to the University of Fort Hare. He was editor of the magazine "Africa", then associate editor of "Drum". When he lost his job with this magazine he taught at an Indian High School in Fordsburg. He then taught at a high school in Manzine, Swaziland, and died there in autumn 1967. Like many South African writers, he was already banned from publishing or being quoted in any South African newspaper or publication.

In 1953 Can Themba won the first prize in a writing competition of the magazine "Drum".

Can Themba published articles and short stories in "Drum" and "The Classic" which were collected posthumously in the volume *The Will to Die*, London 1972.

Tiendrébéogo, Yamba   Upper Volta

Yamba Tiendrébéogo was born in 1907 in Wagadugu, Upper
Volta, as son of Dimbé Tiendrébéogo, who, in 1897, became
Larhallé-Naba (Second Minister) of Naba Siguiri, King of the
Mossi. From 1910 to 1923 his father was chief of the region of
Kudugu, and thus Yamba grew up there, and was educated the
traditional way. It was only in 1923, and only for two years,
that he received a French education. When his father died in
1928, Yamba Tiendrébéogo succeeded him in the position of
Larhallé-Naba. Since 1947 he has been vice-president of the
Union of Traditional Chiefs and since 1961 has also been Fourth
Assistant of the Mayor of Wagadugu.

Yamba Tiendrébéogo is well known among the Mossi population as a musician and story-teller. Many of his stories are
broadcast by Radio Upper Volta.

Yamba Tiendrébéogo is the author of a collection of traditional stories, *Contes du Larhallé,* published by the author in 1964
in Wagadugu.

Timi of Ede, the
vid. '*Laoye I, John Adetoyese; the Timi of Ede*

Tippoo Tib
vid. *Hamed bin Muhammed el Murjebi*

Tippu Tip
vid. *Hamed bin Muhammed el Murjebi*

Tjokosela, Joseph I. F.   Lesotho

Born about 1911, Joseph Ivory Fox Tjokosela is a teacher at St. Joseph's Training College in Maseru, Lesotho, and a prolific Catholic writer. He published the stories *Mohale o tsoa maroleng* (2145) and *Sarah* (2147), and *Mosonngoa* (2146), a novel, that "describes the life of a pagan girl, with particular emphasis on courtship and marriage customs" (Albert S. Gérard, all three in Sotho.

Touré, Sékou   Guinea

Born in 1922 in Faranah near the source of the Niger, district Faranah, Guinea, Sékou Touré is the son of poor Muslim farmers. He claims as his grandfather Almami Samori, the almost legendary hero who until 1898 resisted French occupation.

Sékou Touré was educated at a Koran and a primary school. He then went to the French Technical School in Conakry in 1936. The following year he was expelled for leading a food strike, and he continued to educate himself. In 1940 he was employed by the French business firm Niger Français. In 1941 he passed an examination qualifying him for work in the Post and Telecommunication services (PTT). He became Secretary General of the PTT Workers' Union in 1945 and helped to create in Guinea an organization closely connected to the CGT (Confédération Générale des Travailleurs). In 1946 he was a founding member of the RDA (Rassemblement Démocratique Africain) formed in Bamako under the leadership of Houphouet-Boigny. By 1952 he had the Guinea branch of his party, the PDG (Parti Démocratique du Guinée) well organized. In 1956 he became Mayor of Conakry. Building up his power in his party and his trade union he decided to vote "non" to the de Gaulle referendum, choosing complete independence rather than a limited autonomy within the French Community. On October 2, 1958, Guinea became independent and Sékou Touré was elected President. He has held this position ever since, in spite of several attacks on his life.

Sékou Touré's only creative work is a small volume of political poetry, *Poèmes militants* (1107). But he published numerous political writings and speeches like *Expérience Guinéenne et Unité Africaine*, Paris 1959, *L'Afrique et la Révolution*, Conakry s. a., *Défendre la Révolution*, Conakry s. a., *Le pouvoir populaire*, Conakry s. a., and many others.

Traoré, Bakary   Senegal

Born on August 19, 1928, in Saint-Louis, Senegal, Bakary Traoré was educated at the famous Ecole William Ponty at Gorée. In 1951 he went to Paris and studied at the Ecole Pratique des Hautes Etudes de la Sorbonne until 1961, from 1961 to 1962 at the Institut des Etudes Politiques in Paris, and from 1958 to 1964 at the Faculty of Law of the Sorbonne, Paris. Since January 1, 1966, he has been Assistant Professor at the Faculty of Law of the University of Dakar, Senegal.

His book, *Le théâtre négro-africain et ses fonctions sociales* (SW 341), was the first introduction to the oral theatre of West Africa and the beginnings of playwriting in French.

Traoré, Mamadou   Guinea

Born on December 16, 1916, in Mamou, Mamou region, Guinea, Mamadou Traoré received his elementary education in his home town. From 1931 to 1934 he attended the Ecole Primaire Supérieure in Conakry, then he was at the famous Ecole William Ponty at Gorée, Senegal. From 1937 to 1947 he was a teacher in Guinea. He had to leave the civil service because of his anticolonialist articles written under the pen-name Ray Autra. In 1947 he became a merchant's clerk in Conakry and an active trade unionist. Because of this activity he was shunted off to Niger, then to Dahomey. With independence of Guinea in 1958 he became one of the leading personalities in the UGTAN (Union Générale des Travailleurs de l'Afrique Noire). In 1961 he was accused of having participated in the "teachers' plot" and was sentenced to hard labour. Freed in 1965 he was appointed Ambassador of Guinea to Algeria. He later became Director of the Technical School at Kindia, a position he is still holding.

His poetry was compiled in a volume, *Vers la Liberté* (1109), published in Peking.

Tshibamba, Paul Lomami
vid. *Lomami-Tshibamba, Paul*

Tutuola, Amos   Nigeria

Born in 1920 in Abeokuta, Western State, Nigeria, Amos Tutuola started school at the Salvation Army School, Abeokuta, in 1934, and continued in 1936 at Lagos High School, Lagos, attending for two years, and passing from Standard II to Standard V. But he left the school and Lagos, because he could no longer bear the severe punishments of his guardian for whom he worked as servant in compensation for the school fees. Tutuola went back to Abeokuta and continued school there, passing from Standard V to VI. In 1939 his father died, and "there was none of my family who volunteered to assist me to further my studies".

Tutuola took over his father's farm, hoping to yield such a crop as to pay for his school fees, but failed. So he returned to Lagos in 1940 and began apprenticeship as a blacksmith. Two years later he joined the Royal Air Force as a smith and was discharged after the war as a grade two blacksmith. In 1946 he was employed by the Department of Labour as messenger, then joined the Nigerian Broadcasting Service as a storekeeper. In 1957 he was transferred to the Ibadan branch and has remainded there since.

Tutuola wrote six popular novels in English, depending largely on oral tradition, but mingling his stories with the paraphernalia of modern life, such as television, shillings and pence. His first work, which immediately became a success, was *The Palm-Wine Drinkard and his Dead Palm-Wine Tapster in the Dead's Town* (1114). It achieved nine translated editions, and was followed by *My Life in the Bush of Ghosts* (1115), *Simbi and the Satyr of the Dark Jungle* (1116), *The Brave African Huntress* (1117), *Feather Woman of the Jungle* (1118), and *Ajaiyi and his Inherited Poverty* (1119).

"It seems quite ironical, but true that the more popular the books get abroad, the more unpopular they become (at least until recently) at home" (E. N. Obiechina).

"One cannot perhaps help feeling that having to write in English somehow impoverishes the author's style and that he would probably have expressed himself far better in Yoruba" (Ola Balogun).

"With Tutuola and the other African writers we assist at the birth of a new and very important literature" (John Henrik Clarke).

"Tutuola's books are far more like a fascinating cul-de-sac than the beginning of anything useful to other writers. The cul-de-sac is full of wonders, but is nonetheless a dead end" (Gerald Moore).

"It was the personal decision of Sir Geoffrey Faber that Tutuola's English should not be 'normalized', thus permitting a work of major significance to reach the public in all the striking and often breathtaking originality of its prose" (Robert P. Armstrong).

"The book *(The Palm-Wine Drinkard)* is deeply Nigerian in character and style, yet written in English. The result is good literature but bad English. A fresh attempt to resolve this particular conflict between an indigenous and a borrowed culture has now been made. The novel has been adapted by a Yoruba actor-manager, into a Yoruba play which is as fresh and entertaining as its original" (Dorothy Schwarz).

"The Nigerian readers' failure to appreciate Tutuola largely arises from their own inadequate linguistic awareness and incompetent knowledge of the theory, principles, and practice of literary art" (A. Afolayan).

"Tutuola, sensitizing all matter, transmutes it. All substances, human, animal, plant, and mineral, metamorphose, slice into one another, as through graphic exaggeration he pushes the bounds of beliefs and creates his real, superreal world. All phenomena too are at play, made real through activity, concretized by the author's vision of reality. All realm merge and run together, space is shattered, and time is pushed back into the beginnings of all folklore" (Wilfred Cartey).

"If there is any writer on whom we need more informed, more rigorous and more ambitious criticism, it is Tutuola" (Bernth Lindfors).

Portrait on Plate IX.

Udechukwu, Obiora   Nigeria

Born in 1946 in the East Central State, Nigeria, Obiora Udechukwu attended the Dennis Memorial Grammar School at Onitsha. In 1965 he enrolled at the Ahmadu Bello University, Zaria. In 1966, during the disturbances in Northern Nigeria, he transferred to Nsukka University, where, in 1972, he was a final-year student in Fine Art.

While still at grammar school, Obiora Udechukwu showed an early talent in painting and drama. In 1966 he founded, together with Enukaoha Okoro, the "Nkisi Theatre Group" at Onitsha. During the Civil War he worked as an artist in the Cultural Affairs Division at Ogwa where he was one of the founding members of the "Odunke Community of Artists", contributing the first movement and the epilogue of the play, *Veneration to Udo.* Since 1972 he has been President of "Odunke".

His poetry has been published in German, in the anthology "Gedichte aus Biafra" (AW 133), in the United States, and in the anthology "Nsukka Harvest", Nsukka 1972.

uHadi Waseluhlangeni   South Africa

uHadi Waseluhlangeni (The Harp of the Nation) is the pseudonym of Jonas Ntsiko, a blind catechist of the St. John's Mission at Umtata, Transkei, Cape Province, South Africa. He
was well known as a hymn writer. Nineteen out of a collection
of 130 hymns of the Church Xhosa Hymn Book, that appeared
in Grahamstown in 1881, are his. For a period of several years,
until 1884, he contributed many articles to "Isigidimi", a
monthly Xhosa journal. He was the most famous and the most
controversial of its contributors. He voiced the discontent of
many of its readers, both in verse and in argumentative prose.
His minimal demand was that the editor allow the African
point of view to be expressed as fully as the official positions of
government and church. In 1884 an article of his that he submitted to "Isigidimi" was rejected by Gqoba, who was then
editor, for being "too hostile to British rule". The young
African intellectuals soon lost all confidence in the paper, and
it lost many of its readers. Many of uHadi's articles have never
been published and remain today in the library at Umtata in
manuscript.

U Tam'si, Tchicaya
vid. *Tchicaya U Tam'si*

Uzodinma, Edmund Chukuemeka Chieke   Nigeria

Born in 1936 in East Central State, Nigeria, Edmund Chukue-
meka Chieke Uzodinma received his education in Eastern and
Northern Nigeria. He later studied at the Universities of Ibadan
and London, England. He was the first Principal of the Aguata
Community Grammar School, and taught in 1967 at Our Lady's
High School in Onitsha.

His novel, *Our Dead Speak* (1128), deals with murder, revenge and mystery. His stories are collected in the volume *Brink of Drawn* (1127).

"As a secondary school text for Nigerian children, the novel could prove useful, but to an international reading public the novel is in parts confusing and superficial, the final impression being one of mediocrity" (Julie Bidwell).

Victor, Geraldo Bessa
vid. *Bessa Victor, Geraldo*

Vieira, Luandino (Angola)

Born in 1937 in Lisbon, José Vieira Mateus de Graca who uses Luandino Vieira as a pen-name, has been living most of his life in Angola. In 1961 he was arrested together with Antônio Cardoso and Antônio Jacinto, and sentenced to fourteen years of detention because of nationalist activity. He was deported to the prison camp Chao-Bom on the Cape Verde Island Sal.

In 1965 the Portuguese Writers Association (Sociedade Portuguesa de Escritores) awarded him the "Grande Premio da Novela" for his volume *Luuanda* (2155) which includes three short stories. The Writers' Association was therefore dissolved by the Portuguese Government and three of its six jury members were arrested.

In his stories, *A cidade e a infância* (2153), *Duas histórias de pequenos burguesas* (2154) and *Luuanda* (2155), Luandino Vieira describes the life of the poor and suppressed people in the slum areas around Luanda.

"It is an 'engaged' work of art, because its subject denounces an oppressive system" (Virgilio de Lemos).

"The work of Luandino Vieira offers the unique feature of being simultaneously the first major native revelation coming from Angola while having qualities comparable to the best Afro-American or Afro-European works of real international interest" (Antonio de Figueiredo).

Vilakazi, Benedict Wallet   South Africa

Benedict Wallet Vilakazi was born on January 6, 1906, in Grout-ville, near Stanger, the site of Shaka's great kraal Dukuza, Zu-luland, South Africa. His parents were Christians, and his father had worked for a commercial firm and had earned enough money to buy a small farm. At six the boy went to the mission primary school and passed Standard IV there, then continued at St. Francis College at Mariannhill, where he obtained a teacher's certificate in 1923. At seventeen he began to teach at Mariannhill and later at the Catholic Seminary at Ixopo, and then at Ohlange Institute where he was closely associated with the Reverend John Dube. "As a student at Mariannhill, Vila-kazi acted as secretary to Father Bernard Huss. It was probably this association more than any other single factor or influence upon him that made Vilakazi long more and more for distant educational horizons" (Cyril L. S. Nyembezi). While teaching, Vilakazi, who had by now become a Roman Catholic, passed the Junior Certificate and the Matriculation Examination by private studies, and obtained a B.A. degree from the University of South Africa in 1934.

In 1932 Vilakazi submitted a novel entitled *Noma Nini* (2158) for the third competition of the International African Institute. The book was awarded a prize in 1933 and printed at Mariannhill two years later. It is a sentimental and rather pointless story which takes place in the late nineteenth century during the reign of Mpande, when the first missionaries reached Groutville. It deals with a girl whose lover goes to work in Durban for bride money and does not come back for years. In the meantime she finds another lover. But her fiancé comes back in time to marry her and all ends well and happy.

More important is his first collection of poetry, *Inkondlo ka-Zulu* (2157), which was chosen by the Witwatersrand Press as number 1 in their Bantu Treasury series in 1935. The first volume of poetry to appear in Zulu, it contains poems that had previously been published by the newspaper "Ilanga lase Natal". In this collection Vilakazi tries to improve and modernize Zulu poetry through adoption and adaptation of the Western poetic technique of rhyme and metrical composition.

"Vilakazi has been able to convey his feelings of frustration, of longing for the past, his aspirations and deceptions, in a style of his own, which is not that of the traditional poems, and not that found in any European either" (P.-D. Beuchat).

In 1936 Benedict Wallet Vilakazi was appointed to the staff of Bantu Studies Department, Witwatersrand University, Johannesburg, as assistant to Prof. C. M. Doke, thus becoming the first African to teach at university level outside Fort Hare. In October 1936 and September 1937 he attended the first two African Author's Conferences, where he represented Zulu writing, together with Herbert Dhlomo. In 1938 he received his M. A. for his thesis, *The Conception and Development of Poetry in Zulu*. In 1946 he received a doctor's degree in Literature (D. Litt.) with his thesis *The Oral and Written Literature in Nguni*.

Vilakazi's second contribution to creative writing was a novel about Shaka's sponsor and protector, *UDingiswayo kaJobe* (2159). This was followed by a collection of poetry, *Amal'ezulu* (2160) in 1945, which was translated into English in 1962. His third and last novel, *Nje-nempela* (2161) is based on the events of the Bambatha Rebellion of 1906, and is an outstanding depiction of traditional life in a polygamous household.

Besides this work Benedict Wallet Vilakazi assisted C. M. Doke in the compilation of the "Zulu-English Dictionary".

Benedict Wallet Vilakazi died on October 25, 1947, in the Coronation Non-European Hospital in Johannesburg.

Waseluhlangeni, uHadi
vid. *uHadi Waseluhlangeni*

Wheatley, Phillis   Senegal

Born around 1753 in Senegal, Phillis Wheatley was brought as
a slave to America, where she was bought by a well-to-do
trader in Boston, a Mr. Wheatley. The family let her have a
good education. In 1770 she wrote her first poem, *An elegiac
poem, on the death of that celebrated divine, and eminent
servant of Jesus Christ, the Reverend and learned George
Whitefield* ... (1140). In 1773 she travelled to Great Britain
in the company of her master's son, and was the guest of Lady
Huntingdon. She was supposed to be introduced to King George
III, but had to return to Boston on account of bad health.
When her master died and his houshold was dissolved, she was
set free and married John Peters, "a man of her race". She
bore him three children, but her marriage was unhappy. She
became a servant in an inn. Phillis Wheatley died on December
5, 1784.

Phillis Wheatley was a successful poetess in her time. She
published *Poems on various subjects, religious and moral* (1141),
*An elegy, sacred to the memory of that great divine, the Rever-
end and learned Dr. Samuel Cooper* ... (1142), *Liberty and
peace, a poem* (1143), *Poems on comic, serious and moral subjects* (1144), and *A beautiful poem on providence* (1145).

Portrait on Plate I.

Wonodi, Okogbule   Nigeria

Born on August 27, 1936, in Diobu near Port Harcourt, Rivers
State, Nigeria, Okogbule Glory Nwanodi who after his first
publications changed his name into Okogbule Wonodi, had his

primary education at St. Paul's (Anglican) Primary School in Diobu. At the death of his father, in 1945, he had to leave school and work at odd jobs, carrying water, errand boy, being timekeeper at an enterprise. In 1956 he was trained at St. John's (Anglican) Teachers' College in Diobu, where he then taught English and History. In 1960 he went to Enugu to study at the Nigerian College of Arts, Science and Technology. From 1961 to 1965 he studied at the University of Nigeria in Nsukka, and from 1965 to 1966 he attended the Writer's Workshop at the University of Iowa, Iowa City, USA. In 1966 he returned to Nigeria to be a Lecturer in English and Creative Writing at the University of Nigeria, Nsukka. During the Civil War he was working in the Ministry of Information of Biafra. Since 1970 he has been Personal Manager at the Nigerian Tobacco Company Ltd. in Port Harcourt, Nigeria.

Okogbule Wonodi edited and published quite a number of journals: from 1960 to 1961 "Fresh Buds", the verse magazine of the Nigerian College of Arts, Science and Technology, in Enugu; from 1961 to 1963 "The Voice", the magazine of the National Union of Nigerian Students; from 1963 to 1964 "The Pilgrim", the voice of the Students' Christian Movement, University of Nigeria, Nsukka; and from 1966 to 1970 he was publisher and editor of the "Okike Publications" poetry pamphlets.

Besides his book *Icheke, and other poems* (749), he wrote poetry which was published in journals such as "Young Commonwealth Poets", "Nigeria Magazine", "Transition" and "Black Orpheus", and anthologies such as *New Voices of the Commonwealth* (London 1968), *Modern Poetry from Africa* (A 75), and others.

"In *Icheke and other poems,* Mr. Nwanodi attempts to find a common ground for cultures which always seem to conflict. It is not merely that ancient rites and traditions are superceded by modern ways; something new seems to emerge from the interfusion of both" (Theo Vincent).

"Nwanodi at his best does not dwell on a scene but brings us quickly up to it" (Paul Theroux).

Yondo, Elolongué Epanya
vid. *Epanya Yondo, Elolongué*

Zadi, Zaourou   Ivory Coast

Born on February 2, 1938, in Soubré, on Sassandra river, West
Central District, Ivory Coast, Zaourou Zadi was educated at
the primary school in Bingerville from 1951 to 1956, then at
the Collège moderne in Abidjan from 1956 to 1958. He interrupted his schooling and went to work, but continued his education privately. He obtained his Baccalauréat at the Lycée classique in Abidjan in 1962, then studied for his second Baccalauréat at the Centre d'Etudes Supérieures. He founded the
Club Littéraire and edited its journal "Flambeau". From 1962
to 1963 Zadi taught at the Collège d'Agriculture in Bingerville.
In 1964 he was back at his studies at the Centre d'Etudes Supérieures, but was arrested in February and held in prison in Yamoussoukro until January 1965. In July 1965 he left for France
to study Lettres modernes at the University of Strasbourg. Passing his examinations in 1969 he went back to Abidjan and
became an assistant at Abidjan University.

Zadi published two plays, *Sory Lombé*, Strasbourg 1968,
and *Les Sofas*, Strasbourg 1969.

AUTHORS GROUPED BY LANGUAGES

Duodu, Cameron
Easmon, R. Sarif
Echeruo, Michael J. C.
Egbuna, Obi
Egharevba, Jacob U.
Ekwensi, Cyprian
Enahoro, Anthony
Enahoro, Peter
Equiano, Olaudah
Ezuma, Benjamin James
Gatheru, Mugo
Gicaru, Muga
Head, Bessie
Henshaw, James Ene
Higo, Aig
Hoh, Israel Kafu
Horatio-Jones, Edward Baba-
   tunde Bankole
Horton, James Africanus Beale
Hutchinson, Alfred
Ijimere, Obotunde
Ike, Vincent Chukwuemeka
Ikiddeh, Ime
Irele, Abiola
Jabavu, Davidson Don Tengo
Jabavu, John Tengo
Jabavu, Noni
Jones, Eldred Duromisi
Jordan, Archibald Campbell
Kachingwe, Aubrey
Kamera, William
Kariuki, Joseph Elijah
Kariuki, Josiah Mwangi
Kassam, Amin
Kaunda, Kenneth
Kayira, Legson
Kayper-Mensah, Albert William
Kenyatta, Jomo
Kgositsile, Keorapetse William
Kimenye, Barbara
Komey, Ellis Ayitey

Konadu, Samuel Asare
Kunene, Raymond Mazisi
Kyei, Kojo Gyinaye
La Guma, Alex
'Laoye I, John Adetoyese
Leshoai, Benjamin
Liyong, Taban lo
Lubega, Stephen
Luthuli, Albert
Maddy, Pat Amadu
Maimane, Arthur
Maimo, 'Sankie
Marshall, Bill
Masiye, Andreya Sylvester
Matshikiza, Todd
Matthews, James
Maxwell, Highbred
Mazrui, Ali A.
Mbiti, John Samuel
Menkiti, Ifeanyi
Mezu, Sebastian Okechukwu
Modisane, Bloke
Modupe, Prince
Moore, Bai T.
Mopeli-Paulus, Atwell Sidwell
Mphahlele, Ezekiel
Mtshali, Oswald
Mulaisho, Dominic
Mulikita, Fwanyanga Matale
Munonye, John
Mutwa, Vusamazulu Credo
Ngoh, John Emmanuel Akwo
Ngugi, James
Nicol, Abioseh
Njau, Rebecca
Nketia, J. H. Kwabena
Nkosi, Lewis
Nkrumah, Kwame
Ntiru, Richard
Ntuli, Deuteronomy Bhekinkozi
   Zeblon

Nwankwo, Nkem
Nwankwo, Victor
Nwapa, Flora
Nwogu, Matthew Chinke
Nyabongo, Akiki
Nzekwu, Onuora
Obiechina, Emmanuel N.
Oculi, Okello
Odinga, Oginga
Ofori, Henry
Ogali, A. Ogali
Ogieiriaixi, Evinma
Ogot, Grace
Ogunyemi, Wale
Okai, John
Okara, Gabriel
Okigbo, Christopher
Oko, Akomaye
Okpaku, Joseph
Olisah, Sunday Okenwa
Olusola, Segun
Omotoso, Kole
Onyeama, Dillibe
Osadebay, Dennis Chukude
Oyônô-Mbia, Guillaume
Palangyo, Peter
Parkes, Frank Kobina
p'Bitek, Okot
Peters, Lenrie
Phiri, Desmond Dudua
Pieterse, Cosmo
Plaatje, Solomon T.
Reindorf, Carl Christian
Rive, Richard
Rotimi, Ola
Rowe, Ekundayo
Rubadiri, David
Rubusana, Walter B.
Ruhumbika, Gabriel
Samkange, Stanlake
Sancho, Ignatius

Seboni, Michael Ontefetse
    Martinus
Segun, Mabel
Selormey, Francis
Serumaga, Robert
Sithole, Ndabaningi
Solarin, Tai
Soyinka, Wole
Sutherland, Efua Theodora
Themba, Can
Tutuola, Amos
Udechukwu, Obiora
Uzodinma, Edmund Chukuemeka
    Chieke
Vilakazi, Benedict Wallet
Wheatley, Phillis
Wonodi, Okogbule

Ewe

Fiawoo, F. Kwasi
Hoh, Israel Kafu

French

A-Amang, Boé
Adotevi, Stanislas Spéro
Alapini, Julien
Amon d'Aby, François-Joseph
Ananou, David
Andriananjason, Victor Georges
Anozie, Sunday O.
Atta Koffi, Raphaël
Ba, Amadou Hampaté
Badian, Seydou
Balogun, Ola
Bamboté, Pierre
Bebey, Francis
Bengono, Jacques
Beti, Mongo
Bhêly-Quénum, Olympe
Bognini, Joseph Miezan

Nzouankeu, Jacques Muriel
Nzuji, Clementine
Ouane, Ibrahima-Mamadou
Ouologuem, Yambo
Ousmane, Sembene
Owono, Joseph
Oyono, Ferdinand
Oyônô-Mbia, Guillaume
Philombe, René
Pliya, Jean
Pouka-M'Bague, Louis-Marie
Prudencio, Eustache
Rabearivelo, Jean-Joseph
Rabemananjara, Jacques
Rabetsimandranto, Fidélis Justin
Rajemisa-Raolison, Régis
Ranaivo, Flavien
Rifoé, Simon
Sadji, Abdoulaye
Salifou, André
Seid, Joseph Brahim
Sengat-Kuo, François
Senghor, Léopold Sédar
Sinda, Martial
Sissoko, Fily Dabo
Socé, Ousmane
Syad, William J. F.
Tati-Loutard, Jean-Baptiste
Tchicaya U Tam'si
Tiendrébéogo, Yamba
Touré, Sékou
Traoré, Bakary
Traoré, Mamadou
Zadi, Zaourou

German

Amo, Anton Wilhelm
Misipo, Dualla

Hausa

Abubakar Imam, Alhaji
Abubakar Tafawa Balewa,
   Alhaji Sir
Bello, Alhaji Sir Ahmadu

Kamba

Mbiti, John Samuel

Kikongo

Massaki, André

Kinyarwanda

Kagame, Alexis

Krio

Casely Hayford, Gladys May

Latin

Amo, Anton Wilhelm
Capitein, Jacobus Eliza Joannes
Latino, Juan

Lozi

Mulikita, Fwanyanga M.

Luganda

Kigundu, Clement
Kiyingi, Wycliffe
Nsimbi, Michael Bazze

Lwo

p'Bitek, Okot

Malagasy

Dox
Rabearivelo, Jean-Joseph
Rabetsimandranto, Fidélis Justin
Rajemisa-Raolison, Régis

Sotho, Southern

Bereng, David Cranmer Theko
Khaketla, Bennett Makalo
Majara, Simon
Mangoaela, Zakea D.
Mofolo, Thomas
Moiloa, James Jantjies
Mopeli-Paulus, Atwell Sidwell
Motsamai, Edward
Ntsane, Kem Edward
Segoete, Everitt Lechesa
Sekese, Azariele M.
Tjokosela, Joseph I. F.

Spanish

Mopila, Francisco José

Swahili

Hamed bin Muhammed el
    Murjebi (Tippu Tib)
Muhammad Said Abdulla
Robert, Shaaban

Tiv

Akiga

Tonga

Chona, Mainza Mathias

Tswana

Plaatje, Solomon T.
Raditladi, Leetile Disang
Seboni, Michael Ontefetse
    Martinus

Tumbuka

Phiri, Desmond Dudwa

Twi

Danquah, Joseph Kwame
    Kyeretwie Bakye
Martinson, Andrews Pardon Adu
Nketia, J. H. Kwabena
Opoku, Amankwa Andrew

Xhosa

Bokwe, John Knox
Gqoba, William Wellington
Guma, Enoch Silinga
Jabavu, Davidson Don Tengo
Jabavu, John Tengo
Jolobe, James J. R.
Jordan, Archibald Campbell
Mqhayi, Samuel Edward Krune
Ndawo, Henry Masila
Ntsikana
Rubusana, Walter B.
Sinxo, Guybon B.
Soga, John Henderson
Soga, Tiyo
Sontonga, Mankayi Enoch
uHadi Waseluhlangeni

Yoruba

Ajao, S. A.
Aromire, Abayomi
Babalola, Adeboye
Delano, Oloye I. O.
Fagunwa, Daniel Olorunfemi
Faleti, Adebayo
Ijimere, Obotunde
Ladipo, Duro
Odunjo, Joseph Folahan
Ogunde, Hubert
Ogunmola, Kola
Ogunyemi, Wale
Oladiti, F. O.
Philips, Femi
Soyinka, Wole

Zulu

Dhlomo, R. R. R.
Dube, John Langalibalele
Mncwango, Leon(h)ard L. J.
Ngcobo, Moses John

Ntuli, Deuteronomy Bhekinkozi
  Zeblon
Nxumalo, Otty E. H. Mandla
Nyembezi, Sibusiso
Vilakazi, Benedict Wallet

AUTHORS GROUPED BY COUNTRIES

Angola

Andrade, Fernando Costa
Andrade, Mario de
António, Mario
Bessa Victor, Geraldo
Cardoso, António
Cruz, Tomaz Vieira da
Cruz, Viriato da
Daskalos, Alexandre
Guerra, Henrique
Jacinto, António
Lima, Santos
Massaki, André
Matta, Joaquim Dias Cordeiro da
Neto, Agostinho
Osório, Ernesto Cochat
Ribas, Oscar Bento
Santos, Arnaldo
Silva, María Perpétua Candeias da
Vieira, Luandino

Botswana

Raditladi, Leetile Disang
Seboni, Michael Ontefetse Martinus

Cameroon

A-Amang, Boé
Bebey, Francis
Bengono, Jacques
Beti, Mongo
Dipoko, Mbella Sonne
Ela, Jean-Marc
Eno-Belinga, Samuel-Martin
Epanya Yondo, Elolongué
Epée, Valère
Ikelle-Matiba, Jean
Kuoh Moukouri, Jacques
Maimo, 'Sankie
Matip, Benjamin
Mbumua, William Eteki'a
Médou Mvomo, Rémy
Misipo, Dualla
Mongo, Pabé
Mveng, Engelbert
Ndedi-Penda, Patrice
Ndzaagap, Timothée
Nganthojeff, Job
Ngoh, John Emmanuel Akwo
Njoya, Martin
Noumé, Etienne B.
Nyunaï, Jean-Paul
Nzouankeu, Jacques Muriel
Owono, Joseph
Oyono, Ferdinand
Oyônô-Mbia, Guillaume
Philombe, René
Pouka-M'Bague, Louis-Marie
Rifoé, Simon
Sengat-Kuo, François

Cape Verde Islands

Anahory, Terêncio
Barbosa, Jorge
Fonseca, Aguinaldo
Gonçalves, António Aurélio
Lopes, Baltasar
Lopes, Manuel
Lopes da Silva, José
Mariano, Gabriel
Martins, Ovídio de Sousa

Ivory Coast

Amon d'Aby, François-Joseph
Atta Koffi, Raphaël
Bognini, Joseph Miezan
Dadié, Bernard B.
Demand Goh, Gaston
Diallo, Mamadou
Doutéo, Bertin B.
Gadeau, Germain Coffi
Koné, Maurice
Kourouma, Ahmadou
Loba, Aké
Nokan, Charles
Zadi, Zaourou

Kenya

Asalache, Khadambi
Gatheru, Mugo
Gicaru, Muga
Kariuki, Joseph Elijah
Kariuki, Josiah Mwangi
Kassam, Amin
Kenyatta, Jomo
Mazrui, Ali A.
Mbiti, John Samuel
Ngugi, James
Njau, Rebecca
Odinga, Oginga
Ogot, Grace

Lesotho

Bereng, David Cranmer Theko
Khaketla, Bennett Makalo
Majara, Simon
Mangoaela, Zakea D.
Mofolo, Thomas
Motsamai, Edward
Ntsane, Kem Edward
Segoete, Everitt Lechesa

Sekese, Azariele M.
Tjokosela, Joseph I. F.

Liberia

Besolow, Thomas E.
Dempster, Roland Tombekai
Moore, Bai T.

Madagascar

Andriananjason, Victor Georges
Dox
Rabearivelo, Jean-Joseph
Rabemananjara, Jacques
Rabetsimandranto, Fidélis Justin
Rajemisa-Raolison, Régis
Ranaivo, Flavien

Malawi

Chafulumira, English William
Kachingwe, Aubrey
Kayira, Legson
Ntara, Samuel Yosia
Phiri, Desmond Dudwa
Rubadiri, David

Mali

Ba, Amadou Hampaté
Badian, Seydou
Cissoko, Siriman
Dembele, Sidiki
Diabaté, Massa Makan
Gologo, Mamadou
Ouane, Ibrahima-Mamadou
Ouologuem, Yambo
Sissoko, Fily Dabo

Mauritius

Maunick, Edouard J.

Okara, Gabriel
Okigbo, Christopher
Oko, Akomaye
Okpaku, Joseph
Oladiti, F. O.
Olisah, Sunday Okenwa
Olusola, Segun
Omotoso, Kole
Onyeama, Dillibe
Osadebay, Dennis Chukude
Philips, Femi
Rotimi, Ola
Segun, Mabel
Solarin, Tai
Soyinka, Wole
Tutuola, Amos
Udechukwu, Obiora
Uzodinma, Edmund
    Chukuemeka Chieke
Wonodi, Okogbule

Rhodesia

Chakaipa, Patrick
Chaparadza, L. Washington
Chidyausiku, Paul
Khumalo, Philios Mtshane
Kuimba, Giles
Marangwanda, John Weakley
Ribeiro, Emmanuel F.
Samkange, Stanlake
Sibanda, Amos M. P.
Sigogo, Ndabezinhle S.
Sithole, Ndabaningi

Rwanda

Kagame, Alexis
Naigiziki, Saverio

São Tomé

Costa Alegre, Caetano da
Espírito Santo, Alda do

Tenreiro, Francisco José

Senegal

Dia, Amadou Cissé
Diagne, Ahmadou Mapaté
Diakhaté, Lamine
Diallo, Bakary
Diop, Alioune
Diop, Birago
Diop, Cheikh Anta
Diop, David
Diop, Massylla
Gueye, Lamine
Kane, Cheikh Hamidou
M'Baye, Annette
Ndao, Cheik
Niang, Lamine
Ousmane, Sembene
Sadji, Abdoulaye
Senghor, Léopold Sédar
Socé, Ousmane
Traoré, Bakary
Wheatley, Phillis

Sierra Leone

Akar, John
Bart-Williams, Gaston
Cole, Robert Wellesley
Easmon, R. Sarif
Horton, James Africanus Beale
Jones, Eldred Duromisi
Maddy, Pat Amadu
Nicol, Abioseh
Rowe, Ekundayo

Somalia

Syad, William J. F.

South Africa

Abrahams, Peter

Bokwe, John Knox
Brutus, Dennis
Dhlomo, Herbert I. E.
Dhlomo, R.R.R.
Dolamo, Elon Ramarisane
Dube, John Langalibalele
Fula, Arthur Nuthall
Gqoba, William Wellington
Guma, Enoch Silinga
Head, Bessie
Hutchinson, Alfred
Jabavu, Davidson Don Tengo
Jabavu, John Tengo
Jabavu, Noni
Jolobe, James J. R.
Jordan, Archibald Campbell
Kgositsile, Keorapetse William
Kunene, Raymond Mazisi
La Guma, Alex
Leshoai, Benjamin Letholoa
Luthuli, Albert
Maimane, Arthur
Matsepe, Oliver Kgadime
Matshikiza, Todd
Matthews, James
Mncwango, Leon(h)ard L. J.
Modisane, Bloke
Moiloa, James Jàntjies
Mopeli-Paulus, Atwell Sidwell
Mphahlele, Ezekiel
Mqhayi, Samuel Edward Krune
Mtshali, Oswald
Mutwa, Vusamazulu Credo
Ndawo, Henry Masila
Ngcobo, Moses John
Nkosi, Lewis
Ntsikana
Ntuli, Deuteronomy Bhekinkozi
  Zeblon
Nxumalo, Otty E. H. Mandla
Nyembezi, Sibusiso

Plaatje, Solomon T.
Rive, Richard
Rubusana, Walter B.
Sinxo, Guybon B.
Soga, John Henderson
Soga, Tiyo
Sontonga, Mankayi Enoch
Themba, Can
uHadi Waseluhlangeni
Vilakazi, Benedict Wallet

South West Africa vid. Namibia

Tanzania

Hamed bin Muhammed el
  Murjebi (Tippu Tib)
Kamera, William
Muhammad Said Abdulla
Palangyo, Peter
Robert, Shaaban
Ruhumbika, Gabriel

Togo

Ananou, David

Uganda

Amar, Andrew Richard
Bazarrabusa, Timothy B.
Bukenya, A. S.
Kigundu, Clement
Kimenye, Barbara
Kiyingi, Wycliffe
Liyong, Taban lo
Lubega, Stephen
Nsimbi, Michael Bazze
Ntiru, Richard
Nyabongo, Akiki
Oculi, Okello
p'Bitek, Okot
Serumaga, Robert

BIBLIOGRAPHY

African Biographies, Bonn-Bad Godesberg 1967.

Anozie, Sunday O., *Sociologie du roman africain*, Paris 1970.

Araujo, Norman, *A Study of Cape Verdian Literature*, Boston 1966.

Brench, A. C., *The Novelists' Inheritance in French Africa*, London 1967.

Cartey, Wilfred, *Whispers from a Continent*, New York 1969.

César, Amândio, *Parágrafos de literatura ultramarina*, Lisbon 1967.

Cornevin, R., *Le théâtre en Afrique noire et à Madagascar*, Paris 1970.

Dictionnaire bio-bibliographique du Dahomey, Port-Novo 1969.

Ephson, I. S., *Gallery of Gold Coast Celebrities*, Accra 1969.

Gérard, Albert S., *Four African Literatures*, Berkeley 1971.

Heywood, Christopher (ed.), *Perspectives on African Literature*, London 1971.

Jahn, Janheinz, *A History of Neo-African Literature*, London, New York 1968.

July, Robert W., *The Origins of Modern African Thought*, London 1968.

July, Robert W., *A History of the African People*, London 1970.

Kunene, Daniel P. and Kirsch, Randal A., *The Beginning of South African Vernacular Literature*, Los Angeles 1967.

Laurence, Margaret, *Long Drums and Cannons*, London 1968.

Mbelolo ya Mpiku, *Joseph, Le roman sénégalais de langue française: la période de formation*, Université de Liège 1969 (mimeographed).

Moore, Gerald, *Seven African Writers*, London 1962.

Moser, Gerald M., *Essays in Portuguese-African Literature*, Pennsylvania State University 1969.

Mouralis, Bernard, *Individu et collectivité dans le roman négro-africain d'expression française*, Abidjan 1969.

Pageart, Robert, *Littérature négro-africaine*, Paris 1966.

Roscoe, Adrian A., *Mother is Gold*, London 1971.

Segal, Ronald, *Political Africa*, London 1961.

Zell, Hans and Silver, Helene, *A Reader's Guide to African Literature* London 1972.

ACKNOWLEDGEMENTS

Acknowledgement is made to the following for kind permission to reproduce the portraits included in this volume:
"Equiano's Travels", edited by Paul Edwards, Heinemann Educational Books London; "Latinus — Amo — Capitein", Kraus Reprint, Nendeln, Liechtenstein; "The Poems of Phillis Wheatley", edited by Julian D. Mason, The University of North Carolina Press, Chapel Hill; "Letters of the late Ignatius Sancho, an African", Dawson of Pall Mall, Folkestone; "The Origins of Modern African Thought", by Robert W. July, Faber and Faber Ltd., London; "A History of the African People", by Robert W. July, Faber and Faber Ltd., London; "Afrikaner erzählen ihr Leben", by Westermann, Essener Verlagsanstalt; "Anthologie négroafricaine", edited by Kesteloot, Marabout université, Éditions Gerard, Brüssel; "Emergency" by Richard Rive, Faber and Faber Ltd., London; The Transcription Centre, London; dpa; Deutsche Afrika-Gesellschaft, Bonn; "Noite de vento" by António Aurélio Gonçalves, Ediçao do centro de informaçao e turismo, Cabo Verde; Institut national des Arts de la République de Côte d'Ivoire; Editions du Seuil, Paris; Cultural Events; "Africa, a subjective view" by Abioseh Nicol, Longman Group Limited, London; Nigeria Magazine, Lagos; Heinemann Educational Books, London; Valerie Wilmer, London; John Goldblatt, London; Centre de Littérature Evangélique, Yaunde; West Africa, London; "1° Encontro de escritores de Angola", Ediçao de 'Publicaçoes imbondeiro', Angola; Horizon; Keystone, Paris; Irmelin Lebeer, Paris; J. G. Jang, Berlin; "J. J. Rabéarivelo" by Valette, Fernand Nathan Editeur, Paris; Editions de l'Université Lovanium, Kinshasa.
The remaining portraits, taken by the author himself, were provided by Mr. Janheinz Jahn's archives.

The editor and the publishers thank the following for permission to quote from their publications:

Faber and Faber Ltd., London, for quotations from Robert W. July "The Origins of Modern African Thought", and Robert W. July, "A History of African People"; Stevens and Sons Ltd., London, for quotations from Ronald Segal, "Political Africa"; The University of California Press for quotations from Albert S. Gérard, "Four African Literatures", and Kunene/Kirsch, "The Beginning of South African Vernacular Literature".